NORTHMEN

JOHN HAYWOOD was educated at the universities of Lancaster, Cambridge and Copenhagen. He is an expert on the history of Dark Age Europe. He is the author of the *Encyclopedia of the Viking Age*, *The New Atlas of World History* and *The Penguin Atlas of the Vikings*.

NORTHMEN

THE VIKING SAGA
793–1241 AD

JOHN HAYWOOD

HEAD of ZEUS

First published in 2015 by Head of Zeus Ltd
Copyright © John Haywood 2015

1 3 5 7 9 10 8 6 4 2

A catalogue record for this book is available from the British Library.

ISBN (HB) 9781781855232
ISBN (E) 9781781855225

Designed and typeset by Broadbase

Printed and bound in Germany by GGP Media GmbH, Pössneck

Head of Zeus Ltd
Clerkenwell House
45–47 Clerkenwell Green
London EC1R0HT
www.headofzeus.com

CONTENTS

Maps   viii

Preface   xiv

Introduction   1

1   Thule, Nydam and Gamla Uppsala
The origin of the Vikings   9

2   Lindisfarne, Athelney and York
The Vikings in England 789–954   42

3   Dorestad, Paris and Rouen
The Vikings in Francia 799–939   77

4   Iona, Dunkeld and Orkney
Vikings in Scotland 795–1064   109

5   Dublin and Cashel
The Vikings in Ireland 795– 1014   136

6   Seville and Luni
Vikings in Spain and the Mediterranean 844–61   164

7   Kiev, Constantinople and Bolghar
Vikings in Eastern Europe to 1041   174

8   Thingvellir, Brattahlid and L'Anse aux Meadows
The Norse in the North Atlantic 835–1000   210

9   Maldon, London and Stamford Bridge
England's second Viking Age 978–1085   247

10   Hedeby, Jelling and Stiklestad
The Scandinavian kingdoms to 1100   270

11   Palermo, Jerusalem and Tallinn
From Viking to Crusader   314

12   Largs, Reykholt and Hvalsey
The Viking Twilight   328

Chronology   *353*
Viking Kings and Rulers *c.* 800–1100   *356*
Further Reading   *361*
List of Illustrations   *369*
Index   *370*

SCANDINAVIA

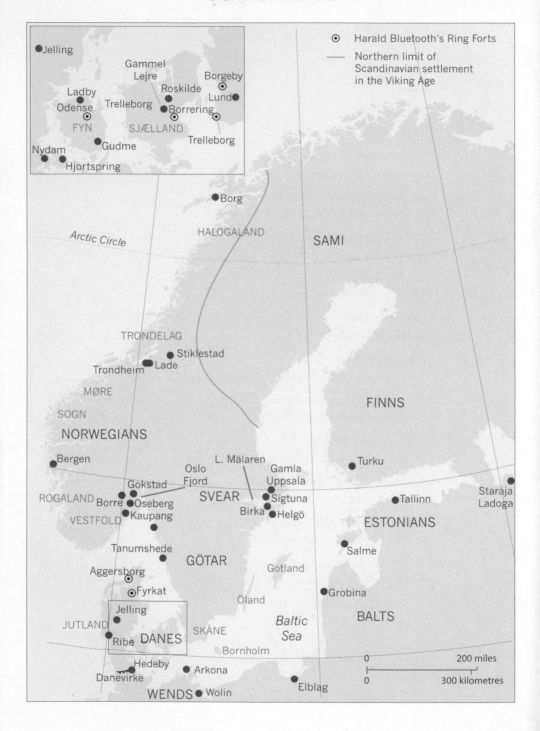

⊙ Harald Bluetooth's Ring Forts

── Northern limit of
Scandinavian settlement
in the Viking Age

Jelling

Gammel
Lejre
Roskilde   Borgeby
Ladby   ⊙
Odense   Trelleborg   Lund
⊙   Borrering
FYN   SJÆLLAND
Nydam   Gudme
         Trelleborg
Hjortspring

Borg

HÅLOGALAND   SAMI

Arctic Circle

TRØNDELAG

Stiklestad
Trondheim Lade

MØRE

SOGN   FINNS

NORWEGIANS

Bergen   Turku
              L. Mälaren
         Oslo   Gamla
         Fjord   Uppsala
Gokstad   Staraja
ROGALAND Borre SVEAR Sigtuna   Ladoga
        Oseberg Birka Helgö
VESTFOLD Kaupang   Tallinn

                               ESTONIANS
        Tanumshede
                          Salme
Aggersborg GÖTAR Gotland
⊙
 ⊙Fyrkat
                               Grobina
Jelling   Öland
JUTLAND   SKÅNE   BALTS
Ribe DANES   Baltic
           Bornholm   Sea
Hedeby   Arkona
Danevirke   0   200 miles
WENDS Wolin   Elblag   0   300 kilometres

ENGLAND AND IRELAND

0   80 miles

0   130 kilometres

—— Border of Danelaw, 902

Shetland

Orkney
Birsay
Kirkwall

Sutherland

Caithness

Hebrides

Portmahomack
Forres

Kingdom of
the Picts

Kingdom of
the Scots

Dunkeld

North
Sea

Iona

Dunadd
Dumbarton
Largs

Strathclyde   *Tweed*

Lindisfarne
Bamburgh

Ailech

*Northern
Uí Néill*   Ulster

Gall-Gaedhill
(Galloway)

Tyne

Northumbria

Armagh

Tynwald

Isle
of Man

Gosforth

Stainmore

Connacht

Meath

Linn
Duchaill

*Southern
Uí Néill*   *Boyne*

Shannon

Liffey   Dublin

Wirral

Cuerdale

Chester

Ouse

Kingdom
of York

York

Humber

Torksey
Lincoln

Dál Cais

Limerick

Leinster

Gwynedd

Tettenhall

Nottingham
Derby

Trent

Stamford

Munster

Waterford   Wexford

Repton

Leicester

Thetford

Cork

Welsh
Kingdoms

Severn

Mercia

Danelaw

East
Anglia

St David's

Alney
Chippenham

Oxford

Maldon

Thames

London

Ashingdon

Countisbury
Hill

Athelney

Edington

Wedmore

Winchester

Hastings

Exeter

Wessex

Portland

English
Channel

*Atlantic
Ocean*

WESTERN EUROPE C. 800

KINGDOM OF THE SCOTS

KINGDOM OF THE PICTS

STRATHCLYDE

Atlantic Ocean

IRISH KINGDOMS

NORTHUMBRIA

North Sea

KINGDOM OF DENMARK

Hedeby

WELSH KINGDOMS

MERCIA

EAST ANGLIA

Frisia

Hamburg

WENDS

Bremen

Elbe

WESSEX

Thames

Dorestad

Flanders

Quentovic

Dyle

Aachen

Cologne

Saucourt

Coblenz

Normandy

Rouen

Trier

Brittany

Pont de l'Arche

Paris

Avaux

Îsle de Groix

Nantes

Angers

Loire

FRANKISH EMPIRE

Danube

Noirmoutier

Poitiers

Rhine

KINGDOM OF GALICIA & ASTURIAS

Bay of Biscay

La Coruña

Bordeaux

Clermont

Santiago de Compostela

Gijón

Aquitaine

Valence

Garonne

Pamplona

Toulouse

Rhône

Nîmes

Arles

Luni

Adriatic Sea

Narbonne

Pisa

Fiesole

Ebro

Tiber

Lisbon

EMIRATE OF CÓRDOBA

Rome

Balearic Islands

Minorca

Seville

Córdoba

Ibiza

Majorca

Niebla

Guadalquivir

Murcia

Mediterranean Sea

Asilah

Palermo

0   500 miles

0   500 kilometres

ICELAND

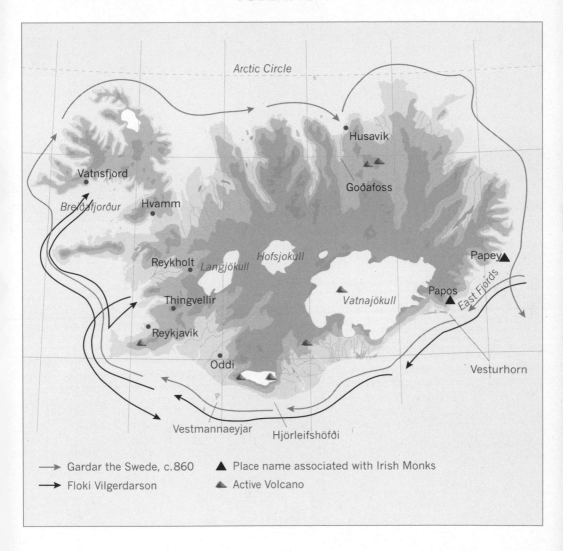

Arctic Circle

Husavik

Goðafoss

Vatnsfjord

Breiðafjorður   Hvamm

Reykholt   Langjökull   Hofsjokull   Papey

Vatnajökull   Papos   East Fjords

Thingvellir

Reykjavik   Vesturhorn

Oddi

Vestmannaeyjar   Hjörleifshöfði

→ Gardar the Swede, c.860   ▲ Place name associated with Irish Monks
→ Floki Vilgerdarson   ▲ Active Volcano

THE VINLAND VOYAGES

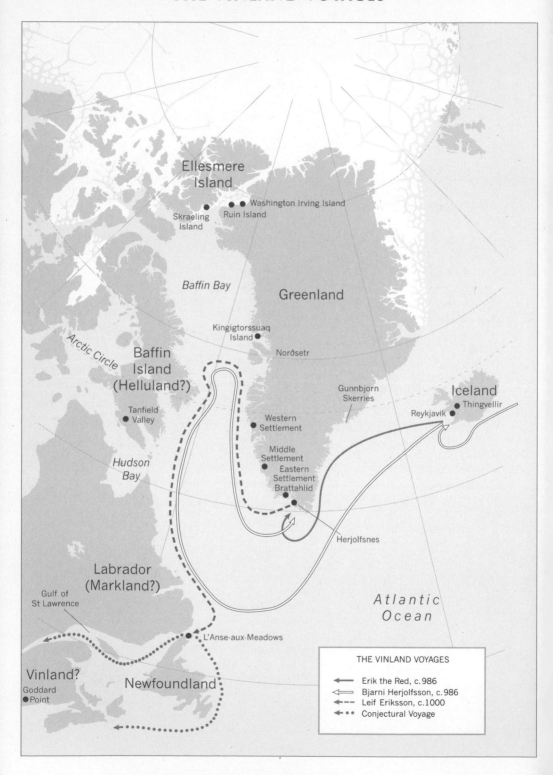

Ellesmere
Island

Washington Irving Island
Skraeling
Island
Ruin Island

Baffin Bay

Greenland

Kingigtorssuaq
Island
Norðsetr

Arctic Circle

Baffin
Island
(Helluland?)

Gunnbjorn
Skerries

Iceland
Thingvellir
Reykjavík

Tanfield
Valley

Western
Settlement

Hudson
Bay

Middle
Settlement
Eastern
Settlement
Brattahlid

Herjolfsnes

Labrador
(Markland?)

Gulf of
St Lawrence

Atlantic
Ocean

L'Anse-aux-Meadows

Vinland?
Goddard
Point

Newfoundland

THE VINLAND VOYAGES

⟶ Erik the Red, c.986
⟸ Bjarni Herjolfsson, c.986
⟵ - - Leif Eriksson, c.1000
⟵ • • Conjectural Voyage

THE EASTERN ROUTES

White Sea

FINNS

Karelia
Lake Onega
FINNS
Lake Ladoga
Beloozero
Gulf of Finland
Staraja Ladoga
Tallinn
Volkhov
Novgorod
Lake Peipus
Pskov
Yaroslavl
Rostov
Izborsk
Volga
VOLGA
Bolghar
BULGARS
Dvina
RUS
Gnezdovo
Dnepr
SLAVS
Chernigov
Korosten
Kiev
Don
Volga
Dnepr Rapids
Sarkel
Itil
PECHENEGS
Berezan Island
Sea of Azov
Caspian Sea
Danube
Pereyslavets
Dorostolon
Black Sea
GEORGIA
Preslav
Sasireti
Barda
DANUBE
BULGARS
Constantinople
Amastris
Ardebil
Arcadiopolis
ARMENIA
Abaskun
Sea of Marmora
Nicomedia
Manzikert
TABARISTAN
BYZANTINE EMPIRE
Caucasus Mountains
ABBASID
CALIPHATE
Tigris
Zagros Mountains
Baghdad
Sidon
Acre
Jerusalem

– – – Area under Rus
control c.900

CHANGING PERSPECTIVES ON THE VIKINGS

The Vikings were an unprecedented phenomenon in European history, not for any technological, military or cultural innovation that they contributed to – in most respects they were really rather backward and even their shipbuilding methods were conservative – but for the vast expanse of their horizons. No previous Europeans had ever seen so much of the world as the Vikings did. From their Scandinavian homelands, Vikings sailed east down the great rivers of Russia crossing the Black Sea to Constantinople and the Caspian Sea to reach Baghdad. In the west, Vikings were active along the entire coastline of Western Europe, founding settlements in Scotland, England, Ireland and France. Vikings even penetrated the Mediterranean to attack Italy and North Africa. Other Vikings crossed the Atlantic, leaving settlements along the way in the Faeroe Islands, Iceland and Greenland, to become the first Europeans known to have set foot in North America. It is these far-flung connections, and the daring spirit that created them, that give the Vikings their enduring appeal.

Attitudes to the Vikings have shifted over the years. The main chroniclers of medieval Europe were monks and understandably, as

they were frequent victims of it, they dwelled on the Vikings' plundering, burning and captive-taking (they had little to say about
rape, perhaps because, as men, they had little to fear from them on
that account, at least). Vikings remained frightening barbarians, on
a par with the Vandals and the Goths who had plundered ancient
Rome, until the nineteenth century era of national romanticism. The
medieval image of the Vikings as all-conquering sea rovers came to
be seen in a positive light. The Scandinavian kingdoms had become a
European backwater, lacking influence on the world stage and playing
no part in the global empire-building activities of countries like Great
Britain and France. The temptation for Scandinavians to hark back
to a more heroic era when it was they who bestrode the world was
irresistible. It was in this period that the word 'Viking' subtly changed
its meaning. If they used the term, medieval writers used 'Viking'
specifically to describe someone who went *í víking* (plundering), that
is a pirate, and not necessarily a Scandinavian one at that. The word is
thought originally to have meant 'men of the bays', perhaps because
that is where pirates lurked hoping to ambush an unwary merchant
ship. Under the influence of national romanticism, however, 'Viking'
became a synonym for 'early medieval Scandinavian' and the usage has
stuck. It was also during this era that Vikings were equipped with their
romantically barbaric, but historically inaccurate, horned helmets
(the error originated in the misidentification by early Antiquarians of
Bronze Age horned helmets as Viking helmets). The helmets too have
stuck in the popular imagination.

    In the second half of the twentieth century this essentially military
image of the Vikings came under increasing scrutiny. Archaeology
uncovered evidence of peaceful Viking enterprise in the fields of crafts,
trade, exploration and settlement, leading to a more balanced view of
their lives. However, there was also a tendency to underplay the violent
aspects of the Viking Age as mere monkish exaggeration. Partly, this
was an over-reaction to the established view, and partly because after
the two horrific world wars, conquest and empire-building no longer
seemed such praiseworthy activities to Europeans. However, violence
was always at the heart of the Viking Age, their trade was fuelled by the
spoils of war – especially their slaving activities – and their peaceful

settlements were preceded by bloody conquest. This book is not an attempt to paint a balanced picture of Viking life – it has little to say about their artistic achievements, their everyday lives or the role of women, for example, rather it is intended to place the Vikings in their wider geographical and historical context, from their prehistoric pagan origins to their transformation into Christian Europeans. This approach reveals that the Viking Age begins and ends at different times in different places. In the English-speaking world the Viking Age is conventionally dated from around 793 (the sack of Lindisfarne) to around 1066 (the battle of Stamford Bridge) but history is not really so neat. In Scandinavia and the Baltic, the Viking Age was clearly underway more than a century earlier and, in many ways, had still not ended a century later. In the Scottish isles, the last recorded Viking raid did not take place until as late as 1240. In the Norse Iceland and Greenland colonies, Viking Age government institutions and social structures survived into the thirteenth century. The Vikings did not burst out of nowhere and they lived through a long twilight. It is a long journey that starts in Asgard at the creation of the world and ends at a wedding in fifteenth-century Greenland.

A note about spellings.
For the benefit of non-academic readers, in this book I have used established modern English or Scandinavian spellings for place-names and personal names. However, I have not thought it appropriate to commission anglicisms where none exist already and in these cases Old Norse forms have been used.

ASGARD
THE VIKING WORLD VIEW

Cattle die, kinsmen die, eventually you will die,
But glory never dies for the man who achieves it.

The foolish man thinks he will live forever,
If he keeps away from fighting;
But old age won't grant him a truce
Even if the spears do.

Hávamál, trans. Carolyne Larrington

ife for most Viking Age Scandinavians involved hard work on the land, constant insecurity and an early death in their thirties or forties. For those Scandinavians who chose to become Vikings in the literal sense of the word, that is a pirate or a plunderer, or who set out on voyages of trade or colonisation, life could be shorter still. All faced the very real prospect of drowning at sea as their fragile ships foundered in a storm or were smashed to matchwood against a rocky shore. Merchants always ran the risk of being attacked by pirates and for every Viking warrior who went home with a sack of silver or won a farm for himself on newly conquered land, there must have been at least another who was hacked to pieces on a battlefield or died of disease in an unsanitary winter camp. Vikings clearly were willing to take incredible risks in the quest to acquire land, treasure and fame. This daring and enterprising society was underpinned by a world view which actively discouraged the avoidance of risk. The world the pagan Norse inhabited did not exist to fulfil any purpose and, if it was true that the gods had created humans,

they did so only for their own benefit, so that there would be someone
to sacrifice to them. If men's lives were to have any meaning in this
world, they had to provide it for themselves by achieving something
for which they would be remembered.

The creation of the world

The Norse believed that the centre of the universe was a vast evergreen
ash tree called Yggdrasil whose branches overspread the heavens and
linked together the separate worlds of the gods, frost giants, fire giants,
elves, dwarfs, humans and the underworld. No myth tells of the origins
of Yggdrasil or of its ultimate fate, its existence is taken for granted and
it was perhaps thought to be eternal. Despite this, Yggdrasil does not
feature at all in the Norse creation myth, in which the cosmos is born
from the interaction of mutually hostile forces. At the beginning of
time there were just two worlds, fiery Muspel in the south and freezing
Niflheim in the north. Between the two worlds was the yawning void
of Ginnungagap. Where the heat of Muspel met the ice of Niflheim, the
ice began to melt and drip. The heat caused life to quicken in the drops
and they took the form of a giant who was given the name Ymir. While
Ymir slept, a male and a female giant formed from the sweat under
his left armpit, and one of his legs fathered a son on his other leg. In
this way Ymir became the ancestor of the race of frost giants. As the
ice continued to melt a cow emerged. This cow was called Audhumla.
Audhumla was nourished by licking the salty ice, and the four rivers of
milk that flowed from her teats fed Ymir.

Audhumla's licking revealed another giant, whose name was Búri.
Big, strong and beautiful, Búri fathered a son called Bor – no mother
is mentioned but she was presumably a frost giant as they were the
only other beings around at the time apart from Audhumla. Bor took
Bestla, the daughter of the frost giant Bölthorn, as his wife and together
they had three sons, Odin, Vili and Vé, the first of the gods. Odin and
his brothers killed Ymir and used his dead body to make the land, his
blood to make the ocean. Then the gods took Ymir's skull and set it
up over the earth to make the sky. The gods caught some of the sparks
and molten embers that were blowing out of Muspel and they set them

in the sky to light the heavens and the Earth. The gods set the dark giantess Nótt ('night') and her bright and beautiful son Dag ('day') in the sky to follow each other around the world once every twenty-four hours. The gods took the beautiful brother and sister, Máni ('moon') and Sól ('sun'), and set them in the sky also. By their movements, the days, months and years, could be counted.

The gods made the world a great circle. The part around the edges the gods gave to the giants as a home. This was Jotunheim, where the giants plotted vengeance for the slaying of Ymir. In the middle, surrounded by the ocean, the gods used Ymir's eyelashes to build a fortress against the hostile giants. This they called Midgard, or 'Middle Earth'. Finally, the gods took Ymir's brains and cast them into the sky to make the clouds. With this, the gods completed their recycling of Ymir. Odin, Vili and Vé walked along the newly created seashore and found two logs. From these the gods created the first two humans, naming the man Ask ('ash') and the woman Embla ('elm'), and from them all of the human race was descended. The gods gave Ask and Embla Midgard to live in. After they had created humans, the gods created their own realm of Asgard, a celestial city high above Midgard, and built the fiery rainbow bridge Bifröst to link the two realms so that they could pass to and fro between them. As to how long before their own day the Vikings believed these events to have taken place, the myths give no clue. Like most pre-literate peoples, the Vikings lacked formal dating methods and any events that had happened before the time of living memory probably existed in something akin to the Aboriginal Dreamtime.

Asgard, home of the gods

Within Asgard's walls are dozens of magnificent halls and temples where the gods feast and meet in council. From the throne in his silver-roofed hall Válaskjálf, Odin watches over the whole of creation, sending his ravens Hugin and Mumin out every dawn to gather news from the world. Like any Viking chieftain, Odin has his own retinue of household warriors, *einherjar*, who are chosen exclusively from the ranks of the bravest warriors who fell in battle. The *einherjar* dwell in

Valhalla ('the hall of the slain'), a vast hall with 540 doors each of which is so wide that 800 warriors can march through them abreast. Valhalla shines with gold, has spears for rafters and a roof made of shields and mail coats. Every morning, the *einherjar* march out of Valhalla to spend the day fighting. In the evening the fallen are miraculously healed and all return to Valhalla to spend the night feasting on pork and drinking mead. The *einherjar* are waited on by the valkyries ('choosers of the slain'), beautiful supernatural females who wear armour and carry a shield and spear. At Odin's command, valkyries ride swiftly through the air, descending on battlefields to decide the victors and choose the warriors who are to fall and conduct the bravest of them to Valhalla. There they will be welcomed with cups of mead and tumultuous table-thumping from the *einherjar*. Viking warriors knew that they had to earn their lord's hospitality on the battlefield. For the *einherjar* the price of Odin's hospitality was to fight for him at Ragnarök, a great battle which he knows is fated to happen at the end of time in which the gods and their implacable enemies, the giants, will annihilate one another with fire and flood and destroy the universe itself before a new cycle of creation begins.

Appeasing the gods

In the myths they told about their gods, the Norse never held them up as examples of morality worth emulating. The Norse gods were above human morality, they happily cheated and lied if it suited them, especially in their dealings with the giants. Nor did the Norse claim divine authority for their law codes, maintaining an orderly society was a human responsibility and one they took seriously despite the mayhem they created abroad. Of the gods only Odin was seen as a source of wisdom. Odin gave humans the knowledge of runes, the gift of poetry, the battle fury of the berserker, and the dangerous magic called *seiðr*, which gave the gift of prophecy and other more sinister powers. Odin's wisdom is embodied in *Hávamál* ('The Sayings of the High One'), a collection of anonymous Viking Age gnomic verses supposed to have been composed by Odin and preserved in a single thirteenth century Icelandic manuscript. *Hávamál* is not concerned with metaphysical questions, only with the kind of pragmatic common-sense wisdom valued by practical people. Cultivate friendships, never take hospitality for granted and repay gifts with gifts. Do not make enemies unnecessarily or pick foolish fights. On campaign, keep your weapons close to hand. Do not drink too much mead or ale, it robs a man of his wits. If you do not know what you are talking about, keep quiet: it is better to listen. Exercise caution in business and always beware of treachery and double dealing. Always deal honestly yourself except with your enemies: deceive them if you can. The advice is sometimes contradictory: *Hávamál* berates the coward who thinks he will live forever if he avoids fighting while also declaring that it is better to be a live dog than a dead lion.

Like all pre-industrial farming peoples the Norse were desperately vulnerable to the vagaries of nature and they looked to their gods for help in their struggle to survive. The gods always needed to be propitiated and could only be won over with prayers and offerings. Central to worship were the sacrificial feasts, called a *blót* ('blood-offering'), which were held in autumn, midwinter and spring. Norse paganism had no priesthood, so these sacrifices were presided over by the local king or chieftain. Pigs and horses were the animals most often sacrificed. The blood of the slaughtered victims, which was splashed on the idols of the gods, on the walls of temples and on the participants themselves, was believed to strengthen both gods and humans. Afterwards, the meat was boiled in great cauldrons and eaten at a sacred feast at which the gods were believed to be present. Prayers and toasts were offered for fertility, good health and prosperity. Human sacrifice, usually by hanging, was also sometimes practiced, particularly in honour of Odin, who had sacrificed himself by hanging from Yggdrasil for nine days to discover the secret of the runes. Cold and calculating, Odin was favoured by kings, warriors and poets, but he was feared rather than loved. The most popular god was probably Odin's son, the mighty thunder god Thor. Thor was rather short-tempered and none too bright – most of the stories told about him humorously illustrate the limitations of brute strength – but he was unambiguously well-intentioned towards humans. Thor protected humans against the giants, who stood for chaos, smashing their brains out with his magic hammer, Mjöllnir. Farmers and seafarers prayed to him for good weather. Miniature Thor's hammers were worn as protective amulets by travellers, rather like Christian St Christopher medallions. The fertility god Freyr controlled the sun, rain and the fertility of the soil and was prayed to and sacrificed to by those seeking peace and a good harvest. Of the goddesses, Freyr's sister Frejya, who was associated with sex and love, and Odin's wife Frigg, invoked by women in childbirth, were probably the ones most actively worshipped. Sacrifices were also offered to the dísir, a group of nameless supernatural females who were associated with fertility and death. Dísir could assist at childbirth and each human family had its own protective dís. If angered, however, the dísir were dangerous so they were appeased by an annual feast and sacrifice known as dísablót, which took place at the beginning of winter in Norway and Denmark and in late winter in Sweden. Elves could make a nuisance of themselves in various ways and they were sometimes also appeased with blood sacrifices.

Fame is the one true afterlife

The promise of Valhalla did not, as might be supposed, make most Viking warriors reckless in battle. Although it may have been a comfort to a warrior facing death in battle, what he really wanted to do was live and enjoy the fruits of victory. Only for the berserkers, fanatical devotees of Odin, was death in battle actually desirable. Before going into battle, berserkers worked themselves into a trancelike rage (*berserksgangr*, 'going berserk'), howling and biting their shields, which left them immune to the pain of wounds. They wore no armour and their complete disregard for their own safety made them terrifying opponents, but most inevitably found the violent death they craved. Aside from the concept of Valhalla, Norse beliefs about the afterlife were vague and mostly rather gloomy. The common practice of burying grave goods, sacrificed animals and even slaves with the deceased suggests that the Norse believed that the afterlife would resemble this life, complete with its distinctions of social status, and that the dead somehow lingered on as ghostly presences in their graves. Alongside this there was a belief that those who died of illness and old age, that is almost everyone, would go to the freezing-fog realm of Niflheim, where they would spend a cheerless afterlife sharing the meagre fare offered by the decaying goddess Hel. The souls of un-wed girls were claimed by Freyja, who took them to dwell in her own realm of Fólkvangr: Odin allowed her to take a share of his warriors to keep them company. Death by drowning was an obvious risk for a Viking warrior. The souls of the drowned were netted by Rán, who took them to dwell in Hlésey, the hall of her husband the sea god Aegir. Happily for those destined to spend their afterlives with him, he was the best brewer among the gods. Perhaps as a result of Christian influence during the Viking Age, Norse paganism developed a concept of reward and punishment in the afterlife, although this was a judgment of the dead without a judge. The souls of the righteous would dwell in the golden-roofed hall of Gimlé in Asgard. Or perhaps they would go instead to another hospitable hall, Sindri in the underworld's Niðafjöll Mountains. Oath-breakers and murderers had the miserable time they deserved in Nástrandir, a frightful hall in Niflheim made of woven serpents dripping with venom. The most wicked souls were cast into the underworld well of Hvergelmir, to be fed on by the serpent Niðhöggr, the corpse-tearer. For most people these various afterlives offered nothing to come that was better than what they had in the here and now – even the most favoured warriors faced ultimate annihilation in a battle they could not win – so it was best to live for the present day.

Knowing that nothing was ever forever, not even the gods or the afterlife, gave the Viking Age Norse a fatalistic outlook and an indifference to death. The Viking warrior was expected to face death with a shrug of the shoulders and some black humour to show that he had kept his presence of mind and not given in to fear. Life was not so much to lose and if it was his fate to die, there was nothing he could do about it anyway.

The pagan Norse believed that female deities called Norns were present at the birth of every child to shape its life. Their fate-making was likened to spinning a thread or making a mark on wood and once a person's fate had been decided it was unalterable. The Norns were the highest power in the universe and not even the gods could challenge their verdict. In some cultures such beliefs might have encouraged apathy. However, with the Norse they encouraged the spirit of risk-taking and enterprise without which the Viking Age would never have happened. For good or ill, the Norns determined a man's fate but they did not determine how he faced it. He could play safe and keep as far away from danger as he could but this would not save his life: he would die at his appointed time whether he was snug in bed or in the thick of battle. The man who recognised and accepted this knew he had little to lose by taking risks. Death came to everyone and all that would survive of a man was his reputation, which, therefore, was far more important than his life. When a Viking warrior fought to the death alongside his lord and comrades, he did so not because he hoped to go to Valhalla but to protect his reputation from being dishonoured by the taint of cowardice. A man without honour was a *niðingr*, literally nothing, who would deservedly be forgotten even by his own family. The man who risked nothing achieved less than nothing. Better by far to be bold and adventurous and strive to win fame, wealth and glory by daring voyages and heroic deeds in battle. Such a man could die secure in the knowledge that the skalds ('court poets') would sing his praises in the feasting halls for generations to come: this was the only sure afterlife a man could hope for.

CHAPTER 1

THULE, NYDAM AND GAMLA UPPSALA

THE ORIGIN OF THE VIKINGS

The Vikings did not spring into life fully formed at the end of the eighth century, even if it may have seemed that way to their startled and appalled victims. In reality, the breaking out of Viking raiding was the consequence of centuries of social and political evolution, which had created in Scandinavia a violent and predatory society. If these developments passed largely unnoticed in the rest of Europe it was only partly because of Scandinavia's remoteness. In the literate Greco-Roman world of Classical antiquity, a deep cultural prejudice against the 'barbarian' meant that the peoples of northern Europe were little studied and rarely written about. This prejudice survived into the Christian era, when Scandinavians were doubly damned for being pagans as well as barbarians. As Scandinavians themselves did not develop a fully literate culture until after their conversion to Christianity at the end of the Viking Age, contemporary written evidence of Scandinavia's historical development before the Viking Age is extremely scarce: Scandinavia's prehistoric period was a long one.

Pytheas' voyage to Thule

Scandinavia's earliest known literate visitor was the Greek explorer Pytheas of Massalia, who made a long voyage in the northern seas in

the years around 320 BC. On his return home Pytheas wrote an account
of his travels entitled *On the Oceans*. Unfortunately, this was lost in
antiquity and is known today only from extracts preserved in the
works of later Greek and Roman geographers. These show Pytheas to
have been a scientifically minded traveller who estimated the latitude
of the places he visited on his journey by measuring the height of the
sun at noon and by the length of the days. In his own time, however,
Pytheas was believed by many to have invented the whole story, so
fantastic did it seem.

Pytheas' home port of Massalia (now Marseilles), was founded in
600 BC by settlers from the Greek city of Phocea. The sheltered natural
harbour was an obvious attraction and it was close to the valley of
the river Rhône, which at that time was a major trade route bringing
British tin and Baltic amber to the Mediterranean. The Phoceans had
the reputation of being the most adventurous Greek seafarers. Soon
after founding Massalia they had sailed through the fabled Pillars of
Hercules – the Straits of Gibraltar – into the Atlantic Ocean to trade
with the mineral-rich Iberian kingdom of Tartessos. One of them,
Midacritus, was rumoured to have gone even further and brought
back tin from Britain. However, around 500 BC the Phoceans were shut
out of the Atlantic when the powerful North African city of Carthage
gained control of the Pillars of Hercules. Carthage lived by trade and
did not welcome foreign merchants in its sphere of influence. Pytheas'
expedition, therefore, was probably commercial, to seek out new trade
routes for Massalia in areas not controlled by Carthage.

When he set out, Pytheas probably bypassed hostile Carthaginian
territory by travelling overland from Massalia to the Bay of Biscay and
there chartered a ship from one of the local Celtic tribes to take him
on to Britain. The Veneti of Brittany were particularly well-known
for building sturdy wooden sailing ships with which they carried on
a brisk trade in tin with Britain. Pytheas landed at Belerion – Land's
End – and travelled the whole length of Britain. Everything the Greeks
knew about Britain up until then was based on hearsay. For the first
time Pytheas added some reliable facts. His estimate of Britain's
circumference as around 40,000 stades, approximately 4,500 miles, is
remarkably close to the actual distance of around 4,700 miles. The next

stage of Pytheas' journey took him far beyond the edge of the known world. Setting out from an unidentified island off Britain's north coast, Pytheas sailed north for six days until he reached the land he called Thule. Pytheas' observation that the sun was below the horizon for only two or three hours at midsummer fixes Thule's latitude at about 64° north. However, Pytheas had no means of calculating longitude. There is no doubt that Thule was a land in the far north but where exactly? The uncertainty of its location has made Thule more a symbol of ultimate hyperborean remoteness than a real place.

Iceland or even Greenland have been proposed as possible locations for Thule but, as this comment on Pytheas' account by the Greek geographer Strabo (c. 63/64 BC–AD 24) makes clear, Thule was inhabited by farming peoples:

> '[Pytheas] might possibly seem to have made adequate use of the facts as regards the people who live close to the frozen zone, when he says that, the people live on millet and other herbs, and on fruits and roots; and where there are grain and honey, the people get their beverage, also, from them. As for the grain, he says, since they have no pure sunshine, that they pound it out in large storehouses, after first gathering in the ears thither; for the threshing floors become useless because of this lack of sunshine and because of the rains.'
> The Geography of Strabo, bk IV 5.5 (Loeb Classics, 1917).

Greenland was inhabited only by early Inuit hunter-gatherers at this time, and Iceland by no one at all, so neither could have been Pytheas' Thule. This means that Pytheas' landfall must have been somewhere around Trondheim Fjord on Norway's west coast. Despite its northerly latitude, the Norwegian coast has a relatively mild climate thanks to the influence of the warm Atlantic Gulf Stream current, which makes farming possible even north of the Arctic Circle. Trondheim Fjord's sheltered south and east shores have some of Norway's most fertile soils and farmers were settled on them as early as 2800 BC. Pytheas sailed still further north and his observations make it clear that he crossed the Arctic Circle. He also claimed that a day's sail north of Thule was the Frozen Sea, though it is not clear if he actually saw this for himself or merely reported what other seafarers had told him.

Following his visit to Thule, Pytheas headed south to explore the

Baltic, which he must have reached via the Skagerrak, the Kattegat and one of the passages through the Danish islands. Pytheas visited the unidentified island of Abalus from whose shores amber was collected. A translucent fossil resin with a fiery colour, amber had been prized in the Mediterranean world for thousands of years, not only because of its beauty but because of its seemingly magical electrostatic properties: called electrum by the Greeks, amber has given us the word 'electricity'. The origins of amber were the subject of several myths but Pytheas was the first to establish its true source. Abalus has been identified as the Danish islands of Sjælland or Bornholm, the Samland peninsula near Kaliningrad (the richest source of amber today), and the North Sea island of Heligoland. Heligoland seems unlikely as Pytheas says that Abalus was a day's sail from the lands of the Goths, who at that time lived on the Baltic coast. Pytheas explored the Baltic at least as far east as the Vistula, before returning to Massalia by a round-about route, following the River Tanais (Don) south to the Black Sea, where he would have had little difficulty finding a ship to take him home at one of the many Greek colonies there.

Brief though it is, Strabo's extract from Pytheas, quoted above, is the earliest eyewitness account of the lives of the Vikings' ancestors that we have, but beyond telling us that they enjoyed drinking mead and ale and had to dry their grain indoors, it doesn't tell us much. If Pytheas did have more to say about the languages, customs and social institutions of the people of Thule, his readers did not think it worth preserving. To learn anything meaningful about the Vikings' earliest ancestors we have to turn to archaeology.

Scandinavia in the Stone and Bronze Ages

The ancestors of the Vikings were most likely Stone Age farmers who began to colonise Scandinavia around 6,000 years ago, displacing or assimilating hunter-gatherers whose own ancestors had arrived at the end of the last Ice Age some 6,000 years earlier. These pioneer farmers belonged to the Corded Ware Culture (named for the way its pottery was decorated by pressing twisted cords into the wet clay), which originated on the north German plain. Although the connection will probably never be proven beyond doubt, this culture is associated with the early spread of the Germanic, Slavic and Baltic languages. If true, the settlers probably already spoke an early form of the modern Scandinavian languages, which all belong, with modern German, English, Dutch and Frisian, to the Germanic language family. The close genetic similarity between modern Danes, Norwegians and Swedes on the one hand, and modern north Germans on the other, strengthens rather than weakens this conclusion. No convincing evidence exists for any further substantial migration into Scandinavia before the later twentieth century. Scandinavia would make its mark on history as an exporter of population.

About 1800 BC bronze artefacts began to appear in Scandinavia. Bronze is an alloy of copper and tin, neither of which were available in Scandinavia at that time (Sweden's rich copper reserves were not discovered until the Middle Ages). Scandinavians were, therefore, completely dependent on imported bronze. At first, finished bronze artefacts were imported, but after Scandinavian smiths mastered the skills of bronze casting they probably relied on imported bronze ingots, which were widely traded around Europe. This was the period when amber first began to be traded widely in Europe, so it was probably the commodity the early Scandinavians used to pay for their bronze. The high value placed on amber ensured that bronze was never in short supply in the north. The increase in long distance trade helped stimulate the development of a more hierarchical society, as demonstrated by the appearance of small numbers of richly furnished elite burials marked by earth barrows. Stone suitable for toolmaking is widespread but bronze's exotic origins, and the specialised skills needed to make and cast it, allowed its distribution to be monopolised by a small elite whose power and status were thereby greatly enhanced. In the more fertile areas of southern Scandinavia, farms began to cluster in small villages. The typical dwelling was a longhouse – a long narrow building in which the family and its livestock lived under one roof, the people at one end, the animals in a byre at the other. The livestock helped keep the house warm in winter. The presence of a single large dwelling among otherwise smaller dwellings indicates that villages were dominated by a single headman or chief. In Norway and

much of Sweden, dispersed settlement remained the norm until the end
of the Viking Age.

Bronze tools were a great advance on stone tools but bronze was
even more important for making status symbols, such as weapons,
jewellery, razors, horned helmets, lurs (horns) and fittings for wheeled
vehicles, and cult objects such as the magnificent 'Sun Chariot' from
Trundholm in Denmark, a model of a four-wheeled horse-drawn
wagon carrying a brilliantly gilded sun disc. The horned helmets,
misinterpreted by antiquarians in the nineteenth century, helped give
rise to the romantic, but mistaken, belief that Vikings wore horned
helmets. Sadly, Vikings never wore horned helmets. The Bronze Age
elite probably also achieved close control over the use and distribution
of amber. Amber beads and other ornaments are common offerings
in Stone Age graves in Scandinavia, but they are virtually absent from
those of the Bronze Age. Amber is so light that it floats in salt water –
another property that made it remarkable to the ancients (it also burns)
– and is washed up on beaches around the North Sea and the Baltic for
anyone to pick up. However, it appears that the elite claimed ownership
of all amber washed up in their territories and could prevent others
using it so they could prioritise its use for export.

Petroglyphs

It is during the Bronze Age (*c.* 1800 BC – *c.* 500 BC), that the importance
of seafaring in Scandinavia first becomes obvious. No Bronze Age
ships have yet been found in Scandinavia but representations of them
are everywhere, carved on rocks and etched into bronze vessels and
tools such as razors, and most prominently as stone ship-settings. The
latter are groups of large stones arranged to form the outline shape
of a ship that were used to mark graves. Sometimes taller stones are
placed at the ends of the settings to give the impression of raised prows
and, more rarely, there are raised stones in the position where, in a
real ship, a mast would have been. Most ship-settings range in length
from around 6 feet (1.8 m) to 50 feet (15.25 m) but the longest, the
now largely destroyed setting at Jelling in Jutland, is about 1,100 feet
(335 m) long. Over 2,000 settings survive, with a major concentration

on the Swedish island of Gotland, but these are probably only a fraction of those originally built. Many of the survivors are now incomplete as a result of farmers removing stones to build walls or clear land for the plough, and it is likely that many more have been completely destroyed in this way. The first ship-settings were built in the second half of the Bronze Age and they continued to be built almost until the end of the Viking Age, nearly 2,000 years later. It is impossible to be certain what beliefs were associated with these symbolic ships or, for that matter, that those beliefs remained the same throughout the long period in which the settings were built, but they were probably intended in some way to transport the soul of the deceased to the afterlife. The use of real ships in burials, which began in the centuries immediately before the Viking Age, was probably a development of these beliefs.

Even more numerous than ship settings are petroglyphs showing large canoe-like boats crewed by warriors armed with spears and axes, as well as wheeled vehicles, animals and sun discs. The boats are always shown in silhouette and have distinctive double beaked prows at each end. No other details of the boats' construction are shown on the petroglyphs, however. The boat petroglyphs are usually carefully sited in natural channels on the rocks, along which rainwater and melted snow would flow to create a lifelike scene. It is unlikely that the petroglyphs were carved simply because Bronze Age people liked to see pictures of boats. They probably depict mythological scenes or had some ritual purpose. The ships are often associated with petroglyphs of sun discs which, with artefacts like the Trundholm Sun Chariot, should probably be interpreted as evidence of a solar cult. Solar cults were widespread in later Bronze Age Europe and are indicative of an increasing importance of sky gods, which were, of course, the dominant gods of the Norse pantheon in Viking times. Another religious change that affected much of Europe in this period was the adoption of cremation as the normal way to dispose of the dead. This was accompanied by a decline in the practice of placing grave goods in burials. Clearly these developments must reflect a major change in attitudes to afterlife. The valuable metalwork that would have gone into graves was now buried as votive hoards in bogs. As places where the separate realms of earth, water and air mingled, bogs were seen as

particularly numinous places. However, votive hoards were not merely
a way of appeasing the gods; they helped maintain the status of the elite
by creating an artificial shortage of metals.

Because of environmental changes most Bronze Age petroglyphs
cannot now be appreciated in their original context. A good example
is the UNESCO World Heritage site of Tanumshede in Bohuslän on
Sweden's west coast, where there are around 600 petroglyphs spread over
a 126 acre (51 hectare) site. When originally carved the Tanumshede
petroglyphs were on the shore of a shallow fjord, but they are now well
inland and surrounded by pine forest. During the Ice Age, the enormous
weight of the Scandinavian ice sheet depressed the land surface by
over 2,000 feet (610 m). When the ice sheets melted, sea levels rose
and this vast depression flooded, forming the Baltic Sea. Relieved of
its burden, the land, more slowly, began to rebound and will continue
to do so for thousands of years to come. This process, which is known
to geologists as isostatic uplift, means that Scandinavia's coastline has
been constantly changing throughout human history. Fishing and
trading communities that depended on access to the sea have often
been forced to relocate themselves as the uplift has left them high
and dry. The Baltic Sea is steadily shrinking and in about 2,000 years
time its northern arm, the Gulf of Bothnia, will be mostly dry land.

During the Iron Age (500 BC–AD 800), Scandinavian society grad
ually acquired the characteristics that directly caused the Viking
expansion. The Scandinavian Iron Age is conventionally divided into
three periods, the early or pre-Roman Iron Age (500 BC–AD 1), the
Roman Iron Age (AD 1–400), and the Germanic Iron Age (400–800).
The introduction of iron had an immediate and dramatic impact in
Scandinavia. Scandinavians had been totally reliant on imported
bronze to make tools and other artefacts but bog iron, a low grade, easily
worked, iron ore that accumulates in bogs and marshes, is abundant
throughout Scandinavia. This new-found self-sufficiency caused the
decline of the long-distance trade systems that had sustained the
Bronze Age elites. With their control over the distribution of metals
broken, their status and power collapsed, and it is five centuries before
there is evidence for the re-emergence of a social elite.

The wider availability of metal tools contributed to agricultural expansion and a rising population, and an increase in conflict. In the late second century BC population pressure led directly to the first of what would be many migrations out of Scandinavia. Faced with a critical shortage of farmland, around 120 BC two tribes from northern Jutland, the Cimbri and the Teutones, set out on a migration in search of new homelands. Their search took them on a destructive rampage across much of central and western Europe before they invaded Italy in 102 BC and were finally annihilated by the Romans. Although it ended in disaster, this migration was just a foretaste of what was to come. Many of the Germanic tribes who invaded the Roman Empire in the fifth century traced their legendary origins to Scandinavia. The Goths believed they had originated in Götaland in southern Sweden; the Burgundians from the island of Borgundarholm, now Bornholm in Denmark; and the Vandals from Jutland. The Angles and Jutes, who joined the Saxons in settling Britain, both certainly came from Jutland. Writing around 550, the Gothic historian Jordanes described *Scandza* as 'the womb of peoples' because it had given birth to so many tribes. The Viking expansion was really just the last phase of an extended period of migrations out of the north.

The genesis of the longship

Conflict is the essence of what is possibly the single most important archaeological find of the early Iron Age: a near-complete 'war canoe' and a hoard of weapons that were buried together in a bog at Hjortspring on the Danish island of Als around the time of Pytheas' travels. The boat itself is the oldest plank-built boat yet found in Scandinavia and has enormous significance as the earliest known ancestor of the Viking longship. What is immediately most striking about the Hjortspring boat is its distinctive double beaked prows, which closely resemble those of the boats depicted in the Bronze Age petroglyphs, so it is likely to represent a well-established tradition of boat building. The boat was 56 feet (17 m) long by 6 feet (1.8 m) broad and was built from just five lime wood planks: a broad bottom plank with two overlapping planks on each side. This method of building a hull from overlapped planks, known variously as clinker, lapstrake or

Nordic construction, is what marks the Hjortspring boat out as the earliest known ancestor of the Viking longships, whose hulls were built in the same way. The ends of the Hjortspring boat were closed with two carved wooden blocks that served as stemposts. The function, if any, of the projecting beaks is unknown. They may have been intended to ride up over the gunwales of an enemy boat and capsize it, or they may simply be a hangover from an earlier stage in the development of the Nordic boat-building tradition that were retained for cosmetic reasons: they do give the boat a racy appearance. No metal was used in the boat's construction: the planks were sewn together and fastened to internal strengthening ribs with ropes made of lime tree bast. The boat was paddled by a crew of twenty – a useful number for a raiding party – who sat on thwarts set at the level of the gunwale. There was a steering oar at both ends, so the boat could be sailed in either direction. This would have been a great advantage for raiding because the boat could run right up a beach and the crew would not have had to turn it around if they needed to make a quick getaway. The boat was skilfully built to be as light as possible and sea trials with a replica have shown that it was fast, stable and relatively seaworthy. The boat was sunk in the bog with enough weapons to equip a small army: 138 iron tipped spears, thirty-one bone- or antler-tipped spears, eleven iron swords, sixty to eighty shields, and around twenty coats of mail, all but one of which survived only as rust prints in the peat. Plates from a bronze cauldron and the bones of a horse, a dog and a puppy, a lamb and calf were also found. Both ship and weapons survived thanks to the acidic and anaerobic (oxygen deficient) conditions found in peat bogs, which preserve organic materials like wood, textiles and leather by pickling them, while the lack of oxygen retards the rusting of iron.

The Hjortspring find is one of the earliest examples of a practice of sacrificing the spoils of war that became widespread in Scandinavia and adjacent areas of north Germany during the early Iron Age. No other known sacrifice approaches the Hjortspring find in scale, however, and its deposition must commemorate a major battle. The most likely scenario is that the ship and weapons belonged to a large army that invaded Als only to be defeated by the local inhabitants, who offered their plunder to their gods as a thank-offering for victory. There are enough weapons to equip at least eighty warriors, so the invaders would have needed a fleet of at least four Hjortspring-type boats and, of course, we don't known how many of them escaped. It is clear, at least, that raiding by sea was already a serious business in early Iron Age Scandinavia.

It was not only weapons and boats that were sacrificed in bogs, people were too. No bog bodies have been found in Norway or Sweden but over 200 have been found in Denmark and neighbouring areas of northern Germany. Though the acidic conditions in the bogs have often completely dissolved the victims' bones, in many cases their hair, skin and internal organs are so well-preserved that post mortem examinations have revealed much about their health, diet and causes of death. One surprise is that seafood appears not to have been an important part of the Danish diet in early Iron Age times. Most bog bodies show signs of a violent death, like Tollund Man, killed *c.* 400 BC by hanging, and Grauballe Man, whose throat was cut from ear to ear around 100 years later. Some of the victims were found pinned down in the bogs by heavy branches. In *Germania*, a treatise on the Germanic peoples written in AD 98, the Roman historian Tacitus says that this was one of the methods used by the German tribes to execute criminals.

The warlike character of Scandinavian society intensified in the course of the Roman Iron Age. Many Roman weapons have been found in votive hoards, especially in Denmark, suggesting that Scandinavians frequently fought with their German neighbours to the south, who had direct access to Roman weaponry. The increasing importance of war in society is indicated by the appearance of warrior graves furnished with weapons, evidence that a warrior elite now dominated Scandinavian society. A small number of these graves are furnished with imported luxury goods, such as Roman silverware, jewellery and glass, indicating the rise within this elite of a class of chieftains or petty kings. Everyday Roman goods, like pottery and coins have also been found in some quantity in Scandinavia, show that trade with the Roman Empire was not confined to luxuries. There may have been direct trade with the empire by sea, but it is perhaps more likely that Roman goods reached Scandinavia through intermediaries in Germany. Not surprisingly, Roman artefacts are most common in Denmark, but they are not evenly distributed over the country. One remarkable concentration of Roman goods is found in the Stevns area of the island of Sjælland, suggesting that this was the centre of a powerful chiefdom or small kingdom, which could control trade over a wide area. Another striking site from the later part of the period is Gudme on the island of Fyn, where evidence for a 154-foot (47 m) long hall has been found: the largest known in Scandinavia from this period, it has been called 'the King's Hall' and, certainly, a hall of such size implies the existence of a strong central authority. Over 1,000 Roman coins, including twenty gold denarii, have also been found at the site. Gudme means 'god's home', so the place may have been a cult centre. Closely associated with Gudme is a seasonal port and trading place at Lundeborg, where Roman coins and other imports have been found, along with evidence of shipbuilding. This close association between religion and trade is also seen at the Iron Age trading place at Uppåkra near Lund in southern Sweden, where the remains of a wooden temple have been found. It is likely that trade fairs were held during religious festivals when plenty of visitors could be expected.

Sacrifices in Nydam Moss

No single place has provided more spectacular evidence of the warlike character of Scandinavia in the Roman Iron Age than Nydam Moss in southern Jutland. Now just north of the Danish-German border, in the Iron Age Nydam was probably in the territory of the Angles, the Germanic tribe from whom the English get their name. The moss is now a rather soggy meadow but in Roman times it was a reed-fringed lake. In the 1830s, local farmers digging peat from the by then silted up lake began to find old iron weapons and shields. These discoveries eventually caught the attention of antiquarians and between 1859 and 1863 the moss was excavated by the Danish archaeologist Conrad Engelhardt, who discovered large quantities of weapons, two intact clinker-built ships, one built of oak and one of pine, and another oak ship which had been deliberately broken up before its deposition. The excavations were brought to an end by the outbreak of war between Denmark and Prussia in 1864, after which the area remained under

German rule until 1920. During the war the pine ship was chopped up for firewood by German soldiers and burned. Systematic re-excavation of the site in 1984–97 produced thousands more artefacts.

The modern science of dendrochronology, the analysis of the pattern of tree rings preserved in ancient timbers, has dated the oak ship's construction very precisely to 310–320. The ship was not new when it was sacrificed, so it was probably sunk in the bog around 350. The larger of the two ships, the oak ship, was around 70 feet (921.3 m) long by 12 feet (3.65 m) broad and was propelled by a crew of thirty oarsmen. The ship was double-ended, with long raking prows and was steered by a side rudder, which was only loosely attached to the hull. Like the Hjortspring boat, which was found only a few miles away, the oak ship was built of overlapping planks, but instead of being sewn together they are fastened using iron clench nails. Internal strengthening frames were lashed to the hull planks using lime-bast rope as on the Hjortspring boat. No fittings for a mast were found so the oak ship did not have a sail. Drawings made of the pine boat before its destruction show that it was about 61 feet (18.6 m) long by 10 feet (3 m) broad, had a crew of about twenty two oarsmen and was built in a generally similar way to the oak ship. There was no evidence that the ship had a mast. The modern re-excavation of the site discovered many fragments of the pine ship, the most important of which was a side rudder, which had been attached firmly to the side of the ship on a wooden boss. This type of side rudder continued to be used on longships until after the end of the Viking Age. Rudders were always fitted to the right-hand side of the ship, hence 'starboard' (from Old Norse *styri*/steer and *borð*/side of the ship). A shield found in the ship was made of timber felled in 296, so the ship was probably sacrificed in the early fourth century. Most of the third ship is thought still to be in the bog, but it was certainly rowed rather than paddled and its planks were fastened with iron clench nails. This ship was built of wood felled in AD 190, so it was probably sacrificed in the early third century.

The change since the early Iron Age from paddling to rowing is significant. For raiding, paddling has the advantage that all the crew can see where they are going, can keep a look-out for the enemy, and can disembark and re-embark more quickly than a crew of oarsmen.

On the other hand, rowing is much more energy efficient than paddling so its adoption made it possible to raid further afield. The pine ship is evidence for this as it was probably built in Sweden. Pines large enough for shipbuilding did not grow in southern Scandinavia at this time and the ship's timbers were decorated with patterns that are also found on contemporary inscribed stones in Sweden. The timing of the transition is uncertain but the earliest evidence for the use of oars is a rowlock found in a bog in Hordaland in Norway, which dates to *c.* 30 BC–AD 250. The question of the timing of the adoption of the sail in Scandinavia is a controversial one because the evidence is inconclusive. The Celtic peoples of Gaul, Britain and Ireland certainly used sailing ships in pre-Roman times and in his *Histories,* Tacitus describes the German tribes of the North Sea coast using sailing ships in their wars with Rome in the first century AD. However, in *Germania*, he also says that the *Suiones* (the Swedes) used neither sails nor oars on their ships. The two Nydam ships, of course, also used oars but not sails. At the time the ships were sacrificed, the Angles' southern neigh-bours, the Saxons, were using sailing ships for pirate raids on Roman Britain and earning notoriety for their practice of sacrificing Roman prisoners to obtain a fair wind home. The Scandinavians cannot, therefore, have been ignorant of the sail in the fourth century. Many Scandinavian mercenaries and merchants must also have been familiar with Roman sailing ships. Despite this, the earliest clear evidence for the use of sails in the region is a seventh-century inscribed stone from Karlby on Jutland's east coast showing a Nydam-type ship under sail.

The sail and Scandinavia

The slow adoption of the sail in Scandinavia is hard to explain, especially as the technology itself is not complex: a woollen blanket or leather cloak, two wooden poles and some rope are all that would have been needed to make a rudimentary sail. The most commonly advanced theory, that the keels of ships like the Nydam ships were too weak to support the stresses of sailing, has never been tested experimentally and seems unconvincing given that, globally, sails have been fitted to all manner of watercraft, a great many of which have been technologically far less sophisticated than either of the Nydam ships. The argument usually advanced is that if the sail was not adopted it was because there was no perceived need for it. Warships needed large crews anyway and a sail would simply make a raiding ship more conspicuous (Vikings sometimes lowered their sails when approaching a hostile coast to increase their chances of landing unobserved), so it may not have seemed so advantageous for short range raiding in sheltered fjords and coastal waters. Chiefs and kings may also have seen commanding a crew of oarsmen as an expression of their own power. However, rowing long distances is hard work even for those accustomed to it, so these arguments are not really convincing. Perhaps it was only when Scandinavians began setting out on raiding and trading voyages beyond Scandinavian waters in the fifth century that the benefits of the sail become obvious to these technologically conservative seafarers?

The ships were only part of the Nydam find. Excavations have uncovered thousands of weapons, or parts of weapons, including swords, spears, lances, axes, and bows and arrows, elaborately decorated wooden scabbards, silver fittings from scabbards and belts, silver bars, and other personal items like combs and wooden storage boxes. The largest number of weapons were found in and around the ships but there were also many other weapon sacrifices in the bog. Most consisted of only a few spear or lance heads but one, which was surrounded by a fence of thirty-six swords thrust down into the bog, contained over 1,000 objects. Deposited *c.* 450–475, this was the last known weapon sacrifice at Nydam and one of the last in Scandinavia. Beliefs were changing again, bogs lost their significance as sacred places and the custom of bog sacrifices died out.

Runes and magic

The finds from Nydam Moss illustrate another change in the north, the beginnings of literacy. The early Germans and Scandinavians wrote using runes, an alphabet of twig-like characters known as the *futhark* after the names of its first three characters. Though often inscribed on stone and metalwork, runes were originally designed to be carved on wood because the characters avoid horizontal lines, which would not have been clearly distinguishable from the grain. The oldest known runic inscription reads *harja*, a man's name, and was found on a comb from Vimose bog on the Danish island of Fyn, which was made *c*. AD 150. The largest concentration of early runic inscriptions has been found in southern Scandinavia but it is not certain that this was the area where they were invented as runes were used by all the Germanic peoples. The origin of runes is surrounded by myth. In the Viking Age Scandinavians believed that runes were a gift of Odin, who had hanged himself, impaled on a spear, from the World Tree Yggdrasil for nine days to learn their secret. They are now more prosaically thought to be derived from Latin letters, which early Germans could easily have become familiar with through contacts with Roman merchants or during mercenary service in the Roman army.

Runes were certainly not for everyone's use in Iron Age Scandinavia. Of the thousands of artefacts recovered from Nydam Moss only ten carry inscriptions in runes. Most are on war gear, arrow and lance shafts, a lance head, a decorative bead from a sword, a scabbard, a silver belt fitting is the only inscribed artefact without an exclusively military function. This suggests that runes were associated with high social status. The inscriptions are all very short, only one or two words, and the majority simply record names, either of the artefacts' presumed owners, the craftsmen who made them, or the runemasters who carved the runes. For example, the scabbard – found in the pine ship, carries the inscription *harkilaR ahti*. The meaning of *ahti* is unknown but *harkilaR* is a man's name. Swords were rare and expensive at that time, so was *harkilaR* the defeated commander of the pine ship? One runic inscription, on a lance shaft, does not spell out a word but is just a sequence of runes and rune-like symbols. This hints at how runes were seen, that the individual characters were at least as significant as the words they spelled.

In most civilizations, the main impetus to the development of writing was the need to keep records when society became too large and complex for unaided human memory to keep all the information needed for good government. Utilitarian lists and tax records came first. Memorials, literature, historical, religious and philosophical texts all came later. The Germanic-Scandinavian world was nowhere near this level of complexity in the Roman Iron Age, so writing fulfilled a different function. Rune means 'secret' or 'something hidden', so there was something esoteric about them. In the Viking Age, runes were believed to have magic properties. Each rune had its own name, embodying gods, ideas and powers. The act of writing a rune harnessed that power. Carving one of the runes named after gods, such as the 'T'-shaped Tiwaz rune associated with the war god Tiwaz or Tyr, was an invocation for the god's protection. In this way the act of carving a runic charm on an object turned it into a protective amulet. However, not just anyone could carve protective runes, they had to be carved by a trained runemaster if they were to be effective. Errors would make them impotent or even harmful. In Scandinavia, the use of runes remained limited to names and charms until the Viking Age, when longer commemorative inscriptions began to be made. Viking graffiti of the 'Halfdan was here' variety has been found across the Viking world, from Greenland to Greece, suggesting that by that time literacy in runes had become widespread. Because they had pagan overtones, most of the Germanic peoples gave up using runes and adopted the Latin alphabet soon after they converted to Christianity. However, they continued to be used in medieval Scandinavia, when even law codes and other texts were written in runes. In the Dalarna district of central Sweden, a tradition of writing runic charms survived into the twentieth century.

Roman influence in the north

The indirect cause of Scandinavia's changing society was Roman influence on the German tribes to the south. By the end of the first century BC the Germanic tribes and the Roman Empire shared a common frontier along the Rhine and Danube rivers. Despite incursions by both sides on each other's territory, this frontier remained stable for 400 years. Contact with the Roman Empire had a great impact on those tribes closest to the border. Plunder from raids, Roman subsidies to friendly tribes, trade, and wages for mercenary service enriched the border tribes. Tribes further north raided and traded with the border tribes, so becoming enriched in turn. Those who led successful raids or gained control of the distribution of trade goods were soon set apart from the rest of society by their greater wealth and status. Roman writers, such as Tacitus, attest that the *comitatus* or war band became the central institution of Germanic society in this period. Known in Viking Age Scandinavia as the *lið* or *hirð*, the *comitatus* was made up of young warriors who entered the service of a chief or king. In return for their loyalty and military service the warriors of the *comitatus* expected to receive food and lodging, gifts of weapons and jewellery, and a share of war booty. The warriors swore loyalty to their chief for life but their loyalty was conditional on the chief fulfilling his side of the bargain. A chief who did not, or could not, reward his warriors would not have a *comitatus* for long. Chiefs who were poor warriors fell by the wayside, those who were good warriors consolidated their power because their success attracted more warriors, and a stronger *comitatus* led to more success in war. This dynamic created a violent and predatory society in which war was the surest route to wealth, status and power. Another effect was to concentrate power in fewer and fewer hands, increasing competition between ambitious men within a tribe, and to encourage the merging of tribes. In some cases this was because a stronger tribe conquered and absorbed a weaker one, but just as often it was done voluntarily. Many tribes allied, forming coalitions to wage war more effectively. When their unity was cemented by success in war, these coalitions became the basis for new ethnic identities. The Saxons and the Franks, for example, both developed from tribal coalitions in this way.

The Germanic Iron Age (400–800) was Scandinavia's heroic age, a proto-historical period that was half remembered in legendary traditions of dragon-slaying warriors and great battles. At the beginning of the period the process of centralisation that had transformed the Germanic world had still not progressed far in Scandinavia. Jordanes listed more than twenty tribes living in the 'island of Scandza' in his history of the Goths, and this doesn't include the Angles and Jutes who lived in Jutland, which he didn't count as part of Scandza. Jordanes' list is based ultimately on the testimony of Rodulf, the exiled king of a Norwegian tribe called the Rani. According to Jordanes, two tribes had already become pre-eminent, however: the Swedes or, as they called themselves, the Svear, and the Danes, whose territory then included Skåne and Blekinge in the far south of modern Sweden. Also prominent were the Götar, who lived between the Swedes and the Danes in Sweden's densely forested Southern Uplands. Around eight tribes lived in Norway; their homelands can be identified with some certainty because they are etymologically related to the names of regions of modern Norway. The Raumarici most likely lived in Romerike, the Alogi in Hålogaland north of the Arctic Circle, the Rugi in Rogaland, and so on. Rodulf's Rani probably lived in Romsdal, the valley of the River Rauma, in the west of the country. Thanks to its rugged geography, Norway remained a land of local tribes even at the beginning of the Viking Age. Elsewhere, most of the tribes named by Jordanes had vanished by this time. The Danes had absorbed the Angles and Jutes and another tribe mentioned by Jordanes called the Heruls, who lived between the Götar and the Danes. The Swedes and Götar had absorbed the rest. This was certainly not a peaceful process. Fortresses proliferated across Scandinavia – over 1,500 are known from this period. On the 80-mile-long island of Öland, nineteen stone ring-forts were built around this time so no one would have been more than two or three miles from a refuge. At the same time there was a general movement of settlement away from the coast, a sure sign that piracy was endemic. The Viking Age may not have started in western Europe until 793 but something like it was already well under way in the Baltic Sea.

The first half of the Germanic Iron Age is known as the Migration Period (400–500), after the series of Germanic migrations that resulted in the complete collapse of the Western Roman Empire in 476. The ultimate cause of the Germanic migrations was the arrival c. 370 in eastern Europe of the Huns, a ferocious Turkic nomad people from Central Asia. Those tribes who could took flight in a desperate search for safer homelands, displacing other tribes and setting almost the whole Germanic world in motion. Some tribes were broken up and absorbed by others, and new ethnic identities were forged from ad hoc coalitions. Many tribes, including the Goths, Vandals, Burgundians and Suevi, sought refuge in the Roman Empire, overwhelming its border defences and founding new kingdoms on its territory. The Huns never reached Scandinavia but the political chaos

of the age created opportunities for the enterprising. Britain slipped
out of Roman control in 410 and was left exposed to the Saxons, who
seized land and began to settle the rich lands of the south-east and
the Midlands. Saxons also took advantage of the chaos the invasions
caused in Roman Gaul, settling in the Pas de Calais, Normandy, and
on the River Loire. At the same time they raided as far north as the
Orkney Islands, as far west as Ireland, and as far south as Aquitaine.
The Angles soon joined the Saxons in Britain, settling along the east
coast from East Anglia north to the Firth of Forth. So too did the Jutes,
whose main settlements were probably in Kent. Another tribe from
southern Scandinavia, the Heruls, launched pirate raids as far afield as
Aquitaine and northern Spain but they made no known settlements. A
branch of this well-travelled people had already migrated to Ukraine
in the third century, and from there launched pirate raids around the
Black Sea and the eastern Mediterranean. Those Heruls who remained
in Scandinavia were conquered by the Danes in the sixth century.
This is most likely the period that sailing ships began to be used in
Scandinavia as it is scarcely credible that the Angles, Jutes and Heruls
should have undertaken such long voyages of settlement and piracy in
rowing ships, taking weeks or months, when their Saxon neighbours
were crossing the same seas, for the same purposes, in much swifter
sailing ships.

The age of Beowulf

Scandinavian raiders were also busy much closer to home, raiding Frisia,
a region on the North Sea coast now divided between Germany and
the Netherlands. In *c.* 528, Frisia was raided by the Scandinavian king
Hygelac, who went on to sail down the Rhine as far as Nijmegen before
he was defeated and killed by the Franks. It is a sign that Scandinavia
was now truly beginning to emerge from prehistory that Hygelac's
raid was recorded in four independent literary sources, including
Gregory of Tours' near contemporary *History of the Franks* and the
eighth-century Anglo-Saxon epic poem 'Beowulf'. Unfortunately, the
sources don't agree whose king Hygelac was. Gregory of Tours, and
two other Frankish sources, describe Hygelac as a king of the Danes

– their earliest appearance in history – but in 'Beowulf' he is called king of the Geats, that is the Götar, from southern Sweden, or even the Jutes of Jutland. In the poem the hero Beowulf is said to have taken part in the raid, swimming home after his king's defeat, in full armour, underwater. Beowulf goes on to save the Danish king Hrothgar from the man-eating troll-like monster Grendel and his equally awful mother, become king of the Geats, and finally die slaying a dragon that was ravaging his lands. 'Beowulf' also describes another Danish raid on Frisia as does another early Anglo-Saxon poem, the fragmentary 'Finnsburg'. A Frankish poem, composed c. 570, records another major raid by Danes but this was also driven off by the Franks. No further Danish raids on Frisia are recorded until the Viking Age, so this defeat appears to have deterred them from interfering in what the Franks regarded as their sphere of influence for 200 years.

The Migration Period was a quite literal golden age for Scandinavia. In the course of their migrations, the Germans and Huns relieved the Romans of enormous amounts of gold and silver, either as plunder or payments of tribute. Much of this gold eventually found its way to Scandinavia, whether by trade or plundering raids across the Baltic, or in the pockets of homeward-bound mercenaries. One of the routes by which much of this gold reached Scandinavia was through Eastern Europe and across the Baltic to the islands of Bornholm, Öland and Gotland, where several treasure hoards dating to this period have been found. The richest hoard of the period, however, was found in the eighteenth century at Tureholm in Södermanland in central Sweden and contained 26.5 pounds (12 kg) of gold. Treasures may be buried for two reasons: ritual offerings to the gods or, in the days before banks, for security. However, in the second case, the owner's intention was eventually to recover the treasure, not leave it in the ground as an expensive time capsule for modern archaeologists or metal-detectorists to discover. There is no evidence that most of these treasures were buried for ritual reasons so the failure of the owners to recover so many hoards is best seen as yet another sign of the pervasive insecurity of the period. These islands would have been particularly exposed to piracy and the owners of the unrecovered hoards may well have been killed in raids or captured and carried off for the slave markets.

Most of the imported Roman gold was melted down and turned into spectacular jewellery and other prestige objects for the aristocracy. It was in the early part of the period that goldsmiths and silversmiths in southern Scandinavia developed the Scandinavian-Germanic animal art style, which used the stylised and enormously elongated bodies of real and imaginary animals to create interlaced patterns of astonishing complexity. The new art was probably a response to the turbulent times, creating a new language of symbols that were full of meaning to those who had the knowledge to read them. Unfortunately, that knowledge is now lost. Taken to Britain by the Anglo-Saxons, the animal style merged with indigenous Celtic art styles to create the hybrid Hiberno-Saxon style, whose finest expressions are found in illuminated manuscripts such as the *Lindisfarne Gospels* and the *Book of Kells*. In Scandinavia, animal art developed through a succession of styles until it was replaced by the imported Christian Romanesque style at the end of the Viking Age.

One of the characteristic items of Migration Period jewellery are bracteates, gold medallions modelled loosely on Roman medallions, which were worn as pendants. Bracteates frequently have the motif of a man's head and a horse – thought to represent Odin and his steed Sleipnir – and sometimes also runic inscriptions, most of which have defied interpretation. Few artefacts, however, could have displayed the wealth of their owner more impressively than the two ornate gold drinking horns found at Gallehus in Jutland, the larger of which was 30 inches (75.8 cm) long and weighed over 7.7 pounds (3.5 kg). Horns like this, together with other precious tableware, fine jewellery and weapons, would have been displayed at the lavish warrior feasts that were, after wars, a chief's or king's most important opportunities to enhance their reputations by feeding their followers heroic portions of meat, filling them with ale or mead, and showering them with valuable gifts. Another example of Roman influence in this period are *guldgubber* ('old men of gold'). These are tiny gold foil votive plaques impressed with figures of men or, more rarely, women or couples, which are thought to be inspired by Roman temple money. Around 75 per cent of the 3,000 guldgubber found so far come from Sorte Muld, a trade and cult centre on Bornholm. Guldgubber were mass produced as many were clearly stamped with the same moulds.

The turbulent times shaped Norse legend as well as metalwork. It was in this period that the *Volsunga Saga*, the most important of the Norse legendary sagas, began to take shape. The saga centres on the deeds of the legendary hero Sigurd, the forging of his magical sword Gram, his slaying of the dragon Fafnir and his acquisition of its cursed treasure hoard, and his eventual murder at the instigation of his spurned Valkyrie lover Brynhild. While a plot like that is unlikely to have any basis in historical fact, several of the saga's leading characters are historically identifiable figures from the Migration Period. Brynhild's husband Gunnar is based on the Burgundian king Gundahar, who was killed in battle with the Huns in 437; King Atli, who kills Gunnar is a barely disguised Attila the Hun (d. 453); and Jormunrek, the husband of Sigurd's daughter Svanhild, is inspired by Ermanaric, a king of the Goths who committed suicide after being defeated by the Huns in 375. Sigurd himself is thought by some to be based on the Frankish king Sigibert (d. 575), who was murdered as a result of family feuding between his wife, his brother and his brother's lover. If so, Sigibert's Burgundian wife Brunhilda may, then, be the inspiration for Brynhild.

The first Scandinavian kingdoms

The Late Germanic Iron Age (550–800) saw the emergence of powerful regional kingdoms in Denmark and Sweden. Scandinavia was still largely beyond the horizons of literate Europeans so these kingdoms' existence is deduced primarily from archaeological evidence such as major defence works, planned settlements, richly furnished burials and feasting halls, all of which point to the presence of strong central-ised authorities that controlled considerable material and human resources. One of these kingdoms was probably centred in southern Jutland where a 19-mile long (30 km) earth and timber rampart, known today as the Danevirke, was built across the neck of the peninsula between Hollingstedt and Schleswig. Although the Danevirke is now in Germany, in the early Middle Ages, this sparsely populated area's marshlands and infertile heaths made it a natural frontier between the Danes and the Saxon tribes to the south. The Danevirke began as a simple earth bank, built around the middle of the seventh century. About eighty years later the height of the rampart was raised and a timber palisade was built on top, turning it into a much more effective obstacle. Thanks to the science of dendrochronology the date of the palisade's construction can be fixed precisely – the timbers used to strengthen the rampart were felled in 737. The Danevirke, which still survives to a height of nearly 20 feet (6.1 m) in places, was strengthened several more times during the Middle Ages before it fell out of use in the fourteenth century. The construction of the Danevirke was probably overseen from a recently discovered high-status settlement at Flüsing, near Schleswig. An eighth-century feasting hall, roughly 100 feet (30.5 m) long by 30 feet (9.1 m) broad, excavated here was surrounded by up to 200 smaller buildings, which could together have accommodated up to 1,000 warriors on a temporary basis.

Another construction work possibly commissioned by the same king is a canal across an isthmus on the island of Samsø, off Jutland's east coast. This has been dated by dendrochronology to exactly 726. It was probably built to make it easier for warships to control the sea routes on both sides of the island. The foundation of Scandinavia's oldest town, Ribe on Jutland's west coast, can also be dated to this period. A site about 220 yards (201 m) long and 70 yards (64 m) wide was drained, levelled with a layer of sand over 2 feet thick, and divided up into rectangular plots. Oak planks from a timber-lined well date the event to between 704 and 710. Around 720, a central street was laid out and this was paved with planks around 730. No traces of permanent buildings have been found on the site but there are signs of temporary huts and craft workshops so Ribe functioned at first as a seasonal market place. The market place was surrounded by a ditch and fence. These were too small to be for defence so were probably intended to make it easier for Ribe's ruler to manage access and collect tolls.

Ribe was linked in to extensive trade networks, extending to Italy, Byzantium and Norway, but the most common imported artefacts originated in the Frankish kingdom: lava quernstones from the Eifel Mountains, and glass and pottery from the Rhineland. Large amounts of unworked amber have been found on the site so this was presumably an important export. There is evidence that large quantities of cattle were brought to the market, so perishable goods like hides were probably also exported. Ribe's foundation demonstrates the existence of a ruler who could control where and when trade was conducted in his territory and presumably also guarantee traders' security when visiting the site. Scandinavia's earliest coins, imitations of a Frisian coin type known as a *scaetta*, were produced at Ribe *c.* 720, so this ruler could also to some extent control the means of exchange. A permanently inhabited site about 250 yards (229 m) south-east of the market may have been the ruler's compound. The identity of the ruler cannot be ascertained with certainty but there is a good chance that it was Angantyr, a Danish king who was visited by the Anglo-Saxon monk Willibrord on the first Christian mission to Scandinavia in *c.* 725. Willibrord's biographer described Angantyr as 'crueller than a wild animal and harder than a stone', but he greeted the missionary politely enough even though he showed no interest in converting to Christianity.

Angantyr was not the only king in Denmark. In 'Beowulf', the hero's Danish host, Hrothgar, is described as a member of the Scylding dynasty. The same dynasty appears in semi-legendary saga traditions and in the *Gesta Danorum* ('Deeds of the Danes') by the twelfth century Danish historian Saxo Grammaticus as the Skjöldungs. Opinion about the historical reality of the Skjöldungs has wavered over the years: the consensus today is that the dynasty really did exist but that the stories that have come down to us belong more to the realm of legend than fact. Traditionally, the Skjöldungs were associated with the village of Gammel Lejre ('Old Lejre') on the island of Sjælland. An extraordinary concentration of impressive prehistoric barrows, dating from the Neolithic through to the late Viking Age, surround the village, marking it as a place that once possessed intense and enduring spiritual significance. In the last thirty years, archaeological excavations at Gammel Lejre have revealed that a succession of great timber feasting halls were built there between the sixth and tenth centuries, confirming that it was also a royal power centre in the period when the first Danish kingdoms were being forged. The attraction of the site for the kings of Sjælland must have been its many ancient monuments: they will have hoped to strengthen their authority by associating themselves with a place of such obvious ancient power.

Halls and *hørgs*

The earliest hall at Gammel Lejre was built at Fredshøj, close to a prominent Bronze Age burial mound on a low ridge overlooking the marshy valley of the Lejre river. The bow-sided hall was around 150 feet (45 m) long and 20 feet (7 m) wide and has been dated to around the second quarter of the sixth century. If Hrothgar was a real historical figure, this would likely have been his hall. Nearby was a *hørg*, a sacrificial offering place or altar made of a pile of stones. Pits surrounding the *hørg* contained the remains of broken pots and thousands of sacrificial animals. In the early seventh century, Fredshøj was abandoned in favour of Mysselhøjgård about 550 yards (500 m) to the south. Like the Fredshøj site, this was also on a ridge overlooking the river and was 160 feet (48.5 m) long by 38 feet (11.5 m) wide, covered an area of 600 square yards (500 sqm), and was subdivided into a central hall and storerooms and residential rooms. Several large houses around the hall were probably built to accommodate household warriors and guests. A timber palisade surrounded the hall and houses so that access to them could be easily controlled.

Outside the royal compound there was a small colony of craft-workers who supplied the royal family with the prestige metalwork they needed to display their own status and to hand out as gifts to their warriors. A large farm about 550 yards (500 m) to the north would have supplied the community's food. As at Fredshøj, there was a *hørg*, close to the feasting hall. The German Thietmar of Merseburg, writing around 1016, described a religious festival involving the sacrifice of ninety-nine humans, the same number of horses and an unspecified number of dogs and cocks, which was held at Gammel Lejre every ninth year on 6 January. So far, no evidence of human sacrifice has been found at the site. During the period when Mysselhøjgård was occupied the largest of all the religious monuments at Gammel Lejre was built. This is a now incomplete 282-foot (86 m) long stone ship that was used for burials and religious ceremonies. The Mysselhøjgård compound remained in use for over 350 years. During this time the feasting hall and its secondary buildings were completely rebuilt many times, replaced by a new hall of approximately the same size and plan.

This too was eventually pulled down and replaced by a new hall sited a few yards to the north. Halls continued to be pulled down and rebuilt at Gammel Lejre until around 1000, when the site was abandoned, probably because of its pagan associations, in favour of the new Christian centre of Roskilde, five miles to the north.

Prehistoric monuments frequently become associated in folklore with historical or legendary figures. Until it was proven to date to the Neolithic, one of the barrows at Gammel Lejre was believed locally to be the burial place of the most famous of the Skjöldung kings, Harald Hildetand ('Wartooth'). Harald most likely lived around the same time as Angantyr of Ribe, so the barrow could not have been raised for him, and, in any case, the legendary traditions agree that he is buried in Sweden on the site of the Battle of Bråvalla, in which he was killed fighting against the Swedish king Sigurd Ring. The location of Bråvalla, the greatest battle of Scandinavia's proto-historical period, is unknown but was traditionally thought to have been near Bråviken Fjord, in Östergötland. Harald had no political motives for invading Sweden. He had enjoyed a long and successful career of raiding, conquest and plundering, but having reached the ripe and improbably old age of 150, he was becoming seriously worried that he would die in bed and so forfeit the chance to go to Valhalla. Harald's sole motive was, therefore, to seek an opportunity to die fighting in battle. In some versions of the story, Harald was felled by the hand of Odin himself, who battered him to death with a club. The victors burned Harald on a funeral pyre, bidding him ride straight to Valhalla, together with the fifteen kings and 30,000 other warriors who had fallen in the battle. Plenty of mead would have been drunk that night in Valhalla.

Gamla Uppsala and the kingdom of the Swedes

In Sweden the last period of the Germanic Iron Age is known as the Vendel Period after a remarkable cemetery of fourteen high status graves at the modern village of Vendel, a few miles north of Uppsala in Uppland in central Sweden. This fertile region was the homeland of the Swedes. The burials at Vendel are the richest in Sweden for this period and most probably belong to members of a royal dynasty. The

bodies were interred, without cremation, in large boats of up to 32 feet
(10 m) in length, perhaps to transport them to the realm of the dead,
and were surrounded with valuable grave goods, food and cooking
gear for the journey, glass, superb weapons and armour, including a
bronze-decorated iron helmet, hunting dogs, horses and saddles and,
in one grave, a falcon. The distinctive animal-interlace ornament found
on much of the metalwork gave its name to the Vendel art-style. Also
near Vendel is a 16 feet (3 m) high barrow known as Ottarshögen
('Ottar's barrow') after King Ottar of the Swedish Yngling dynasty
who, like the Danish Skjöldungs, belong to the shadowlands between
legend and history. The barrow contained the remains of a man and a
woman. A well-worn Roman gold *solidus* minted in 477 was found in
the burial, probably dating it to the sixth century. Ottar is the Swedish
King Ohthere who is mentioned in 'Beowulf' as a contemporary of the
eponymous hero, so it is not impossible that the barrow could really
be his grave.

In the semi-legendary Icelandic saga traditions the Ynglings were
descended from the fertility god Freyr and his consort, the giantess
Gerðr. The dynasty's name comes from Freyr's alternative name,
Yngvi (Yngling means 'descendent of Yngvi'). The site most closely
associated with the Ynglings is Gamla Uppsala ('Old Uppsala'), which,
in the Viking Age, was a major cult centre dedicated to Freyr, Thor
and Odin. The site lies a few miles north of the modern university
town of Uppsala on the fertile plain of the River Fyris. In the Viking
Age, Gamla Uppsala was easily accessible by ship from Lake Mälaren
to the south, which was at that time a long, shallow fjord penetrating
deep inland from the Baltic Sea – the gradual post-glacial rebound of
the land turned Mälaren into a lake around 1200. The most striking
monuments at Gamla Uppsala are three enormous burial barrows
traditionally associated with the Yngling kings Aun, Egil and Adils.
The two mounds that have been excavated, those associated with Aun
and Egil, each contained the cremated remains of a high ranking male
and warrior gear including poorly preserved helmets decorated in the
Vendel style. Hundreds of smaller burial mounds surround the three
great mounds. These are just the few survivors of centuries of farmland
improvements: originally there were as many as 3,000 burial mounds

around Gamla Uppsala. Those burials that have been investigated date consistently to the sixth century or later. A low flat topped mound to the east of the great barrows, known as the Tingshögar ('thing-mound'), is probably where the Disting was held in historical times. This was the annual thing ('assembly') of the Swedes, which got its name because it was held at the same time as the late-winter Dísablót, a sacrifice in honour of the Dísir, a group of female fertility spirits. Underneath Gamla Uppsala's twelfth century church are the remains of an earlier wooden structure. These are thought to be of a wooden temple that contained idols of Freyr, Thor and Odin: the temple was said to covered with gold in the late Viking Age. According to the German ecclesiastical writer Adam of Bremen (d. c. 1080), a festival in honour of the three gods was still being celebrated in this temple in the 1070s. The festival was held once every nine years around the time of the spring equinox and lasted for nine days. On each day one human male was sacrificed, together with other male animals, including horses and dogs, so that all together the gods were offered seventy-two living creatures. The bodies were hanged in a sacred grove near the temple and left to putrefy. On one occasion, according to saga traditions, the Yngling king Domalde was sacrificed to appease the gods after he had presided over two years of failed harvests. Recent excavations have discovered the traces of two rows of wooden poles, the longest of which is around 1,000 yards (915 m) long. Probably erected in the fifth century, the rows' purpose is as yet unknown but some of the post holes contained animal bones, possibly from sacrifices.

In the sixth century a large feasting hall, around 164 feet (50 m) long, was built on an artificial platform south of the temple. The hall had a bow-sided plan, similar to the halls at Gammel Lejre, and may have looked rather like an upturned boat. The hall had several grand entrances, one of which was decorated with wrought iron spiral ornaments. The hall burned down in the eighth century and was not rebuilt. The area around the hall was densely populated by craftworkers. There is evidence of gold, silver, lead, bronze, glass and garnet working.

The kingdom of the Swedes was connected to an extensive network of trade routes through the island trading post of Helgö in Lake Mälaren, which developed in the fifth century. Helgö means 'holy

island' and gold foil plaques decorated with gods and monsters similar
to others found at religious sites in Denmark, suggest that the island
was a pagan cult centre where markets were held at festival times. No
other site in Sweden of the period has produced so much evidence of
trade and manufacture. Jewellery making was a particularly important activity: thousands of broken moulds used for casting bronze
brooches have been found. Iron working was also carried on. A hoard
of seventy-six sixth-century Byzantine gold coins suggests that Helgö
had trade links with the Mediterranean, possibly it was a market for
furs. In the seventh and eighth centuries, more exotic objects turned
up, including a bronze crosier from Ireland, baptismal spoons from
Egypt, and a bronze statuette of the Buddha from India. These objects
may have passed through many hands on their way to Helgö, so they
are not evidence that Swedish merchants were ranging as far as India.
However, Swedish merchants had already begun to establish bases
east of the Baltic and explore the Russian river systems, which in the
Viking Age they would follow to the Black and Caspian Seas. Grobina
in Latvia, where three Scandinavian cemeteries dating to 650–800
have been found, was one of the earliest Swedish colonies in the east.
One of the cemeteries contained warrior burials with artefacts similar
to those found in the Vendel cemetery, while artefacts from the other
two shows links to Gotland. There is evidence too that a Scandinavian
colony was established at Elblag in Poland as early as *c.* 650.

Swedish penetration of the Russian river system began early in the
eighth century and by 750, Scandinavian merchants were living side by
side with Finns and Slavs at the fur trading centre of Staraja Ladoga, on
the Volkhov River near where it flows into Lake Ladoga. Scandinavians
also headed east to plunder as a remarkable double ship burial found
recently at Salme in Estonia spectacularly demonstrates. All previously
discovered ship burials contained the remains of only one or two
people – a high status individual and sometimes a sacrificed slave
to accompany them in the afterlife. These two ships between them
contained around forty individuals, all well-built mature males, many
of them with obvious battle injuries. Weapons and jewellery decorated
in the Vendel style identify the dead as Swedes and date the burial to
c. 750. The ships were poorly preserved but enough evidence survived

confidently to identify the larger of the two as a sailing ship, the oldest so far found in the Baltic region.

State formation in Norway

Norway's rugged geography proved to be a major obstacle to state formation. Overland travel through the mountains was all but impossible for much of the year because of snow so the main links between regions was by sea. Thousands of islands and skerries created a sheltered inshore passage along the coast, the 'North Way' from which the country got its name, but despite this seafaring came to an end every October and did not resume until the end of March. Ships were hauled onshore to be stored for the winter in boatsheds and *nausts* (sheltered hollows). The relative isolation of communities bred local independence and the impressive archaeological evidence for state formation in the immediate pre-Viking period that is seen in Denmark and Sweden is absent from Norway. However, here too political power was gradually being centralised. The best evidence comes from Borre in the Vestfold, the sheltered region on the west side of Oslo Fjord, where there is a cemetery of seven large barrows and twenty-five smaller ones (the *Borrehaugene*). There probably were once many more as some are known to have been destroyed by quarrying for road stone in the nineteenth century. One of those destroyed contained a warrior's ship burial but it was not scientifically excavated. In the same area, a great timber hall was built at Huseby in the mid-eighth century. In the Viking Age the area around Huseby was known as Skiringssal, a power centre associated in the saga traditions with a Norwegian branch of the Yngling kings. Less than 2 miles from Huseby at Kaupang ('trading place') on Viksfjord, a semi-urban trading place and craft centre had developed by 800, no doubt due to the stimulus provided by the nearby royal centre. Evidence for state formation is more limited but a major barrow cemetery with several burned ship burials, now largely destroyed, at Myklebust on Nordfjorden, points to another power centre in the west of Norway, and other impressive barrows are found at Raknehaugen in Romerike, north of Oslo, and at Svenshaug in Hedmark, in east-central Norway.

The Viking impulse

At the end of the eighth century, the Scandinavian kingdoms were all still highly unstable. Scandinavia had a relatively numerous class of men who could aspire to kingship. In theory, Scandinavian kingship was elective and any man possessed of royal blood, whether from his father's side or his mother's side, was eligible for kingship. Illegitimacy was no bar. However, as power became ever more concentrated, as chiefdoms were subordinated to kingdoms and lesser kingdoms were subordinated by larger kingdoms, the opportunities to rule were becoming ever fewer. With many potential claimants for a throne, succession disputes were common. Joint kingship was a common solution where two rival claimants enjoyed equal support and were willing to compromise, but disputed successions often led to destabilising civil wars. If they were fortunate enough to survive, the losers of these conflicts would be forced into exile but, being possessed of the charisma of royal blood, all was not lost to them. Early Scandinavian rulers were primarily rulers of men rather than territory so any man of royal blood who could attract a warrior following might be recognised as a king by his men even if he did not actually have a kingdom. These 'sea kings' could turn pirate and, with luck, might win a fortune, a reputation as a great warrior, and loyal armed following with which to make a new bid for power at home. Or, as the Viking Age progressed, win a new kingdom for himself abroad. A reigning king might also find it expedient to go on Viking raids, to bolster his own reputation and to gain extra wealth to reward his own warriors and keep them loyal so that he could fight off challenges to his authority. Members of the chieftain class, the jarls (regional lords) and hersar (local chiefs) were faced with the same necessities as the growth of royal power began to encroach on their traditional independence. Any man rich enough to own a longship and raise a crew to man it had a strong incentive to go on Viking raids. At the same time western Europe was becoming an attractive target for Viking raids. The long economic recession that followed the collapse of the Western Roman Empire in the fifth century was coming to an end as political stability began to return. As trade with the north increased, Scandinavian merchants had ample opportunities to learn about western Europe's rich, and largely unguarded, ports and monasteries. The potential spoils of raiding the west would amply repay the increased risks of sailing further afield. The violence that for so long had characterised Scandinavian society was about to spill over into the rest of Europe.

CHAPTER 2

LINDISFARNE, ATHELNEY AND YORK
THE VIKINGS IN ENGLAND
789–954

early in 793 the people of the Anglo-Saxon kingdom of Northumbria witnessed strange apparitions in the sky. Immense flashes of lightning terrified the people, and fiery dragons flew through the air. Famine followed. Bloody rain fell from a clear sky onto the northern end of St Peter's cathedral in York, Northumbria's capital. It was a sign, surely, that something terrible was going to come from the north. Then, on 8 June, the dreadful omens were fulfilled: Viking pirates sacked the wealthy and influential Northumbrian monastery on the island of Lindisfarne. In a letter written shortly after the attack, the distinguished Northumbrian scholar Alcuin (*c.* 735–804) expressed his anguish and shock:

> 'We and our fathers have lived in this fair land for nearly three hundred and fifty years, and never before has a such an atrocity been seen in Britain as we have now suffered at the hands of a pagan people. Such an attack was not thought possible. The church of St Cuthbert is spattered with the blood of the priests of God, stripped of all its furnishings, exposed to the plundering of pagans – a place more sacred than any in Britain. ... Who is not afraid at this?'
> (trans. Stephen Allott, *Alcuin of York* (York, 1974)).

If there was anyone who was not afraid, they soon would be, for this was just the beginning.

The holy island

Low lying and largely covered with sand dunes, Lindisfarne lies in the North Sea, just a mile off the mainland to which it is joined for a few hours twice a day at low tide by sand flats. Today Lindisfarne feels remote, especially when the tide is in and tourists cannot reach it, but it is only 5 miles by sea from Bamburgh castle, one of the main strongholds of the Northumbrian kings. It was because of its closeness to this seat of power that Aidan, an Irish monk, founded a monastery and bishopric here in 635 as a base for the evangelisation of the still pagan Angles of Northumbria. On his death in 651, Aidan was buried at Lindisfarne and was soon recognised as a saint. A veritable factory of holiness, Lindisfarne's next eight bishops were also recognised as saints, the most famous of them being St Cuthbert (d. 687), so gentle a man that he was supposedly even befriended by the local otters.

Monasteries were the main centres of literacy and book production in early medieval Europe and Lindisfarne was home to an outstanding scriptorium where monks ruined their eyesight producing books so intricately illuminated that later generations thought them the work of angels. Of all the monasteries in Britain only the Scottish monastery of Iona rivalled Lindisfarne's reputation for sanctity. The relics of Lindisfarne's many saints were its greatest treasures and the foundation of its reputation for holiness. Kings, seeking the monks' prayers and the intercession of the saints for the benefit of their peoples' and their own, usually rather sinful, souls gave the monastery generous grants of land. Visiting pilgrims seeking miraculous cures and spiritual merit made their lesser donations. Lindisfarne became wealthy as well as spiritually powerful. This wealth was displayed for the glory of God: silk vestments for the priests, gold and silver communion vessels, crucifixes, croziers, reliquaries and book covers all encrusted with precious stones. The monastery would inevitably have attracted merchants and craftsmen to cater for the monks' needs for food, clothing, vellum for writing, and precious objects for display. And all this was completely undefended. No wonder it was attractive to the Vikings. Perhaps most valuable of all were the many healthy, well-fed, unarmed monks who they could be confident would fetch a good price at the slave market.

Divine retribution

It is difficult today to understand exactly how shocking this attack was:
even the reaction to the 9/11 attacks on New York and Washington DC,
which robbed Americans of their sense of invulnerability, falls short
as a comparison. Americans may trust in God but they do not make
Him responsible for their defence policy: early medieval Christians
did. Belief in the power of the saints to intercede with God to protect
their holy places was absolute. All over Europe monasteries were
completely undefended and, certainly, no Christian would have dared
risk divine retribution by violating them. The monks of Lindisfarne
must have been aware of the danger of Viking attack. About four years
earlier three ships from Hordaland in western Norway attacked the
port of Portland in the south of England, killing a royal official called
Beaduheard, the earliest known casualty of a Viking raid. It is likely that
there had been other, unrecorded raids on England too, because the
powerful Mercian king Offa ordered the preparation of coast defences
for Kent in 792. Yet such was their confidence in God's protection that
still they took no precautions. Of course, as pagans, the Vikings felt no
qualms about attacking monasteries, that was the kind of behaviour
to be expected of barbarians, but why had God not punished them for
their sacrilegious act? This, more than the raid itself, was what really
frightened Christians. 'What assurance can the churches of Britain
have,' asked Alcuin, 'if St Cuthbert and so great a company of saints do
not defend their own?' Alcuin felt defenceless.

In reality Alcuin was in no immediate physical danger – he was
teaching in the school at the Frankish emperor Charlemagne's palace
at Aachen in Germany – but like all medieval Christians he believed
that even the mightiest empires existed only as long as they enjoyed the
favour of God. This was what was understood to have been the fate of
the Roman Empire. God had permitted its creation to make the spread
of Christianity easier but it was a sinful state and when it had served
its purpose, God allowed it to fall. Alcuin's response was, therefore, not
to see the Viking raid as a military problem but as a moral problem.
When God allowed bad things to happen to His followers it was His
just chastisement for their sins. Alcuin wrote to the survivors of the

raid urging them to examine their own conduct. Wealth, he thought, might have led the monks to relax monastic discipline by eating and drinking to excess, wearing fine clothes and neglecting to care for the poor. Northumbria's king Æthelred also came in for even harsher criticism for allowing injustice and immorality to flourish under his rule. 'A country has no better protection,' Alcuin said, 'than the justice and goodness of its leaders and the prayers of the servants of God.' He reminded Æthelred that just one prayer from the good and just Hebrew king Hezekiah secured the destruction of 185,000 Assyrians in a single night. If Æthelred would just reform his ways, and those of his subjects, God would surely smite the Vikings in the same way.

The next year, Vikings attacked another prestigious Northumbrian monastery, Jarrow, once home to the Venerable Bede (d. 735), England's earliest historian. This time the Vikings were not so lucky: local forces captured and killed their leader and a storm wrecked their fleet as it tried to escape. Those survivors who made it ashore were quickly slaughtered by the angry locals. A just punishment, gloated the monkish chroniclers, but this impressive manifestation of the power of the saints did not deter the Vikings. In 795, Vikings plundered in Scotland and Ireland, sacking Iona and another monastery on the island of Rechru off the Irish coast. In 799, Vikings extended their activities to the Frankish Empire for the first time. It would be more than 200 years before the people of Western Europe could look out to sea and see a sail on the horizon without at least a frisson of fear. Was that a Viking longship?

In the short term, however, life on Lindisfarne soon returned to normal. Many monks, including the bishop Higbald, survived the attack, so too did the monastery's precious relics and many of its other treasures, such as the magnificent intricately ornamented *Lindisfarne Gospels*, now displayed in the British Library in London. It is likely that the monks had at least some warning of the attack and managed to hide many of the monastery's valuables – a small rocky hill nearby, now occupied by a castle, would have made a fine look-out point. As Alcuin makes no mention of burning or wanton destruction, the monastic buildings may have escaped undamaged and the community was re-established within the year. It is even possible that the kidnapped monks eventually made it home. Alcuin wrote to Higbald to tell that him that Charlemagne would try to ransom the captured monks: we don't know if he succeeded. After the failure of the attack on Jarrow, no further Viking raids against England are recorded for over thirty years. That does not mean that there weren't any. In 804, the monks of Lyminge in Kent, a few miles inland from the Channel coast, took the precaution of acquiring a refuge in the relative security of nearby Canterbury. Five years later, Vikings audaciously captured the papal legate Ealdwulf at sea while returning to the Continent from a mission to Northumbria. Recognising that they had captured someone of importance, the Vikings immediately took Ealdwulf back to England where the Mercian king Coenwulf paid his ransom. However, a few small-scale raids around the coast were trivial affairs compared to the many battles recorded in this period between the four Anglo-Saxon kingdoms, Northumbria, Mercia, East Anglia and Wessex. The rivalry was most intense between Mercia and Wessex, each of which aspired to be recognised as the dominant kingdom of Britain. Their rivalry culminated in 825 with the great battle of Ellandun in Wiltshire, at which King Egbert of Wessex defeated King Beornwulf of Mercia and became recognised as *Bretwalda*, an ill-defined title probably signifying 'overlord of Britain'.

The raids intensify

The 830s saw a step-change in the nature of the Viking threat to England. The attack on Portland in 789 involved just three ships and was a classic example of what the Vikings called *strandhögg*, 'hit and run'. It is likely that this was typical of early Viking raids. Then, in 836, a fleet of twenty-five or thirty-five Danish ships (sources disagree about the number) arrived in the west of England. King Egbert gathered an army and met them in battle at Carhampton in Somerset. Both sides fought hard but in the end it was the Anglo-Saxons who broke and, as the *Anglo-Saxon Chronicle* put it, 'the Danes had possession of the place of slaughter'. The Anglo-Saxons soon had the opportunity for revenge. In 838 a Danish fleet arrived in Cornwall, which at that time was an independent Celtic kingdom. Egbert had devoted much of his reign to trying to conquer the Cornish, so, not surprisingly, they welcomed the Danes as allies and together they planned to attack Wessex. Egbert moved fast, however, and attacked first, defeating the alliance at the Battle of Hingston Down. It was Egbert's last victory. He died the next year, having made Wessex the leading Anglo-Saxon kingdom and set a precedent of effective resistance to the Vikings that his successors would exploit.

In 850 there came another escalation in Viking activity when a Danish army occupied the Isle of Thanet in Kent and settled down to spend the winter there in a fortified camp. So far raiding had been a seasonal activity, confined to the summer months, and by September the Vikings were heading home to avoid getting caught at sea by autumn gales. By wintering in their victims' territory, Vikings could extend the raiding season into the autumn and make an earlier start the following spring. Spring 851 saw the arrival of a new Viking fleet in Kent. Reported to be 350 ships strong, this was by far the largest Viking fleet to attack England so far. This formidable force sacked Canterbury, England's premier ecclesiastical centre, and then the growing port of London. Mercia's king Beorhtwulf brought the Vikings to battle but was heavily defeated. Buoyed by their success, the Vikings crossed the Thames and invaded Wessex, only to be defeated in battle at the unidentified location of *Aclea* ('Oak Field'). It was the greatest slaughter of heathen raiders the Anglo-Saxon chronicler had ever heard of.

In the same year Æthelstan, a son of King Æthelwulf of Wessex, defeated a Viking fleet in a naval battle at Sandwich harbour and captured nine ships. Naval battles were exceptionally rare in the Viking Age. Ships of the period could not remain at sea for extended periods to patrol for enemy fleets so the chances of intercepting a Viking fleet on the open sea was negligible. Naval battles, when they did occur, usually took place when one fleet managed to trap another in a harbour or estuary, as Æthelstan's seems to have done here. These victories bought England only a year's respite and in 853 the Vikings were back on the Isle of Thanet. Yet despite the unrelenting raids, Æthelwulf of Wessex felt that his kingdom was secure enough for him to go on a year-long journey to Rome to visit the pope in 855, taking with him his favourite youngest son, Alfred. The Vikings were a severe nuisance but they were not, so far, seen as an existential threat.

The Viking way of war

After more than half a century of Viking raids, the Anglo-Saxons appeared to be meeting the Viking challenge. True, many important towns had been sacked but they would certainly have been well aware of how much more severely Ireland and the Frankish Empire were suffering at the Vikings' hands. The Anglo-Saxons had never run away from a fight and when they had brought the Vikings to battle they had won more often than they had lost. Despite their ferocious reputation, Vikings were not invincible military supermen. Their weapons were no better than those of the Anglo-Saxons or Franks and nor did they use innovative battle tactics. On a battlefield it would have been hard to tell the Anglo-Saxons and Vikings apart. Both fought on foot and relied on the shield and spear as their main weapons, and both formed up for battle in a linear formation known as the shield wall, in which each warrior stood in rank with his shield slightly overlapping that of the man next to him. Depending on the size of the army, the formation could be several ranks deep, with the men in the rear ranks adding weight to the formation when it came to the pushing and shoving when battle was joined, and stepping forward to fill the front rank when men were cut down. It was essential to maintain the integrity of the shield wall. The critical point of many battles came when one side began to lose its nerve and tried to withdraw. If the shield wall remained intact the defeated army could withdraw in good order to lick its wounds without suffering heavy casualties. If the shield wall collapsed it was every man for himself and casualties would be heavy because the victors could strike the exposed backs of their fleeing enemies.

The real secret to the Vikings' success was their mobility, which meant that they, rather than the defenders, usually held the initiative. In pre-modern times, travel by water was always faster than travel by land. Viking longships had only a shallow draught so a raiding fleet could make a landing almost anywhere on the open coast or penetrate far inland on rivers. If they found local forces alert and waiting, the Vikings could just move on and try somewhere else, and sooner or later they would catch somebody off guard. When that happened, the Vikings could plunder and be well away before sufficient local forces could gather to oppose them. By collecting their forces to oppose the Vikings in one place, the defenders necessarily left other areas exposed to attack. This tended to undermine the defence. In most western European kingdoms, the Scandinavian kingdoms included, adult free men had to perform levy service when called out by their lords or kings. Men willingly turned out when a campaign involved invading a neighbouring state because of the opportunities for plunder that it brought: the Vikings were not at all unique in early medieval Europe in seeing war as an opportunity to profit. In contrast, defensive campaigns brought no such benefits to offset the risks and costs of war, and men were also naturally reluctant to leave their own families and farms unprotected. As a result, the call to arms often went unanswered.

Full-scale battles were relatively rare in the Viking Age. Thanks to their mobility, Vikings could generally avoid fighting if they thought the odds were unfavourable to them. However, the pay-off from victory could be very high so Vikings were not shy about fighting when it suited them. Plundering could most efficiently be done by splitting an army up into smaller bands to rove widely over the countryside. However, such bands were always vulnerable to being picked off by local forces. If the defender's army could be engaged and decisively defeated first, the Vikings were free to plunder unhindered. Apart from loot, and a strong hand when it came to negotiating tribute payments with the vanquished, victory in battle also enhanced a Viking leader's reputation, securing the loyalty of his warriors and attracting new ones. Conversely, the defenders were acutely aware of the awful consequences of defeat. Just maintaining an army in the field at least inhibited Viking activity, so the defenders were usually more cautious about seeking battle than the Anglo-Saxons. This may seem a cowardly strategy, but they had a lot more to lose than the Vikings so it was often safer to pursue a policy of damage limitation than to risk everything on a battle.

The 'great heathen army'

In 865 it was finally England's turn to feel the full fury of Viking attack. Early in the year, a Viking fleet once again settled on Thanet. The long-suffering people of Kent had had enough of being raided by now and instead of resistance they offered the Vikings tribute in return for peace. This was the first time that what came much later to be called Danegeld was offered by the Anglo-Saxons. The offer of tribute was a sign that in the worst affected areas morale was beginning to break, but the money was never actually paid. The Vikings were merely using negotiations to lull the people of Kent into a false sense of security before launching a surprise attack on them. The Vikings had calculated that they could get more by plundering than from negotiating. Far more serious, the same year saw the arrival in East Anglia of a 'great heathen army' from Denmark. So far the Vikings had only been after plunder. This army was different, its objective was to conquer and settle.

The leaders of the Danish army were an alliance of landless 'sea kings', the most prominent of whom were Ivar, Halfdan and Ubba. Ivar and Halfdan were certainly brothers: Ubba may have been their brother but the evidence is inconclusive. Contemporary sources have nothing to say about any of the leaders' origins, but in Danish and Icelandic sources of the thirteenth and fourteenth centuries Ivar had become identified with the enigmatically named Ivar the Boneless, a son of the legendary Viking Ragnar Lodbrok ('hairy breeches'). Whether there is any truth in the tradition is anyone's guess. Ragnar is one of those legendary characters who, like King Arthur and Robin Hood, may well be based on real historical people but whose actual lives have become buried under such a deep accretion of later legends that separating any facts from the fiction is now completely impossible.

Ragnar's career, as told by Saxo Grammaticus, begins in a credible enough fashion, with him fighting off a host of rivals to become king of Denmark. Like real historical Viking kings, Ragnar consolidated his position by leading great plundering raids, but the range of his activities is improbable, he plundered everywhere from Britain and Ireland to the Mediterranean, the Byzantine empire, Russia and the Arctic. Ragnar earned his nickname for the shaggy trousers he wore for protection when he killed two enormous venomous serpents that were ravaging Sweden. Ragnar married three times but to no ordinary women: one of his wives was Lathgertha, a shieldmaiden (a type of Viking Amazon and just as legendary; women did not fight in real

Viking armies). Another wife, according to Icelandic traditions, was the daughter of the mythical dragon slayer Sigurd Fafnisbane and his valkyrie wife Brynhild. Ragnar was survived by enough sons to crew a small longship, among them, according to Saxo, Regnald, Fridlef, Rathbarn, Dunvat, Daxon, Björn Ironside, Sigurd Snake-in-the-Eye, Hvitserk, Ubbi, Erik Wind-Hat and Agnar, as well as Ivar the Boneless. Most of these sons probably belong as much to the realm of legend as their father.

The Danish army wintered at Thetford in East Anglia and in the spring struck a peace deal with the locals. The East Angles would provide the Danes with horses and they would ride off and plunder someone else. This indifference to Viking raiding in the other Anglo-Saxon kingdoms was typical. On only one occasion did one Anglo-Saxon kingdom ally with another against the Vikings, and it worked greatly to the Vikings' advantage as they were able to concentrate all their efforts on one kingdom at a time. Acquiring horses gave the Danes much the same mobility on land as they had previously enjoyed on water, with all the tactical advantages that went with it. The Danes used their horses to invade Northumbria, which was wracked by a civil war between rivals for the throne: Vikings always exploited political divisions when they could. Northumbria's capital city, York, fell to the Danes without a fight on 21 November. Recognising the seriousness of the threat, the two kings, Ælle and Osberht, made common cause and together they attempted to recapture York in March 867. York's defences were not in good condition and the Northumbrians stormed in, but once inside the city the battle turned against them and both kings were killed along with most of their followers. According to the colourful, but unreliable, medieval Scandinavian traditions, Ælle was responsible for the death of Ragnar Lodbrok. Ælle captured Ragnar after he was shipwrecked and had him thrown into a pit of adders to be bitten to death. Ragnar warned Ælle that 'the piglets would be grunting if they knew the plight of the boar', meaning that his sons would avenge him. When they captured Ælle at York, Ragnar's sons sacrificed him to Odin by making a 'blood eagle' of him, that is cutting open his ribcage either side of the spine and pulling out his lungs to create the appearance of bloody wings. Scholars have endlessly debated whether this was a genuine

Viking practice or merely the product of a fertile skaldic imagination. The sacrifice seems no more horrific than the old English punishment for traitors of hanging, drawing and quartering, so it would be foolish to rule out the possibility that it was sometimes actually performed: *víking* was not an activity for the squeamish, after all.

As well as two kings, much of Northumbria's military aristocracy died in the Battle of York. Deprived of leadership, those Northumbrians who survived submitted to the Danes, who appointed an obscure Northumbrian nobleman called Ecgberht as a puppet king. The Danes remained quietly at York for the next twelve months before invading Mercia in spring 868. Mercia's king, Burgred, put aside old rivalries and appealed to King Æthelred of Wessex for help. The two kings laid siege to the Danes in Nottingham, but they seem to have lacked resolve. The Danes refused to come out and fight, while the allies were unwilling either to storm the fortified city or to starve them out by a long siege. Burgred made his peace with the Danes, probably paying tribute in return for their withdrawal to Northumbria. It is likely that Æthelred preferred a more confrontational policy because the two kingdoms never co-operated against the Vikings again.

In 869, the Danes returned to ravage East Anglia, burning and destroying every monastery they came to and slaughtering their monks. In November, Ivar and Ubba crushingly defeated the East Angles at Hoxne, captured their king, Edmund, and brought the whole kingdom under their control. According to later hagiographical traditions, Ivar and Ubba offered to allow Edmund to rule East Anglia as a tributary king if he would become a pagan. Edmund refused and was tortured by being shot full of arrows, like St Sebastian, before being beheaded. Edmund's head was thrown into the wood, where it was later found safe, supposedly guarded by a wolf calling 'here, here, here'. Miracles followed and Edmund was quickly considered to be a saint. It is probable that the Danes appointed a caretaker puppet king, as they had in Northumbria, while they planned their next expedition. It is likely that sometime over the winter Ivar died, as he is not mentioned again in Anglo-Saxon sources.

Alfred the Great and the Danes

In 870 the Danes invaded Wessex and seized the town of Reading, which they used as their base until spring 871. However, the Danes' further advance into Wessex was strongly resisted by king Æthelred and his brother Alfred. Eight or nine battles were fought across Wessex over the next year, none proved to be decisive and both sides suffered heavy casualties. The West Saxons lost an ealdorman and a bishop in the course of the battles, the Danes a king and nine jarls. In April 871, King Æthelred died and was succeeded by Alfred, the only king the English have thought worthy of being described as 'the Great'. Alfred's biographer and adviser bishop Asser would later describe his reluctance to accept the throne because he felt inadequate to the task of defeating the Danes unless God gave him support. A good Christian king should be modest and pious, of course, and Asser was determined to present a favourable image of his employer. In fact, almost all the sources on which we depend for our knowledge of Alfred's struggle with the Danes were written by people who were close to the king or who were writing under his direction. We only have Alfred's side of this story.

Around the time of Alfred's accession, the Danes were reinforced by a new fleet under Guthrum, Anund and Oscetel, which sailed up the Thames to Reading. After suffering two defeats in quick succession, Alfred made peace with the Danes on condition they would depart. The terms of the deal are not known but Alfred probably paid them tribute, as the men of Kent had done in 865. The Danes finally left Reading in the autumn, but they only went as far as London, which they seized from the Mercians. Alfred was probably lucky that a rebellion by their Northumbrian puppet king forced the Danes to hurry back to York early in 872. Ecgberht was dealt with quickly enough for the Danes to invade Mercia and winter in a camp near Torksey on the River Trent. Recent excavations have discovered large quantities of hacked-up Arab *dirhems* on the site. This is probably evidence that Scandinavian merchants with links to the eastern trade routes visited the camp, most likely to buy slaves captured by the army. With the Vikings, trade and war were always closely linked. The large size of the camp, estimated at

64 acres (26 hectares), confirms that the Anglo-Saxon chronicler was not exaggerating when he described the Danish army as a 'great' army, probably several thousand strong.

In 873 the Danes took a fleet up the Trent and captured the main Mercian royal centre at Repton, where they spent the winter. The site of the Danish winter camp at Repton has been the subject of intensive archaeological investigation. The Danes built a slipway on the river-bank so they could draw their ships ashore for the winter, as was normal Viking practice. To protect the ships from attack, the Danes constructed a roughly semi-circular ditch and rampart, about 200 yards (183 m) long, which opened onto the riverbank. The rampart incorporated a pre-existing church building as a strongpoint. Viking fortifications of this kind were common in Ireland, where they were known as *longphuirt* ('ship landings', singular *longphort*). Covering only one acre, this longphort is very small compared to known Irish longphuirt, and to the previous winter's camp at Torksey, so was clearly not intended to house the whole army. Just outside the rampart was a unique mass burial containing the skeletal remains of at least 249 individuals, 80 per cent of which were robust males aged between fifteen and forty-five. These were arranged around the body of a single male, thought to have been one of the leaders of the Danish army. None of the skeletons showed evidence of battle injuries, so it is likely that they were victims of an epidemic – in pre-modern times disease often caused more casualties in an army than enemy action. Coins found in the burial confirmed that it dated to the time that the Danish army wintered at Repton. Several individual burials were also found near the site, including a man who had died from a blow to the hip. The man was buried with a sword, a Thor's hammer amulet and a symbolic penis to replace the one he must have lost in combat.

The loss of their capital led to the collapse of Mercian resistance and King Burgred fled into exile in Rome where he later died. The pope was probably not overjoyed to see him: he had only recently written to Burgred telling him that his kingdom's troubles were his own fault for allowing all manner of fornication to flourish. As they had done in Northumbria and East Anglia, the Danes appointed a caretaker puppet king, a nobleman called Ceolwulf, to rule until such time as they decided what to do with the kingdom. In just eight years the Danes had conquered three of the four Anglo-Saxon kingdoms. Only Wessex remained, but it would not have to face the full might of the Danish army again. By now, many of the Danes wanted to settle down and enjoy the fruits of victory and in 874 Halfdan left the army and took his followers back to York to consolidate his control of Northumbria. In 876, Halfdan divided the kingdom into two parts. The northern province of Bernicia (extending from the Tees to the Firth of Forth) remained independent under native rulers based at Bamburgh. The southern province of Deira (roughly equivalent to Yorkshire) Halfdan shared out between his followers and York became the capital of a Viking kingdom. Halfdan probably did not reign for long, because this is the last time he is mentioned in Anglo-Saxon sources. It is likely that he is to be identified with Alband, a Danish chief who, according to Irish sources, was killed at Strangford Lough fighting against the Dublin Vikings in 877. Little is known about Halfdan's immediate successors. One, 'Airdeconut' (probably Harthacnut), is known only from a single coin discovered in a hoard at Silverdale, Lancashire, in 2011.

The rest of the Danish army, now under the leadership of Guthrum, Oscetel and Anund, moved to Cambridge, in the east of Mercia, where they spent a year before invading Wessex late in 875. This took Alfred by surprise and the Danes successfully evaded the West Saxon army, crossing the kingdom to winter at the nunnery at Wareham in Dorset, an easily defended site between two rivers. Alfred laid siege to the Danes but, just as at Nottingham, a stalemate ensued. Negotiations followed and in 876 a peace agreement was reached, which probably involved Alfred paying tribute to persuade the Danes to leave his kingdom. Hostages were exchanged as a demonstration of good faith and the Danes sealed the deal with oaths sworn on a sacred ring dedicated to Thor. Pagan Scandinavians kept such rings, reddened with sacrificial blood, in temples specifically for the swearing of oaths. It is surprising that such a devoutly Christian king as Alfred was willing to sanction a pagan ceremony, but he presumably believed that this way the Danes would feel more bound by their oaths than if they had been made over Christian relics. If so, he was wrong. The Danes did not regard oaths sworn to Christians as binding and they had simply used the peace agreement to lull Alfred into a false sense of security. They killed the West Saxon hostages and, abandoning the hostages they had given Alfred to their fate, set out for Exeter in Devon, part of the army riding overland, part going by sea. Alfred pursued the mounted army but failed to catch it before it reached the safety of the city walls. Those Danes who went by sea were less fortunate: their fleet was caught by a storm and 120 ships were lost.

This disaster changed the military balance. Alfred spent months outside the walls of Exeter but it was now he who had the initiative. When the Danes finally gave in, Alfred did not need to pay them to leave the kingdom: they gave hostages again and in August 877 withdrew to Gloucester in southern Mercia. They now called on Ceolwulf to divide the kingdom with them. Ceolwulf was allowed to keep the western half of Mercia, while the Danes took the east. Anund and Oscetel were probably among those who took lands there as they are not heard of again. Danish settlement was densest around the towns known as the Five Boroughs: Derby, Nottingham, Lincoln, Leicester and Stamford. It is unlikely that the Danish settlement resulted in large-scale displacement of the Anglo-Saxon peasantry. The ranks of the Mercian nobility and freeman classes would have been thinned by the wars and the Danes simply took over their lands: the local peasants just got new landlords. Many monastic communities had been destroyed so their lands were also available for sharing out among the conquerors. Guthrum did not take lands: he still had his eyes on Wessex.

Alfred takes refuge at Athelney

In the Middle Ages, campaigning usually ceased during the winter months. Seas were rough, roads became impassable with mud or snow and there was no grazing for horses so, as the nights lengthened, Vikings and their opponents alike headed for winter quarters. But as Alfred settled down to celebrate Christmas at Chippenham, Guthrum was preparing to attack. Shortly after Twelfth Night (5 January) in 878 Guthrum left Gloucester and made a surprise attack on Chippenham. Alfred only narrowly evaded capture and, with his family and retainers, fled south-west to take refuge in the great wetlands of the Somerset

Levels. Now largely drained for agriculture, in Alfred's day the Levels were an area of twisting river channels, reedy fens, willow woodland, shallow lakes, and peat moors interrupted by low ridges and islands of dry land. When Alfred fled there in mid-winter, the Levels would have been completely flooded, but in summer they dried out enough for parts to be used as rough grazing. It was from this practice that the county of Somerset got its name, from *Sumersaete*, the 'summer country'. Alfred hunted in the area and knew it intimately but it was effectively impenetrable for outsiders, so for the time being he was safe. Guthrum's failure to capture Alfred was a serious setback. Guthrum lacked the forces to occupy all of Wessex so his best chance to control it was by persuading Alfred to rule as his puppet or, if he refused, kill him and appoint someone who would. This approach had been successful in Northumbria, Mercia and East Anglia, it likely would have worked in Wessex too.

Alfred's flight into the wetlands became the stuff of legend. A story first told in the eleventh century, *Life of St Neot,* tells how Alfred took refuge in the house of a peasant woman. The woman prepared some cakes and set them by the fire to bake. Telling the king to watch the cakes, she went out to collect firewood. However, the careworn king nodded off and the woman returned to find the cakes had burned. She angrily scolded the king, telling him that he was happy enough to eat them but was too lazy to help her cook them. Alfred took his scolding with the grace and humility expected of a pious king. Another story of Alfred's time in the wetlands is that St Cuthbert appeared to Alfred in a vision promising help against the Vikings who had chased him out of his home at Lindisfarne. This was a politically convenient vision if ever there was one: if Northumbria's patron saint had transferred his support to the Wessex dynasty, was this vision not a sign that he wanted the Northumbrians to do the same? A third tale tells how Alfred disguised himself as a minstrel so he could infiltrate Guthrum's camp and learn all of his plans. All these stories emphasise not just Alfred's moral qualities but also the desperate circumstances to which he is supposed to have been reduced. Yet, as subsequent events showed, he still retained the loyalty of his subjects and had substantial resources at his disposal.

Around Easter, Alfred established a fortress on the Isle of Athelney, a small island – barely half a mile long – in the southern reaches of the Levels. Athelney's name is derived from Old English (the language spoken by the Anglo-Saxons) *Æthelinga íeg*, meaning the 'island of princes', so it was probably part of a royal estate. Alfred really had no need to lodge with peasants and ruin their cooking. Only after the most severe flooding, as in the very wet winter of 2013–14, does Athelney ever resemble an island today, but before modern draining of the Levels it was a natural fortress.

Athelney's potential was first recognised in prehistoric times when each end of the island was fortified with a bank and ditch. These ready-made defences, which could easily have been refurbished, must have been part of the island's attractions for Alfred. Archaeological evidence of ironworking on the island in Anglo-Saxon times suggests that the king may have used it as a secure centre for weapons production. A causeway linked the western end of the island to dry land at the *burh* ('fortified town') of East Lyng to the west. Anyone hoping to attack Athelney from this direction would have to take East Lyng first. Just a mile north-east of Athelney is the strikingly abrupt hill of Burrow Mump. Though only 79 feet (24 m) high it has a commanding view over the surrounding Levels. A medieval church and a Norman motte have obliterated any evidence of earlier structures that may have been on its summit, but Alfred would surely have built a watchtower here to cover the northern approaches to Athelney.

Alfred ensured that his subjects knew that they had not been abandoned, as the Mercians had been, by launching raids out of the fens to harass the Danes. Athelney's position near the southern edge of the Levels not only put the wetlands between Alfred and the Danes, it also gave him good communications with Devon, Dorsetshire and Hampshire, which remained unoccupied. Ubba led a strong raid into north Devon, perhaps with the intention of outflanking Alfred, but he was defeated and killed with 800–1,200 of his men by a smaller West Saxon force under Odda the ealdorman of Devon at Countisbury Hill. Ubba had forced the West Saxons to take refuge in a hastily constructed fort on the hill. The West Saxons lacked food and water so, rather than attack the strong position, Ubba decided to wait and let hunger and thirst force their surrender. The West Saxons weren't ready to give in, however, and they launched a surprise dawn attack and massacred the drowsy Danes. Only a handful of the Vikings managed to escape back to their ships.

The turning point

While this was happening, Alfred's agents were travelling the country-side secretly preparing to raise a new army against the Danes. In early May, Alfred left Athelney and rode to Egbert's Stone near Selwood in Wiltshire where he met with the levies of Somerset, Wiltshire and Hampshire, who gave him a rapturous reception. Knowing that news of the gathering would soon reach the Danes, Alfred moved fast. Camping only one night at the stone, the next day he marched his army to 'Island Wood', which was probably near Warminster, around 10 miles to the north-west. The next morning, Alfred broke camp and advanced another 8 miles to Edington, where he met the Danes in battle:

> 'Fighting fiercely with a compact shield wall against the entire Danish army, [Alfred] persevered resolutely for a long time; at length he gained the victory through God's will. He destroyed the Danes with great slaughter, and pursued those who fled as far as the stronghold, hacking them down'. (Bishop Asser, *Life of King Alfred*, trans. Simon Keynes.)

The unnamed stronghold is usually reckoned to have been Chippenham, but that is over 12 miles from Edington, a very long way for a hot pursuit after what was clearly a hard-fought battle. It may be more likely that the Danes actually took refuge in Bratton Camp, an Iron Age hillfort only 2 miles from Edington. After a two-week siege, Guthrum capitulated, agreeing to leave the kingdom, hand over hostages and accept baptism.

Three weeks later Guthrum and thirty of his leading men were baptised at Aller, not far from Athelney. Alfred personally raised Guthrum from the font and adopted him as a godson. Guthrum and his men wore the white robes of baptism for eight days, their heads bound by white cloths where they had been anointed with holy oil.

After their heads were ceremonially unbound at the royal manor at nearby Wedmore, twelve days of festivities followed at which Alfred gave Guthrum and his men 'many excellent treasures'. In the autumn, Guthrum kept his word and withdrew to Cirencester in Mercia for the winter and then, in 879, to East Anglia, which he ruled as king until his death in 890. It is impossible to be sure how sincere Guthrum's conversion was but, at least outwardly, he ruled as a Christian king, issuing coinage under his baptismal name Æthelstan. Alfred would later commemorate his triumph over Guthrum by founding an abbey at Athelney, but it never prospered. When the abbey was dissolved in 1539 it was completely dismantled for building stone, fetching just £80. Only a modest stone monument to Alfred (with no public access) marks Athelney as a place of significance to the history of the Viking Age.

How many Vikings?

Determining the size of the Viking armies that came so close to conquering England has proved very difficult. Contemporary annalists, both in England and elsewhere in Europe, tended to describe the size of Viking armies in terms of the number of ships they arrived in, rather than numbers of warriors. Most sources agree that the numbers of ships involved increased sharply in the 840s, from fleets of three to about thirty-five ships before this date to ones of 100–350 after. Assuming these figures are accurate, they still raise obvious questions. How big were the ships? How many Vikings were there in each ship? Some Vikings did take their wives and children with them on campaign and they are known sometimes to have transported horses in their ships. This would have reduced the numbers of warriors carried in each ship. Two almost complete longships from this period were discovered in the nineteenth century in burial mounds at Oseberg and Gokstad in Norway. The older of the two is the Oseberg ship, which was built around 820 or perhaps earlier. This extremely ornate and elegant ship was 71 feet (21.6 m) long by 16.7 feet (5.1 m) broad and 5.25 feet (1.6 m) deep and had fifteen pairs of oars and, like all Viking ships, a single square sail. Sea trials with a replica have shown that the Oseberg ship was not very seaworthy so it is unlikely to have been a raiding ship. The

Gokstad ship, built around 895–900, is a better candidate for a raiding ship, especially as the skeletal remains of the king or chieftain buried in it show clear signs that he was killed in battle. The ship was 76.5 feet (23.3 m) long by 17 feet (5.2 m) broad and 6.5 feet (2 m) deep and had sixteen pairs of oars. However, a rack along the gunwale carried sixty-four shields, suggesting that it carried a double crew. Unlike the Oseberg ship, the Gokstad ship was very seaworthy indeed: a replica has been sailed across the Atlantic. The oldest known Danish longship, from Ladby on Fyn, is roughly contemporary with the Gokstad ship. Like the Gokstad ship, the Ladby ship had sixteen pairs of oars and, at 68 feet (20.6 m) long, was nearly the same length. However, at only 9.5 feet (2.9 m) broad and 2.3 feet (0.7 m) deep, its hull was also much narrower and shallower than the Gokstad ship's. Although it would have carried fewer men and been less seaworthy than the Gokstad ship, the Ladby ship would in many ways have been a better raiding vessel as it drew less water and would have been much faster under oars. If this ship was typical of those used by the Danes raiding England in Alfred's time, we could conclude that a large Viking army must have numbered at least a few thousand (but probably not tens of thousands) of warriors. This seems all the more credible because we know from reliable literary and archaeological sources that Alfred's Wessex could muster around 30,000 armed men.

A major Viking army of this period did not have a hierarchical structure with a single supreme commander. The basic Scandinavian military unit was the *lið* (or, in the late Viking Age, the *hirð*), a kings' or chieftain's personal retinue of warriors the size of which depended on the wealth and status of its leader. The warriors of a *lið* formed a sworn fellowship or *félag*, which was bonded together by oaths of mutual loyalty. Formal discipline in the ranks was unnecessary. Viking warriors regarded their honour and reputations as their most valuable possessions and had to be defended at all costs. Any warrior who abandoned his comrades in battle would lose his honour and become *niðing*, literally 'nothing', a non-person. Most Vikings would have preferred an honourable death to becoming *niðing* – at least this preserved a man's posthumous reputation and protected his family's honour. For a *víking* expedition, a chieftain could supplement his *lið*

with men recruited from the local defence levies. With the promise of
loot and land, there was probably no shortage of volunteers. Armies
like that, which invaded England in 865, were essentially just groups
of *liðr* which had come together for a common purpose. Decision-
making was consensual with the greatest weight being accorded to
the most successful war leaders and those with royal blood. When a
campaign was over, armies simply broke up into their respective *liðr* to
settle, return home or join another army somewhere else.

After Alfred's victory at Edington, England enjoyed a respite from
major Viking raiding. Most of those Vikings who were not busy settling
moved across the Channel to Francia in search of easier pickings. Alfred
used this period of relative peace to embark on a thorough reform of
his kingdom's defences. A problem with fighting the Vikings was that
it took time to raise an army. Alfred set up a rota so that a third of
his thegns (military aristocracy) and a half of the peasant levies were
always in arms. The thegns were expected to supply their own horses, so
they could form a rapid reaction force, and everyone had to bring sixty
days' supplies with them so that the army could stay in the field longer.
Alfred built a fleet to take on the Vikings at sea: it immediately proved
its worth in battles with small raiding forces around the coast. The
most important element of Alfred's reforms was his system of *burhs*,
'fortified towns', often built at strategic river crossings, which acted
as refuges for country folk and secure operating bases for his army.

Together, Alfred's reforms were intended to deny the Vikings freedom of movement and ensure that they would be pursued everywhere
they went, preventing them from plundering effectively, reforming
the army and building a fleet to take on the Vikings at sea. A devout
Christian, Alfred believed that no amount of military reforms would
defeat the Vikings unless he also had the support of God, so he introduced educational reforms to raise the standard of the clergy. Alfred
invited scholars from abroad and personally translated several major
works, including Pope Gregory the Great's *Pastoral Care*, into English.
He was also responsible for beginning the *Anglo-Saxon Chronicle*. This
is the major source for the events of the Viking Age in England, but
modern readers need to be aware that, despite the chronicle's matter-
of-fact style, its main purpose was to glorify the West-Saxon dynasty's

role in saving Christian England from the pagan Vikings.

Alfred's reforms got their first test in 885 when a large Viking force arrived in Kent and laid siege to Rochester. When Alfred turned up with his army, the Vikings fled to their ships, abandoning their prisoners and all the horses they had brought with them from Francia in anticipation of harrying the countryside. Guthrum had broken the peace by supporting the invaders so, in 886, Alfred seized London in retaliation, which had been under Danish control since the fall of Mercia, rebuilt its Roman walls and installed a permanent garrison. By doing so he effectively closed the Thames to Viking fleets. In the same year Alfred was recognised as king by all the Anglo-Saxons who were not living under Danish rule. It was probably at this time that Alfred agreed a peace treaty with Guthrum, the text of which still survives. In return for treating the Anglo-Saxons under his rule equally with Danes, Alfred recognised the borders of Guthrum's kingdom as running 'up the Thames, and then up the Lea, and along the Lea to its source, then in a straight line to Bedford, then up the Ouse to Watling Street' (an old Roman road). The agreement was most advantageous to Alfred, as it effectively recognised his annexation of all of western Mercia. Alfred had prepared the ground for this already by marrying his daughter Æthelflæd to the ealdorman Æthelred, who had been the ruler of Mercia since Ceolwulf's death in 879 or 880.

Hastein's invasion

The arrival of two large Viking armies from Francia in 892 tested Alfred's new defences to the limit. The larger of the two armies built a camp at Appledore on Kent's Channel coast. The smaller of the two sailed into the Thames estuary and built a fort at Milton Regis in northern Kent. The leader of this army was Hastein, a brilliant commander who had made his name leading a daring Viking raid in the Mediterranean in 859–62 (see ch. 7) and had spent most of the previous thirty years plundering in Francia. A Norman monk, Dudo of St Quentin (*c.* 960–*c.* 1043), would later describe Hastein in lurid terms as a 'cruel and harsh, destructive, troublesome, wild, ferocious, infamous, destructive and inconstant, brash, conceited and lawless,

death-dealing, rude, ever alert, rebellious traitor and kindler of evil',
and every bit the freebooting Viking of the popular imaginative.
Hastein certainly lived the Viking dream, a peasant boy who made
good through sheer guts but whose lack of royal blood prevented him
from reaching the pinnacle of Scandinavian society by conquering a
kingdom of his own.

Alfred responded to the invasion by placing his army in mid-Kent
between the two Viking armies. A long stand-off followed. Alfred
could not concentrate his forces against one Viking army without
leaving the other free to plunder as it wished but, with a large Anglo-
Saxon army in the field, the Vikings were also reluctant to stray far
from their camps. At some point Alfred entered negotiations with
Hastein. These resulted in the baptism of Hastein and his family and a
payment of tribute in return for his promise to withdraw. In the event,
Hastein took the money and stayed. The stalemate was finally broken
when a third Viking army, this one from York, arrived in Devon in
spring 893 and occupied Exeter. This left Alfred no choice but to split
his forces. The new Viking army spent the summer besieged in Exeter
before breaking up in the autumn, some to return to York, others
going to Ireland. This diversion gave the two Viking armies in Kent the
opportunity to escape. Alfred had easily contained the Vikings in Kent
so both armies decided to move across the Thames estuary to East
Anglia, where they could expect support from local Danish settlers.
Hastein built a new fort at Benfleet in Essex, while the Vikings from
Appledore sent their ships to Mersea Island, also in Essex, and then set
out to join them by marching overland through Wessex, plundering
as they went. Heavily burdened with booty, the Vikings moved slowly
and were intercepted by Alfred's son Edward at Farnham in Surrey.
Rather than abandon their booty and run, the Vikings fought and
were defeated. The survivors escaped to Mersea but their king had
been badly injured in the battle and could no longer provide effective
leadership, so most of them defected to Hastein at Benfleet.

Encouraged by this reinforcement to his army, Hastein set out on a
plundering expedition in east Mercia. While he was gone, ealdorman
Æthelred raised an army from London and stormed Hastein's camp at
Benfleet, capturing all his ships and booty, along with his wife and two

sons. Many of Hastein's ships were taken to London and Rochester, the rest were broken up and burned. Charred ships' timbers found by navvies building a railway bridge at South Benfleet in 1855 may have belonged to the Danish ships destroyed after the battle. Hastein built a new fort at Shoebury, 10 miles east of Benfleet, where he received new reinforcements from the East Anglian Danes. Undeterred by the defeat at Benfleet, Hastein launched a raid across west Mercia to the Welsh border. Harried by Mercian and Welsh forces, he was besieged at Buttington on the River Severn, near Welshpool in Powys. Hastein fought his way out but suffered heavy casualties and retreated back to Shoebury. Reinforced by more East Anglian Danes, Hastein set out for Mercia again in the autumn. This time he occupied the old Roman legionary fortress at Chester, but the Mercians had cleared the surrounding countryside of food. Short of supplies and with winter coming on, Hastein again retreated, this time to Mersea Island. Alfred now released Hastein's family but his conciliatory gesture was not reciprocated. In 894 Hastein sailed up the Thames and built a new fort on the River Lea, north of London, but was forced to abandon his ships in 895 when Alfred built a stockade to block the river. Another raid into west Mercia that summer also failed while Alfred's new fleet won victories over several small raiding fleets from York and East Anglia. Though Hastein had never suffered a decisive defeat, Alfred's reformed defences had denied him the freedom to plunder. Frustrated, the Danish army broke up in 896, some to settle in East Anglia, others to return to Francia with Hastein, where it is likely he settled. A relieved chronicler wrote: 'The raiding army had not, by God's grace, greatly afflicted the English people to a very great extent, but they were much more severely afflicted during those three years by the mortality of cattle and men.' Wessex had weathered the storm.

Alfred had never enjoyed good health and he lived only three more years. In the late Anglo-Saxon period, Alfred's reputation was overshadowed by those of his son Edward the Elder and grandson Æthelstan. Alfred's reputation began to grow in the twelfth century, thanks to his almost hagiographical treatment by the chronicler William of Malmesbury (c. 1095–c. 1143) but it was not until the sixteenth century that he acquired his unique title 'the Great'. Certainly, with the benefit of hindsight, Alfred's reign can be seen as decisive in English history, marking the beginning of a national kingship. In his combination of political, military and scholarly abilities, Alfred stands alone among the rulers of early medieval Europe.

The Danelaw

While Wessex's survival still lay in the balance, the Danes consolidated their control over their conquests in East Anglia, the east Midlands and Yorkshire. Because different legal customs, introduced by the Danes, prevailed there, the area subsequently became known as the Danelaw. The scale of Danish settlement is difficult to assess. Danes certainly formed the social and political elite of the Danelaw, what is unclear is if there was also widespread settlement of Danish peasant farmers. Genetic studies of the modern population of the Danelaw have failed to shed light on this because the Danes came from much the same area that the Anglo-Saxons originally hailed from, so the two populations were not genetically distinct. However, place-names of Danish origin are very common in the Danelaw, strongly suggesting that Danes did settle in substantial numbers. Two of the most common place-name elements are -*by*, as in Grimsby ('Grim's village'), and -*thorpe*, as in Kettlethorpe ('Ketil's outlying farm'). Danish place-names are not spread evenly throughout the Danelaw so it would seem that many areas saw little or no Danish settlement. The military nature of the Danish settlement is reflected in the local government of the Danelaw. In Anglo-Saxon England, the basic unit of local government, for taxation and defence was the hundred, a unit of land considered sufficient to support a hundred families: in the Danelaw it was the much larger wapentake, from Old Norse *vápnatak* ('weapon taking'). The Anglo-Saxon hide (the area of ploughland needed to support one peasant family) was generally known as the ploughland (Old English *plogesland*). The law of the Danelaw was distinguished from English law by procedural differences, heavy fines for breach of the king's peace, and the use, unknown in England at the time, of sworn aristocratic juries of presentment to initiate the prosecution of criminal suspects in the wapentake courts. While under contemporary English law, trial by ordeal was used for the most serious crimes. In the Danelaw trial by combat was normal. There were also major differences in landholding in the Danelaw, with much larger numbers of peasant freeholders, or 'sokemen' than in the rest of England. In Lincolnshire freeholders accounted for nearly 50 per cent of the population and in the rest of the Danelaw counties they averaged around one third.

Assimilation of the Danes with the native population began with conversion to Christianity. This was a diplomatic necessity at the top levels of Danish society because it made relations with English rulers easier. The Danish kings of East Anglia issued coins in the name of St Edmund as early as 890, but this may have been intended to appeal their English subjects as much as it was a genuine show of piety. It is not clear how quickly Christianity was adopted by the rest of the Danish population but pagan burial customs had died out by around 950. There probably still were pagans in England after this date, however, because the Anglo-Saxon chronicler criticised King Edgar (r. 957–75) for allowing heathen ways. Assimilation was made easier because the Old Norse and Old English languages were to a limited extent mutually intelligible (this is particularly the case with the Old English dialects spoken in East Anglia and Northumbria). Although it was the Danes who finished up speaking English in the end, it was not a linguistic one-way street as hundreds of Danish words were adopted into the English language. Modern English words pronounced with a *sk*, as in skin, sky, skirt and scrape, are usually of Danish origin as are words pronounced with a hard *k* or *g*, like kid, get, give and egg.

While the establishment of the Danelaw was an undoubted triumph for the Danes, it came at a price. By taking land and settling down, the Danes lost their main military advantage over the English, their mobility. Now that the Danes had farms and families to protect they became vulnerable to English retaliation. The Danes were also vulnerable because they were divided into many small politically unstable kingdoms. The changed balance of advantage soon became apparent in the reign of Alfred's son and successor Edward the Elder (r. 899–924). Edward's first three years as king were spent suppressing a rebellion by his cousin Æthelwold, whose claim to the throne was supported by the East Anglian Danes. Æthelwold's death in battle in 903 freed Edward to take the offensive against the Danes. In 909 Edward attacked the Danes of York: the following year they retaliated by invading Mercia only to be defeated by the combined levies of Mercia and Wessex at Wednesfield, near Tettenhall in Staffordshire. Danish casualties were heavy and included three kings and eleven jarls.

Following his victory, Edward, aided closely by his sister Æthelflæd of Mercia, embarked on the methodical conquest of the Danelaw. Danish resistance crumbled after an unnamed king of East Anglia was killed in battle at Tempsford in Bedfordshire in 917, and by the end of 918 all of the Danelaw south of the Humber was under Edward's control. Edward was generous in victory. The Danish settlers were not dispossessed of their lands and were allowed to retain their own laws and customs. The Danelaw would retain a distinctive identity within England until well after the Norman Conquest. Vikings were not political nationalists. Laws and customs were the true markers of ethnic identity in early medieval Europe, not states, and these concessions helped bind the Danes more closely to the English crown. In parallel with his campaigns in the Danelaw, Edward steadily absorbed Mercia into Wessex, seizing London, Buckinghamshire and Oxfordshire in 911 and the rest of the kingdom in 919 following the death of Æthelflæd. Edward consolidated his conquests by extending Alfred's system of fortified *burhs* north. When Edward died in 924, it was clear that he had set his sights on eliminating the last bastion of Danish power in England, the kingdom of York.

The Viking kingdom of York

York originated as a Roman legionary fortress, founded in AD 71 on a low, level ridge between the confluence of the rivers Ouse and Foss. The Romans named the fortress Eboracum, a name of Celtic origin probably meaning the place of the alders or yews. York had two great attractions to the Romans: it lay at the heart of a large and fertile plain, the produce of which could feed the garrison, and the Ouse was easily navigable to the ships of the day so it could be reached from the North Sea. Like most Roman fortresses, York soon attracted merchants, craftsmen, innkeepers and brothelkeepers eager to relieve the soldiers of their wages and a civilian settlement, or *vicus*, developed on the west bank of the Ouse, opposite the fortress, to which it was linked by a bridge. The *vicus* had grown to such an extent that by 237 it had been formally recognised as a city. It was in York, in 306, that Constantine the Great, Rome's first Christian emperor, was proclaimed emperor by his troops following the death there of his father Constantius.

With the end of Roman rule in Britain in 410, York ceased to be a major population centre but the fortress, at least, was not completely abandoned. The fortress walls remained intact and the legionary headquarters building continued to be used, probably as a palace for the rulers of the small British kingdom of Deira. York began to recover after it became the capital of the Anglian king Ælle, who conquered Deira around 581. Around 604, Ælle's successor, Æthelfrith united Deira with the neighbouring Anglian kingdom of Bernicia to create the kingdom of Northumbria, which stretched from the Humber north to the Firth of Forth. The Anglian kings continued to maintain the walls and use the legionary headquarters until it was destroyed by fire around the time of the Viking conquest. As trade between Britain and the Continent began to revive in the seventh and eight centuries, trading ports, known as *wics*, began to develop on navigable rivers. At York, known to the Anglo-Saxons as *Eoforwic*, a *wic* developed to the south of the fortress along the banks of the Foss.

With the conversion of the Angles to Christianity in the early seventh century, York became an ecclesiastical as well as a royal centre. The Northumbrian king Edwin was baptised there in a newly built wooden church in 627: this was replaced by a stone church *c.* 670. The establishment of an archbishopric at York in 735 made it the second most important ecclesiastical centre in Britain after Canterbury. A school associated with the cathedral developed in the eighth century into a major centre of scholarship with a vast library and an inter-national reputation. In 781 Alcuin, the principal master at the school, met the Frankish king Charlemagne at Parma in the course of a mission to Rome. Recognising his talents, Charlemagne recruited Alcuin to found a school at his palace at Aachen. The fate of York's cathedral school and library under Danish rule is not known for certain but they are unlikely to have survived, if, indeed, they were still functioning at the time of the conquest. The disruption caused by Viking raiding to the church – the main provider of education in the early Middle Ages – had already led to a dramatic decline in the standards of learning in England by the 830s.

Under Danish rule York, or *Jórvik*, as it was called by the Danes, was the capital of the most powerful of the kingdoms of the Danelaw, controlling an area roughly equivalent to modern Yorkshire and parts of Lancashire and Cumbria. Despite their paganism, the Danish kings tolerated the church and it is more than likely that they made use of its literate personnel in administering their kingdom. It would have been in the archbishops' interests to collaborate as this would offer some protection to church property and personnel as well as the opportunity to spread its teachings among the Danes. York's second Danish king, Guthred, may have been an early convert as he is known to have been buried in the cathedral after his death in 895. The Danish kings also adopted the city's mint, issuing coins bearing both Christian and pagan symbols, which were obviously intended to appeal to both settlers and natives. York's trade links under its Anglian rulers had been mainly with Frisia and the Rhineland. To these established links, the Danes brought new connections with Scandinavia, Ireland and further afield: coins from Samarkand, Byzantine silk and Baltic amber have been found in excavations. The Danish rulers actively promoted trade, which they could tax for their own benefit. Their success in stimulating commercial activity is demonstrated by the fact the silver content of the city's coinage increased and by rapid growth of the city's population, including re-occupation of the old Roman vicus west of the Ouse. The Roman walls were refurbished and in places extended to protect newly settled areas. Effective urban planning is suggested by the laying of regular tenement blocks and streets in parts of the city in the early tenth century. Archaeological excavations have revealed evidence for a wide range of craft and industrial activities, including glass-making, metallurgy, weaving and manufacturing items of bone, antler, wood, leather and jet.

By the late tenth century, York's population had reached around 10,000, making York a large city by contemporary standards and, in the British Isles, second in size only to London. Despite this, any merchants visiting from the more urbanised Mediterranean or Arab worlds would not have been impressed by its appearance. Only the city's churches were built of stone and these were mostly modest structures, without towers (the appearance of the cathedral at this time is not known but it was probably the largest building in the city). Most buildings in the city were built of perishable materials: timber, wattles, clay and thatch. Life in the crowded waterfront areas was damp, muddy and unhygienic – latrines were often dug within feet of wells used for drinking water. These waterlogged conditions are ideal for the preservation of organic materials such as leather, cloth and wood, because of the lack of oxygen. Thanks to this, excavations in these parts of the city, notably in the Coppergate area in the 1980s, have revealed a vivid picture of everyday life in the Viking city.

Vikings in north-west England

Danish control of York first came under threat not from Wessex but from the Norwegians. In 902, the Irish expelled Norwegian Vikings from their fortified settlement at Dublin and many of the refugees fled east across the Irish Sea to north-west England. Some of these refugees, led by Ingamund, tried to seize the island of Anglesey, but were expelled by the Welsh. Ingamund then invaded Mercia, but was defeated by ealdorman Æthelred after his Irish followers defected to the English. Ingamund appealed to Æthelred's wife Æthelflæd for lands, and she allowed him to settle on the Wirral peninsula near Chester. A few years later, Ingamund attempted to seize Chester, but he was driven off by the inhabitants who quite literally threw everything they had at the Vikings, including their beehives. Little is known about the Norwegian settlement in the rest of the north-west. An anonymous *History of St Cuthbert* written at Durham records the flight across the Pennines of an abbot and of a nobleman called Alfred son of Brihtwulf, who were escaping the Vikings, so the settlement probably involved the expulsion of the Anglo-Saxon landowning class. Place-names of Norwegian origin are common in Wirral, the Fylde in west Lancashire, the Lake District, and just across the modern Anglo-Scottish border in Dumfriesshire. Fell (*fjall* = 'mountain'), beck (*bekr* = 'stream'), thwaite

(*tveit* = 'clearing'), and side (*saetr* = 'shieling', i.e. a summer settlement)
are common place-name elements of Norwegian origin in these areas.
The settlers also left a long-lasting genetic legacy. After excluding
recent immigrants, a recent DNA study found that around 50 per cent
of the population of Wirral share distinctive genetic markers with the
people of Norway.

Another legacy of this migration may be the Cuerdale hoard, with
over 8,600 objects and weighing 176 pounds (80 kg), the largest Viking
treasure hoard found anywhere outside Russia. The hoard was discovered in 1840 by workmen digging on the bank of the River Ribble at
Cuerdale, near Preston in Lancashire. The hoard was buried in a lead-
lined chest and contained 7,500 silver coins from all over the Viking
world. Around 40 per cent of the coins were silver pennies issued at
York by its Danish kings Sigfrid and Cnut, but others came from as far
away as Spain and Afghanistan. The latest coins in the hoard are fifty-
five pennies of Edward the Elder, a papal coin of Benedict IV dating
to 901–3, and coins of king Louis of Provence dating to 901–5. These
suggest that the hoard was buried not long after 905. As well as the
coins, the hoard contained over 1,000 pieces of jewellery and hacksilver. Vikings put no great store by the artistic merit of the precious
objects they looted and usually hacked them up into smaller pieces to
make the loot easier to share out. Most of the hacksilver and jewellery
came from Ireland and Cuerdale is only a few miles inland from the
Irish Sea. It is likely, then, that the hoard was buried by Viking refugees
from Ireland, who must have come to a bad end not to have recovered
such a valuable stash.

The Norwegian settlers in the north-west probably followed a
similar trajectory of assimilation and conversion to Christianity to
that of the Danes further east. The remarkable sculptured stone cross
at Gosforth in west Cumbria gives some insights into the process
of Christianisation. Tall (15 ft/4.5 m) and very slender, the cross is
decorated in the distinctive Viking Borre art style, which dates it to
the first half of the tenth century. The likely Irish origin of the local
Norse settlers is betrayed by the head of the cross, which has a ring
around it, which is usual in Irish sculptured crosses but not English
ones. Although the cross carries a depiction of Christ's crucifixion, it is

dominated by scenes from Norse pagan mythology showing Ragnarok, the battle at the end of time when the gods will be overthrown and a new cycle of the universe will begin. The mixture of pagan and Christian imagery represents an early stage of conversion, where Christ was worshipped alongside the old gods. Missionaries accepted this as an essential first step: convincing converts that only Christ to be worshipped could come later. The choice of Ragnarok as a subject for the cross is therefore not really the concession to the old religion that it at first seems to be. It is a graphic reminder to pagans that their gods are mortal and are ultimately doomed to be overthrown. Eternity belongs to Christ.

The unification of England

In 910 the Danes of York invaded Mercia. They were retaliating against a raid into the kingdom of York by Edward the Elder's army the year before. The Danes got as far as Tettenhall in Staffordshire before they were met by the combined levies of Wessex and Mercia. In the battle that followed, the Danes suffered a crushing defeat. The deaths of their three kings, Halfdan, Eowils and Ivar, in the battle left the kingdom of York without a ruler. This created the opportunity for Ragnald, the son of Ivar I, a king of Dublin, to seize control by a coup in 911. Ragnald had just enough time to issue some coins in his own name before the Danes drove him out, but he returned in 919 and ruled York until his death in 921. The Irish-Norse dynasty was never able to establish itself securely at York, however. Following the death of King Sihtric Cáech ('squinty') in 927, king Æthelstan of Wessex (r. 924–39), Edward's son, seized York, thereby bringing, for the first time, all of England under a single ruler. An attempt by Sihtric's nephew Olaf Guthfrithsson to recapture York in alliance with Constantine II of Scotland and Owen of Strathclyde was defeated by Æthelstan at the hard-fought battle of Brunanburh in 937. So great was the victory that the *Anglo-Saxon Chronicle* abandoned its usual matter-of-fact style and burst into heroic verse. Unfortunately, while strong on blood-thirsty images of slaughter, it does not give any details of the conduct of the battle itself. When the Vikings and their allies finally fled they left the bodies of five minor

Norse kings, seven jarls, and Cellach, the son of King Constantine of the Scots, as well as countless warriors. King Owen was probably also among the dead. 'Never yet in this island,' the *Chronicle* exulted, 'was there a greater slaughter of people felled by the sword's edges... since Angles and Saxons came here from the east and seized the country from the Welsh'. Brunanburh's location has never been located but a credible candidate is Bromborough on the Wirral peninsula. Lying on the Mersey estuary, its accessibility from the Irish Sea would have made it a convenient mustering place for Olaf and his allies, who could also have expected a friendly reception from the local Norse settlers.

Æthelstan's achievement was threatened after his death in 939, when Olaf returned with Scottish support and not only recaptured York but conquered Northumbria and the important Five Boroughs of the Danelaw. Olaf did not live long to enjoy his victory: he died on campaign in 941 and his successor, his cousin Olaf Sihtricsson, was unable to hold on to his conquests. Æthelstan's successor Edmund (r. 939–46) recaptured the Five Boroughs in 942 and York was back in English hands by 944. York was returned to Scandinavian rule for the last time by the exiled Norwegian king Erik Bloodaxe in 948. For the next six years he struggled for control with Olaf Sihtricsson, who had become king of Dublin in 945, and King Eadred (r. 946–55) of England. However, it was the people of York itself, perhaps wearying of his violent ways, who finally drove him out for good in 954. Erik fled west across the Pennine hills but was ambushed and killed by the otherwise unknown Maccus on the bleak Stainmore Pass: a ruined medieval cross, the Rere Cross, was traditionally regarded as having marked the site of Erik's death, that is, before it was moved to its present location in a litter-strewn layby to make way for a road improvement scheme. Eadred, apparently unopposed, took back control of York. Osulf of Bamburgh, who had orchestrated the coup against Erik, was rewarded by being made ealdorman of Northumbria. England's unity was never again seriously threatened. The Wessex dynasty's unification of England was achieved not only in the face of opposition from the Vikings and their British and Scots allies but also that of many of the Anglo-Saxons who lived in the Danelaw. Local traditions of independence died hard and East Angles, Mercians and Northumbrians sometimes fought with the Danes against the West Saxon conquerors. For them, a local Viking ruler was preferable to a distant West Saxon one. One of the most consistent supporters of Scandinavian rule at York was its archbishop, Wulfstan I (d. 956). Wulfstan may have feared that the status of his seat would be diminished in a united England and he was implicated in several conspiracies against the West Saxon kings. After Erik's overthrow, Eadred allowed Wulfstan to keep his office but had to exercise it from a monastery in the south of England, where he would have no opportunities to plot to restore northern independence under Viking rule.

The unification of England by the Wessex dynasty was undoubtedly one of the most important consequences of the Viking Age. It is by no means certain that this would have happened (and certainly not in the way that it did happen) without the intervention of the Vikings, which completely disrupted England's existing power structures and, by eliminating its rivals, opened the way for Wessex to unify the country. There was already some sense of a common English identity before the Viking Age, but it had found no political expression. As early as the seventh century, Frankish chroniclers who found it difficult to tell the difference between the Angles and Saxons had coined the expression Anglo-Saxons (*Angli-Saxones*), to describe all the Germanic settlers in Britain. At this time, the Anglo-Saxons were divided politically into seven kingdoms (reduced to four by the beginning of the Viking Age), but they all shared a common culture and spoke closely related dialects of a Germanic language that they called *Englisc*. Known to linguists as Old English, this still had a long way to go before it would be intelligible to modern English-speakers. Attempts to articulate a common English identity began with the *Ecclesiastical History of the English People*, written by the Venerable Bede at the beginning of the eighth century. Bede saw common Christian religion as being as much of a unifying factor as language and culture, and this proved very much to be the case in the struggle against the pagan Vikings during which the Anglo-Saxons began to describe themselves collectively as *Anglecynn* ('Englishkind'). One of the reasons Alfred deserves his reputation for greatness is that he recognised the political potential of this developing concept of Englishness and consciously exploited it in his own nation-building project. The creation of the unified 'Kingdom of the English' by Alfred's successors was only the beginning of the creation of a common political identity. Local allegiances remained strong and the cultural assimilation of the Scandinavian settlers was only just beginning, but even a resurgence of Viking raiding later in the tenth century did not seriously threaten the unity of England.

CHAPTER 3

DORESTAD, PARIS AND ROUEN

THE VIKINGS IN FRANCIA 799–939

On Christmas Day 800, Pope Leo III crowned the Frankish king Charlemagne (r. 768–814) Roman emperor in St Peter's basilica in Rome. According to Charlemagne's biographer Einhard, the king had no idea what was going to happen and that if he had only known he would never have set foot in the church. However, this was only the formal modesty expected of a good Christian emperor. In reality the event was long planned, Charlemagne having made up his mind to claim the inheritance of the Roman Empire at least a year beforehand. Comprising modern France, Germany, the Low Countries, Austria, Switzerland, Italy, and parts of Spain, Slovenia, Hungary and the Czech Republic, Charlemagne's empire, known as the Carolingian empire (from Latin *Carolus* = Charles), was the largest and most powerful state to have existed in Europe since the fall of the Western Roman Empire over 300 years before. The peace and security that Charlemagne's rule brought to this vast area led to the growth of trade and a revival of cultural life known as the Carolingian Renaissance. Significantly, this was focussed not on the Mediterranean, the centre of Classical civilisation, but on the north, on the Rhineland, the Low Countries and the fertile farmlands of northern France. The impact of this rising prosperity extended well beyond Charlemagne's domain, stimulating trade in Britain and Scandinavia as well. It was partly to feed markets in the Frankish lands that Swedes were forging new trade routes along the rivers of Eastern Europe. Many Scandinavian merchants must have seen the empire's rich and undefended ports and monasteries, and wondered if there weren't other ways to share in its prosperity.

The limits of power

Charlemagne's coronation was, of course, a celebration of his achievements but he was well aware that his empire faced many challenges, one of which was the threat of Viking piracy: he had, after all, tried to ransom the monks of Lindisfarne who had been captured by Vikings in 793. As a pious Christian, he must have found this attack on such a holy place as deeply disturbing as any churchman.

The first recorded Viking attack on the Frankish Empire did not come until 799. The raid was not a great success. The Vikings plundered an island off the coast of Aquitaine, probably Noirmoutier, an important centre for the salt and wine trades and home to the important monastery of St Philibert, but some of the Vikings' ships were wrecked, an occupational hazard, and over a hundred of them were killed by the Franks. This did not make Charlemagne complacent. Writing with the benefit of hindsight, the monk Notker the Stammerer (d. 912), one of Charlemagne's less reliable biographers, says that the great warrior wept on hearing the news of the first Viking raids on the empire, not because he feared them himself but because he foresaw the trouble they would cause his successors. The story is probably a monkish invention, meant to shame Charlemagne's less able successors, but his response to the raid was certainly vigorous. In March 800, Charlemagne set out from his palace at Aachen for Boulogne on the Channel coast where he personally oversaw the preparations for defence against the Vikings. Further measures followed in 802, 806 and 810. Showing a clear understanding of the nature of the Viking threat, Charlemagne concentrated his forces – fleets, coastguards and fortifications – at the mouths of the empire's major rivers. These were highways into the empire's economic heartlands, lined with towns, monasteries and the richest farmlands. Charlemagne's defences were intended to deny their use to the Vikings.

However, there was little that he could do to protect the open coastline. An incident recorded in the *Royal Frankish Annals* in 820 illustrates both the strengths and weaknesses of Charlemagne's defences. A fleet of thirteen Viking ships landed in Flanders, but the coastguards drove the pirates off before they could do much damage. The Vikings moved on to the Seine, but the coastguards were ready here too and again they were driven off after losing five of their number in skirmish. But the initiative was always going to be with the Vikings. They moved on and kept probing, eventually plundering the unguarded village of Bouin on the coast of Aquitaine. The empire's most exposed area was Frisia, which lay only a couple of days' sail from Denmark. The first recorded Viking raid on Frisia came in 810 when the Danish king Godfred, with a fleet of 200 ships, forced the Frisians to pay him 100 pounds (45 kg) of silver in tribute. On hearing news of the attack, Charlemagne immediately ordered the mobilisation of the fleet and the army, but by the time he reached the area, the Danes had already sailed for home. Frustrated, Charlemagne lamented that God had not granted him the opportunity to let his 'Christian hand sport with these dog-heads'. Charlemagne was now aged around seventy and this was the last time he would lead an army in person.

The great *emporium*

Charlemagne's coastal defences provided a large measure of security for the empire and few incidents are recorded in the twenty years after his death in 814. However, in 834 a large Viking fleet suddenly penetrated over 50 miles into the Rhine delta and sacked the Frisian town of Dorestad, the empire's most important *emporium* or trading centre (equivalent to the Anglo-Saxon *wic*). Near modern Utrecht in the Netherlands, Dorestad was founded in the early seventh century as a beach market outside the walls of a ruined Roman fort at the junction of the Rhine and the River Lek. In the agrarian economy of early medieval Europe, tolls and taxes on trade were one of the few ways a ruler could get his hands on hard cash. Self-interested Frankish

kings offered privileges to encourage merchants and traders to settle
at Dorestad and by Charlemagne's time a town stretched for about
2 miles along the bank of the Rhine, covering an estimated area of
around 1 square mile. With a population of around 2,000 people, it
was probably the largest town in northern Europe at the time. Enough
silver passed through Dorestad for it to have its own mint. The town's
silver coins acknowledged its maritime links, carrying stylised images
of single-masted sailing ships with strongly curved hulls.

Dorestad's appearance was typical of the north European trading
places of its day, an untidy collection of houses, warehouses and
workshops built entirely from wood, clay and thatch, cut by muddy
streets roughly paved with split logs. Apart from two wooden churches,
no public buildings have been identified. Dorestad was divided into an
upper and lower town. The upper town, centred on the old Roman
fort, was the administrative centre: governance was shared between
a count and the bishops of nearby Utrecht, who owned a large part
of the town. The lower town, stretched along the riverbank, was the
commercial and industrial quarter. The riverbank was divided into
long, narrow plots to give the maximum number of traders access to
the river. Causeways of earth and timber stretched out into the river
to give access to timber jetties. As the course of the river gradually
changed, swinging away from the town, these jetties grew ever longer,
eventually stretched over 150 yards from the riverbank. Excavations
have uncovered evidence of a wide variety of manufacturing activities.
Weavers, metalworkers and jewellers, comb-makers, basket weavers
and shipbuilders all plied their trades here. The town's merchants
acted as middlemen, importing high quality lava quernstones, glass,
metalwork, wheel-thrown pottery, and wine from the Rhineland, and
re-exporting it to Britain and Scandinavia. What they received in
return is not known. Baltic amber has been found on the site but most
imports were probably perishable goods such as hides and furs. Behind
the waterfront was a less densely settled area of farms, which supplied
food and other animal products to the town. Just outside the town was
a fortified enclosure, protected by a ditch and bank, which may have
been a refuge for the townsfolk in times of war or the compound of a
local aristocrat. The town itself was not fortified, a sign of the peaceful

conditions that prevailed in Charlemagne's empire.

Exactly how much damage the Vikings inflicted on Dorestad in 834 is unclear. Frankish chronicles paint a familiar picture of burning, killing and captive and tribute taking, but the Vikings thought it worth their while to return again in 835, 836 and 837. Clearly the town was able to recover quickly from Viking raids and output from Dorestad's mints actually peaked in the period 838–40 and continued to be high throughout the 840s. It is quite possible that Dorestad was profiting indirectly from Viking raids elsewhere. As wealth flowed back to Scandinavia from Western Europe it stimulated greater trade, more than compensating for the damage caused to Dorestad itself: the Vikings were great redistributors of wealth.

A troubled empire

That Vikings were able to penetrate as far inland as Dorestad is a sign that Charlemagne's coast defence system had broken down. The reasons for this have little to do with the increasing strength of Viking fleets in this period. They are instead related to internal political developments in the Frankish empire. Frankish tradition dictated that on the death of a king, his kingdom should be divided equally between all his surviving legitimate sons. Since its foundation by the Merovingian dynasty in the fifth century, the Frankish kingdom had experienced frequent partitions, but a vigorous tradition of dynastic murder kept the number of potential heirs in check and prevented it breaking up permanently. When the Carolingians overthrew the Merovingians in the mid-eighth century, they continued the tradition and Charlemagne provided for the empire to be divided between his three sons Charles, Pippin and Louis the Pious after his death. In the event, Charles and Pippin died before their father, so the empire passed intact to Louis the Pious (r. 814–840). In 817, following an accident in which he narrowly escaped death, Louis made provision for the succession. Under the influence of the church, which saw the empire as an instrument of God for promoting the unity of the Christian people, Louis broke with Frankish custom and, instead of providing for an equal division of the empire between his sons, he appointed his eldest son Lothar as co-emperor and granted his younger sons Pippin and Louis subkingdoms in Aquitaine and Germany. This settlement unravelled when Louis decided to marry Judith of Bavaria in 819 after the death of his first wife the year before. Had Louis been less pious and made do with mistresses, the future of the Frankish empire might have been much less troubled. In 823 Judith bore Louis another son, Charles (the Bald, as he would later become known).

Louis could only provide Charles with a suitable inheritance at the expense of his elder brothers. When Louis granted Charles his own subkingdom in 829, Lothar, backed by his brothers, rebelled and deposed him. Charles was excluded from the succession but this seemed grossly unjust to Frankish traditionalists. With their support, Louis was restored in 830, but the problem of the succession continued to fester for the remainder of his reign, steadily undermining the strong royal authority on which Charlemagne's military system was based. Following Louis' death in 840, a civil war broke out between his three surviving sons, Lothar, Louis and Charles (Pippin died in 838), which resulted in a tripartite division of the empire at the Treaty of Verdun in 843. This settlement did not bring stability. In the decades that followed, the empire went through a succession of partitions before it broke up for good in 888. Throughout this period, the Vikings often came a poor third in the Frankish kings' list of priorities: combating dynastic rivals and trying, generally unsuccessfully, to prevent the counts from usurping royal powers always came first.

When not distracted by his troublesome sons, Louis did his best to shore up the coast defences and put diplomatic pressure on Danish kings to restrain their subjects, with some success: in 836 and 838 King Horik executed the leaders of Viking raids against the empire (see ch. 11). After the first Viking attack on Dorestad, Louis ordered the construction of forts to protect the Frisian coast and the Rhine delta. One of these forts, on the island of Walcheren, was captured by the Vikings in 837 while on their way to sack Dorestad for the fourth time. Frankish casualties were heavy and two dukes and other men of rank were captured. Louis cancelled a planned trip to Rome, so seriously did he take this setback. An enquiry into the disaster pinned the blame on the local Frisians for ignoring their military duties and not opposing the Vikings. Fortunately in 838, a fifth attack on Dorestad was prevented when the Viking fleet was destroyed by a storm before it got there. By this time, however, Vikings were active along the empire's entire northern coastline.

The Frankish defences collapse

Vikings were never slow to exploit political weakness and their raids intensified during the civil wars between Louis' sons. The monk Ermentarius described how the strife: 'gave encouragement to the foreigners. Justice was abandoned, and evil advanced. No guards were mounted on the ocean beaches. Wars against foreign enemies ceased and internal wars raged on. The number of ships grew larger, and the Northmen were beyond counting. Everywhere there were massacres of Christians, raids, devastations and burnings.' Of the three kingdoms set up by the Treaty of Verdun, it was Charles the Bald's kingdom of West Francia that was most vulnerable to Viking raids, having a coastline that extended from Flanders to the Pyrenees and many navigable rivers, including the Seine, Loire and Garonne. Lothar's kingdom extended from Rome to the North Sea and included Frisia and the Rhine delta and was therefore also vulnerable to raids. Louis the German's kingdom of East Francia lay between the Rhine and the Elbe and was the least vulnerable to Viking raids, having only a short coastline on the North Sea: apart from frequent raids on the important military and ecclesiastical centre of Hamburg, it was relatively untroubled by the Vikings.

Lothar (r. 840–855) attempted to solve his Viking problem by using fire to fight fire. In 850 Roric, a Danish Viking leader, brought a fleet to Frisia. Unable to expel him, Lothar granted Roric part of Frisia and the town of Dorestad as a fief, making him responsible for defending it against other Vikings and collecting the taxes and handing them over to the royal treasury. There was nothing nationalistic about the Vikings. They were quite happy to fight other Vikings if the price was right. It is questionable how effective an ally Roric proved to be – Vikings ravaged Frisia in 851, 852 and 854, and in 857 when Dorestad itself was sacked yet again – but his loyalty seems never to have been seriously

questioned by any of the four kings he eventually served. At some
point Roric converted to Christianity and one of the empire's most
important churchmen, archbishop Hincmar of Reims, took a personal
interest in his spiritual welfare. In 855, Lothar supported Roric in a
bid to seize the Danish throne but was unable to establish himself and
was back in Frisia by the end of the year. Roric's greatest failure came
in 863 when a fleet of 252 Viking ships sailed down the Rhine as far as
Cologne, sacking Dorestad on the way. Roric negotiated the Vikings'
withdrawal but a rumour spread that he had colluded with the raiders
and in 866 the Frisians rebelled and drove him out. However, he kept
the confidence of his lord, who by now was Lothar's son Lothar II, and
he was soon restored to his fief. When Lothar II died in 869, Roric's
fief was divided between Charles the Bald and Louis the German, but
he reached agreements with them both despite the brothers' mutual
antipathy. Roric is last heard of in 873 and it is not known when he died.
The experiment was obviously deemed a success by the Franks because,
by 882, the new emperor Charles the Fat (r. 881–7) had granted Roric's
lands to another Dane called Godfred. This turned out to be a mistake.
Despite being baptised and married into the royal family, Godfred did
nothing to prevent Viking raids and was murdered at the instigation
of a group of local nobles in 885. By this time Dorestad was largely
deserted. Viking raiding was probably not the critical factor, however.
Dorestad's position in a conflicted borderland between the East and
West Frankish kingdoms disrupted trade even more than Viking raids,
while the shifting course of the river left the town high and dry.

A question of priorities

Charles the Bald's (r. 843–77) authority was the most precarious of
Louis' three sons. Throughout his reign Charles had to contend with
the hostility of his brothers and rebellious counts, as well as intensive
Viking raiding, problems he dealt with in roughly that order of
priority. This may seem puzzling but Charles was determined above
all to defend his throne and, judged from this perspective, his policy
towards the Vikings becomes more comprehensible. Viking raids, no
matter how destructive, would have been of little consequence to him

if he had allowed his brothers or vassals to depose him. Unfortunately, the way Charles protected his throne just made life worse for his subjects. Charles often paid tribute to the Vikings, to buy them off while he dealt with more direct threats to his authority, but this simply encouraged more raids, and made him unpopular with his subjects, who were doubly impoverished by being both taxed and plundered. He refused to allow the building of castles and city walls, which would have given protection to his subjects from Viking raiders, because of a well-justified fear that they might also be used against him by his rebellious counts.

The counts were central to Charles' problems. The county was the basic administrative subdivision of the Frankish kingdoms. Each count was responsible for administering justice, collecting tax revenues on behalf of the crown, and for mobilising and leading those freemen liable for military service in wartime and supplying troops for the royal army as required. Under Charlemagne, counts were usually appointed for life but as royal authority waned after his death the office became hereditary, passing from father to son. This wasn't necessarily a bad thing for the county: often the best candidate for the job would be the son of the old count. He had been brought up in the area, knew the land, and knew, and was known by, the people. For the king, however, it represented a loss of control and patronage if he could not dismiss an ineffective or disobedient count, or reward a loyal vassal by promoting him to county. Once their office became hereditary, counts treated their counties as if they were their own personal principalities. They were reluctant to send troops to join the royal army and leave their own lands exposed to attacks by Vikings or, indeed, neighbouring counts who saw a chance to expand their lands at someone else's expense. This trapped Charles in an ever-tightening vicious circle. The king relied on the counts for troops. Without their co-operation, Charles could depend only on the resources of his own personal estates. With limited forces at his command, the king could neither combat the Vikings nor enforce his authority over disobedient counts. Under these circumstances it is not surprising that Charles was also very reluctant to confront the Vikings in battle. A defeat would not only allow the Vikings to plunder the countryside at will, it might also encourage a rebellion or an attack by his dynastic rivals while his forces were weakened. However, unavoidable though they were, Charles' policies were ultimately self-defeating. Protection was the most important thing that medieval people expected of their kings and his failure to provide it only accelerated the decline of royal authority.

Though few parts of the West Frankish kingdom escaped raids – Vikings even attacked its Mediterranean coastline – the Vikings concentrated their activities on the rich and easily accessible lands of the Loire and Seine river valleys. The Seine was the first to be penetrated by Vikings. In May 841, while the civil war raged between Charles the Bald and his brothers, a Norwegian Viking leader called Asgeir took a fleet up the Seine and sacked Rouen, together with the wealthy abbeys of Jumièges and Fontanelle, where sixty-eight monks were captured and ransomed for 26 pounds (11.8 kg) of silver. The whole campaign took just two weeks. In 842, Vikings sailed down the river Canche, further north along the coast from the Seine, and sacked Quentovic, after Dorestad the most important trade centre in the Frankish lands. Some of the town's inhabitants saved their property by paying ransom to the Vikings. Like Dorestad, Quentovic survived the raid and when it was finally abandoned in the tenth century, it was because the river on which it lay had silted up.

Exposed islands off the mouth of the Loire had been targeted since the earliest days of Viking raiding. In 830, the abbot of St Philibert's on Noirmoutier built a castle as refuge for his monks, so often had it been raided. Soon after this the monks began to retreat to the mainland during the summer raiding season, returning to their island monastery only in the winter when they hoped bad weather would keep the Vikings away. By 836, the abbey had been raided so often that the monks dug up the precious body of their patron saint and, to prevent its desecration by the pagan Vikings, abandoned Noirmoutier and fled with it to find a new home on the mainland. In 843, Vikings sailed up the Loire for the first time. On 24 June a fleet of sixty-seven ships fell upon Nantes while the population were celebrating the feast of St John the Baptist. Vikings burst into the cathedral during a service and massacred the congregation, killing bishop Gunhard at his altar. The timing of the attack is unlikely to have been a coincidence:

attacking during a religious festival, when the population would likely be off guard, was a stratagem the Vikings used more than once. The people of Nantes had felt secure from Viking attack, believing that no strangers could navigate their way through the maze of shoals in the Loire's estuary. However, these Vikings had been supplied with a pilot by Lambert, a local count, who was in rebellion against King Charles and hoped the Vikings would help him get his hands on Nantes. Lambert got his city, or what was left of it anyway. It was a hundred years before Nantes recovered its former prosperity. The Vikings spent the rest of the summer plundering the Loire valley before withdrawing to the security of Noirmoutier where, for the first time, they wintered in Francia. Many of the Vikings had brought their families with them and clearly meant to stay long-term: the Loire would not be free of Vikings until 939.

Charles' defence of the Loire was frequently undermined by rebellious vassals. In 844, Charles' nephew Pippin, the sub-king of Aquitaine, guided a Viking leader called Oskar up the Garonne to help him capture Toulouse. Oskar also scouted the area for opportunities for plunder and in 845 returned and seized Bordeaux. Unfortunately for Pippin, this damaged his credibility and in 851 he was captured and handed over to Charles, who imprisoned him in a monastery. Pippin escaped in 854 and tried again to seize Aquitaine. While Pippin and Charles were fighting, the Loire Vikings plundered the countryside at will, sacking Poitiers, Angoulême, Périgeux, Limoges and Clermont. Pippin failed to establish himself securely and in 864 threw in his lot with the Vikings. A Frankish chronicler even accused him of giving up his Christian faith and becoming a devotee of Odin. If true, Odin proved to be no help. Pippin was captured by Charles later in the year and died in prison. For Nomenoë, the duke of Brittany, the Vikings were a welcome distraction. Vikings often raided Brittany's long, indented coastline but it was a poor country and Vikings found the rich lands of the Seine and Loire much more attractive. The Bretons were unwilling subjects of the Franks and in 845-9, Nomenoë took advantage of Charles' many distractions to assert his country's independence. Even the most effective defender of the Loire, Count Robert the Strong of Angers, who inflicted many defeats on Viking raiding parties, was in rebellion against Charles between 856 and 861. Robert was eventually killed fighting an alliance of Bretons and Vikings at Brissarthe in 866.

The threat to Paris

In 845 the Vikings returned to plunder the Seine valley with a fleet of 120 ships under a leader called Ragnar, who is perhaps the most credible prototype for the legendary Viking Ragnar Lodbrok of the saga traditions. King Charles at least tried to stop the Vikings, stationing troops on both sides of the river just downstream from Paris. Ragnar attacked the smaller of the two Frankish forces with his whole army, which is likely to have been 3,000–4,000 strong given the size of his fleet, and routed it. Ragnar took 111 of his prisoners to the riverbank and hanged them in full view of the other Frankish force, who promptly got the message and fled. Ragnar moved on to sack Paris, at that time just one of many market towns along the Seine, not yet the capital city it would one day become. Early medieval kings spent their lives moving with their courts from one estate to another so no one place was crucial to the administration of a kingdom: the government was wherever the king was. Charles did not think Paris was worth fighting over, he wanted to husband his troops to fight the rebellious Bretons, and simply paid the Danes 7,000 pounds (3,175 kg) of silver to leave the city. While Charles may not have been over-concerned about the Vikings, God, so monkish chroniclers believed, was and He sent an epidemic to punish them for plundering so many holy places. Over 600 of them died according to the *Annals of Xanten*. According to another monastic tradition, an impious Viking who had plundered the abbey of St Germain outside Paris died after his bones miraculously shriveled away.

This divine intervention may have deterred the Vikings for they kept away from the Seine until 852, when a large fleet under Godfred, a son of the Danish king Harald Klak, plundered Frisia and Flanders before settling down for the winter at Jeufosse, mid-way between Rouen and Paris. Charles laid siege to Godfred's camp, but his troops refused to fight and at New Year he withdrew leaving the Danes to ravage the countryside savagely. In July, Godfred moved on to the

Loire, sacking Nantes again and raiding upstream as far as Tours. Danes again returned to the Seine in August 856 and plundered their way upstream, re-establishing their winter camp at Jeufosse. Then, on 28 December, they attacked Paris again and burned it. Every church was destroyed except St Stephen's cathedral, the church of St-Denis, and the church of SS-Vincent and Germain, which were saved when the clergy paid a large ransom in cash. Abbot Louis of St-Denis and his brother Gauzlin, who were captured by the Danes, were themselves ransomed for the incredible sum of 686 pounds (311 kg) of gold and 3,250 pounds (1,474 kg) of silver. Following the attack, the Danes established a new and more secure camp on the island of Oissel, in the Seine 8 miles south of Rouen. There they held out against King Charles, who besieged them fruitlessly for three months during the summer of 858. By this time the peasants of the lower Seine had had enough, both of the Vikings and of their own ruler's failure to defend them. They formed armed bands and began to fight the Vikings, with some success. However, for Charles and his nobles alike, peasants taking the law into their own hands was an unacceptable challenge to their authority. The peasants' reward for resisting the Vikings was to be slaughtered by their own lords. The sense of despair permeated throughout society. The theologian Paschasius Radbertus wrote mournfully: 'Who among us would ever have believed or even imagined that in so short a time we would be overwhelmed with such fearful misfortunes? Today we tremble as we think of these pirates arrayed in raiding bands in the very vicinity of Paris and burning churches along the banks of the Seine. Who would ever have believed, I ask, that thieving gangs would perpetrate such outrages? Who would have thought that a kingdom so glorious, so fortified, so large, so populous, so vigorous would be so humiliated and defiled by such a base and filthy race.' Then in his early seventies, Paschasius was old enough to remember the glory days of Charlemagne.

Since his own troops were only good for fighting peasants, in 860 Charles agreed to pay 3,000 pounds (1,360 kg) of silver to Volund, the leader of a Viking army that was ravaging the countryside around the River Somme, to attack the Vikings at Oissel. Volund took the money and left to invade England and only after the English defeated him in battle did he remember his deal with Charles. The following year, Volund sailed up the Seine with a fleet of 200 ships and laid siege to Oissel. In addition to the silver he had already given Volund, Charles levied another payment of 6,000 pounds (2,722 kg) of silver on his subjects and ordered them to supply his army with grain and cattle, 'so that the realm should not be looted.' Attracted by the generous payments, another Danish fleet of sixty ships came to join Volund. Where Charles had failed, Volund succeeded. Starvation forced the Danes on Oissel to surrender and hand over to Volund 6,000 pounds of gold and silver. The two forces then combined and set out for the open sea. It was now late in the year and winter storms prevented their departure. The army split up into its component fellowships, which were billeted on towns and monasteries along the whole length of the Seine as far as Paris and beyond to the fortress of Melun. Splitting up like this made provisioning the army easier, but it also made the isolated groups of Vikings more vulnerable to Frankish attack, so the arrangement must surely have been made with Charles' agreement.

Charles used the winter respite to position troops along the Seine and its tributaries, the Marne and Oise, to prevent the Danes plundering. This foresight won him a bloodless success when the Danes wintering at Fossés near Paris took a few ships early in 862 and set out to plunder Meaux on the Marne. Unable to catch them, Charles built a barrier across the river behind them to block their escape. Trapped, the Danes gave hostages, released all the captives they had taken and agreed to leave the Seine or help Charles fight any other Danes who failed to keep the agreement made the previous year. About three weeks later Volund and other Danish leaders met with Charles and renewed their oaths to leave. As winter drew to a close, the Danes withdrew as far as Jumièges to repair their ships and, after the spring equinox, the traditional beginning of the sailing season, they returned to the open sea, split up and went their separate ways. Some Danes went to Brittany and allied with Duke Salomon to fight the Franks again. Others went to the Loire and allied with Robert the Strong to fight the Bretons. Volund stayed on the Seine with his family, converted to Christianity and entered Charles' service. He was killed in 863 in a duel with another Dane who had accused him of treachery.

Building bridges

By summer 862, Charles had seen off or outlived his most dangerous dynastic rivals and now began to take the Viking threat more seriously. Charles did not mind too much if Vikings ravaged the lands of his rebellious vassals, but now that they were at the gates of Paris, his own royal estates in the Île de France were acutely vulnerable. Something had to be done. Charles called an assembly at Pîtres, on the Seine just south of Rouen and ordered the construction of a fortified bridge across the river at nearby Pont de l'Arche. Forts of stone, earth and timber were to be built at each end of the bridge for permanent garrisons to bar the passage of Viking fleets up- or downstream. Orders were also given for the construction of fortified bridges on the Marne, Oise and Loire rivers. Arguments about who should build the bridges and garrison them meant that Charles' orders were not carried out. Charles held another assembly at Pîtres in June 864, where he issued the same proclamation. At the same time he ordered towns to pull down any walls they had built to protect themselves from Viking attack. From Charles' perspective it was safer to leave a town exposed to Viking attack than to run the risk that a rebel vassal might hold it against him if it was fortified. This time work on the bridge at Pont de l'Arche seems actually to have started, but it was still incomplete the next summer when it was seized by the Danes. In September, the Danes sent a 200-strong raiding party to Paris in an unsuccessful quest to find supplies of wine. In October, they again sailed up the Seine and sacked the abbey of St-Denis, just outside Paris. They were duly punished for their impiety with an outbreak of dysentery. And in January 866, the Danes sailed right past Paris to attack Melun again. A Frankish army sent to stop them just ran away without fighting.

Charles once again resorted to payments of tribute to get rid of the Danes. This time it was 4,000 pounds (1,814 kg) of silver, as weighed on their own scales, and a supply of wine. To raise the money a levy was imposed on every household in the kingdom. The free paid six denarii, serfs three (a denarius was a silver coin weighing about 0.06 of an ounce/1.75 g: it could purchase twelve two pound (900 g) wheat loaves), merchants the equivalent of one tenth of their goods, and even priests had to pay. Various other taxes were also raised to help pay the tribute. In addition any captives who had been enslaved by the Danes and had been lucky enough to escape were to be returned to their new masters or ransomed at a price set by the Danes. Charles also agreed to pay compensation for any Danes who had been killed by Franks during the campaign. It took until June to raise the silver, but once they had been paid the Danes kept their side of the unequal bargain, set sail down the Seine and reached the open sea in July. Charles followed them as far as Pîtres, taking with him workmen and carts to complete the bridge at Pont de l'Arche 'so that the Northmen might never again be able to get up the Seine beyond that point'. Those who lived downstream from the bridge must have watched the construction work with mixed feelings: they were being taxed to pay for the bridge but were, essentially, being abandoned to the Vikings in future. All too typically, work on the bridge once again languished and it was not actually completed until 873. Fortunately for the Franks, England became the main focus of Viking attentions for the next decade.

In the same year that the bridge at Pont de l'Arche was completed, Charles inflicted a severe defeat on the Loire Vikings at Angers, which bought several years' peace to the region. However, Charles' interest in fighting Vikings was short-lived: playing dynastic politics suddenly promised to be much more rewarding. When his nephew Louis II, the king of Italy, died in 875, Charles invaded, seized control of his kingdom and was crowned emperor in Rome. While crossing the Mont Cenis pass in the Alps on his way home from Italy in autumn 877, Charles fell ill and died. Charles' last wish was to be buried at the abbey of St Denis, which a few years earlier he had fortified to protect it from Viking raids, but his followers were forced to bury him hurriedly at Nantua Abbey near Lyons, because the stench of his rotting corpse had become unbearable.

Though he had succeeded in defending his throne, Charles' reign was an almost unbroken series of disasters for his people: even those who weren't raided by Vikings were punitively taxed to buy them off. Charles has come in for plenty of criticism over the centuries for failing to make combating the Vikings a priority. In his own defence, Charles would probably have argued that if he had succeeded in his goals of re-establishing royal authority and reuniting the empire, dealing with the Vikings would have been easy. He might have been right but his failure to protect his subjects left royal authority in freefall.

Following Charles' death, the Frankish empire was divided between his sons and nephews. They died one by one, young and heirless, until by 882 the sole survivor, Charles the Fat, became the first ruler since the death of Louis the Pious forty years before to rule the whole empire. Charles went so far as to issue coins with the Latin legend *Carolus Magnus*, 'Charles the Great', but he was not destined to be the second Charlemagne his supporters hoped. His ineffectiveness in dealing with raids by Viking and Arab pirates quickly destroyed what little prestige was retained by the Carolingian dynasty.

Flanders ravaged

The Vikings were not people to let a good crisis go to waste. In 878, a new army of Danish Vikings arrived in England, just in time to learn about Alfred the Great's decisive victory over Guthrum at Edington. Clearly, the days of easy pickings in England were over so, after spending the winter in a camp at Fulham on the Thames, the Danes crossed the Channel to Flanders, hoping to take advantage of the dynastic instability in the Frankish kingdoms. For the next ten years the lands between the Seine and the Rhine were devastated with an intensity so far not seen anywhere. In the next four years: Thérouanne (twice), St Bertin, Ghent, Tournai, Marchiennes, Condé, Valenciennes, St Quentin, Laon, Reims, Courtrai, Arras, Cambrai, Péronne, St Omer, Cassel, Amiens, Corbie, St Valéry, St Riquier, Tongres, Liège, Maastricht, Neuss, Cologne, Bonn, Koblenz, Trier and Metz, in roughly that order. Even Charlemagne's favourite residence, his palace at Aachen, was plundered and burned. The chronicler of the abbey of St Vaast at Arras, an eyewitness to the devastation wrought by the Danes, wrote:

> 'The Northmen did not stop capturing and killing Christians or destroying churches, pulling down fortifications, or setting villas on fire. The corpses of clerics, laymen, nobles, women, young people and children were lying on every road. There was no road or place in which the dead did not lie and lamentation and sadness filled everyone, seeing that Christians were massacred.'

Monasteries, already sorely battered by years of Viking raiding and pervasive insecurity, virtually collapsed across the whole of northern Francia. The modest revival of cultural life fostered by Charlemagne fizzled out.

The Vikings seemed able to roam at will, seldom meeting organised resistance. Impressive Frankish victories at Saucourt in 881 and at Avaux, near Reims, in October 882 were not followed up and the plundering continued unabated. On one occasion the Danes mocked a Frankish army for its reluctance to join battle with them, saying: 'So why did you come to see us? It was not necessary. We know who you are and what you want, so let us visit you. Let us do that for you.' But even this did not goad the Franks into action and the army returned home 'in great shame'. In the summer of 885 the Danes moved south to the Seine valley, which had had ten years to recover from the Danes' earlier depredations and was now ripe to be plundered again. The Danes occupied Rouen on 24 June and built a fortified camp on the opposite side of the river from the town. A Frankish army confronted them there but after Ragnold, the duke of Le Mans, was killed with a few of his men in a skirmish, the rest of the army withdrew, a testament, perhaps, to the effectiveness of Viking field fortifications as much as to the lack of resolve of the Franks. The presence of the army had at least restrained the Danes; now that they had fled, they could plunder wherever they wished. The Franks built fortifications by the Seine to impede the progress of the Danish ships upriver, but their garrisons' lack of resolve meant that they were useless. Archaeological excavations have shown that the bridge at Pont de l'Arche was burned around this time, as was another fortress built to block the River Oise at Pontoise.

The Vikings besiege Paris

On 24 November, the Danes arrived outside Paris. The Danes probably expected a rapid capitulation, that was what they had come to expect, but they became bogged down in a year-long siege, which, in retrospect, came to be seen as the turning point of the Frankish struggle against the Vikings. A monk, Abbo the Twisted, who was present in Paris throughout, later wrote a detailed and colourful account of the siege in Latin verse. The day after their fleet arrived at Paris, the Danes' leader Sigfred approached Gauzelin, the city's bishop, to negotiate free passage upstream. According to Abbo, Sigfred pleaded with Gauzelin to spare himself and his flock the horrors of war. If he granted the Danes free passage so that they could ravage the countryside beyond Paris, Sigfred promised that they would do no harm to the city and respect all property. Gauzelin refused. He had been made responsible for the city's defence by his king Charles the Fat, he told Sigfred, and he would not betray that trust. When Gauzelin asked him rhetorically what treatment he thought he would deserve if it was he who had been entrusted with defending the city and tamely allowed an enemy to pass, Sigfred told him: 'I should deserve that my head be cut off and thrown to the dogs. Nevertheless, if you do not give in to my demand, I must tell you that tomorrow our war machines will destroy you with poisoned arrows.'

Gauzelin's defiance was more than simple bravado. In the years of peace since Paris was last attacked by the Danes, Gauzelin had overseen the construction of substantial fortifications. At this time Paris was mainly confined to the Île de la Cité, a long narrow island in the Seine. The island was protected by walls so the Danes could not easily land on it. A wooden bridge, the Grand Pont, linked the island to the north bank of the Seine. The approach to the bridge was protected by a still incomplete stone tower. Another wooden bridge, the Petit Pont, connected the island to the south bank. The approach to this bridge was protected by a wooden tower. Together the two bridges completely blocked the river to all shipping. The defence of the city was led by its count Odo, the son of Robert the Strong. Odo commanded only a small garrison of 200 soldiers, but he was an inspiring leader and just as determined not to give in as the bishop was. The defenders also possessed mangonels (giant catapults) and balistas (giant crossbows). The size of the Danish army that opposed them is unknown. According to Abbo, the Danes came in 700 ships and were 40,000 strong, but this number must be a gross exaggeration. No other chronicler of the period records such large fleets and it would, in any case, have been impossible to keep such an enormous force in the field for so long under early medieval conditions. The army was certainly not large enough to invest the city completely because messengers were able to leave and return throughout.

Knowing that mobility was the key to their success, Vikings generally avoided sieges. But the Franks had not held any fortification against them for long, so Sigfred probably expected Paris to fall quickly. True to his word, Sigfred launched an assault on the city at dawn on the day after his meeting with Gauzelin. The Danes concentrated their attack on the incomplete tower that guarded the Grand Pont, battering it with catapults and battering rams. The battle raged all day, and count Odo, his brother Robert and another count, Ragenar, were always in the thick of the fighting encouraging the defenders. Gauzelin planted a crucifix on the ramparts and fought with a bow and an axe, in spite of his priestly vows, which forbade the shedding of blood. Gauzelin probably felt that pagan blood did not count. An abbot, Ebolus, was wounded by an arrow fighting on the ramparts. At nightfall the Danes withdrew carrying their dead with them. The tower had suffered serious damage and Odo and Gauzelin worked through the night organising repair work and adding an extra storey in timber so that when the Danes renewed their assault the next day they found it half as high again as it had been originally. This time the Danes first attempted to set fire to the tower and then tried to undermine its foundations by digging. The diggers fled when the Franks poured a mixture of boiling oil, pitch and wax onto them. Some of them tore their scalps off in agony and many died from burns. A single bolt from one of the Franks' balistas reportedly skewered seven Danes together. When the dispirited Danes retreated, the jeers of their wives and concubines sent them back to try again but at nightfall they gave up the assault. The presence of women in a Viking army was not unusual. Though they did not fight, the women made life in camp bearable, cooking, washing and repairing clothes, and caring for the sick.

Having failed to intimidate Paris into surrender or take it by a quick assault, the Danes set up a fortified winter camp at the abbey of St Germain l'Auxerrois on the north bank of the Seine, not far from the bridgehead of the Grand Pont. It was not until the last day of January 886 that the Danes launched another attack. This time the Danes divided their forces into three groups. One group attacked the bridgehead tower on the Grand Pont while the other two attacked the bridge itself from ships. The Danes fought for three days to capture the tower, trying to fill its moat in with earth, logs, straw bales and even the bodies of dead animals and captives so that that they could push three mobile siege towers close enough to storm the ramparts. The defenders sallied out and destroyed two of the towers but a few Danes managed somehow to break into the city, only to be quickly killed. The Danes now tried to break the bridge by sending three fireships crashing against it, but it failed to catch light. The weather seemed to be on the side of the Danes, however. On 6 February the Seine flooded and debris smashed the Petit Pont. During the night Gauzelin sent a hand-picked unit across the river to guard the now isolated tower on the south bank so that they could begin to repair the bridge at first light. They were seen by the Danes who at daybreak began to assault the tower. The rest of the garrison could do nothing but watch helplessly as the Danes set fire to the tower and slaughtered everyone in it before throwing the bodies into the river.

It was now possible for the Danes to sail past Paris on the south side. The Danes moved their camp across the river to the abbey of St Germain-des-Prés, Abbo's monastery. While part of the Danish army maintained the siege other bands raided far and wide, to Chartres in the west and Evreux to the south. Dismayed by the loss of the bridge, Gauzelin sent messengers out with an urgent appeal for help to Henry of Franconia, the count of Saxony. Henry arrived with an army but his soldiers were weakened by the winter weather and he withdrew after the Danes repulsed a half-hearted attack on their camp. Sigfred was rapidly losing enthusiasm for the siege and he and his personal following left after Gauzelin agreed to pay him a face-saving tribute of 60 pounds (27 kg) of silver. After fighting so long and hard, most of the Danes were not willing to be bought off for so little and the siege continued. No contemporary annal names the leader of these diehards, but according to later traditions it was Rollo, who would become famous as the founder of Normandy.

Like so many of the great Viking leaders, Rollo's origins are uncertain. In Icelandic saga traditions he was identified with Hrolf the Ganger ('walker'), a son of the Norwegian jarl Rognvald of Møre, who got his nickname because he was so tall that no horse could be found that could carry him. However, the Norman historian Dudo of St Quentin believed that Rollo was a Dane. According to Dudo, Rollo arrived on the Seine as early as 876 and at some point after that captured Rouen, making it his permanent base.

The end of the siege

Hunger and disease began to take a heavy toll on the Parisians in spring 886. By April there was not enough space in the city to bury the dead. One of those who succumbed was Gauzelin, who fell ill and died on 16 April, striking a severe blow to the Parisians' morale. The Danes must have had sympathisers within the city walls because they heard the news of Gauzelin's death before most of the townsfolk. Hugh, abbot of St Germain l'Auxerrois, took over spiritual leadership of the city but he too died three weeks later, casting the Parisians into despair. Odo secretly left Paris and rode to meet the emperor to beg him to lead an army in person to lift the siege. Odo received no firm assurances and on his return to Paris was ambushed outside the gates of the battered tower on the north bank, the Danes having learned in advance of his return. Odo's horse was killed under him but he and the soldiers who accompanied him fought their way through to safety.

It was not until October that Charles, urged on by the archbishop of Reims, who warned him that if he lost Paris he would lose his kingdom, raised an army and marched to relieve the city. On route, Henry of Franconia was killed in a skirmish with the Danes after his horse fell into a ditch. Charles set up camp at the foot of Montmartre but, to the dismay of the Parisians, he simply opened negotiations with the Danes, giving them exactly what they had asked for at the beginning of the siege: permission to sail past Paris and spend the winter ravaging the Burgundians, whose count had proved disloyal. This may have made sense to Charles but it seemed like betrayal to the Parisians and they refused to let the Danes pass (presumably they had repaired the Petit Pont by this time). The Danes were forced to drag their ships overland and launch them back into the river upstream of Paris. Come the spring, Charles made it even less likely that he would get any credit for his relief of Paris when he paid the Danes 700 pounds (318 kg) of silver to leave the Seine. Some of the Danes did indeed leave but a large contingent under Rollo remained behind.

Charles the Fat's behaviour at Paris left him looking weak and incompetent and he quickly lost support. While he was holding a council at Frankfurt in November 887, Charles was deposed by his nephew, Arnulf of Carinthia (r. 887–99), who was elected king in his place by the East Franks. Deserted even by his servants, Charles retired to his estate at Donaueschingen in the Black Forest where he died on 13 January 888: it was rumoured that he had been strangled on Arnulf's orders. Charles' death triggered the final break-up of Charlemagne's empire. Arnulf's coup was recognised only by the East Franks. The nobles of Burgundy, Provence and Italy all elected their own kings, as did those of West Francia, who chose Odo (r. 888–98), the hero of the siege of Paris and the first king of the Franks who was not a Merovingian or a Carolingian. West and East Francia would never be reunited, developing instead into the medieval kingdoms of France and Germany.

Arnulf and Odo both proved to be energetic rulers and their reigns saw a marked decline in Viking activity in the Frankish kingdoms. Arnulf won a major victory over the Danes at the battle on the River Dyle, near Louvain in modern Belgium, in September 891. This was the same Danish army that had laid siege to Paris in 885–6. The Danes had built a fortified camp on the riverbank. Led by Arnulf himself, the East Franks stormed the camp. The Danes panicked and tried to escape across the river but in the free-for-all hundreds, if not thousands, were crushed to death or drowned, their corpses damming the river 'so that it seemed to run dry'. Among the dead was a king called Sigfred, but it is not clear if he was the same Sigfred who led the Danes at the siege of Paris. The survivors retreated to Boulogne, from where they crossed to England in 892 in ships provided by the locals, who no doubt thought them a small price to pay to see the back of the Vikings. A factor that is likely to have influenced their decision just as much as defeat on the Dyle was a famine in Flanders, which meant the army could not live off the land. Unfortunately for the Danes, they found England well prepared for them.

The foundation of Normandy

Odo was not a Carolingian and their supporters frequently challenged his authority. In 893, the Carolingian Charles the Simple, the posthumous son of King Louis the Stammerer, was crowned king in opposition to Odo. A long civil war followed but the Danes were busy in England and there was no resurgence of Viking raiding. Odo finally triumphed in the war in 897 and Charles withdrew his claim to the throne. However, when Odo died in 898, Charles took the throne without opposition, restoring the Carolingian line. Charles' kingdom was still host to Viking armies on the Loire and the Seine. The Frankish kings had never regained effective control of either area since Danish Vikings first arrived in force in 841. The Seine Vikings were the greater threat because Rollo's base at Rouen was too close to Paris and the royal estates in the Île de France. Rollo's depredations in the area only finally came to an end in 911, when he was defeated in an attack on Chartres. The next year Rollo met with Charles the Simple (whose nickname means 'sincere' not simple-minded) at the village of St-Claire-sur-Epte, and the two men negotiated a peace deal. In return for his homage, conversion to Christianity, and agreement to defend the Seine against other Viking raiders, Charles appointed Rollo as count of Rouen. It was a mutually advantageous arrangement. Charles got recognition of his sovereignty over lands he did not actually control, while Rollo's de facto rule over the lower Seine was legitimised. This was, of course, not the first time a Frankish ruler had come to this kind of agreement with a Viking leader. Charles may have expected that it would prove to be a temporary expedient and that Rollo's tenure would be as short-lived as Roric's and Godfred's had been on the lower Rhine. However, Rollo's principality, soon to become known as Normandy, from *Nordmannia* meaning 'Northman's Land', not only survived but flourished, coming to play an influential role in European history as part of the Viking Age's 'long tail'.

Rollo stuck to his side of the agreement and kept other Viking

raiders out of the Seine, but he was determined to be no more obedient
to his king than he really had to be. A story told about the meeting at
St-Claire-sur-Epte by Dudo relates that Rollo was required to kiss King
Charles' foot as a condition of the agreement, but he was too proud to
do so. 'The bishops said to Rollo, "you who receive such a gift ought to
kiss the king's foot." And he said: "I shall never bend my knees to the
knees of another nor shall I kiss anyone's foot". Compelled, however,
by the prayers of the Franks, he ordered another warrior to kiss the
king's foot. This man immediately seized the king's foot and put it to
his mouth and kissed it while the king was still standing. The king fell
flat on his back. This raised a great laugh and greatly stirred up the
crowd.' It is easy to read this most likely apocryphal tale as evidence
of Rollo's freebooting Viking spirit, but in his desire to pay no more
than lip service to his overlord, he was really no different to any other
independent-minded Frankish count. Rollo left Paris alone but he
was always on the look-out for opportunities to expand his territories,
attacking the neighbouring county of Flanders several times, though
without success. In 922, Charles the Simple was deposed and a civil war
broke out. The political turmoil gave Rollo an opportunity to secure
control of Caen and Bayeux, almost doubling the size of Normandy.

Rollo's agreement with King Charles gave Danes the security to
settle in Normandy and put down permanent roots. The first settlers
were Rollo's own warriors and their families. Rollo distributed the
land in much the same way that a Viking leader would have shared
the loot from a successful raid, keeping the largest share for himself
and giving the more important warriors larger estates than the rank
and file warriors. These first settlers were soon joined by others from
England, where the West Saxon conquest of the Danelaw was in full
swing. One of these refugees was jarl Thorketill, who arrived with his
followers from Bedford in 920. Little is known about the nature of the
Danish settlement but, as happened in England, they probably took
over the abandoned estates of local nobles and monasteries: the local
peasants simply got new landlords. It is clear from the distribution
of Danish place-names that Danes did not settle in all of the lands
granted to Rollo, and that even in the areas they did settle they must
have been a minority among the native population. The densest

clusters of settlement seem to have been around Rouen and Caen and in the Pays de Caux between the Seine estuary and the fishing port of Fécamp on the Channel coast. The settlers left little archaeological evidence of their presence, indicating that they quickly adopted the material culture and burial customs of the native population. So far, the only certain pagan Viking burials found in France are a female burial discovered near Pîtres and a chieftain's ship burial on the Île de Groix off the coast of Brittany.

Viking Brittany

While Rollo was consolidating his position in Normandy, a Viking leader called Rognvald established another Viking colony in Brittany. By the beginning of the tenth century, the Franks were getting the measure of the Vikings, and so too were the English and the Irish. Brittany's relative poverty had protected it in the ninth century but it now began to look increasingly like a soft target. When the settlement of Rollo and his followers in Normandy in 911 closed the Seine to raiders, the Vikings turned their full fury on Brittany. As monastery after monastery was sacked, Breton monks fled en masse to seek safety in France and England, taking with them whatever books and treasures they could carry. After Rognvald captured Nantes in 919, Breton resistance collapsed completely. The aristocracy followed the monks into exile in France and England and Brittany became a Viking kingdom with its capital at Nantes. Nothing is known about Rognvald's earlier career, but it is clear that, unlike Rollo, he was no statesman, making no effort either to legitimise or institutionalise his rule. Rognvald seems to have seen Brittany as no more than a base from which to launch plundering raids on Francia. While York, Dublin and Rouen prospered as trade centres under Viking rule, Nantes, whose location at the mouth of the Loire should have ensured its prosperity too, was allowed to become semi-derelict: its cathedral was abandoned and became overgrown with brambles.

In 924–5, Rognvald raided deep into the Auvergne but was defeated by the Franks and made a fighting retreat to Nantes where it is thought he died soon after. According to the *Miracles of St Benedict*, Rognvald's death was divine punishment for attacking the saint's abbey at Fleury on the Loire. Fittingly, for a man who had inspired such terror in his lifetime, Rognvald's death was marked by dreadful portents, lights in the sky, moving rocks and apparitions. It is not known who, if anyone, succeeded Rognvald as leader of the Vikings in Brittany. The pirate state began to unravel. When the Vikings gathered in Nantes to launch a major raid up the Loire, the peasants of Brittany rebelled. Lacking strong leadership and military skills, the peasants were defeated but the revolt encouraged Alain Barbetorte ('twistbeard'), a Breton noble living in exile in England, to lead an invasion of Brittany in 936 with a fleet supplied by king Æthelstan. Landing from the sea, Alain enjoyed complete surprise, capturing and executing a party of Viking revellers celebrating a wedding near Dol. A Viking fort at Péran, further west along the coast, was destroyed by fire around this time, possibly as a result of fighting during Alain's reconquest. Alain captured Nantes after a fierce battle in 937 and the Bretons stormed the Vikings' last stronghold, at Trans, in 939. The destruction of the Viking colony doubly benefited the Franks. The last major Viking threat to the Frankish kingdom was eliminated, while Brittany never fully recovered and drifted permanently under Frankish influence.

Conversion and assimilation

Although Rollo was still a pagan when he won control of Rouen, it appears that he allowed what was left of the church to function in the area under his control much as the Danish rulers of York had done. Pagan Vikings were rarely positively hostile to Christianity; sacking churches and monasteries and selling their occupants into slavery was just good business. Even after his baptism in 912 Rollo, like many first generation Viking converts to Christianity, hedged his bets and worshipped the pagan gods alongside Christ. Shortly before he died, Rollo ordered 100 Christians to be beheaded as an offering to the pagan gods, but he also gave 100 pounds (45 kg) of gold to the churches of Rouen. Conversion was the normal price Christian rulers from the time of Louis the Pious onward demanded of pagan Viking leaders and their followers before entering into treaties with them. Many such conversions were probably completely insincere. The custom of giving baptismal gifts of clothes and weapons on these occasions certainly encouraged some Vikings to be baptised more than once. Notker tells the story of a Dane who complained to Louis the Pious about the quality of his baptismal robe, the worst he had ever been given – it turned out that he had been baptised twenty times already. The church was philosophical about this sort of backsliding as it pursued a policy akin to entryism. It was relatively easy for a polytheist to accept Christ as just one more god. Once the convert had got into the habit of believing in Christ, the church could get to work convincing him or her that the old gods were false gods. Most of the earliest Scandinavian converts to Christianity were settlers in countries, like Francia, that were already Christian and baptism marked the first step of their assimilation into the native population.

Rollo died some time around 928 and was succeeded by his son William Longsword (d. 942). As a traditional Viking leader Rollo never imposed his authority on his followers by force – in keeping with Scandinavian custom, their allegiance was entirely voluntary. William took a more forceful line in imposing his authority over the Danish settlers in Normandy. This provoked a rebellion in 933 by settlers who felt that William was becoming too Frankish in his behaviour and was favouring Frankish advisers over Danes. It did not help that he had a Frankish mother, Poppa of Bayeux, and a Frankish name. William reacted forcefully and the rebellion collapsed after he defeated their leader Riulf in a battle near Rouen. William continued his father's expansionist policy and in 933, King Rudolph granted him the Cotentin peninsula. Cotentin was not much loss to the king as it had not been under Frankish control since 867, when Charles the Bald ceded it to Brittany after his defeat the previous year by a Breton-Viking alliance at the Battle of Brissarthe. The northern part of the Contentin was settled by Norwegians rather than Danes, as in the rest of Normandy. Place-name evidence shows that many of the settlers had previously been living in Gaelic-speaking Ireland or the western isles of Scotland. The arrival of the Norwegians in the Cotentin is undocumented and they may well have arrived before the area formally became part of Normandy. Possibly they were, like the Norwegians who settled north-west England, refugees from the great Irish offensive which saw the Vikings expelled from Dublin and their other bases around Ireland in 902.

Like Rollo, William also aspired to expand into Flanders but he was equally unsuccessful. Tiring of William's attacks, Arnulf, the count of Flanders, invited him to a parley on an island in the River Somme where Arnulf's followers ambushed and killed him in December 942. William's death threw Normandy into chaos. King Louis IV confirmed Richard's ten-year-old illegitimate son Richard the Fearless (r. 942–96) as count but placed him in custody with the count of Ponthieu at Laon as a prelude to restoring full Frankish control of Normandy. Louis occupied Rouen and divided Normandy between himself and the powerful count Hugh the Great of Paris. Some Normans swore allegiance to Louis, others to Hugh, but others remained loyal to Richard. The situation was further complicated by the arrival on the Seine of a new Danish army under Sihtric of Hedeby. This encouraged many Normans to abandon Christianity and return to paganism. Louis defeated Sihtric and his pagan Norman allies near Rouen, but his plans began to unravel when he was captured by the Norman leader Harald of Bayeux. Harald handed Louis over to Count Hugh, who only agreed to release him after he had made territorial concessions. While Louis was imprisoned, Richard was rescued from his imprisonment by a group of Normans led by Osmund de Centville. Richard swore allegiance to Count Hugh and with his backing regained control of Normandy by 947. Perhaps because the beginning of his rule had been so turbulent, Richard abandoned the aggressive stance of his predecessors and concentrated on building his own authority in Normandy. Richard repaid Hugh's early support in 987 by helping his son Hugh Capet seize the throne on the death of the last Carolingian king Louis the Lazy. Hugh's Capetian dynasty would rule until 1328, ultimately making France (as it is now usual to call the West Frankish kingdom) Europe's strongest kingdom.

Although Frankish chroniclers described Richard as *piratarum dux* ('pirate leader') it was during his long reign that Normandy began its transformation from a Viking colony into a Frankish principality. Richard introduced Frankish feudal institutions, binding the leading

Normans to him as his vassals. Although the archbishopric of Rouen had continued to function at some level through the worst ravages of the Vikings, monasteries across Normandy were abandoned and ruined: Richard refounded them with generous endowments. Apart from a trickle of settlers from England's Danelaw, Scandinavian immigration all but ceased. However, Rouen retained strong links to the north through trade: coins minted in tenth-century Rouen have been found everywhere along the Vikings' trade routes from Ireland to Russia. Normandy continued to be part of the northern world under Richard's successor Richard II 'the Good' (r. 996–1026), his son by his Scandinavian second wife Gunnor. Richard, the first ruler of Normandy to use the title 'duke', was deeply involved in French politics, taking part in King Robert II's wars with Burgundy, working to reform the Norman church, and forging marriage alliances to bring Brittany within the Norman sphere of influence. However, Richard still maintained strong ties to the north, allowing the Danish king Svein Forkbeard to use Normandy as a base for attacks on England in return for a share of the plunder and recruiting Viking mercenaries into his army. The Norman elite now fought in the French style, as armoured cavalry, however. Norman soldiers also joined Viking armies, fighting in the battle of Clontarf near Dublin in 1014. Richard must have had good contacts in Scandinavia because in 1000 he was able to secure the release of the wife of the count of Limoges who had been captured by Vikings.

In 1002, Richard married his sister Emma to the English king Æthelred, in effect backing both sides in the unfolding Anglo-Danish struggle. After Æthelred's death in 1014, Emma remained in England, marrying Svein's son Cnut after he became king of England in 1016. Despite this, relations between Richard and Cnut seem not to have been close and Normandy's links with the north quickly faded. The last vestige of Scandinavian influence is the visit of Sigvatr, an Icelandic skald (court poet), to the ducal court at Rouen in 1025. Sigvatr's presence implies that there were still Normans who could understand the Old Norse language but most by now must have spoken French. Most of Rollo's followers had been single men who, after they took lands in Normandy, had married Frankish women: their children would, therefore, have grown up as French speakers even if they had also learned Old Norse from their fathers. The severing of ties with the north is mirrored in coin hoards from Normandy which, after Richard's death, mostly contain coins from France and Italy. At the same time, coins minted at Rouen disappear from hoards found in Ireland, England, Scandinavia and Russia. By the time William the Conqueror became duke in 1035, Normandy was culturally and linguistically part of France and the Normans had begun describing themselves as *Franci* or French.

The end of the Viking Age in Francia

Following the establishment of Normandy and the failure of the Viking colony in Brittany, Viking activity in the West Frankish kingdom declined rapidly. Occasional raids continued into the eleventh century, but these were mere irritants compared the great raids of the ninth century: by *c.* 950 the Viking Age in Francia was effectively over. Francia was no longer an easy place to raid. This had nothing to do with a resurgent Frankish monarchy. The authority of the West Frankish kings continued to decline throughout the period. When Hugh Capet seized the throne in 987, his authority did not extend beyond the Île de France. The counts and dukes who ruled the rest of his kingdom paid homage to the king as vassals, but his resources were so slender that he was powerless to enforce their obedience. The counts and dukes ruled their principalities in virtual independence, waging private war on one another, and obeying the king only when it would serve their interests. No Frankish king of the tenth or eleventh centuries could have reconstituted Charlemagne's coastal defence system, even had they wanted to.

The lack of strong central authority, however, did not mean that the West Frankish kingdom was weak. The decline of royal authority freed the Franks to take their defence into their own hands. Towns were free to build defensive walls (or, often, to refurbish old Roman walls) and small earth and timber castles proliferated across the countryside, providing refuges and secure bases for harassing invading Viking armies. The counts and dukes may have paid scant attention to their kings but they often ruled their own principalities effectively and could react more quickly to an attack than the more centralised Carolingian system. The decline of royal authority was accompanied by the growth of feudalism and the appearance of a new military class of professional armoured cavalrymen or knights. Only the very wealthiest could afford to equip themselves to fight in this way so most knights were vassals of the counts and dukes, who granted them estates for their maintenance in return for military service. In battle, Frankish knights invariably proved superior to even the most determined foot soldiers, as the English would discover to their cost in 1066. It was this combination of castles and cavalry that had turned Francia into a no-go zone for Vikings. How far the Vikings were responsible for the changes in Frankish society is a moot point. The driving force of the break-up of Charlemagne's empire was dynastic and the Frankish laws of partible inheritance made this more or less inevitable. However, the decline of royal authority that accompanied the empire's break-up was at the very least accelerated by the Vikings, who time and again had demonstrated the Frankish kings' powerlessness to defend their subjects.

CHAPTER 4

IONA, DUNKELD AND ORKNEY

VIKINGS IN SCOTLAND
795–1064

Scotland's Viking Age began, like England's, with attacks on exposed monasteries, but the raiders were very quickly followed by settlers who put down deep roots: the Viking influence lasted longer here than anywhere else in the British Isles. No part of Scotland was immune to Viking attacks, but it was the northern and western isles that bore the brunt of the early raids and then, after their colonisation by Scandinavian settlers, became bases from which raids could be launched further south. While the Viking armies that ravaged England and Frankia were dominated by Danes, Scotland, with Ireland, was always in the Norwegian sphere of interest.

At the beginning of the Viking Age, Scotland in the modern sense did not exist. The greater part of the modern country, from the Firth of Forth north to the Shetland Islands was occupied by the kingdom of the Picts, descendents of ancient Britons who had held out in the north against Rome. The south-east of the country was part of the Anglo-Saxon kingdom of Northumbria, while in the south-west was the Welsh kingdom of Strathclyde. In the west, the district of Argyll and the Hebridean islands were occupied by the Scots, a Gaelic-speaking people who had immigrated from northern Ireland under the Dál

Riata dynasty at around the same time that the Anglo-Saxons were arriving in Britain from northern Germany. Despite frequent wars, a stable balance of power existed between the four kingdoms: this would be shattered by the arrival of the Vikings.

St Columba's island

No historical annals that were actually written in Scotland have survived from before the late tenth century. Most of the contemporary records of Scotland's Viking Age were written in Irish monasteries and they have a strong bias towards events on the Gaelic-speaking west coast and to the sufferings of their brother monks. The first recorded attack on Scotland came in 795 when Vikings plundered St Columba's monastery on the small Hebridean island of Iona before going on to raid in Ireland. Thereafter, raids in the Hebrides became almost annual events, with monasteries bearing the brunt of the attacks. Vikings returned to Iona in 802 and this time they burned the monastery after they had plundered it. There is no mention of killing during these raids, but in the course of a third raid in 806, sixty-eight monks were slaughtered. Just a year later, Iona was sacked for a fourth time.

St Columba's was, arguably, the most famous and influential monastery in the whole of Britain and Ireland. Born in 521, its founder Columba was an energetic, powerfully-built, hot-tempered Irishman from a noble family from Ulster. Joining the church at an early age, Columba soon earned a reputation for piety and learning. However, his temper almost destroyed his career. In 561 a dispute over a sacred manuscript that Columba had illicitly copied escalated out of control, leading to a battle in which a great many people were killed. A synod called to judge Columba considered excommunicating him but in the end sentenced him to exile. In 563 Columba left Ireland and sailed to Scotland with twelve companions, resolving to atone for his errors by winning as many souls for Christ as had been lost in the battle. Columba was welcomed by his kinsman King Conall of Dál Riata, who gave him Iona as a base from which to evangelise the pagan northern Picts. As well as piety, Conall probably had some very worldly motives. In medieval Europe, political power often followed the church.

Bringing the Picts under the influence of the Irish church could open the way to bring it under the political influence of Dál Riata.

Columba's voyage to Scotland was an expression of one of the most important traditions of the Celtic church, *peregrinatio*, a penitential journey in which the monks placed their fate into the hands of God. Irish monks became skilled seafarers, usually sailing in *curachs*, small but seaworthy sailing boats made of greased leather stretched over a wicker frame. Using these boats, Irish monks searched for ultimate solitude to contemplate the glories of God, founding spartan monasteries – often no more than a few dry-stone 'beehive' huts – on remote islands all along the coasts of Ireland and Scotland. Some went further, discovering the Faeroe Islands and Iceland some 200 years before the Vikings. The Vikings often encountered Irish monks (and not usually to the monks' advantage) during their voyages and place-names derived from *papar*, as the Vikings called them, are widespread in the Hebrides, Northern Isles and even Iceland. The largest group of *papar* place-names are islands. Four islands in the Outer Hebrides are called Pabbay (from *papar* and ø), meaning 'island of the papar', as is another off the Isle of Skye. There are also islands named for the *papar* in the Orkney and Shetland Islands and off Iceland.

Like Lindisfarne, Iona seems a remote place today, but the sea lanes were the main roads of the early Middle Ages and seen from this point of view it was an excellent choice for an active evangelist like Columba. Ireland lay only 70 miles away to the south, an easy day's sail in fair weather. Even more important for Columba's ambitions, Iona was within easy reach of the Great Glen, the main west–east overland route through the northern Highlands, which led directly to the main power centres of the northern Picts around the Moray Firth. In modern terms, Iona was about as inaccessible as a shopping mall at a motorway intersection. The narrow sound that separates Iona from the much larger neighbouring island of Mull provided sheltered anchorages and landing places, which the Vikings no doubt also appreciated. Though mostly covered with rock, heather moor and bog, Iona has large areas of fertile *machair*, pasture formed on raised beaches with light soils of lime-rich shell-sand, so the community could be self-supporting.

Columba's personality made him a force to be reckoned with and by the time of his death in 597 his abbey was the dominant church not only of Dal Riata and Pictland but also of much of northern Ireland, where even bishops were subordinated to his authority. Columba's death only enhanced Iona's influence by making it a place of pilgrimage. When King Oswald of Northumbria wanted to make his kingdom Christian, it was to Iona, rather than Rome, that he turned to ask for missionaries. The abbot sent Aidan, the founder of St Cuthbert's monastery on Lindisfarne. Iona became a centre for crafts, including glass, metalwork, sculpture and book production. The *Book of Kells*, one of the finest illuminated gospel books of the early Middle Ages, was made at Iona. Iona's greatest treasure was, however, the magnificent jewelled reliquary that held Columba's remains, the priceless source of the monastery's power.

Martyred by the Vikings

After the second raid on Iona, abbot Cellach bought land at Kells, well inland in Ireland, for use as a refuge for the monks in the event of further attacks. After the massacre in 806, Cellach left to oversee the construction of a new monastery on the land the community had bought at Kells. When work was completed in 814, most of the community moved to Kells, which became the seat of the abbot. Iona was not abandoned completely, however. Cellach resigned his abbacy and returned to Iona with a small group of monks who were willing to accept the risk of death at pagan hands: Irish monks saw their calling as a manly one, requiring courage and fortitude. The all-important relics of St Columba also stayed on Iona. In 824 an Irish monk called Blathmac became head of the community on Iona. Blathmac was not afraid of the Vikings. His biographer, a German monk called Walafrid Strabo (d. 849), says that he was actively seeking martyrdom at pagan hands because he 'wished to endure Christ's wounds'. Blathmac did not have to wait long to achieve his ambition: the Vikings returned to Iona in 825. When warning of Viking raiders reached the abbey, Blathmac allowed those monks who did not think they could endure martyrdom to leave: he remained with a hardcore of willing martyrs. The raiders arrived while Blathmac was celebrating morning mass. Bursting into the church, the Vikings immediately killed Blathmac's companions. The Vikings were after the precious reliquary that contained Columba's relics, but the monks had removed it from its pedestal in the church and hidden it under a stack of peat. No amount of torture could persuade Blathmac to reveal its hiding place and in the end the enraged Vikings hacked him to pieces and left empty handed.

Amazingly, this savage attack was not the end of monasticism on Iona. The monks who had fled returned, buried Blathmac and restored St Columba's reliquary to its place. Columba's relics remained at Iona until 849, when they were divided, half going to Kells, the other half being sent to the cathedral of Dunkeld, north of Perth in Scotland. Politics was more important in this decision than security, however (see below), as Iona had not been raided again after Blathmac's killing. Even then, Iona's glorious history ensured that some sort of monastic community continued throughout the Viking Age as at least three Scots kings were buried there in the later ninth century; Iona was just too prestigious to be abandoned completely. In this respect, Iona was more fortunate than most other Scottish monasteries, almost all of which were abandoned after repeated Viking attacks. A Pictish monastery at Portmahomack in Easter Ross on Scotland's east coast is one of the few monasteries of this period that has been systematically excavated. This community thrived in the seventh and eighth centuries as a centre for book production, metalworking, glassworking and sculpture. Over-lying all the occupation layers was a layer of soot and charcoal dated to around 800, showing that the monastery was abandoned after suffering a catastrophic fire, almost certainly, given the dating, the result of a Viking attack.

Raiders become settlers

Because of its fame, Viking raids on Iona were recorded in Irish annals but it is more than likely that Vikings were active in Scotland before 795. Almost certainly, the first places in Scotland to be raided by Vikings were in the Northern Isles (the Shetland and Orkney Islands) as they are the natural first landfall for ships sailing west across the North Sea from Norway. Shetland is 250 miles west of Norway, less than two days' sail in good conditions, and from there it is only 60 miles south to Orkney, from where Viking raiders could choose to sail south down Britain's east coast, or head west and south to the Hebrides and Ireland. The Vikings who raided Lindisfarne in 793 and Iona in 795 would have sailed via Shetland and Orkney. These routes were probably already well-known to the Norwegians. There is strong archaeological evidence for trade between the Northern Isles and Norway before the Viking Age – combs made of Scandinavian reindeer antler have been found in the high-status Pictish settlement at Birsay in Orkney, for example – so the first Viking raiders knew where they were going.

Within a very short time of their earliest recorded raids in Scotland, Vikings began to seize land in Scotland for settlement. This settlement went unrecorded in contemporary chronicles, no doubt because Viking raids on Scottish monasteries had dispersed or killed the monks who might have written them. In the absence of written sources, the most important source of evidence about its geographical extent are place-names of Scandinavian origin. Scandinavian place-names are most common in the Northern Isles, and Caithness in the far north-east of the Scottish mainland. Almost all place-names here are of Scandinavian origin. Scandinavian place-names are also common throughout the Hebrides and along Scotland's deeply indented west coast, showing that this area too saw substantial settlement. Scandinavian place-names in all of these areas are overwhelmingly of Norwegian origin, pointing to the origins of most of the Viking settlers. Norwegian place-name elements such as –staðir, as found in Grimista ('Grim's place'), and –bolstaðr, as in Isbister ('eastern farm'), are especially common in the Northern Isles. Other common elements found in the Northern Isles, the Hebrides and along the west coast include fjall, as in Askival ('ash mountain'); fjord, as in Laxford ('salmon fjord'); sker, as in skerry (i.e. a reef); dalr ('dale'); vik, as in Lerwick ('muddy bay'); and ø, an island, as in Sanday ('sandy island'). Dating these settlements is not easy. It is thought that the Northern Isles were settled very early, possibly as early as 800, while the Hebrides – the Sudreys or 'South Isles' to the Vikings – were settled around 825. There were certainly well-established Norse communities in these areas by the second half of the ninth century. Place-names of both Norwegian and Danish origin also show that there was Scandinavian settlement in the Isle of Man and in Galloway and Dumfries in south-west Scotland. The settlements in Dumfries are probably best considered as an extension of the Scandinavian settlements in north-west England, which took place in the early tenth century.

Viking DNA

As might be expected, given their proximity to Norway, the Viking impact was strongest in the Northern Isles. The islands must have looked to Norwegians like attractive places to settle. The environment is similar to western Norway's so settlers could easily transplant their traditional pastoral-farming way of life. The Shetland Islands are predominantly covered with peat moors and rough pasture, but the Orkney Islands, though windswept and treeless, have large areas of good arable land, which was in short supply in Norway. The islands also had the advantages of good communications, being located not too far from the support of family and also providing good bases for Viking raids further south. The isolated Pictish communities there stood no chance of organising a co-ordinated defence against Viking raiders and they would have been overwhelmed quickly and easily. At least some of the native Picts had something more than land to seize as a major hoard of eighth-century silver jewellery, sword fittings and drinking bowls found buried near a ruined Pictish monastery on St Ninian's Isle in Shetland shows. The date of this hoard makes it likely that it was buried to hide it from Viking raiders. That such a valuable hoard was not recovered suggests its owner came to a bad end.

The Northern Isles were unique in the history of Scandinavian settlement in the Viking Age. In all areas which Scandinavians settled in this period that already had an indigenous population, the fate of the settlers was, ultimately, to be assimilated into the local population in around three generations. This is what happened in England and Normandy. However, the Northern Isles developed into an enduring extension of the Scandinavian world, becoming completely Norse in culture and language. Until recently it was thought that this was because the Vikings had actually slaughtered or expelled most of the

Pictish population. The Viking settlement certainly seems to mark a
clear break in the islands' history. No Pictish place-names survive (a
few Norse place-names may have Pictish roots, but this is disputed),
no Pictish settlements show evidence of continuing occupation after
c. 800, though some, as at the Brough of Birsay, were later built over by
Norse settlements. Very few Pictish artefacts have ever been found in
Norse settlements, indicating that there was little interaction between
settlers and locals. It might appear that the Picts disappeared without
trace. Thanks to the new science of DNA profiling, the genes of the
modern population of the Northern Isles tell a subtler story. Analysis
of the male population's Y chromosomes, which are passed only
through the male line from father to son, showed that 44 per cent of
men in Shetland and 33 per cent of men in Orkney carry a distinctive
genetic marker called the M17 haplotype, which is also carried by a
majority of Norwegian and Swedish (but not Danish) men. Factoring
out post-medieval immigration, this indicates that more than half the
male population of the isles in the Viking Age was of Scandinavian
origin. Studies of mitochondrial DNA, passed only through the female
line, found that the same proportion of women in Shetland and
Orkney have Scandinavian ancestry. This indicates that the settlers
came as family groups, a sign that they felt secure and unthreatened by
native resistance. What happened to the Picts? The process of conquest
must have thinned their numbers in various ways, some were killed
in battle, others took their boats and fled, and many more would
have been rounded up for the slave trade and sold off the islands. The
outnumbered survivors, reduced to a servile condition, were soon
assimilated by the Norse.

The nature of the Scandinavian settlement in the Hebrides was
strikingly different in nature. Genetic profiling shows that around 25
per cent of the modern male population of the islands can trace their
origins back to Norway, but only 10 per cent of the female population
can. Even allowing for modern immigration, Scandinavian settlers
must always have been a minority among the native Gaelic-speaking
population. It is also clear that the majority of the Scandinavians were
single men who found wives locally. Settlement here was, therefore,
probably seen as a riskier proposition than going to the Northern Isles,

not a place that a man would feel comfortable bringing his wife and children. Icelandic saga traditions seem to bear this out as many of the earliest settlers of Iceland, like Aud the Deep-Minded and Helgi Magri, were Hebridean Norse who were finding it hard to maintain their positions. Place-names in the Hebrides point to the eventual fate of the settlers: Scandinavian place-names are common but often difficult to recognise for what they are because they survive in Gaelicised forms, such as Roineabhal ('rough-ground fell'), or as hybrids incorporating Norse and Gaelic elements, such as Skerryvore ('the great skerry') from the Old Norse *sker* and Gaelic *mhor* ('big'). The settlers were eventually assimilated by the native Gaels but it took centuries, not the two or three generations that it took for the Danish settlers in England and Normandy to become assimilated to their host populations. Partial assimilation of the Norse settlers began early. Because so many of the settlers had taken local wives, their children grew up bilingual, speaking both Old Norse and Gaelic. This hybrid Gaelic-Norse population became known to the Irish as the Gall-Gaedhil, the 'foreign Gaels', and the Hebrides became the Innse Gall, the 'islands of the foreigners'. The same process of partial assimilation took place in Galloway, which gets its name from the Gall-Gaedhil. True Gaels probably saw the Gall-Gaedhil as being more Norse than Gaelic as the Irish bard Urard mac Coise (d. 990) described their stumbling attempts to speak the Gaelic language as *gioc-goc*, meaning gibberish. This assimilation is also visible in material culture, especially jewellery styles, which blend Celtic forms with Norse ornament. The popular Celtic penannular brooch, a type of fastening for cloaks and dresses, was adapted to the Norse taste by becoming plainer in style but much larger.

Perhaps because so many of them had taken Christian wives, the Scandinavians who settled in the Hebrides were among the earliest to accept Christianity. However, several Viking pagan burials have been discovered in the area too, including a tenth-century boat burial at Port an Eilean Mhóir, in Ardnamurchan on the west coast of the mainland. According to Irish sources, some of the native Gaels even renounced Christianity and adopted the paganism of their new rulers. After the violence of the initial Norse conquest, pagans and Christians probably lived peacefully side by side as they did in other areas settled by Scandinavians. One Hebridean Viking, Helgi the Lean, managed to believe in both Christ and Thor at the same time, and this kind of syncretism may have been very common. This could explain why, after 825, Iona was not raided again for 160 years. When Vikings eventually returned, in 986, the attackers were outsiders, Danes making a rare foray into the western seas. The abbot and fifteen monks were killed in this attack: a hoard of tenth-century silver coins found on Iona may have been buried by one of the victims. The survival of so many papar place-names may be evidence that Iona was not the only monastic community to survive the Viking raids: some must have survived long enough at least for the papar place-names to 'stick' in common usage.

The process of assimilation and co-existence between Scandinavian and native Gael is also clearly seen in the Isle of Man. The evidence of pagan burials, containing weapons and sometimes human sacrifices and boats, indicates substantial pagan Scandinavian settlement in the mid-ninth century. This is borne out by genetic studies, which indicate that around 40 per cent of the modern population have Norse ancestry. The native Christian Gaelic-speaking population was not exterminated but the distribution of typical Scandinavian place-names shows that the settlers appropriated the better, lower-lying land for themselves and left the rougher hill areas to the Gaels. Possibly they were relegated to servile tasks, such as tending the conquerors' sheep and cattle on the upland pastures. The settlers used Christian cemeteries for pagan burials as a symbolic way of demonstrating their power over the natives. After they adopted Christianity in the mid-tenth century, the settlers erected a series of fine carved stone memorial crosses that incorporated Irish, English and Scandinavian decorative styles, and both pagan and Christian imagery. Inscriptions on these crosses are always in runes but several commemorate people with Gaelic names, a sign of intermarriage between the two populations. One bilingual inscription, in Old Norse and Gaelic (written in the ancient Irish ogham alphabet), is also known.

The Gall-Gaedhil retained their distinctive identity until the thirteenth century. The reason for this is partly political – the Hebrides were remote from any major centres of centralised political power that could impose authority on either the Norse settlers or indigenous

Gaelic leaders. Norse dominance of the sea lanes also meant that the settlers were in constant contact with other Norse colonies in the Northern Isles and Ireland and also with Norway, so they could constantly reinforce the Norse element in their cultural identity. Only when these links with Norway were broken after the Scots won control of the Hebrides and Man in 1266, were the Gall-Gaedhil thoroughly and finally Gaelicised.

Scots and Picts

The arrival of the Vikings in Scotland had the effect of destabilising the established power structures. Northumbria lost almost half its territory to the Danish kingdom of York and ceased to be a major influence in northern Britain. Strathclyde too entered a permanent decline after the sack of its capital in 871. The Viking intervention impacted most seriously on the Picts, indirectly leading them into complete extinction. The Scots of Dál Riata also lost considerable territories to the Vikings, yet they ultimately became the great winners of Viking Age Scotland, turning the situation to their advantage, conquering the Picts, the Welsh of Strathclyde, and the northern Northumbrian district of Lothian to create the kingdom of Scotland.

Dál Riata began as a colony of the minor Dál Riata dynasty, which ruled Antrim in Northern Ireland. Traditionally, King Fergus Mór mac Eirc (d. 501) was considered to be the conqueror of Argyll, but as its coast lies barely a dozen miles east of Antrim, the area may have been under Irish influence long before his time. Scottish Dál Riata was ruled as part of Irish Dál Riata until the reign of Domnall Brecc (r. c. 629–42), when the kingdom split after suffering a succession of military disasters. From then until the beginning of the Viking Age, Dál Riata led a precarious existence, first as a dependency of Northumbria and then, from c. 736, as a dependency of the kingdom of the Picts. The Scots regained their independence in 768 after the Picts had been weakened by a disastrous attempt to conquer Strathclyde, but the arrival of the Vikings in the 790s brought further setbacks. The Scots lost control not only of the Hebrides but of the mainland district of Kintyre and, probably, of Morvern and Ardnamurchan too. The Scots'

capital and inauguration place of the Dál Riata kings at Dunadd, only
2 miles inland from the west coast, was dangerously exposed despite
its strong fortifications and it seems to have been abandoned around
this time. It is not even clear who was king of Dál Riata in the decade
after the first attack on Iona, so great was the turmoil. The Scots had a
long tradition of naval warfare and a well-organised fleet levy system
for which each district had to raise a specified number of men and
ships. This system was really only suited to launching raids, however,
and it would have been little use in combating the Vikings. By the time
the fleet had been gathered from the kingdom's scattered territories,
Viking raiders would be long gone. Under pressure by the Vikings
from the west, the Scots turned east to the rich Pictish lands of Fortriu
in southern Pictland. Although some earlier kings of Dál Riata may
have won temporary control of Fortriu, it was King Kenneth mac Alpin
(d. 858) who completed the conquest of the region in 842/3, taking the
title king of the Picts. The rest of Pictland fell to Kenneth soon after.
In 848 or 849, Kenneth transferred half of St Columba's relics from
Iona to the Pictish royal monastery at Dunkeld in Perthshire. It was a
gesture of thanks by the king to the saint for the support of his church
and it also served notice to the Picts that their conquest by the Scots
was spiritual as well as political. St Columba came to Dunkeld not as a
refugee from the Vikings, as is often assumed, but as a conqueror.

The birth of Scotland

Quite how Kenneth achieved his coup is unclear, but he was certainly
a direct beneficiary of a Viking victory over the Picts in 839. This was
a very severe defeat for the Picts, involving heavy casualties. The death
of their king Eóganán and his brother Bran in the battle left them
leaderless. As there was no obvious successor, a three-sided succession
dispute broke out, leaving the weakened kingdom even more vulnerable.
However, it was not only the Picts who were left leaderless by the battle.
One of those killed fighting alongside the Pictish kings was Aed mac
Boanta, the king of Dál Riata. The sources do not explain why Aed
was fighting with the Picts but it would seem that on this occasion
the Scots had allied with them against a common enemy. Following

Aed's death, Kenneth became king of Dál Riata. Kenneth's origins are obscure and it is not even absolutely certain that he was a member of the Dál Riata royal family: he was certainly not close kin to Aed. Had the Vikings not killed Aed, Kenneth might never have had the opportunity to claim the throne. Once he had secured his position as king of Dál Riata, Kenneth seized the second opportunity the Vikings had created for him and invaded Pictland. The divided kingdom was in no state to resist and it fell quickly to the Scots. Kenneth and his immediate successors continued to use the titles 'king of the Picts' and 'king of Dál Riata', but his grandson Donald II (r. 889–900) abandoned this practice and adopted the single title 'king of Scotland' (*rex Scotia* in Latin, or *rí Alban* in Gaelic).

The Picts did not long survive their subjugation. Though the Scots adopted many of the trappings of Pictish kingship, including its inauguration place at Scone in Perthshire, there was no merging of Gaelic and Pictish culture. The Picts had probably long been exposed to Gaelic culture through the activities of the Columban church, but the Scottish conquest resulted in the complete and rapid annihilation of their identity: the last contemporary reference to the Picts dates to 904. The Picts' culture died out completely, their distinctive art styles became extinct and whatever Pictish literature that survived Viking attacks on their monasteries was not preserved: the Pictish view of their own history is unknown. The Pictish language also died out, replaced by Gaelic, and only a few words survive as place names. The sparse contemporary records make it clear that there was great violence involved during the Scottish conquest and later Scottish folk traditions held that the Picts had been exterminated. The Scots remembered the Picts as a race of blue pygmies who lived underground rather than as real people. It is unlikely that the Picts were literally wiped out, but it is likely that during the conquest and its aftermath their aristocracy were killed or exiled leaving the rest of the population without political or cultural leadership and so vulnerable to rapid assimilation by the Scots. The destruction of the Pictish aristocracy may be the subject of Sueno's Stone, a 23-foot (7 m) high sculpted monolith that stands on the outskirts of Forres in Moray. Carved in the later ninth century by a Pictish sculptor, the stone shows scenes of battle and mass executions.

The stone is the latest known work of Pictish sculpture, so it may have been commissioned by Kenneth or one of his immediate successors to celebrate the Scottish victory and send a bleak message to the Picts who survived. This is speculation, of course, as the stone lacks any ins-criptions to make its true purpose clear.

Saint Columba's residence at Dunkeld turned out to be a brief one. Fortriu's wealth made it attractive to the Vikings and it was repeatedly raided. King Constantine I killed Olaf, king of the Dublin Vikings, in 874–5, but was himself killed fighting Vikings in Fife in 877. In 878, Dunkeld suffered Iona's fate and was sacked by Viking raiders. Columba's relics survived, presumably hidden by the monks, but afterwards they took the decision to reunite them with rest of the saint's remains at Kells. This time he really was a refugee from the Vikings: as an Irish annalist put it, his relics 'were taken in flight to escape the foreigners'. It was a wise decision, as Dunkeld was sacked again in 903 and 904. Without Columba's relics, Dunkeld's importance quickly dec-lined and it was superseded in 906 as Scotland's prime religious centre by St Andrews in Fife, which possessed its own potent relics.

Scottish expansion

Kenneth's successors were quick to exploit other opportunities for territorial expansion created by the Vikings. In 870 the Dublin Vikings under their King Olaf laid siege to Strathclyde's strongly fortified capital on Dumbarton Rock, which towers over the mouth of the River Clyde. Recognising that their mobility was their main strength, Vikings were normally reluctant to get bogged down with sieges, but in this case they persevered for four months until the Welsh were forced to surrender when their well ran dry. Olaf's men took a vast number of captives and a great amount of treasure back to Dublin with them. One of the captives was Strathclyde's King Artgal. Artgal might have expected to be ransomed – ransoming high-status prisoners was a profitable sideline for Viking raiders – but Constantine I (Kenneth's son and successor) saw an opportunity to weaken Strathclyde still further and persuaded Olaf to kill him instead. Presumably, Constantine paid Olaf the equivalent of the king's ransom so that he did not lose out by killing such a valuable captive. With Artgal out of the way, Constantine installed the king's brother Run as client king of Strathclyde. Constantine married Run to his sister, so establishing a Scottish claim to the throne of Strathclyde. The kingship of Strathclyde remained in the gift of the kings of the Scots as they slowly tightened their control over the kingdom. It is thought that in the tenth century, Strathclyde became a sub-kingdom that was ruled by the *tanist* (the heir-apparent to the Scottish throne) until he succeeded to the kingship of Scotland. The last known king of Strathclyde was Owen the Bald, who died *c.* 1015, and soon after that Strathclyde was annexed to Scotland.

Another target for Scottish expansionism was Bernicia, the northern half of the Anglo-Saxon kingdom of Northumbria that had remained independent after the Danes seized York in 866. King Constantine II (r. 900–43) sought to bring Bernicia into the Scottish sphere of influence by lending support against Ragnald, the aggressive Norse-Irish king of Dublin who won control of York in 919. However, Bernicia was not just threatened by the Vikings and the Scots. As early as the 870s, Alfred the Great, the king of Wessex, had laid claim to the leadership of all the English in the struggle against the Danes. It is not known what the Northumbrians thought about this but there is no reason to assume that they welcomed it. The Wessex-based *Anglo-Saxon Chronicle* describes the rulers of Bernicia as 'ealdormen' (earls), to imply subordination to Alfred and his successors, but they still considered themselves to be kings. As such, they may have preferred to be sub-kings under the Danes or the Scots than ealdormen under the Wessex dynasty. Bernicia's future was decided in 927 when Alfred's grandson Æthelstan captured York and expelled its Irish-Norse King Guthfrith, who took refuge with Constantine II.

Following his victory, Æthelstan summoned Constantine, together with the kings of the Welsh, and Ealdred, the king of Bernicia to a meeting at Eamont Bridge, near Penrith in Cumbria. The purpose of the meeting was twofold. Firstly, Æthelstan announced Ealdred's deposition and the annexation of Bernicia. This is generally taken to mark the creation of the kingdom of England because, for the first time, it brought all the English under a single ruler. Secondly, the meeting was probably an occasion for the Scots and Welsh kings to acknowledge Æthelstan as high king or overlord of all Britain. Eamont Bridge is the location of three Neolithic henge monuments and numerous megalithic standing stones, marking it out as a place of ancient spiritual power. In later historical times one of these henges was associated with King Arthur, the legendary ruler of Britain. If the henge was already associated with Arthur in Æthelstan's time, it would have been a powerfully symbolic location for the kings of Britain to recognise him as their overlord. Æthelstan had demanded, on pain of war, that Constantine bring Guthfrith with him and hand him over at the meeting. Constantine cannot have welcomed the unification of England: it would not have required great powers of prediction to see that it would make an uncomfortably powerful neighbour for Scotland. Constantine's best opportunity to avert this threat was to help the Vikings regain control of York so, on the way to Eamont Bridge, he allowed Guthfrith to escape back to Dublin. This soured relations between Æthelstan and Constantine and may have played a part in Æthelstan's decision to invade Scotland in 934. Though Æthelstan won no great victories, Constantine went with him when he returned to England at the end of the summer and was still in England the following year, probably not of his own free will.

Guthfrith died in 934, remarkably for a Viking leader, of natural causes. His claim to the throne of York was taken up by his son Olaf Guthfrithsson, who succeeded him as king of Dublin. Despite Olaf's paganism, Constantine gave him one of his daughters as a wife. In 937 Olaf, Constantine and King Owen of Strathclyde became allies and invaded England with the intention of restoring the Viking kingdom of York. It was this grand alliance that Æthelstan crushed at the Battle of Brunanburh in 937. Subsequent attempts by Constantine and his successor Malcolm I (r. 943–54) to prop up Viking rule in York also ended in failure, and in 954 the kingdom came firmly under the control of the Wessex dynasty.

The Wessex dynasty had a difficult task in establishing its authority in the old kingdom of Northumbria. Even York was a long way from the main centres of English royal power, which at this time all lay south of the Thames, and this left Bernicia vulnerable to Scottish takeover. Sometime around 960, the Scottish king Indulf captured the Bernician border fortress of Edwin's Burgh, better known now as Edinburgh. Recognising the difficulty of defending Bernicia, the English king Edgar (r. 957–85) divided the province in 973, ceding Lothian, the northern half lying between the River Tweed and the Firth of Forth, to Scotland's King Kenneth II (r. 971–95) in return for his submission to English overlordship. However, Kenneth did not adhere to his submission and the English recovered control over Lothian in 1006. However, by this time England was suffering a new and devastating Viking onslaught. In 1016, the year that England was conquered by the Danes, Lothian passed permanently to the Scots after Malcolm II (r. 1005–34) won a major victory over the English at Carham in Northumberland. Despite years of warfare in the centuries to come, the Anglo-Scottish border established after Carham has remained little changed to this day.

The conquest of Lothian and the annexation of Strathclyde, which took place around the same time, created a kingdom that approximated to modern Scotland. There were however, regions of this kingdom where royal authority remained purely nominal. Galloway, in the south-west, remained effectively independent under its Norse-Gaelic lords, and Moray, in the far north, was ruled by its powerful *mormaers* ('stewards'), who exercised virtually regal authority. The most famous of the *mormaers*, Macbeth (r. 1032–57) even became king of Scotland in 1040. The Hebrides, Caithness and the Northern Isles remained under Norse control and would do for centuries to come. This ensured that the Viking Age lasted longer in Scotland than it did anywhere else in Europe, including even Scandinavia.

The Earldom of Orkney

The political situation in the Norse settlements in the Hebrides and the Northern Isles is very obscure until the later ninth century. Most probably, the isles were divided between several chiefs or petty kings, each ruling independently over their own immediate followers, free of any overlord. A few, such as Ketil Flatnose and Thorstein the Red who ruled in the Hebrides, are known from saga traditions, but nothing is known about the extent of their territories. Though this pattern of political fragmentation still prevailed in the Hebrides, by around 900 the Orkney and Shetland islands had been united in the powerful semi-autonomous Earldom of Orkney. The earldom was essentially a pirate state because its rulers supplemented their income from their estates with annual summer Viking raids around the coasts of Britain and Ireland. The history of the earls of Orkney is vividly told in *Orkneyinga Saga* ('The Saga of the Orkney Islanders'), which was written by an unknown Icelandic author around 1200. The saga is based on a multiplicity of oral traditions, skaldic poems and written sources, and it is clear that the author was at pains to use only reputable (but not always reliable) sources. Like other historical sagas, *Orkneyinga Saga* includes dialogue and speeches. These are not true records of conversations and should be read in the same way as speeches recorded in the works of Classical historians like Thucydides and Tacitus, who used them as a tool for analysing the character and motives of their subjects.

According to the saga, the Earldom of Orkney was created by the Norwegian king Harald Fairhair (r. *c.* 880-*c.* 930), who conquered the Northern Isles towards the end of the ninth century in order to stop them being used as bases by Vikings, who were raiding their former homeland. Harald ravaged his way south through the Hebrides to the Isle of Man and on his return to Orkney granted the Northern Isles to his ally jarl ('earl') Rognvald of Møre (d. *c.* 895) as compensation for the death of his son Ivar during the campaign. Rögnvald wanted to concentrate on his Norwegian earldom and gave Orkney to his brother Sigurd the Mighty (d. *c.* 892), who should be regarded as the true founder of the earldom. Harald is generally reckoned to have been the first king to rule all of Norway and it is quite credible that he tried to impose his authority over the Norse settlers in the Northern Isles as well. However, the saga account is unlikely to be true because older Irish annals say that it was Rognvald himself who won control over the islands at about the same time that the Danes conquered York (866), much too early for Harald to have had a hand in events.

Sigurd allied himself with the Hebridean Viking ruler Thorstein the Red and together they conquered Sutherland, Caithness and parts of Argyll and Moray. According to the *Orkneyinga Saga*, Sigurd met his death in a most unusual way. Sigurd arranged a peace conference at an unspecified location with a Scottish jarl called Máel Brigte, who was probably the *mormaer* of Moray. Both parties agreed to attend the meeting with no more than forty men, but on the day of the meeting Sigurd decided that he didn't trust the Scots and so he had eighty men mounted on forty horses. Máel Brigte, who had kept his word, spotted the deceit too late. Though he and his men fought bravely, they were overwhelmed and slaughtered. Gaels still practiced the ancient Celtic custom of head-hunting and never considered taking prisoners for ransom. Sigurd adopted this custom and strapped his enemies' heads to the saddles of his horses to show off his triumph. Máel Brigte was nicknamed 'the bucktoothed'. When Sigurd mounted his horse to begin the journey home, he cut his calf on one of the teeth sticking out of Máel Brigte's mouth. This minor wound became infected and Sigurd died of septicaemia: Máel Brigte obviously did not practice good dental hygiene. Sigurd was buried in a barrow near the mouth of the River Oykel, probably at Cyderhall Farm, not far from Dornoch. In the thirteenth century this farm was known as *Syvardhoch*, which is derived from Old Norse *Sigurðar-haugr* ('Sigurd's barrow'), though no barrow is visible there today.

The blood eagle

A period of instability followed Sigurd's death. Sigurd's son Guttorm succeeded him as jarl but survived him for only a year and died childless. Rognvald sent his son Hallad to replace Guttorm, but he proved a weak ruler. Vikings happily preyed on other Vikings and the scattered Norse settlements in the Northern Isles were just as vulnerable to raiders as the Pictish settlements had been. Hallad soon tired of trying to defend the islands and he gave up the earldom and returned to Norway, a laughing stock. Rognvald's youngest son, Einar, volunteered to become the next earl. Ugly, blind in one eye and born to a slave mother, Rognvald had low expectations of Einar, reputedly telling him 'you're not likely to make much of a ruler'. Soon after Einar became earl, Rognvald was killed in a dispute with Halfdan Highleg, one of the many sons of King Harald Fairhair. After the killing, Halfdan fled Norway to escape his father's anger. Arriving in Orkney, Halfdan began to terrorise the islanders and set himself up as king. Einar fled to Scotland but within a year he came back and defeated and captured Halfdan in a sea battle. According to the *Orkneyinga Saga*, Einar made a blood eagle sacrifice of his father's murderer as a victory offering to Odin. On hearing of his son's gruesome death, Harald led an expedition to Orkney and forced Einar to pay him heavy compensation equivalent to sixty marks of gold (approximately 30 pounds (13.6 kg)). Einar turned this situation to his advantage. The Norse settlers held their lands by *óðal* right (freehold). Einar offered to pay the whole amount of compensation from his own funds without levying any taxes if the settlers agreed to surrender their *óðal* rights to him: most agreed and became his tenants. Einar was credited in Orkney tradition with introducing the practice of burning peat ('turf') for fuel in the treeless Northern Isles. For this he was given the nickname *Torf*-Einar.

Einar died peacefully in bed some time around 920 and was succeeded by three of his sons, Arnkel, Erlend and Thorfinn Skullsplitter who ruled jointly. The earls welcomed the exiled Norwegian king Erik Bloodaxe and allowed him to use Orkney as a base for raiding Scotland and for his ultimately unsuccessful attempts to win control of York. Arnkel and Erlend were killed alongside Erik Bloodaxe, fighting at Stainmore in England in 954, leaving Thorfinn to rule alone until his death in *c*. 963. Despite his lurid nickname his rule appears to have been uneventful, a sign, probably, that he was an able ruler. If Thorfinn had a shortcoming, it was that he left too many sons who did not get on with one another. The *mormaers* of Moray took advantage of their political feuding to try to gain control of Caithness, but without success. Stability returned when Thorfinn's grandson Sigurd the Stout became jarl in *c*. 985. Sigurd resisted Scots pressure on the borders of Caithness and Sutherland, defeating Finnlaech, the *mormaer* of Moray, at the Battle of Skitten Mire in Caithness. According to saga traditions Sigurd fought under a magical raven banner woven for him by his mother Eithne, an Irish princess who was reputed to be a sorceress. The banner brought victory from Odin but also guaranteed death to whoever carried it. During the battle, Sigurd was said to have lost three standard bearers before he won the day. In 995 Sigurd was baptised, allowing him to make an advantageous second marriage to an un-named daughter of King Malcolm II of Scotland. Their son

Thorfinn was sent to be brought up a Christian at Malcolm's court in Scotland. Sigurd was probably an insincere convert as he met his end fighting under his enchanted raven banner at the Battle of Clontarf in 1014.

The earldom at its peak

Sigurd was succeed by his sons Brusi and Thorfinn, who shared the earldom uneasily between them. Brusi was a peaceable man but Thorfinn soon showed that he had the makings of a great warrior, leading his first Viking raid when he was fifteen – not an exceptionally young age for a Viking leader of high birth. Because he enjoyed the support of the king of Scotland, Thorfinn was in a stronger position than Brusi. When a dispute over the division of the earldom broke out, Brusi appealed to King Olaf II (St Olaf) of Norway to arbitrate between him and Thorfinn. This was a welcome opportunity for Olaf to re-assert Norwegian sovereignty over the earldom, which had been to all intents and purposes independent since the death of Harald Fairhair a century before. Olaf must have seen that if Thorfinn's relationship to King Malcolm became any closer it might lead to Scotland claiming sovereignty, and he forestalled it by insisting that both he and Brusi swear allegiance to him before he gave judgement. This forced Thorfinn to declare where his allegiance really lay. The agreement stuck until Brusi's death *c.* 1035, after which Thorfinn took control of the whole earldom, ignoring the claims of Brusi's son Rognvald, who was living in Norway.

Thorfinn's close relationship with Scotland did not survive Malcolm's death in 1034. According to the saga tradition, the new Scottish king Karl Hundason occupied Caithness in 1035 and then invaded Orkney with a fleet of eleven longships. No such king as Karl Hundason ever ruled Scotland. The king's name means 'churl son of a dog', so it must have originated as an insulting nickname, but for whom? Malcolm's successor as king of Scotland was his grandson Duncan, Thorfinn's cousin, and he certainly never invaded Orkney. Given that there was already a long history of conflict between the earldom and Moray, it is most likely that Karl was the *mormaer* of Moray, who at this time would have been Macbeth. Thorfinn defeated Karl's invasion fleet in a hard-fought sea battle off Deerness on Orkney's east coast and quickly retaliated by invading Moray. At Tarbat Ness, on the north side of the Moray Firth, Thorfinn won a resounding victory over Karl's army, and afterwards annexed Ross to the earldom, bringing it to its territorial peak.

In 1037–8, Norway's King Magnus the Good gave Rognvald Brusason ships and sent him home to claim his father's share of the earldom. Thorfinn and his nephew shared the earldom amicably enough for eight years, often going raiding together. Eventually, however, they quarrelled about their shares of the earldom. Rognvald maintained that only the king had the right to decide how the earldom should be divided. Thorfinn would not hear of this, as he still resented having submitted to Magnus's father, King Olaf. Rognvald was popular with the common people but, recognising that Thorfinn had more warriors, he went to Norway to seek King Magnus's support. Magnus supplied Rognvald with ships and men but when he returned to Orkney, Thorfinn defeated him in a sea battle in the Pentland Firth. Rognvald escaped back to Norway and returned secretly to Orkney with a single ship just as winter was setting in. Vikings rarely made long sea voyages after the autumn equinox for fear of storms, so Rognvald was able to take Thorfinn by surprise while he was drinking with his men in his hall one night. Rognvald's men covered all the entrances to the hall and set the thatched roof on fire. Trapped inside, Thorfinn's men could do nothing to resist. Rognvald allowed the women and slaves to leave but left Thorfinn and his men to burn. Thorfinn managed to break through the hall's side wall and escape under cover of the smoke. Finding a small boat he crossed the Pentland Firth by night and stayed secretly with trusted friends in Caithness, allowing Rognvald to believe that he had perished in the flames. Surprise was now on Thorfinn's side and just before Christmas he ambushed Rognvald on the small island of Papa Stronsay and killed him. Thirty of King Magnus's men who had come to Orkney with Rognvald were later captured. Thorfinn executed all but one of them, who was sent to take the news to King Magnus. This amounted to a declaration of independence. Already at war with the Danes, Magnus had to accept Thorfinn's coup with as much grace as he could muster. Magnus died soon after and his successor Harald Hardrada was preoccupied with fighting the Danes and let Thorfinn be.

Now unchallenged, Thorfinn was a figure of European stature and he began to behave like any other western European Christian ruler rather than as a Viking chief. Not long after King Magnus's death in 1047, Thorfinn set out on a pilgrimage to Rome, travelling via Norway, Denmark and Germany. On the way he was feasted by King Svein Estrithson in Denmark, and in Germany by the Holy Roman Emperor Henry III, the most powerful ruler in Europe. On his return to Orkney, Thorfinn laid up his longships and devoted his time to providing his earldom with a unifying administrative and ecclesiastical structure. At his hall at Birsay, on the north coast of Mainland, he built a church as a seat for Henry of Lund, the first bishop of Orkney. Earl Rognvald was also a Christian and shortly after he returned to Orkney in 1037–8, he built a church dedicated to Saint Olaf at Kirkwall. This, the church from which the town gets its name (*Kirkjuvágr* = 'church creek'), survives only as a single romanesque arch, now removed from its original site and re-used in a later building down a minor backstreet.

Thorfinn died of old age in 1065. Because of his achievements, Thorfinn became known as 'the Mighty', but he was never a popular ruler and many of his subjects found his rule oppressive, probably because he was more efficient at gathering taxes and tribute than his less administratively capable predecessors. It often happened in medieval Europe that a reaction followed the death of a strong ruler as his subjects tried to claw back some of their lost autonomy. Thorfinn needed a strong successor to hold on to the gains he made but he didn't have one. Thorfinn's sons Paul and Erlend succeeded jointly to the earldom. Neither son was a forceful character and Erlend was positively indolent. The brothers remained on friendly terms and were well liked by their subjects, but they were not warriors and, ultimately, they would fail to preserve the earldom's independence.

The Kingdom of Man

The decline of the Earldom of Orkney created the space for the rise of a second Norse state in the region, the Kingdom of Man and the

Isles, which was ruled from the Isle of Man. Very little is known about the political situation in the Isle of Man for a century or more after its settlement by the Norse, but it is likely that for much of the time it was within the sphere of influence of the Dublin Vikings or of Irish kings. The island has a strategic position in the middle of the Irish Sea, close enough to England, Wales, Ireland and Scotland for them all to be visible in clear weather. The many Viking Age silver hoards that have been found on the island suggest that it prospered as a result, whether by trade or because it was a very convenient base for launching Viking raids. The origins of the Kingdom of Man are very obscure. The earliest known king is generally thought to have been Maccus Haraldsson, a Viking who was active around the Irish Sea between 971 and 984. Maccus was described as the 'king of many islands', but whether the Isle of Man was one of them is uncertain. Maccus had a brother, Godfred Haraldsson, who was also active in the same area and was described in Irish sources as *rí Innse Gall*, 'king of the Islands of the Foreigners', but again the Isle of Man is not specifically mentioned as part of his domain. Godfred was particularly active in Wales, his greatest success being a raid on Anglesey in 987, in which he took 2,000 captives for the slave markets of Dublin. Godfred seems to have outlived his brother by a few years and was killed fighting in Argyll *c.* 989.

The earliest king of Man who can be identified with certainty was Godred Sihtricsson, who died in 1070 and was succeeded by his son Fingal. Fingal's death is not recorded and he may still have been king in 1079 when Godred Crovan, a Norse-Gaelic Viking from Islay, conquered Man and united it as a single kingdom with the Hebrides. Godred first arrived in Man late in 1066 as a refugee, a survivor of the Norwegian king Harald Hardrada's crushing defeat by the English at the Battle of Stamford Bridge near York. Godred Sihtricsson welcomed him, but after his death Godred Crovan returned to the Hebrides and in 1079 raised a fleet and army and invaded Man. Twice the Manxmen defeated Godred and forced him to withdraw. Godred raised a third army and landed at the harbour of Ramsey under cover of night. He prepared an ambush for the Manx, hiding 300 men in a wood on the side of Sky Hill, about a mile from his landing place. The Manx attacked Godred at dawn the next day. When the battle was at its peak, the men concealed in the wood emerged and attacked the Manx from the rear, throwing them into disorder. If Fingal was still king, he was likely killed in the battle. After his victory, Godred allowed his men to plunder the island, then he divided it into northern and southern halves. The south he gave to the surviving Manxmen and the north to the men who had come with him from the Hebrides. No one, Manx or Hebridean, held land as freeholders: Godred claimed all the land by right of conquest so everyone was a tenant of the king. Godred ruled Man and the Hebrides as a single kingdom and later in his reign he gathered tribute from Galloway, and was also accepted as king of Dublin between 1091 and 1094. Godred divided Man and the Isles into five administrative districts, which together sent thirty-two representatives to the annual thing, held at Tynwald on the Isle of Man. The modern Manx parliament still meets here annually, in the open air, to promulgate the laws passed during the preceding year, making it probably the oldest continuously functioning legislature in the world.

Godred died on Islay in 1095, leaving three sons, Lagmann, who inherited the throne, Harald and Olaf, who was still a child. Harald soon rebelled against Lagmann but was captured and blinded and castrated. Regretting his actions, Lagmann abdicated and set out on a penitential pilgrimage to Jerusalem, and died on the way, leaving the kingdom without a ruler. The chieftains of the kingdom appealed to Muirchertach Ua Briain, the powerful king of Munster, to provide a regent to govern until Olaf Godredsson came of age. The regent Muirchertach sent turned out to be a tyrant and after three years he was expelled. Shortly afterwards a dispute between the native Manx and the Hebridean settlers on the Isle of Man led to a battle at Santwat (traditionally identified as St Patrick's Island) in which many of the leading men of the island were killed.

In 1097 King Magnus Barefoot (r. 1093–1103) of Norway sent an agent called Ingemund to the Hebrides to assert his claim to sovereignty. When Ingemund was murdered Magnus decided to take the islands by force. In 1098 Magnus raised a fleet of sixty or 160 ships (the sources differ) and sailed to Orkney, where he deposed earls Paul and Erlend and sent them into exile in Norway where they later died. In their place, he appointed his eight-year-old son Sigurd as earl, ending the earldom's independence. Magnus moved on, laying waste to the Hebrides. Along the way he paused to make a thoroughly respectful visit to Iona before getting back to the real business of burning, killing and plundering. Christianity did not greatly change the ethics of Viking warfare. When Magnus finally landed on the Isle of Man he met no resistance. While he was there, Magnus visited Santwat and found it still littered with the remains of the men who had fallen in the recent battle. Whether it happened now, or perhaps during the earlier conflicts, young Olaf Godredsson went into exile, finding a refuge at the English court.

In the course of his expedition, Magnus gained Scottish recognition of Norwegian sovereignty over 'all the islands off the west coast which were separated by water navigable by any ship with the rudder set'. According to the saga tradition, Magnus tricked the Scots' king Edgar into ceding the Kintyre peninsula by having his ship dragged overland at the narrow isthmus at Tarbert while he sat at the helm. Magnus used the Isle of Man as a base to gather tribute in Galloway and Anglesey, off the north Welsh coast. The Normans were also trying to win control of Anglesey and Magnus defeated two earls, Hugh the Fat of Chester and Hugh of Shrewsbury, in a battle by the Menai Straits. During the battle, Magnus personally killed Hugh of Shrewsbury, hitting him in the face with an arrow.

In 1099, Magnus returned home to deal with a dispute with Sweden but returned to the Isle of Man in 1101 or 1102, and spent a year or two raiding in Ireland in alliance with King Muirchertach. During his time in Ireland, Magnus began wearing the Gaelic kilt instead of the Norse trousers, earning him his nickname 'barefoot' or 'barelegs'. Muirchertach needed Magnus's support against his rival for the high kingship, Domnall king of Ailech, and in return ceded Dublin to him. Magnus was on the brink of achieving the complete domination of the Irish Sea, but his career came to an abrupt end in August 1103 when he was ambushed and killed by the Irish while foraging for supplies in the north of Ireland: he was aged just thirty. Magnus was the last Scandinavian king to be killed on a Viking raid. Many of Magnus's closest advisers thought he was reckless in battle, but he always had an answer, 'a king is for glory, not for long life': it was a fitting epitaph for a Viking Age kingship. The Norse colonies in the Northern Isles and the

Hebrides had finally lost their independence, not to the nearby Scots but to the king of Norway. However, the islands were at the far reach of Norwegian royal power and time would quickly tell if Magnus's successors could hold on to his conquests.

CHAPTER 5

DUBLIN AND CASHEL
THE VIKINGS IN IRELAND
795– 1014

Few places suffered more at the hands of the Vikings than Ireland. For the best part of 200 years the Vikings systematically milked Ireland of its people to supply the slave trade, yet, for all their military success they failed to conquer and settle in any territory besides a few fortified coastal enclaves. This is the conundrum of Viking Age Ireland; it was a land that looked weak but was in reality strong and resilient.

Superficially, Ireland must have looked to the Vikings like an easy target. There is no doubt that in England and Francia internal divisions worked to the Vikings' advantage, and if there, why not even more so in Ireland, which was the most divided country in western Europe? Early medieval Ireland was a complex mosaic of around 150 local kingdoms and a dozen over-kingdoms. The local kingdoms or *túatha* were usually very small – often less than 100 square miles with populations of only a few thousand – and were defined as a 'people' or 'community', rather than as territorial units. The people of a *túath* were, in theory at least, an extended kinship group, or clan, and the king was the head of the senior lineage. The king (*rí túathe*) was responsible to his people for the fertility of their land and cattle, hence their prosperity: this was a legacy of pagan times when a king who failed to deliver would be sacrificed to the gods. Kings also had duties of lawmaking, judgement and leadership in war. In return all the free families of the *túath* owed the king taxes (paid in kind) and military service. Local kings might themselves owe tribute (usually in cattle), hospitality and military service to an over-king (*ruirí*), who in turn might owe it to a high king (*rí ruirech*). Over-kings, therefore, did not exercise direct rule outside their own *túath*, their power rested upon their ability to call on the resources and services of their client kings. The most powerful over-king of the day might be described as High King of Ireland (*rí Érenn*), but this was not really a formal institution with defined rules of succession. The relationships between kingdoms were not fixed. A local king with military ability and ambition could build a strong war band and use it to make himself an over-king by forcing other local kings to become his tributaries. Nevertheless, by the eighth century some stable dynasties of over-kings had emerged, the most powerful of which were the Northern and Southern Uí Néill dynasties of north-east Ulster and Meath respectively. To an outsider, early medieval Ireland would have appeared to be a chaotic and deeply divided country and, indeed, small-scale warfare between its kingdoms was endemic. Yet this highly decentralised political structure was to prove incredibly resilient, well able to absorb the shock of Viking invasions and constantly renew resistance.

In contrast to England and Francia where the Danes dominated, these raids were mainly the work of Norwegians, sailing to Ireland via the Northern Isles and the Hebrides. Viking activity in Ireland developed at first in much the same way as it did in England and Francia, beginning with small-scale hit-and-run raids on exposed coastal monasteries gradually escalating until the Vikings founded permanent bases and became a year-round presence plundering and captive-taking across the whole country. The first recorded Viking raids in Ireland took place in 795 when the same Viking band that sacked Iona sacked a monastery on *Rechru*, which may either be Lambay Island north of Dublin, or Rathlin Island off the northern Irish coast. In the 830s, larger fleets, numbering around sixty ships, began to arrive. Once its island monasteries had been plundered, Ireland's wild and mountainous west coast, so similar to the west coast of Scotland, was generally shunned by the Vikings because of its poverty. The Vikings concentrated their efforts on the more fertile and densely populated east coast and the great midland plain. In 836, a fleet sailed for the first time far inland along Ireland's longest river, the Shannon, and sacked the wealthy monasteries of Clonmacnoise and Clonfert. The following year, a Viking fleet sailed from Donegal Bay into Lough Erne to plunder monasteries around its shores. Another sacked the monastery of Áth Cliath – on the site of modern Dublin – while a third army ravaged on the Boyne, and a fourth was on the Shannon again. Nowhere was safe: 'the sea cast floods of foreigners into Ireland, so there was not a point thereof that was without a fleet', wrote one chronicler.

Although the Irish often fought fiercely, the Vikings' advantage of mobility meant that they often escaped unchallenged: the saints slept and did not protect their monasteries. Monks trembled in their cells and prayed for bad weather to keep the Vikings off the seas. As kings were rarely inclined to help their rivals, the Vikings often benefited from the divisions between the Irish kingdoms. Indeed, most kings took a thoroughly pragmatic view of the Vikings, treating them as just another element in their country's complex political geography, often welcoming them as allies who could help weaken a rival kingdom. Some bands of Irishmen took advantage of the disorder created by the Vikings to go plundering themselves 'in the manner of the heathens'. One such band was destroyed by Máel Sechnaill mac Máele Ruanaid (r. 845–62), the powerful Southern Uí Néill high king of Meath, in 847.

The first *longphuirt*

In 839 there was a step-change in Viking activity. A Viking fleet sailed up the River Bann into Lough Neagh. Instead of plundering and leaving, the Vikings built a fortified ship camp on the lakeshore, which they used as a base to plunder the heart of Ulster for three successive summers. This was the first of many such bases – known as *longphuirt* by the Irish – that Viking armies were to build in Ireland over the next few years as they intensified their raids. The foundation of the longphuirt subtly changed the dynamics of Viking activity in Ireland. The Vikings were now a permanent presence in Ireland and could raid all year round, but at the same time, they lost some of their mobility, making them more vulnerable to Irish counterattack.

The leader of the fleet on Lough Neagh was a warlord who the Irish called Turgeis, that is probably Thórgestr or Thórgils in Old Norse. Turgeis' origins are not known, but he may have come from the Hebrides as he had as his allies the Gall-Gaedhil, those 'foreign Gaels' who were the product of marriages between Norse settlers and the local Gaelic-speaking population. Turgeis' greatest coup was plundering St Patrick's monastery at Armagh three times in 840: after his final attack he burned it down for good measure. Armagh was an especially rich prize; apart from its precious reliquaries and sacred vessels, many Irish kings had their royal treasuries there, hoping that they would enjoy the protection of its powerful patron saint. It would not only have been monks who suffered in these attacks. Armagh was surrounded by a small town of craftsmen, merchants, estate managers and others who serviced the needs of this most prestigious of all Irish ecclesiastical centres. Turgeis' activities are uncertain for the next few years, but he is thought by some historians to have been the leader of the Vikings who in 841 founded what would become the most successful of all the longphuirt at Dublin. In 844, Turgeis led his fleet up the River Shannon as far as Lough Ree, where he built another longphort from which he plundered widely in the midlands. The following year, in the first serious reverse suffered by the Vikings in Ireland, he was captured by Máel Sechnaill, who drowned him in Lough Owel in County Westmeath.

Turgeis' reputation grew with the telling and after his death he became a symbol of everything that was wicked about the Vikings. In the colourful but unreliable twelfth-century history of Ireland's Viking wars, *Cogadh Gaedhel re Gallaibh* ('The War of the Irish with the Foreigners'), Turgeis has become the king of all the Vikings in Ireland, bent on conquering the whole island. This Turgeis is a militant pagan who expels the abbot from Armagh and sets himself up as a pagan high priest. His wife Ota (probably Auðr) is just as bad, performing acts of witchcraft on the altar of the abbey at Clonmacnoise. This story might not be wholly improbable as Ota may have been a *völva*, a Viking seeress with powers to predict the future. According to the Welsh churchman

Gerald of Wales, who travelled in Ireland during the 1180s, Turgeis actually conquered Ireland but was lured to his death by his weakness for women. Turgeis took a fancy to Máel Sechnaill's daughter. The king, 'hiding his hatred in his heart', agreed to hand her over to Turgeis on an island in Lough Owel along with fifteen other beautiful girls. Turgeis was delighted and went to the rendezvous with fifteen of his leading warriors, all of them expecting amorous encounters. But Máel Sechnaill had laid a trap for them. His daughter was waiting for Turgeis on the island not with fifteen girls but with fifteen hand-picked young men, all clean shaven and dressed in women's clothing, under which they carried knives. Turgeis and his unsuspecting warriors were stabbed to death 'in the midst of their embraces'. Gerald probably recorded the story not to flatter the Irish for their cunning but because it chimed comfortably with his own prejudices: he regarded the Irish as a thoroughly deceitful and untrustworthy bunch who always negotiated in bad faith.

More reverses for the Vikings followed. In 848 the Irish won four major battles against the Vikings, killing over 2,000 of them in the process, according the *Annals of Ulster*. Irish annalists described these battle casualties as 'heads': Irish warriors still practiced the ancient Celtic custom of taking enemy heads as war trophies and rarely took prisoners. Then, in 849, Máel Sechnaill captured and plundered Dublin. Discouraged by their defeats, many Vikings left to seek easier pickings in Francia. The Norwegians suffered another blow in 851when a large force of Danish Vikings expelled them from Dublin. The following year the Norwegians suffered another crushing defeat by the Danes in a three-day battle at Carlingford Lough in County Down. The Danish intervention in Ireland was short-lived. In 853 two brothers, Olaf and Ivar, recaptured Dublin for the Norwegians and expelled the Danes.

The kingdom of Dublin

The arrival of Olaf and Ivar at Dublin in 853 was a decisive moment in Ireland's Viking Age. Olaf and Ivar (who are called Amláib and Ímhar in Irish annals) became the first kings of Dublin and under their rule it developed from a rough ship-camp into the dominant Viking power centre of the whole Irish Sea area. Irish sources describe Olaf and Ivar as sons of King Gofraid of Lochlann, which is the usual Gaelic name for Norway, but their origins remain uncertain. Most modern historians identify Olaf with Olaf the White, a king of Dublin who features in Icelandic saga traditions. Attempts to identify Ivar with the legendary Viking Ivar the Boneless are unconvincing: Ivar the Boneless's father was the equally legendary Viking Ragnar Lodbrok who, if he existed at all, was most likely a Dane. What is more certain is that the descendants of Olaf and Ivar, known to the Irish as the Uí Ímair, would dominate the Irish Sea for the next 200 years.

There is not enough evidence about the careers of Turgeis and Tomrair to be sure of their motives: did they aspire to found Viking states in Ireland or were they really just out for the plunder? It is clear, however, that Olaf and Ivar were trying to create a kingdom for themselves because their first actions were to impose tribute on all the Viking armies operating in Ireland. It is hard to work out from the Irish annals exactly how many of these there were but there must have been at least three or four. In their efforts to build a secure power base, the brothers took full advantage of the complex political rivalries of the Irish kingdoms. In 859 Olaf and Ivar allied with Cerball mac Dúnlainge (r. 842–880), king of Osraige, against his overlord Máel Sechnaill. According to saga traditions, the alliance was sealed by a marriage between Olaf and one of Cerball's daughters. A Christian king is unlikely to have married his daughters to pagans, so, if the tradition is true, it is likely that Olaf had at least been baptised. In 858, Ivar and Cerball campaigned together in Leinster, and in Munster against the Gall-Gaedhil. The next year Olaf, Ivar and Cerball together invaded Máel Sechnaill's kingdom of Meath. After Cerball came to terms with Máel Sechnaill, he dropped his Norse allies. Olaf and Ivar soon found a new ally in Áed Finnliath (c. 855–79), the northern Uí Néill king of Ulster. Together they plundered Máel Sechnaill's kingdom in 861 and 862. After Máel Sechnaill's death in 862, Olaf and Ivar switched to supporting his successor Lorcán against Áed. The brothers did Lorcán's standing no good at all when, in 863, they dug open the great Neolithic burial mounds at Knowth on the River Boyne to look for treasure. Although pagan in origin, these ancient mounds were rich in mythological significance for the Irish and this desecration was thought to be shocking behaviour even by the Viking's low standards. The following year Áed captured the discredited Lorcán, blinded him and forced him to abdicate.

Olaf and his brothers had now run out of willing allies in Ireland and, in 866, they took their fleet across the Irish Sea to raid Pictland in alliance with the Gall-Gaedhil. Áed, now high king, took advantage of their absence to plunder and destroy all the Viking longphuirt in Ulster. After a victory over the Vikings on Lough Foyle, Áed took 240 heads home as trophies. The limited extent of Viking territorial control was starkly demonstrated in 867 when Áed's ally Cennétig king of Loigis, destroyed Olaf's border fortress at Clondalkin just 5 miles from Dublin, which he then went on to plunder. Olaf now allied with the southern Uí Néill and Leinster against Áed. Áed crushed the alliance at the Battle of Killineer (Co. Louth) in 868: among the dead was one of Olaf's sons. Olaf struck back at Áed in 869, brutally sacking Armagh and leading off 1,000 captives for the slave markets. This was a severe blow to Áed's prestige – he was supposed to be the monastery's protector. After this success, Olaf and Ivar crossed the Irish Sea to Strathclyde and laid siege to its capital, Alt Clut, on the summit of Dumbarton Rock, overlooking the River Clyde. Alt Clut fell after four months and the brothers returned to Dublin with a hoard of treasure. They went back to Strathclyde for more the following year and this time returned 'with a great prey of Angles, Britons and Picts'. Olaf and Ivar were back plundering in Meath in 872, but in the next year Ivar died of 'a sudden, horrible disease'. Olaf survived until 874 or 875: he was killed in battle with Constantine I of Scotland at Dollar in Clackmannanshire.

The deaths of Ivar and Olaf began what the *Cogadh Gaedhel re Gallaibh* dubbed the 'Forty Years' Rest', a long period of reduced Viking activity in Ireland that lasted until 914. Deprived of the strong military leadership provided by Olaf and Ivar, Dublin became politically unstable under a succession of short-lived successors. Olaf's first successor as king of Dublin, his son Oystín (Eystein), lasted barely a year: he was killed when Dublin was captured by a Danish Viking who Irish annalists called Alband. Alband is most likely to have been

Halfdan, the Danish king of York. Áed Finnliath came to the rescue of his Viking allies, quickly expelling Alband and placing Ivar's son Bárðr on the throne. Alband returned to Ireland in 877, but was killed fighting the Dublin Vikings at Strangford Lough. However, his dream of uniting Dublin and York into a trans-Irish Sea kingdom survived. Bárðr died in 881 and was followed by six short-lived kings, none of whom was able to arrest the kingdom's decline. In 902, Cerball mac Muirecáin, king of Leinster and Máel Finnia of Brega launched a co-ordinated pincer attack on Dublin from the north and south, forcing the Norse to flee for their ships after a fierce battle. The refugees fled mainly to North Wales and north-west England. Ireland's first Viking Age was over.

From *longphort* to town

Most of the Vikings' longphuirt were either abandoned, or were destroyed by the Irish, after relatively short periods of occupation. Dublin was one of a small group of longphuirt, which also included Wexford, Waterford, Cork and Limerick, which developed into perm-anent towns. These longphuirt all had in common good tidal harbours. The exact location of the original Viking longphort at Dublin now lies buried beneath later buildings. This has necessarily limited archaeological investigation of the city's origins to rescue excavations on sites that have been temporarily cleared for redevelopment. Evidence for early Viking occupation, including warrior burials, buildings, ship rivets and a possible defensive rampart, excavated from sites at Ship Street Great and South Great George's Street, suggest that the longphort was probably in the area where Dublin Castle now stands, close to the *Dubhlinn*, the 'black pool' from which the city got its English name. This was a now-vanished tidal pool at the confluence of the River Liffey and its small tributary the Poddle. Dublin was already a place of some importance before the longphort was built as a monastic centre and the site of the lowest ford across the River Liffey: its Gaelic name Áth Cliath means 'the ford of the hurdles'. This ford made Dublin a natural focus of overland routes and, with its good harbour and short sailing distances to Wales, north-west England, Galloway and the Isle of Man, it was ideally situated to become a successful port and trading centre. The same geographical advantages also made Dublin an ideal base for raiding, not only in eastern Ireland but around the whole Irish Sea region. No other longphort in Ireland had the same combination of advantages: it was almost inevitable that Dublin would become Ireland's dominant Viking centre.

Early Dublin was probably similar to the well-preserved longphort at Linn Duchaill, about 40 miles further north, near the village of Annagassan in County Louth. Founded in the same year as Dublin, this longphort was built on the site of a minor monastery on the banks of the River Glyde, close to its estuary into the Irish Sea. The Vikings occupied the longphort until 891, when the Irish expelled them. Vikings reoccupied the site c. 914 only for it to be abandoned for good in 927. The site has been open farmland ever since so, unlike Dublin, this longphort's remains have seen little disturbance. Covering about 40 acres (16 hectares), the longphort at Linn Duachaill was large enough to accommodate an army that was several thousand strong. A rampart and ditch, ¾ of a mile long, protected the landward side of the fort and there was a small citadel on higher ground within the fort. Excavations yielded large numbers of ships' rivets, testifying to ship repair and perhaps shipbuilding on the site. Pieces of hacksilver and the remains of scales show that loot was divided up here and an iron slave chain dredged from the river is evidence of slave raiding. A shuttle and spindle whorl provide evidence of spinning and weaving in the fort. As these were not occupations for Viking warriors, women must have lived there. Geophysical surveys suggest that the waterfront was densely built-up but this has not yet been confirmed by excavations. Linn Duachaill did not have the good harbour that Dublin had, and it was that which probably prevented it ever developing into a permanent town.

The Viking slave trade

Archaeological evidence indicates that by 902 Dublin had begun to outgrow the longphort and become a true town rather than an armed camp. Significantly, following the Irish conquest in that year, Dublin was not abandoned: there is clear evidence of continuity of settlement through to its recapture by the Norse in 917. That there was an exodus of Scandinavians from Ireland at that time is not in doubt, so this is probably evidence that Dublin had a significant Irish population living alongside the Norse and that they were allowed to remain: they may even have been the majority because genetic studies have found scant evidence of Scandinavian DNA in the modern Irish population.

Dublin owed its transformation to a town to trade. Pre-Viking Ireland did not play a large part in international trade so it had no trading towns to compare with the likes of Dorestad or York. Coinage was not used either. Ireland was not poor, however. The hoards of magnificent gold and silver liturgical vessels from Ardagh and Derrynaflan stand testimony to the wealth of Ireland's monasteries in the early Middle Ages. Major Irish monasteries like Armagh or Clonmacnoise were much more than communities of monks, they were also centres of political power and economic activity. Secular communities of craftsmen and merchants grew up around the more important monasteries and by the eighth century a few were becoming small towns. Kings, seeking the authority and safety that close association with the saints was believed to confer, often had residences, treasuries and garrisons in these monastic towns. All of this was more than enough to justify the Vikings' attentions, but their main interest was in Ireland's people.

Crude estimates based on a count of known settlements suggest that Ireland's population was about half a million when the Viking Age began. Thanks to the country's mild winters, cool summers and reliable rainfall, grass grew all year round so cattle and sheep did not have to be kept inside during the winter. The Irish did not bother to gather hay in the summer as it was so rarely necessary. Despite occasional famines caused by cattle epidemics and severe weather, the Irish population was generally well nourished and very few people were desperately poor. The Vikings rounded up these people in their thousands to be ransomed or sold as slaves according to their wealth and status. Slavery was rare in pre-Viking Ireland – it was used mainly as a form of debt bondage – so there was no slave trade. Plundering in wars between the Irish was usually confined to cattle rustling, so Viking slaving added a new form of suffering to the experience of warfare. Perhaps inevitably,

Irish kings soon began to take captives during their wars and sell them
to the Vikings. Irish captives who were not lucky enough to be ransomed
by their relatives could expect to be sold abroad. Anglo-Saxon England
and the Frankish kingdoms both had active slave trades but most Irish
captives probably finished up in Scandinavia or the Moorish kingdoms
in Spain and North Africa. Through developing the slave trade, the
Vikings drew Ireland into fuller participation in the international trade
networks. This is usually presented as one of the positive impacts that
the Vikings had on Ireland, but it is unlikely that their victims were
quite so sanguine about it.

We know enough about the horrors of the trans-Atlantic slave trade
of the eighteenth century to guess at the human misery Viking slaving
must have caused. Its economic impact is harder to estimate but it is
likely that Vikings targeted the young and healthy rather than infants
and the elderly. The kidnapping and breaking-up of communities of
learned monks must have had a far more serious impact on Ireland's
flourishing monastic culture than ever the destruction of books, sacred
vessels and buildings did. As mere commodities, the voices of slaves
are rarely heard in the historical record, but two remarkable accounts
have survived about the experiences of Irishmen who were captured by
Viking slavers. One relates to a Leinsterman called Findan whose sister
was captured by Viking raiders some time around the middle of the
ninth century. Findan's father sent him to the Vikings to arrange his
sister's ransom, but they immediately clapped him in irons and carried
him off to their ship too. After keeping him without food and water
for two days, the Vikings discussed what to do with him. Luckily, his
captors decided that it was wrong to capture people who had come
to pay ransom, no doubt because it would discourage others from
doing so, and they let him, and presumably his sister, go. A short time
afterwards Findan got caught up in another Viking raid but evaded
capture by hiding behind the door of a hut. For Findan it was third time
unlucky, because in his next encounter with the Vikings he was taken
prisoner and sold into slavery. After changing hands several times,
Findan finished up on a ship bound for Scandinavia. Findan gained
his owner's confidence by helping the crew fight off some pirates and
he was released from his leg irons. When his owner made a stop-over

in Orkney, Findan seized the opportunity to jump ship and escape. Findan eventually made his way to Rome as a pilgrim and ended his life as a monk at the monastery of Rheinau in Switzerland: one of his fellow monks recorded his life story shortly after he died.

The second story concerns an Irishman called Murchad, a married man with a daughter, who was captured by Vikings and taken to Northumbria, where he was sold as a slave to a nunnery, with comical consequences. After he had seduced several of the nuns and turned the nunnery into a brothel, Murchad was expelled and cast adrift on the sea in a boat without oars or a sail as a punishment for his impiety. Murchad was rescued by Vikings, who took him to Germany and sold him to a roguish widow, who paid for him with counterfeit money. Murchad seduced her too, of course. After many more adventures, Murchad eventually returned to Ireland, was reunited with his family, and took up a career teaching Latin grammar. How much real history there is in this tale is hard to tell; perhaps it is really about making the best of hard times. It is unlikely that many captives were as lucky as Findan and Murchad but neither is it likely that all came to bad ends: most of the thousands of Irish slaves who were taken to Iceland later in the ninth century were eventually freed and became tenant farmers, for example.

Division is strength

By the early tenth century, Vikings had conquered and colonised substantial parts of England, Scotland and Francia, as well as the uninhabited Faeroe Islands and Iceland. Yet for all the fury of their onslaught, in Ireland the Vikings had not even been able to retain a toehold. Appearances can be deceptive. Ireland's divisions might have been a handicap in combating plundering raids but they also made it all but impossible for the Vikings to conquer and hold territory. On the face of it, it would have seemed that Ireland's disunity should have made it more vulnerable to conquest by the Vikings than England, which was divided into only four powerful centralised kingdoms. In fact the opposite was true. In early medieval Europe it was always the centralised kingdoms that got conquered most easily. After the 'Great

Army' of Danish Vikings invaded England in 865, the kingdoms of Northumbria and East Anglia both collapsed as soon as their kings had been killed in battle. Mercia too collapsed when its king decided he would prefer not to get killed and fled the country. Only Wessex survived to prevent England becoming Daneland. The centralised nature of the Anglo-Saxon kingdoms meant that it was relatively easy for the Vikings to destroy the small ruling class and take over; just one battle might do the trick, as it did, more or less, in 1066. Little trouble would then be expected from the leaderless peasantry. Ireland, however, had dozens of kings and even more lineages from which new kings could be chosen. No victory, therefore, could ever have the decisive knockout effect it could in a country like England. Nor was there much chance of a lasting peace agreement with so many kings to negotiate with because what one agreed was not binding on the others.

The military resources of the Irish should not be underestimated either. Most Irish local kingdoms could raise armies of around 300 men. This was inadequate to deal with anything but a small Viking raiding party, but there were a great many local kingdoms. Local kings owed military service to their over-kings, so an over-king who could enforce the obedience of his vassals could raise a very large army indeed. However, in a clash of shield walls an Irish warrior was no match for a well-equipped Viking. The Irish fought almost naked without armour or iron helmets, armed with spears and using only bucklers (small round shields) for protection. The Irish recognised the superiority of the Viking warrior and they usually avoided formal battle in favour of irregular tactics, harassing raiding parties and wearing them down with sudden ambushes before melting away into the woods and bogs. In this kind of fighting, their lack of armour was an advantage to the Irish, making them more agile than a mail-clad Viking. A weary Viking raiding party returning home burdened with loot, captives and stolen cattle would have been particularly vulnerable to these tactics.

The Irish countryside was scattered with as many as 50,000 ring-forts, but these were probably less of a hindrance to Viking raiders than Ireland's warriors. Ringforts varied in size according to the status of their inhabitants. An over-king might have a substantial stone structure like the Grianán of Aileach in Donegal, a stronghold of the

Northern Uí Néill dynasty. Built in the eighth century, the Grianán's 15 foot (4.5 m) thick stone walls enclose an area 75 feet (23 m) in diameter. But although it is an impressive structure, modern experiments have shown that it would not have been at all easy to defend so it may have been built mainly as a ceremonial centre rather than to withstand a siege. Local kings and aristocrats had more modest forts, sometimes as little as 30 feet (9 m) in diameter, with earth ramparts and a palisade, containing its owner's house and ancillary buildings. The ramparts of these small forts were primarily markers of status, for they were barely adequate for keeping livestock in, never mind keeping raiders out. More secure were crannogs, high status dwellings built on artificial islands in the middle of lakes. Communal fortifications like the English *burhs*, intended to provide refuges for the general population, were unknown.

During the course of the Viking Age, monks began to provide their monasteries with tall, slender, stone round towers. These were primarily used as bell towers and treasuries but they were also refuges against Viking raids. Over eighty round towers are known to have been built: the tallest surviving round tower, at Kilmacduagh in Galway, is 113 feet (34.5 m) tall. The towers' entrances were set well above ground level so that they could only be entered with a ladder. The entrances of some towers show signs of fire damage, which is likely a result of Viking attacks. Having no source of water, or battlements from which to fight off attackers, round towers could not withstand a long siege but a small Viking raiding party could not really afford any delay.

The Vikings return

During Ireland's 'Forty Years' Rest', the bulk of Viking forces were busying themselves plundering England and Francia. By the first decade of the tenth century, the English and Franks were finally getting the measure of the Vikings so Ireland once more began to look attractive to them. In 914 Ragnald, a grandson of Ivar I, appeared in the Irish Sea and defeated a rival Viking leader in a sea battle off the coast of the Isle of Man before going to set up a longphort at Waterford in south-east Ireland. The Vikings were back and with a vengeance. In 917, Ragnald's brother Sihtric Cáech ('squinty') recaptured Dublin and in 919 smashed an Irish counter-attack at Islandbridge, killing the Úi Néill High King Niall Glúndubh and five other kings. In 922, Tomar mac Ailche (Thormódr Helgason) re-established Viking occupation at Limerick and around the same time other Viking leaders established themselves at Cork and Wexford. As was the case in the ninth century, the Vikings made no extensive territorial conquests or settlements outside their heavily fortified towns. Dublin came to control the most extensive territory: known as *Dyflinnarskíri* or 'Dublinshire', it extended along the coast from Wicklow (*Vikinglo*) in the south to Skerries (from Old Norse *sker* meaning a 'reef') in the north, and as far inland as Leixlip (Old Norse *lax hlaup* meaning 'salmon leap') on the River Liffey. A dearth of Norse place-names in the countryside of Dublinshire supports the conclusion that there was little or no Viking settlement outside Dublin and its immediate environs.

The history of the revived Viking kingdom of Dublin is frequently entangled with that of the Viking kingdom of York across the Irish Sea. While the Norse had been exiled from Ireland, Ragnald had briefly held power in York and now he wanted it back. Using Dublin as a base to campaign in northern England, Ragnald recaptured York in 919. York must have seemed a greater prize than Dublin because when Ragnald died in 921, Sihtric gave up the kingship of Dublin to another brother, Guthfrith, and took up the kingship of York. An aggressive ruler, Guthfrith immediately launched a furious campaign of plundering and slaving raids against the Irish, culminating in a curiously respectful sack of Armagh in November. Guthfrith spared the monks, the sick and the monastic buildings, 'save for a few dwellings which were burned through carelessness.' It may be that Guthfrith was a Christian. If so, Guthfrith's show of respect for St Patrick did him no good because he was intercepted on his way home by Muirchertach of the Leather Cloaks (r. 919–43), the king of the Northern Uí Néill, and heavily defeated. This set the tone for Ireland's second Viking Age: the days when Vikings might criss-cross Ireland without meeting serious opposition were gone. Muirchertach won another victory over the Dublin Vikings at Carlingford Lough in 925, when 200 of them were captured and beheaded, and the following year he killed Guthfrith's son Alpthann (Halfdan) in another battle at Linn

Duchaill. Muirchertach besieged the survivors in the longphort there until Guthfrith brought an army north from Dublin to rescue them. The longphort was afterwards permanently abandoned.

What had changed since Ireland's first Viking Age? The shock of Viking raiding had forced change upon the Irish. Irish society became increasingly militarised and those kings who offered the most effective military leadership against the Vikings enhanced their status and power and, as they tightened their grip over their sub-kings, they could raise larger armies and enhance their power even more. It was the same virtuous circle of success that was driving political centralisation and state formation in contemporary Scandinavia. Irish kingship was gradually becoming more territorial and many local kings found themselves reduced to the status of local chieftains. At the same time, the Irish had learned from the Vikings, making greater use of swords and axes in battle. Though they still lacked armour, this went some way to evening the odds on the battlefield. War was also waged with a new ruthlessness, against both the Vikings and other Irish kingdoms. Ravaging and burning had been rare before the Viking Age, but now Irish kings used it routinely as a weapon against their foes irrespective of whether they were Irish or Norse.

After Sihtric's death in 927, Guthfrith went to York, whether to claim the throne for himself or to support his brother's son Olaf Cuarán is not known. Both were quickly expelled by Æthelstan of Wessex. Guthfrith returned to lay siege to York, but was forced to surrender to Æthelstan, who allowed him to return to Dublin, which he ruled until his death in 934. Guthfrith's son and successor, Olaf Guthfrithsson, established dominance over all the Norse in Ireland when he defeated the Limerick Vikings in a naval battle on Lough Ree in 937. It was in the same year that he allied with the Scots and the Welsh of Strathclyde in another attempt to win the kingdom of York only to be defeated by Æthelstan at the Battle of Brunanburh (see p. 124). Muirchertach sacked Dublin the following year, taking advantage of its weakness after Olaf's defeat in England. However, Æthelstan's death in 939 finally gave Olaf the chance to seize York and unite it with Dublin in a single kingdom. Olaf did not enjoy his success for long: he died shortly after raiding the Northumbrian monasteries at Tyninghame and Auldhame in 941, a victim, it was said, of divine displeasure. A tenth-century Viking burial discovered in the monastic cemetery at Auldhame almost certainly belongs to a high-status Viking who was involved in these raids. It has been speculated that the burial was even that of Olaf himself. As Olaf was married to the daughter of King Constantine II of Scotland he must have been at least a nominal Christian. The king might therefore have been buried on consecrated ground as a posthumous act of penance. Following Olaf's death his cousin Olaf Cuarán became king of York, while his brother Blácaire succeeded him at Dublin.

Blácaire was an active raider. On 26 February 943 he defeated and killed Muirchertach at the Battle of Glas Liatháin and five days later sacked Armagh. Muirchertach's death was mourned by the Irish, the *Annals of Ulster* described him as 'the Hector of the western world' and lamented that his death had left the 'land of the Irish orphaned'. Irish retaliation was swift. The following year, the newly acknowledged High King Congalach Cnogba captured and burned Dublin, carrying away a vast amount of booty. Four hundred Vikings were said to have been killed in the fighting and Blácaire fled into exile. In his absence, Congalach installed Olaf Cuarán, recently expelled from York by the English, as king of Dublin. Olaf's dependence on Congalach was such that when the pair were defeated by a rival for the high kingship in 947, Blácaire was able to depose him and reclaim his throne. After his death in battle against Congalach in 948, Blácaire was succeeded by his cousin Godfred, another son of Sihtric Cáech. In 951 Godfred led an enormously successful expedition in the Irish midlands, plundering half a dozen monasteries including Kells. According to the *Annals of Ulster*, 'three thousand men or more were taken captive and a great spoil of cattle and horses and gold and silver was taken away'. Divine vengeance followed swiftly, of course. A severe epidemic, described in the annals as dysentery and leprosy, broke out in Dublin on Godfred's return and the king was one of its victims.

While Godfred had been plundering in Ireland his brother Olaf had briefly regained control of York before being expelled by the Norwegian Erik Bloodaxe in 952. Olaf now succeeded as king of Dublin but the dream of uniting Dublin and York was dead. The Dublin Vikings would never be a power in England again. It is doubtful that a

Dublin-York axis was ever really viable in the long term. York is much more remote from Dublin than a casual glance at a map would suggest. As York could only be reached by ship from the North Sea, sailing there from Dublin involved a long, dangerous and time-consuming voyage around the north of Britain. The only alternative would have been to sail from Dublin to north-west England and then trek across the Pennine Hills to York. However, it is far from clear how much, if any, control the kings of York actually exercised west of the Pennines. And, fighting off the English and the Irish at the same time must have been way beyond the resources of the Dublin Vikings.

Olaf was not a peaceable king but neither was he a traditional freebooting Viking, as he rarely raided unless he was acting in alliance with an Irish king. Olaf was also closely linked to Irish dynasties by marriage – made possible by his baptism in England as part of a peace deal with king Edmund in 943. Olaf's first wife was Dúnlaith, the sister of the high king Domnall ua Néill (r. 956–80) and, after her death, he married Gormflaith, daughter of Murchad mac Finn, king of Leinster. Olaf seems to have gained little, if any, political advantage from his marriages because his reign was dominated by conflicts with Domnall and with successive kings of Leinster (some of whom Olaf held hostage in Dublin). On Domnall's death in 980, Dúnlaith's son by an earlier marriage, Máel Sechnaill mac Domnall, the king of Meath, succeeded his uncle as high king. Máel Sechnaill clearly had no love lost for his stepfather as he had begun his reign as king of Meath in 975 with an attack on Dublin, in which he burned 'Thor's Wood' (a pagan sacred grove) outside the city. Shortly after becoming high king, Máel Sechnaill heavily defeated a force of Vikings from Dublin, Man and the Hebrides in battle at the Hill of Tara, the traditional inauguration place of the high kings. Máel Sechnaill followed up his victory by laying siege to Dublin, which surrendered after three days. Máel Sechnaill imposed a heavy tribute on the citizens and deposed Olaf, who went into retirement as a monk on Iona, where he died soon afterwards. In his place, Máel Sechnaill appointed his half-brother Jarnkné ('iron knee') (r. 980–9), Olaf's son by Dúnlaith, as tributary king. There was no disguising Dublin's loss of independence.

The Vikings in Wales

One side effect of the strength of Irish resistance was to increase Viking interest in Wales. At its closest points, Wales was only a day's sail away from Dublin, Waterford and Wexford, and from the Viking colony in the Isle of Man, but despite this had so far suffered relatively little from Viking raids. A combination of strong military rulers such as Rhodri Mawr (r. 844–78) of Gwynedd, difficult mountainous terrain, and Wales' poverty compared to England, Ireland and Francia, seem to have deterred any major Viking invasions in the ninth century. Only a dozen Viking raids are recorded in the period 793–920, compared to over 130 in Ireland in the same period. This was fewer than the number of English invasions of Wales in the same period. Place-name evidence points to areas of Viking settlement in the south-west, in Pembrokeshire and Gower, but, as they are undocumented, it is not known when they were made. There was also a small area of Viking settlement in the far north-east, modern Flintshire, most probably by refugees from Dublin following its capture by the Irish in 902. This was probably overspill from the successful Viking colony a few miles away across the estuary of the River Dee in Wirral (see p. 71).

In the first half of the tenth century, Wales was dominated by Hywel Dda (r. 915-50), the king of Deheubarth in the south-west. During his long reign Hywel came close to uniting all of Wales under his rule but his death in 950 was followed by a civil war and the break-up of his dominion. This was a signal to Vikings based in Ireland, the Isle of Man and the Hebrides to launch a wave of attacks on Wales. The area most exposed to Viking raiding was the large and fertile island of Anglesey off the coast of North Wales, which lay only 70 miles due east of Dublin and just 45 miles south of the Isle of Man: raids are recorded in 961, 971, 972, 979, 980, 987 and 993. Another place hit hard was St David's monastery on the Pembrokeshire coast, Wales' most important ecclesiastical centre. Founded c. 500 by St David, the monastery became the seat of the archbishops of Wales in 519. Only 60 miles from Wexford, St David's was first sacked by Vikings in 967, then again in 982, 988 and 998, when they killed archbishop Morgeneu. St David's would be sacked at least another six times before the end of the eleventh century. In 989 the raids had become so bad that King Maredudd of Deheubarth paid tribute to the Vikings at the rate of one silver penny for each of his subjects. Viking raids declined quickly after 1000, perhaps because the Viking towns in Ireland had come under the control of Irish rulers, but raids from the Hebrides and Orkney continued into the twelfth century. Vikings from Ireland also continued to come to Wales, but they did so mainly as mercenaries signing on with Welsh kings to fight in their wars with one another and with the English.

The Rock of Cashel

The end of Ireland's Viking Age is traditionally associated with the rise of the O'Brien (Ua Briain) dynasty of Munster, and of its greatest king Brian Boru (r. 976–1014) in particular. Brian's career certainly had an epic quality about it. Brian was a younger son of Cennétig mac Lorcáin (d. 951), king of the Dál Cais, whose kingdom, which was roughly equivalent to modern County Clare, was subject to the kings of Munster. As a younger son Brian probably never expected to rule and his early life was spent in the shadow of his elder brother Mathgamain. Even Brian's date of birth is uncertain. Some Irish sources claim that he was eighty-eight when he died in 1014, which would mean he was born in 926 or 927, but other sources give dates as early as 923 and as late as 942. Brian's first experience of war came in 967 when he fought alongside his brother at the Battle of Sulcoit against Ivar, king of the Limerick Vikings. The following year the brothers captured and sacked Limerick, executing all male prisoners of fighting age. The rest were sold as slaves. Ivar, however, escaped to Britain and in 969 he returned with a new fleet and regained control of Limerick only to be expelled again by the Dal Cais in 972.

Probably in 970, Mathgamain expelled his nominal overlord, Máel Muad the king of Munster, from his stronghold on the Rock of Cashel. The rock is a natural fortress, a craggy limestone hill rising abruptly and offering a magnificent view over the fertile plains of County Tipperary. The rock is now crowned by the ruins of a medieval cathedral and one of Ireland's tallest surviving round towers, so little evidence of earlier structures survives. In legend, Máel Muad's ancestor Conall Corc made Cashel the capital of Munster after two swineherds told him of a vision in which an angel prophesised that whoever was the first to light a bonfire on the rock would win the kingship of Munster. Conall needed no more encouragement and had hurried to Cashel and lit a fire. This was supposed to have happened around sixty years before St Patrick visited around 453 and converted Munster's then king Óengus to Christianity. During the baptismal ceremony the saint accidentally pierced Óengus' foot with the sharp end of his crozier. The king, thinking it was part of the ritual, suffered in silence.

Mathgamain's success in capturing Cashel promised to make the Dál Cais a major power as Munster was one of the most important of Ireland's over-kingdoms, covering the whole of the south-west of the island. However, before Mathgamain could win effective control of Munster, Máel Muad murdered him and recaptured Cashel. Brian now unexpectedly found himself king of the Dál Cais and quickly proved himself to be a fine soldier. After his expulsion from Limerick in 972, Ivar established a new base on Scattery Island, close to the mouth of the Shannon, from where he could still easily threaten Dál Cais. This sort of tactic had served Vikings well since the 840s, but no more. Brian had learned the importance of naval power from the Vikings and in 977 he led a fleet to Scattery Island, surprising and killing Ivar. A year later Brian defeated and killed his brother's murderer to regain control of Cashel. Very shortly afterwards he defeated his last serious rival for control of Munster, Donnubán of the Uí Fidgente, and the remnants of the Limerick Vikings under Ivar's son Harald. Both Donnubán and Harald were killed. This spelled the end of Viking Limerick. The town now effectively became the capital of Dál Cais, but Brian allowed its Norse inhabitants to remain in return for their valuable military and naval support. In the years that followed, Brian also became overlord of the Viking towns of Cork, Wexford and Waterford.

Now secure in his control of Munster, Brian began to impose his authority on the neighbouring provinces of Connacht and Leinster. Brian's ambitions inevitably brought him into conflict with Dublin's overlord, Máel Sechnaill. Almost every year, Brian campaigned in either Leinster, Meath or Connacht. Limerick and other Viking towns provided Brian with fleets, which he sent up the River Shannon to ravage the lands of Connacht and Meath on either side. When Donchad mac Domnaill, the king of Leinster, submitted to Brian in 996 Máel Sechnaill recognised him as overlord of all of the southern half of Ireland, including Dublin. Brian almost immediately faced a rebellion by Donchad's successor in Leinster, Máel Morda, and the king of Dublin, Sihtric Silkbeard (r. 989–1036). Sihtric was another son of Olaf Cuarán, by his second wife Gormflaith, who was Máel Morda's sister. Brian's crushing victory over the allies at the battle of Glen Mama in 999 left him unchallenged in the south. Brian dealt generously with Sihtric, allowing him to remain king, and marrying Gormflaith, so making him his son-in-law. There was a brief peace before Brian, his sights now set on the high kingship itself, went back onto the offensive against Máel Sechnaill. Sihtric played a full part in these campaigns, providing troops and warships. Finally defeated in 1002, Máel Sechnaill resigned his title in favour of Brian and accepted him as his overlord: it was the first time that anyone other than an Uí Néill had been high king. Two more years of campaigning and every kingdom in Ireland had become tributary to Brian, hence his nickname *bóraime*, 'of the tributes'.

The Battle of Clontarf

Brian's achievement was a considerable one but he did not in any meaningful sense unite Ireland: outside his own kingdom of Dál Cais, Brian exercised authority indirectly, through his tributary kings, and he created no national institutions of government. Nor was the obedience of Brian's tributaries assured: he faced, and put down, several rebellions. The most serious of these rebellions began in 1013 when Máel Mórda of Leinster renewed his alliance with Sihtric Silkbeard, who, despite Brian's conciliatory approach, still hoped to recover Dublin's independence. To strengthen Dublin's forces, Sihtric called in an army of Vikings under Sigurd the Stout, the jarl of Orkney, and Brodir, a Dane from the Isle of Man, which arrived at Dublin just before Easter 1014. Brian quickly raised an army that included several of his tributary kings, including Maél Sechnaill, and a contingent of

Vikings under Brodir's brother Óspak. The two armies met in battle at Clontarf, a few miles north of Dublin on Good Friday (23 April) 1014. Neither Brian nor Sihtric fought in the battle. Sihtric watched the battle from the walls of Dublin, where he had remained with a small garrison to defend the city if the battle was lost. Now in his seventies or eighties, Brian was too frail to take any part in the fighting and spent the battle in his tent. The exact size of the rival armies is unknown but Brian's was probably the larger of the two.

The battle opened around daybreak in heroic style with a single combat between two champion warriors, both of whom died in a deadly embrace, their swords piercing one another's hearts. The fighting was exceptionally fierce but Brian's army eventually gained the upper hand and began to inflict severe casualties on the Vikings and the Leinstermen. Brian's son and designated successor, Murchad, led the attack and was said personally to have killed 100 of the enemy, fifty holding his sword in his right hand and fifty holding his sword in his left hand, before he was himself cut down and killed. Among Murchad's victims was jarl Sigurd. Of the Dublin Vikings fighting in the army, only twenty are said to have survived the battle and the Leinster-Dublin army as a whole suffered as many as 6,000 casualties. By evening, the Leinster-Dublin army was disintegrating in flight and many Vikings drowned as they tried desperately to reach their ships anchored in Dublin Bay. At this moment of victory, Brodir and a handful of Viking warriors broke through the enemy lines and killed Brian as he prayed in his tent. Brodir's men were quickly killed by Brian's bodyguards and, according to Icelandic saga traditions, Brodir was captured and put to a terrible death. His stomach was cut open and he was walked round and round a tree until all his entrails had been wound out. Máel Mórda and one of his tributary kings were also killed in the fighting, as too were two tributary kings on Brian's side.

For the anonymous author of the *Cogadh Gaedhel re Gallaibh*, Clontarf was the decisive battle of Ireland's Viking wars, but this exaggerates its importance. The author of the *Coghad* was essentially a propagandist for Brian Boru's Ua Briain dynasty and he intended, by glorifying his achievements, to bolster his descendents' claim to the high kingship of Ireland, which they contested with the Uí Néills. The true impact of the battle was rather different. The deaths of Brian and Murchad caused a succession crisis in Dál Cais that brought the rise of the Ua Briain dynasty to a crashing halt. Brian's hard-won hegemony immediately disintegrated, Cashel reverted to its traditional rulers, and Máel Sechnaill reclaimed the high kingship. Sihtric found himself back where he had started his reign, a sub-king to Máel Sechnaill. There could have been no clearer way to demonstrate how far gone in decline Viking power in Ireland already was. Sihtric continued to take part in Ireland's internecine conflicts but his defeats outnumbered his successes, and Dublin's decline into political and military irrelevance continued. Dublin continued to prosper as Ireland's most important port, however, making Sihtric a wealthy ruler. In 1029 he ransomed his son Olaf, who had been captured by the king of Brega, for 1,200 cows, 120 Welsh ponies, 60 ounces (1.7 kg) of gold, 60 ounces of silver, hostages, and another eighty cattle for the man who had conducted the negotiations. Though he was quite willing to sack monasteries when it suited him, Sihtric was a devout Christian and in 1028 he made a pilgrimage to Rome. Such journeys were primarily penitential and, as an active Viking, Sihtric no doubt had much to be penitential about. On his return to Dublin he founded Christ Church cathedral but pointedly placed it under the authority of the Archbishopric of Canterbury in England, then ruled by the Danish King Cnut. It was not until 1152 that the diocese of Dublin became part of the Irish church. His alliance with Cnut briefly resurrected Dublin as a power in the Irish Sea, but Cnut's death in 1035 left Sihtric in a weak position. In 1036 Echmarcach mac Ragnaill, a Norse-Gaelic king of the Hebrides, captured Dublin and forced Sihtric into exile: he died in 1042, possibly murdered during another pilgrimage to Rome.

Echmarcach never succeeded in securing his hold on Dublin and in 1052 he was expelled by Diarmait mac Máel, the king of Leinster, who ruled the city directly as an integral part of his kingdom. For the next century Dublin became a prize to be fought over by rival Irish dynasties interspersed with periods of rule by Norse kings from the Isle of Man, the Hebrides, and even Norway.

Ostman Dublin

By the eleventh century the Viking towns had become fully integrated into Irish political life, accepted for the trade they brought and the taxes they paid on it, and their fleets of warships, which made them valuable allies in the wars of the Irish kings. Pagan burial customs had died out during the second half of the tenth century so it is likely that by now the Irish Vikings were mostly converted to Christianity. It was not only kings like Sihtric Silkbeard who had taken Irish wives, and in many cases the children of these mixed marriages were Gaelic speaking. It is even possible that people of Norse descent were minorities in the Viking towns among a population of slaves, servants, labourers and craftsmen that was mostly Irish. The Irish Vikings had become sufficiently different from 'real' Scandinavians to have acquired a new name, the Ostmen, meaning 'men of the east' (of Ireland). The name seems to have been coined by the English, who by this time had had ample opportunities to learn how to distinguish between different types of Scandinavian.

In its general appearance, Ostman Dublin was probably much like other Viking towns of the period, such as York or Hedeby in Denmark. In the tenth century the site was divided up by post-and-wattle fences into long narrow plots along streets. Sub-rectangular houses built of wood, wattles, clay and thatch were built end-on to the streets, with doors at both ends. Though the houses were often rebuilt, the boundaries of the plots themselves remained unchanged for centuries. Irish kings used these plots as the basic unit for levying tribute on Dublin, as Máel Sechnaill did in 989 when he levied an ounce (28 g) of gold for every plot. Paths around the houses were covered with split logs, or gravel and paving slabs. The streets of Ostman Dublin lie under the modern streets, so it is not known what they were surfaced with, but split logs were used in other Viking towns like York. Different quarters of the town were assigned to different activities. Comb-makers and cobblers were concentrated in the area of High Street, while wood-carvers and merchants occupied Fishamble Street, for example. Other crafts, like blacksmithing and shipbuilding, were probably carried out outside the town. The wreck of a Viking longship discovered at Skuldelev near

Roskilde in Denmark proved to have been built of oak felled near Glendalough, 22 miles south of Dublin, in 1042.

The town was surrounded by an earth rampart, which was probably surmounted by a wooden palisade. By 1000, Dublin had begun to spread outside its walls and a new rampart was built to protect the new suburbs. By 1100 it had proved necessary to extend the defences again, this time with a stone wall that was up to 12 feet high. This was such a novelty that a poem of 1120 considered Dublin to be one of the wonders of Ireland. Dublin probably lacked any impressive public buildings – even the cathedral founded by Sihtric Silkbeard was built of wood and it would not be rebuilt in stone until the end of the twelfth century. Dublin's four other known churches were probably also wooden structures. The basic institution of Dublin's government, as in all Viking Age Scandinavian communities, was the thing, the meeting of all freemen. The thing met at the 40-foot (12 m) high *thingmote* ('thing mound'), which was sited near the medieval castle. This survived until 1685, when it was levelled to make way for new buildings. Of the other Ostman towns, only Waterford has seen extensive archaeological investigations. Like Dublin it was a town of wooden buildings laid out in orderly plots within stout defences.

The end of Viking Dublin

Viking Dublin was finally brought to an end not by the Irish but by the Anglo-Normans. In 1167, Diarmait MacMurchada, exiled to England from his kingdom of Leinster, recruited a band of Anglo-Norman mercenaries to help him win back his kingdom. Reinforcements arrived in Leinster in 1169 and, with their help, Diarmait captured the Ostman town of Wexford. In 1170, Richard Fitzgilbert de Clare, popularly known as Strongbow, the earl of Pembroke, brought an army of 200 knights and 1,000 archers to support Diarmait, and within days he had captured another Ostman town, Waterford. On 21 September in the same year, Diarmait and Strongbow captured Dublin. The city's last Norse king Asculf Ragnaldsson (r. 1160–71) fled to Orkney where he raised an army to help him win it back. In June 1171, Asculf returned with a fleet of sixty ships and attempted to storm Dublin's east gate.

The Norman garrison sallied out on horseback and scattered Asculf's men. Asculf was captured as he fled back to his ships. The Normans generously offered to release Asculf if he paid a ransom, but when he foolishly boasted that he would return next time with a much larger army, they thought better of it and chopped his head off instead. Cork was the last Ostman town to fall to the Anglo-Normans, following the defeat of its fleet in 1173.

The Anglo-Norman conquest was a far more decisive event in Irish history than the advent of the Vikings. Despite their long presence in the country, the Viking impact on Ireland was surprisingly slight. Viking art styles influenced Irish art styles, and the Irish adopted Viking weapons and shipbuilding methods, and borrowed many Norse words relating to ships and seafaring into the Gaelic language, but that was about it. The Vikings certainly drew Ireland more closely into European trade networks and by the tenth century this had stimulated the development of regular trade fairs at the monastic towns. However, on the eve of the Anglo-Norman conquest, the Viking towns were still Ireland's only fully developed urban communities. In contrast over fifty new towns were founded in the century after the Anglo-Norman conquest. Sihtric Silkbeard was the first ruler in Ireland to issue coinage in *c.* 997, but no native Irish ruler imitated his example: coinage only came into common use in Ireland after the Anglo-Norman conquest. The impact of Viking raiding did accelerate the slow process of political centralisation in Ireland, but even in 1169 the country still lacked any national government institutions. The high kings still exercised authority outside their personal domains indirectly through their tributary kings (though there were many fewer of them than when the Vikings had first arrived). A true national kingship would likely have emerged eventually, but the Anglo-Norman conquest brought this internal process to a sudden end. English governmental institutions were imposed in those areas controlled by the Anglo-Normans, while in those areas still controlled by the Irish, kingship degenerated into warlordism. There were no more high kings.

Dublin prospered after the Anglo-Norman conquest, becoming the centre of English rule in Ireland. England's King Henry II (r. 1154–89) granted Dublin a charter of liberties based on those of the important

English West Country port of Bristol. This gave Dublin privileged access to Henry's vast British and French lands, spurring a period of rapid growth. One of Henry's edicts took the Ostmen of Dublin and the other Norse towns under royal protection: their skills as merchants and seafarers made them far too useful to expel (though some chose to leave voluntarily). An influx of English settlers gradually made the Ostmen a minority in the city, however. The Ostmen also found that they did not always receive the privileges they had been granted because of the difficulty in distinguishing so many of them from the native Irish. In 1263, the dissatisfied Ostmen appealed to the Norwegian king Håkon IV to help them expel the English, but the collapse of Norse power that followed his death later that year ended any possibility that Dublin would recover its independence. Norse names soon fell out of use and by c. 1300, the Ostmen had been completely assimilated with either the native Irish or the immigrant English communities. A last vestige of the Viking domination of the city survives in the suburb of Oxmantown, a corruption of Ostmantown.

CHAPTER 6

SEVILLE AND LUNI
VIKINGS IN SPAIN AND THE MEDITERRANEAN 844–61

I t was all but inevitable that once the Vikings were established as a
permanent presence on the River Loire in the 840s that they would
sail further south and investigate the possibilities of the Iberian
Peninsula. There was certainly much there to tempt a Viking.
The peninsula was dominated by Western Europe's richest and most
sophisticated state, the Moorish Emirate of Córdoba. Vikings raided
Iberia in strength several times to try to relieve the Moors of their
wealth, but they found the emirate a formidable military power and,
for all their courage and enterprise, they never prospered there.

Al-Andalus

The Emirate of Córdoba was the westernmost outpost of the Islamic
world. Iberia was conquered for Islam in 711–12 and became part of
the Umayyad Caliphate, a vast Arab empire stretching from the Atlantic
Ocean to India. Only in the rugged Cantabrian Mountains in the far
north-west did Christians hold out against the Muslim invaders. The
Muslim conquest was followed by large-scale immigration of Moors
(i.e. Berbers) from North Africa and also by smaller numbers of
Arabs, which completely transformed the culture of the peninsula. The
Umayyad Caliphate was the political embodiment of the Ummah, the

community of all Muslim believers, and a direct link back to the time of Muhammad. However, the caliphate's unity became increasingly strained as it expanded and in 750 the Umayyads were overthrown by the Abbasid dynasty. A general massacre of the Umayyad family followed. One of the few to escape, Abd al-Rahman, made his way to Iberia – *al-Andalus* to the Muslims – and founded a breakaway state at Córdoba. The emirate flourished and Córdoba became, with a population of around 200,000, by far the largest and richest city in Western Europe and probably the fifth largest city in the world. Córdoba was also Europe's most dynamic cultural centre. Jewish and Christian scholars were welcomed alongside Muslims to study the science and philosophy of the Classical world at its many schools.

The emirate was not only wealthy and culturally sophisticated, it also had a very efficient military organisation with a large and well-organised professional standing army of infantry and light cavalry. The army was especially strong in archers and the royal armouries manufactured 20,000 arrows every month. The bow was generally regarded as a secondary weapon by the Vikings, and they used it mainly in skirmishing before a battle started. Both infantry and cavalry wore mail or scale armour, and iron helmets, which were available only to richer Viking warriors. The emirate's elite warriors were the mamluks, slave soldiers, usually bought as children and brought up as warriors. Despite their slave status, mamluks were respected and could become wealthy and influential. The standing army allowed the emirate to react quickly to Viking raids in comparison to Francia or the Anglo-Saxon kingdoms, where it took time to raise and gather levy-based local defence forces. These states also found it difficult to get men to fulfil their military obligations because they were reluctant to leave their homes and families unprotected. This was not an issue with mamluks. A state of near continuous war prevailed between the emirate and the Christian states of the north, the kingdoms of Galicia and Asturias, and of Navarre, and the County of Barcelona. This attracted many highly motivated jihadis. As their survival depended on it, the Christian states were also geared for war and the Vikings would find no easy pickings anywhere in Iberia.

Al-Majus

Muslim chroniclers sometimes refer to Vikings as *al-Urdumaniyin*, meaning 'Northmen', but it is more common for them to be described as *al-Majus*. Derived from 'magi', this was a word originally used by Arabs to describe the Zoroastrians of Persia, but it acquired pejorative overtones and was used in the same way that Christian writers would often simply describe Vikings as 'the pagans'. Modern historians have often claimed that Christian writers exaggerated both the violence of Viking raids and the size of Viking fleets and armies. However, Muslim chroniclers show the same sense of shock at the violence and audacity of Viking raiders and also agree broadly with Christian chroniclers about the size of Viking fleets and armies.

The first recorded Viking raid on the Iberian Peninsula took place in 844. Vikings from the Loire sailed south to the Gironde and, taking advantage of the dispute between Charles the Bald and Pippin of Aquitaine, they sailed up the River Garonne as far as Toulouse without meeting any resistance. After this success, the Vikings moved on to plunder the coast of Galicia and Asturias and, not for the last time, sacked the small port of Gijón. When the Vikings attacked La Coruña they were met by the army of King Ramiro I and were heavily defeated. Many of the Vikings' casualties were caused by the Galicians' ballistas – powerful torsion-powered projectile weapons that looked rather like giant crossbows. Seventy of the Vikings' longships were captured on the beach and burned. More of the Viking force was then lost in a storm. The survivors sailed on, round Cape Finistere and down the coast of modern Portugal, which was then almost entirely under the control of Córdoba. When the Vikings landed near Lisbon in August, the Andalusian chronicler al-Razi says that they still had 108 ships in their fleet (fifty-four large ships and fifty-four smaller ones). This suggests that when it set out from the Loire, the Viking fleet must have numbered around 200 ships. The Vikings plundered the countryside around Lisbon for thirteen days, fighting three battles with Moorish forces before withdrawing.

The sack of Seville

Messengers from the governor of Lisbon rode to Córdoba to raise the alarm. The emir, Abd al-Rahman II, in turn put the governors of all the coastal provinces on alert, but not before the Vikings had sacked the port of Cadiz and the walled hill town of Medina-Sidonia, some 20 miles inland. Part of the fleet sailed to Morocco and sacked the city of Asilah before rejoining the main force. The Vikings then sailed into the River Guadalquivir, which ran through the emirate's most prosperous territories and led ultimately to Córdoba itself. On 29 September, the Vikings set up a base on Isla Menor, an island in the Guadalquivir about 30 miles from the sea: Andalusian sources say that they now had eighty ships. The next day the Vikings sent four ships to plunder the nearby village of Coria del Rio. Many of the inhabitants were killed. On 1 October, the whole fleet sailed 15 miles further up river to Seville. Seville was a prize worth taking. The mythical hero Hercules was said to have founded the city and under Roman rule it became a wealthy river port exporting wine, grain and olive oil. Seville continued to grow under Moorish rule and in the ninth century it was probably the second most important city in the emirate, after Córdoba. The Vikings had seen cities before in Francia but most were the shrunken, depopulated cores of Roman towns that had declined along with the empire that founded them. In Iberia, town life was reinvigorated by inclusion in the vast free trade area that was the Islamic empire. As they approached Seville, the Vikings must have been dizzy at the thought of the riches it must contain. Despite the warnings, Seville's governor seems not to have taken any special measures to protect his city and he fled before the Vikings arrived, leaving the inhabitants leaderless. When lookouts spotted the Vikings disembarking on the riverbank, the townspeople bravely but unwisely left the safety of the city walls and sallied out to fight them. They were little better than an undisciplined mob and soon lost their nerve and panicked when the Vikings attacked, scattering in all directions. In the chaos, the Vikings stormed into the city and spent seven days of unhindered plundering, killing and taking captive those of the inhabitants who had not fled to take refuge in the mountains.

After they had finished looting Seville, the Vikings withdrew back to their base on Isla Menor from where they continued to send out raiding parties towards Córdoba and other cities. A few days later Vikings returned to Seville, hoping that some of the refugees might have returned. Only a few had; they took refuge in a mosque, where the Vikings massacred them. While this was going on, Moorish forces were gathering in the hills above Seville and cavalry patrols were scouring the countryside, harassing Viking foraging parties. One large party (an improbable 16,000-strong, according to the chronicler Ibn al-Kutia) was ambushed and wiped out. On another occasion 500 Vikings were killed and four fully laden ships taken. As October drew on, the Vikings' position became increasingly insecure. On 7 (or 11) November, the Moors used a feigned retreat to draw another large Viking force into an ambush at Tablada, near Seville. Over 1,000 Vikings were killed, including their leader, and 400 were captured along with thirty ships. The Moors hanged many of the dead in palm trees and burned the ships. The captives were all beheaded. The emir sent 200 of the severed heads to his friends in Asilah by way of announcing his victory. The surviving Vikings were trapped and hungry but they still had their prisoners to bargain with. The Moors allowed the Vikings to withdraw after they agreed to release their prisoners in exchange for food and clothes. Moorish chroniclers last recorded what was left of the fleet as it passed Lisbon on its way back to the Loire. It would seem likely that less than a quarter of the Vikings who had set out on the expedition made it back alive.

In the aftermath of the raid, the emir ordered the strengthening of the coast defences and built a new armoury at Seville. He also ordered the construction of a fleet and recruited a force of well-paid sailors. The warships built by the Moors were a type of large, fast, sailing galley known as a dromon. They carried crews of fifty to a hundred oarsmen and as many soldiers, and had two masts mounting lateen sails, which gave a ship a superior windward sailing ability compared to the Viking square sail. The emir ordered that the ships be fitted with catapults that could throw incendiary bombs made with naptha. These alone gave the Moorish warships a decisive advantage over the Vikings' longships.

The great raid of Hastein and Björn Ironsides

The greatest of all Viking expeditions to Spain was led by two of the most famous of all Viking leaders, Björn Ironsides and Hastein. Björn was later believed to be one of the many sons of the legendary Ragnar Lodbrok. When he was a child, Björn's mother was supposed to have given him a magical invulnerability to wounds for which he earned the nickname 'Ironsides'. Hastein was the wily Viking chieftain who later proved to be such a thorn in the side of Alfred the Great. Björn and Hastein left their base on the Loire in 859 with a fleet of sixty-two ships to raid along the coast of Galicia and Asturias. Finding local resistance too strong, the Vikings moved on to pillage the emirate's west coast. Here they evidently enjoyed greater success. The emirate's coastguards captured two longships scouting ahead of the main fleet and found that they were already full of treasure, provisions and captives. The fleet suffered another defeat when it landed at Niebla near Huelva in south-west Spain. The fleet next put into the mouth of the Guadalquivir, perhaps with the intention of sacking Seville for a second time, but it was confronted by the new Moorish fleet. The Vikings had no answer to its incendiary weapons and they fled after several longships were burned. The Viking way was always to move on if resistance proved too strong in one place, knowing that they would eventually catch somewhere off-guard. Finally, at Algeciras, a few miles from Gibraltar, they achieved complete surprise, taking and sacking the town and burning its main mosque.

Björn and Hastein took their fleet through the Straits of Gibraltar into the Mediterranean. Though Vikings had never plundered in the Mediterranean before, the sea was no stranger to piracy, and Italy and Francia suffered frequent raids by Arab and Moorish pirates based in North Africa. The Vikings landed first on the African coast, at Nakur in the vicinity of modern Melilla. Local forces put up only a little resistance before fleeing and the Vikings plundered freely for a week, capturing the harem of a local ruler, which was later ransomed by the emir of Córdoba. The Vikings also captured some black Africans, who they described as *blámenn* ('blue men'), who had probably been brought to North Africa by Arab slave traders. The Vikings found them so exotic that they kept some of them. They were eventually sold again as slaves and finished up in Ireland. From Melilla, Björn and Hastein returned to Spain, plundering the coast of Murcia and then the Balearic Islands. Returning to the mainland, the Vikings continued north along the Mediterranean coast, sacking Narbonne and then setting up a winter camp on an island in the Camargue, a marshy delta of the River Rhône. In the spring, Björn and Hastein sailed over 100 miles up the Rhône, sacking Nîmes, Arles and Valence. After the Franks defeated them in a battle, the pair judged it wise to head back to the open sea and sailed east along the Côte d'Azur to Italy.

Hastein's mistake

According to a colourful but surely legendary account by the Norman monk Dudo of St Quentin, Björn and Hastein landed at the Ligurian port of Luni and mistook it for Rome. Luni had enjoyed modest prosperity in the Roman period as a port for exporting the pure white Cararra marble from the nearby Alpi Apuane, but by the ninth century it was little more than a village and the scant ruins that remain today make it hard to imagine that anyone could ever have mistaken it for Rome. But why spoil a good story? The glory-hungry Vikings were determined to capture the most famous of all cities. Judging the city's defences to be too strong to storm, Hastein came up with a plan to gain entry by a ruse. Viking emissaries approached the townspeople, telling them that they were exiles seeking provisions and shelter for their sick chieftain. On a return visit the emissaries told the townspeople that their chieftain had died and asked permission to enter the city to give him a Christian burial. The unsuspecting townspeople agreed and a solemn procession of Vikings followed their chief's coffin to the grave at which point Hastein, still very much alive and fully armed, leapt out of the coffin and slew the city's bishop. In the resulting confusion, the Vikings sacked the city. When he was told that he had been misinformed, and that he had not after all, sacked Rome, Hastein felt so disappointed that he ordered the massacre of Luni's entire male population. This story was repeated by many later Norman writers and the same ruse was attributed to later Norman leaders such as Robert

Guiscard, Bohemund of Taranto and Roger I of Sicily. It is evidence that medieval warriors admired cunning as much as bravery and skill at arms. The Vikings moved another 60 miles down the Tuscan coast to the mouth of the Arno, sacking Pisa and then, following the river upstream, also the hill-town of Fiesole above Florence. After this the Viking fleet disappears for a year. Björn and Hastein must have wintered somewhere and it may be that they sailed into the eastern Mediterranean to raid the Byzantine Empire. Late Arabic and Spanish sources claim that Vikings raided Greece and Alexandria. If they did it was probably Björn's and Hastein's fleet.

The fleet reappears in 861 when it passed through the Straits of Gibraltar again, this time homeward bound. The straits are only 9 miles wide so the chances of the Vikings slipping through unobserved were slim and the Moorish fleet was ready and waiting for them. Of Björn's and Hastein's remaining sixty ships, only twenty escaped the ambush the Moors had prepared for them. Björn and Hastein may have been unaware that a strong surface current flows constantly through the straits from the Atlantic into the Mediterranean Sea. During the Second World War, sixty-two German U-boats entered the Mediterranean undetected by riding this underwater current with their engines turned off. Not one was ever able to get out again against the current. Björn and Hastein may have had the same problem, their slow progress against it giving the Moors plenty of time to intercept them.

Undaunted by this disaster Björn and Hastein continued raiding as they sailed homewards. Just before they left Spanish waters, they raided the small Christian kingdom of Navarre and sacked Pamplona. In a spectacular coup they captured its King Garcia I, and ransomed him for the incredible sum of 70,000 gold dinars (approximately 679 pounds/308 kg of gold). The survivors of the expedition returned to the Loire in 862 very rich men. After the expedition, Björn and Hastein split up. Björn headed back to Denmark, perhaps intending to use his wealth and reputation to launch a bid for the throne. He never made it and died in Frisia after losing everything in a shipwreck. Hastein stayed on the Loire: he still had a long and profitable career ahead of him.

The daring nature of Björn's and Hastein's expedition secured their reputations as legendary commanders but the cost had been very high: less than a third of those who had set out three years earlier had made it back. This must have given other Vikings pause for thought for, though they continued to raid the Iberian Peninsula until the early eleventh century, there was no return to the Mediterranean. The Straits of Gibraltar had proved to be a dangerous and unavoidable bottleneck for any fleet trying to get into or out of the Mediterranean and in the future the Vikings kept well clear. The Moors defeated major raids in 889, 912–13, 966 and 971. The raiders in 889 got as far as Seville before they were defeated, once again, on the fields of Tablada. The survivors of the raid settled in the surrounding countryside and many subsequently converted to Islam. This was the only known Viking settlement in Iberia. During the course of their expeditions to Iberia, Vikings may have accidentally discovered the Atlantic island of Madeira. The evidence for this comes from an unusual source, the DNA of Madeiran house mice, which indicates that they were introduced to the then uninhabited island from Northern Europe, probably as stowaways, some time between around 900–1050.

An embassy to the king of the Majus

There probably were also more peaceful contacts between the Vikings and the Moors. There was strong demand in the Emirate of Córdoba and in the Moorish states in North Africa for Frankish, Slavic, English and Irish slaves, and many of these would have been supplied either directly or indirectly through middlemen by Viking slave traders. Many of the younger male captives were destined to be castrated: al-Andalus was famous as the main supplier of eunuchs to the Islamic world. In 845, after the Viking attack on Seville, the emir Abd al-Rahman sent an embassy led by al-Ghazal to visit the king of the Majus with gifts for him and his queen. Al-Ghazal described the land of the Majus as an island, three days journey from the mainland. There were other islands in the vicinity, which the king ruled too. Before his audience, al-Ghazal insisted that he should not be asked to kneel before the king. This was agreed, but when he arrived at the king's hall he found that the entrance had been lowered so that he would be forced to enter on his knees. The perfect diplomat, al-Ghazal resolved the difficulty by lying on his back and pushing himself in, feet first. This would very likely have impressed rather than irritated his hosts, who would have recognised something of themselves in his determination not to be humiliated. The king's wife Noud took a fancy to al-Ghazal and seduced him, assuring him that the Majus did not suffer from sexual jealousy and that women were free to leave their husbands at will. Al-Ghazal was correct that Scandinavian women had the right to divorce, but as for the absence of sexual jealousy, this was wishful thinking. A wife's adultery was usually taken very seriously by her husband and in some parts of Scandinavia he had the right to kill both her and her lover if they were caught together: he may actually have mistaken a favoured concubine for a queen. It is not known which king al-Ghazal visited. If he had mistaken the Jutland peninsula for an island he may have visited the Danish king Horik. Alternatively, he may have visited a Viking warlord in Ireland, possibly Turgeis, whose wife was called Auðr, which is not too different to Noud. The purpose of al-Ghazal's embassy is not stated either but it was almost certainly to do with trade – slaves if he had gone to Ireland, furs from the northern forests if he had gone to Denmark.

Ultimately the Vikings had no great impact on the Iberian Peninsula. Their raids were bloody and destructive but both the Christians and the Moors were able to contain them. As a result, the Vikings did not act as a catalyst for change by upsetting the local balance of power as they did in so many other places that they raided. Writing in the 1150s, the Andalusian geographer al-Zuhri summarised the Vikings as: 'fierce, brave and strong, and excellent seamen. When they attacked, the coastal peoples fled for fear of them. They only appeared every six or seven years, never in less than forty ships and sometimes up to one hundred. They overcame anyone they met at sea, robbed them and took them captive'. So, just another bunch of barbarians.

CHAPTER 7

KIEV, CONSTANTINOPLE AND BOLGHAR

VIKINGS IN EASTERN EUROPE TO 1041

It was in the east that the Viking combination of violence and commerce was at its most organised. The great attraction that drew the Vikings east was the *dirhem*, a high quality silver coin minted in huge quantities in the Arab Abbasid Caliphate and other Muslim states. The caliphate's vast wealth drew in luxury goods from across the known world, including slaves, beeswax, honey and furs from Northern Europe. Arab merchants bought these goods from the nomadic Khazars and Bulgars who lived on the steppes north of the Caspian Sea, paying for them with dirhems. These coins began to circulate among the Slavs, Balts and Finns and by around 780 were beginning to turn up at trading places like Staraja Ladoga on Lake Ladoga and Grobina on the Baltic Sea, where they came into the hands of Swedish merchants. This encouraged the Swedes to begin exploring the river systems of Eastern Europe to try to discover their source. The Swedes may have been motivated by commerce but their expansion in the east was no more peaceful than the Danish and Norwegian expansion in the west because most of their trade goods came from slave-raiding and tribute-gathering.

1. **ABOVE, TOP** The three major Viking
pagan gods: (from left) the one-eyed high
god Odin; hammer-wielding Thor; and the
fertility god Freyr as depicted in a twelfth-
century tapestry from Skog, Sweden.

2. **ABOVE** Reconstructed chieftain's
longhouse at Borg in the Lofoten Islands,
Norway. Housing both people and
livestock under one roof, the longhouse
was the typical Viking Age dwelling.

3. **LEFT, TOP** Ancestors of the Viking longship: Bronze Age ships with raiding parties on petroglyphs from Tanumshede, Sweden.

4. **LEFT, CENTRE** Evidence of state formation: the Vendel Period burial mounds at Gamla Uppsala, Sweden, traditionally associated with the proto-historic Yngling dynasty.

5. **LEFT, BELOW** The 23-metre long Gokstad ship, built *c*. 895–900, could carry a crew of around sixty-five men on long open sea voyages.

6. **RIGHT, TOP** The tenth-century Viking helmet from Gjermundbu in Norway is the most complete ever found. There is no evidence that Viking helmets ever had horns.

7. **RIGHT, BELOW** King Edmund of East Anglia is martyred by the pagan Danes in 869, in a fifteenth-century wall painting from Pickering church, North Yorkshire.

8. **LEFT** Irish monastic round tower at Glendalough: used as bell towers, treasuries and emergency refuges, dozens of such towers were built during Ireland's Viking Age.

9. **BELOW** Golden Gate of Kiev, built by Yaroslav the Wise, in 1017–24, as a monumental entry to the Rus capital. The gate was substantially reconstructed in 1982.

10. **RIGHT, TOP** The ruins of Luni, on the coast of Liguria: The city was sacked in 860 by Hastein, who supposedly mistook it for Rome.

11. **RIGHT** Constantinople's mighty fifth-century fortifications made it impervious to attacks by the Rus in 860, 907, 941 and 1043.

12. **BELOW** Modern replica of a *knarr*, a long-distance trade ship, under sail: it was in ships like these that Norse seafarers crossed the Atlantic Ocean.

13. **ABOVE, TOP** Traditional haymaking in the Faeroe Islands. Viking settlers in the North Atlantic were pastoralists, dependent on the hay harvest to see their livestock through the winter.

14. **ABOVE** Thingvellir, Iceland. The sheltered rift was the meeting place of the Icelandic assembly, the Althing, from *c.* 930 until 1798.

15. **RIGHT, TOP** Reconstruction of the Norse settlement at L' Anse aux Meadows in Newfoundland, the earliest known European settlement in the Americas.

16. **RIGHT, CENTRE** Aerial view of Hedeby: in the Viking Age it was Scandinavia's largest town and most important international trade centre.

17. **RIGHT, BELOW** Aerial view of Trelleborg, Sjælland: it was one of several circular forts built by Harald Bluetooth to help impose royal authority across Denmark.

18. **RIGHT** From Viking warlord to patron of the church: King Cnut and his English consort, Aelfgifu, present a gold cross to Hyde Abbey in 1031.

19. **BELOW** Survival of pagan knowledge: the mythological wolf Fenrir and the world tree Yggdrasil from a seventeenth century copy of Snorri Sturluson's *Edda*.

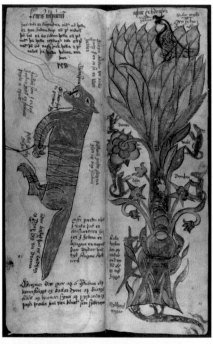

20. **BELOW** Ruins of Hvalsey church. A marriage here in 1408 is one of the last recorded events in the history of the Norse Greenland colony.

Because neither the Scandinavians, nor the Slavs, Balts and Finns who inhabited Eastern Europe had literate cultures at that time, we know far less about the Vikings' military activities in the east than we do about those in the west. The most valuable contemporary accounts come from the writings of Arab geographers and travellers, and Byzantine chroniclers and statesmen, many of which are informed by direct personal experience. Perhaps because they felt less threatened by the Vikings, these writers, especially the Arabs, had a different perspective to western writers, showing much greater interest in Viking customs and trade than in their raids. Viking activities in the east were closely linked to the origins of the Russian state so they were a major theme of the earliest Russian history, the twelfth century *Russian Primary Chronicle*. This is a difficult work to use, however, because it contains much material that is clearly legendary, and because its main purpose was to establish the legitimacy of medieval Russia's ruling Ryurikid dynasty. Viking adventures in the east feature in the Norse saga traditions, but these are the latest of all the main primary sources, not having been written down until the thirteenth century. The only truly contemporary Scandinavian sources for the Vikings in Eastern Europe are ninth–eleventh century Swedish runestones commemorating men who went on expeditions to Russia and Greece.

From Swedes to Rus

By the 830s at the latest, the Swedes had forged trade routes from the Baltic through to the Black Sea and the Caspian Sea. Many had gone much further and sailed across these seas to trade in Constantinople and Baghdad, the capitals of the Greek Byzantine Empire and the Arab Abbasid Caliphate respectively. Along the way the Swedes operating permanently in the east acquired a new name, the 'Rus'. The origins of this name, from which Russia gets its name, is disputed. The most widely accepted explanation is that it is derived from *Ruotsi*, the Finnish name for the Swedes. *Ruotsi* itself probably derives from Old Norse *roðr*, meaning 'a crew of oarsmen'. An alternative view is that the term is of Greek origin, derived from literary references to the *Rusioi* ('blondes'), an alternative name for the well-travelled Heruls from

Jutland who served the Byzantine Empire as mercenaries in the sixth century.

The Rus founded settlements or, probably more often, seized control of existing settlements along the trade routes. These gave Russia its Viking name *Garðariki*, the 'kingdom of cities'. The Rus became the ruling warrior and merchant elite of these settlements, but the majority of their populations were always native Slavs or Finns. The Rus settlements became bases from which to raid the neighbouring Finnish and Slavic tribes for tribute in slaves and furs, both of which the Greeks and Arabs were eager to buy. Arab writers say that the Rus lived entirely by plunder and did not practice agriculture. Winter was the main raiding season, when travel overland was easier because the ground was hard-frozen. Trading expeditions began to gather in the spring, as soon as the ice on the rivers broke up, and returned home in the autumn. The trade routes took the Rus through hostile territory, so they always travelled in groups for safety. The most dangerous places were the portages, places where it was necessary to carry the ships and their cargoes overland to get from one river system into another or to avoid impassable rapids. Because the portages were unavoidable, they made ideal places for ambushes.

The main source of archaeological evidence for a Scandinavian presence in Russia during the Viking Age comes from hundreds of graves furnished with typical Scandinavian artefacts. Both male and female graves have been found, indicating that the Rus travelled in family groups. According to the Arab writer Ibn Hawqal the Rus were divided into three groups, the Kuyavia, Slavia and Arcania, but it is not clear whether he was referring to ethnic or geographical divisions. A group of Rus who visited the court of the Frankish emperor Louis the Pious with a Byzantine diplomatic mission in 839 claimed that they were ruled by a 'khagan', a Turkic word cognate with khan, which they must have adopted as a result of their contacts with the Bulgar and Khazar nomads with whom they often traded. When the Franks worked out that the Rus were really Swedes, they suspected that they were Viking spies and detained them while they decided whether or not they were bona fide travellers. The Rus might have expected to be greeted with suspicion by the Franks and so have used an exotic title to increase their status or to distance themselves from the Vikings who had so recently sacked Dorestad four times.

The foundation of the Rus state

During the second half of the ninth century, the Rus settlements were united into a single kingdom. According to the semi-legendary account of the *Russian Primary Chronicle*, the first Rus state was founded some time around 860–62. The story told in the chronicle is improbable to say the least. The Slavs became tired of their constant internecine wars, so they appealed to the Rus to send them a leader to rule them according to law. They chose three brothers. Rurik, the eldest, established himself as ruler of Novgorod; Sineus became ruler of Beloozero (now Belozersk) on Lake Beloye; and the third brother, Truvor, became ruler of Izborsk near Pskov. When Rurik's brothers died two years later, he inherited their territories and became ruler of all of north-west Russia. Novgorod was not founded until *c.* 930 so Rurik's capital was probably at Gorodische, a former island 2 miles south of the modern city centre, which has produced substantial evidence of Scandinavian occupation in the ninth century. Rurik is supposed to have died *c.* 879 and was succeeded by Oleg (Old Norse Helgi) (r. *c.* 879–*c.* 913). According to the *Primary Chronicle*, Oleg was a kinsman of Rurik but early Novgorod chronicles describe him merely as one of his army commanders. The rulers of the Rus used the title *kniaz*, which is usually translated into English as 'prince', which implies something less than full sovereignty. However, *kniaz* shares a common Indo-European root with English 'king', which more accurately describes their power and status.

At about the same time that Rurik is said to have become ruler of Novgorod, two brothers, Askold and Dir, sailed south down the River Dnepr and captured the town of Kiev from the Poljani Slavs. According to the *Primary Chronicle*, it was Askold and Dir who led the first Rus attack on Constantinople in 860. Like all subsequent Rus attacks on Constantinople, it was defeated. Around 882, Oleg brought an army of Vikings and Slavs down the Dnepr from Novgorod and captured Kiev. Askold and Dir were both killed in the attack. Oleg subsequently moved from Novgorod to Kiev and made it the capital of the Rus state. Russians have traditionally seen the foundation of the Kievan Rus state as marking the origins of the modern Russian state. It therefore remains hard for Russians to accept that the city which they see as the birthplace of their nation is now, as a result of the break-up of the USSR in 1991, the capital of an independent country, Ukraine.

According to the *Primary Chronicle*, Oleg led an attack on Constantinople in 907. If he did no one in Constantinople appears to have noticed because it is not mentioned in any Byzantine sources. The attack may have been invented to explain trade treaties that the *Primary Chronicle* says were agreed between the Rus and the Byzantine government in 907 and 911. The 907 agreement gave Rus merchants the rights to receive food supplies in Constantinople for up to six months, a monthly allowance, the use of public baths, and supplies of anchors and sails for their ships. In return, the Rus paid a toll of twelve grivnas of silver (about 6 pounds/2.7 kg) for each ship they brought. The Rus were not allowed to live within the city walls, could not bring any weapons into the city with them and, when they were in the city, had always to be accompanied by a government official. Rus merchants from Kiev were given priority treatment over those from other centres. In the 911 treaty, the Rus agreed not to plunder Byzantine ships and to give whatever help was necessary to any they found in difficulties. Other clauses concerned crimes committed by the Rus in Byzantine territories, the ransom of prisoners, return of runaway slaves and terms for Rus who wanted to join the Byzantine army. Oleg died soon after these treaties were agreed, probably in 913. The *Primary Chronicle*'s account of Oleg's death is plainly legendary. Having been warned by a soothsayer that his favourite horse would cause his death, Oleg vowed never to ride or even see it again. When the horse died five years later, Oleg mocked the soothsayer for his false prophecy. But when Oleg went to view the horse's skeleton, a poisonous snake slithered out from its skull and fatally bit his foot. In reality, it is more likely that he was killed during an unsuccessful raid in the Caspian Sea.

Oleg was succeeded by Igor (Old Norse Ingvar) (r. *c.* 913–45). Though most modern historians think it is unlikely, the *Primary Chronicle* claims that Igor was Rurik's son, brought up as a foster-son by Oleg after his father's death. Fostering was, however, a common practice in Viking Age Scandinavia, at all levels of society. Igor is the first truly historical ruler of the Rus but his reign was not a great success. In 941, Igor led a disastrous attack on Constantinople. Most of his fleet was destroyed by Byzantine galleys fitted with Greek Fire projectors and he was lucky to escape with his life. He was probably also the leader of a Rus rampage around the Caspian Sea in 943. This expedition too ended in failure after sickness decimated its ranks while it was occupying the Muslim city of Barda in modern Azerbaijan. Igor raised a new army of Rus, Slavs and Pecheneg nomads for another attack on Constantinople in 944, but the *Primary Chronicle* claims that the Byzantines bought him off with an offer of tribute and a new trade treaty in 945. However, the terms offered by the Byzantines were noticeably worse than those won by Oleg in 911, which does not suggest that he was negotiating from a position of strength. The treaty set limits on the amount of silk Rus merchants could buy in Constantinople and banned them from making winter camps on Berezan Island at the mouth of the River Dnepr. This measure was to prevent the Rus becoming a permanent presence in the Black Sea. The poor returns from his expeditions led Igor to double his demands for tribute from his Slav subjects in 945. When he raided the Drevljane for the second time in a month, they attacked and killed him. The Byzantine writer Leo the Deacon records the story that his killers bent two trees together, tied his legs to them and then let them spring apart so that his body was torn in two.

The Drevljane paid a high price for their defiance. Igor's successor, his son Svyatoslav (r. 945–72) was still an infant, so it fell to his for- midable wife Olga (Old Norse Helga) to defend the Kievan state. The *Primary Chronicle* describes the vicious, and probably legendary, reprisals Olga took against the Drevljane. After Igor's death, the Drevljane sent an embassy to Olga to propose that she marry their chief and so unite the two peoples. Olga had them buried alive in a burial mound. A second embassy was sent and Olga burned its members to death in a bath house. Olga next invited 5,000 of the Drevljane to a funeral feast to commemorate Igor's life. The Drevljane must have been remarkably lacking in curiosity about the disappearance of their two embassies to Olga because they turned up. When the Drevljane had got thoroughly drunk, she ordered the warriors of her *druzhina* ('bodyguard', the Rus equivalent of the Viking *lið*) to massacre them. Finally, Olga laid siege to the Drevljane's stronghold of Iskorosten (now Korosten, Ukraine). The Drevljane offered to pay tribute in furs and honey in return for peace, but Olga asked only for three sparrows and three pigeons from each household. When the birds had been delivered, they were given to her warriors, who tied pieces of sulphur to their wings and set them alight. The terrified birds flew straight back to their nests in Iskoresten, setting the whole town ablaze. Fighting so many fires at once was impossible, so the Drevljane fled the city only to be massacred by the vengeful Rus. This stratagem features in many other folk tales about Viking and Norman leaders: Guthrum is said to have captured Cirencester in Wessex in this way, for example. Whatever the truth of these colourful stories, there can be no doubt that Olga proved to be a most able regent, preserving the unity of the Kievan state until Svyatoslav attained his majority *c.* 963.

The river routes of the Rus

The trade routes on which the early Rus state depended began in the Gulf of Finland, the long arm of the Baltic Sea that separates Estonia and Finland. Ships heading for Russia from the west generally took the sheltered passage through the thousands of islands and skerries along the Finnish coast to the mouth of the River Neva, where St Petersburg now stands. Broad and deep, the River Neva gave easy access to Lake Ladoga, Europe's largest lake, about 45 miles inland. Swedish merchants probably first ventured into Lake Ladoga in the first half of the eighth century in order to obtain furs from the local Finns to trade to western Europe. Miniver, the silky white winter coat of the stoat, was particularly prized and commanded high prices. Around 750, a permanent settlement of merchants and craftsmen developed at Staraja Ladoga a few miles from the lake on its major feeder river, the Volkhov. The earliest structures so far discovered on the site have been dated by dendrochronology to 753. The town became known to Scandinavians as *Aldeigjuborg*, from its original Finnish name Aloda-joki ('lowland river'). The Slavic name Ladoga is also derived from the Finnish name. From its foundation, the town had a mixed population of Scandinavians, Finns and Slavs. Each of these ethnic groups had their own cemeteries, suggesting that in life they had been segregated into their own quarters in the town. Grave goods from Scandinavian burials suggest that there were close links to the large Swedish island of Gotland: vast quantities of dirhems have been discovered in silver hoards on this island confirming its key role in trade with Russia and the east. Excavations of the town have revealed evidence for a wide range of manufacturing, including jewellery- and glass-making, blacksmithing, bronze-casting, and amber-, bone- and antler-working. Many of these manufactured goods would have been traded for furs with the Finns, who lacked metalworking skills. Towns were an obvious attraction to raiders (both native and Scandinavian) and Staraja Ladoga was protected by a rampart at an early stage in its development. The town was, therefore, already well-established when the first silver dirhems began turning up there in the 780s. Staraja Ladoga's easy access from the Baltic made it vulnerable to Viking raids from Scandinavia. There is archaeological evidence that the town was burned around 860 and it was sacked by the Norwegian jarl Erik of Lade around 996–7, and probably by his half-brother Svein around 1015.

Until the tenth century, Staraja Ladoga remained the most important of the trade centres under Rus control. This was thanks to its strategic position, close to Lake Ladoga, where the river routes to the Black Sea and the Caspian Sea divided. Merchants who wanted to trade with the Islamic world would sail the few miles back down the Volkhov into Lake Ladoga and sail east along its southern shore until they reached the mouth of the River Svir, Ladoga's most important feeder after the Volkhov. An 80-mile sail up the Svir led into Lake Onega. From Lake Onega the River Vytegra was followed to its headwaters from where boats had to be dragged overland across the Baltic-Caspian Sea watershed into the headwaters of the River Kovzha. The Kovzha was followed to Lake Beloye and the Finnish town of Kisima. In the nineteenth century a canal, the Baltic-Volga waterway, was built across the watershed to link Lake Onega with Lake Beloye. In the tenth century Kisima was abandoned in favour of Beloozero, on the southern shore of the lake at the place where the River Sheksna flows out on its way to join the River Volga. Like Kisima, Beloozero was mainly inhabited by

Finns when it was founded but over the next few centuries they were gradually replaced by Slavs, migrating from the south. Archaeological excavations have produced plenty of evidence of the town's wide-ranging trade connections: jewellery and weapons from Scandinavia, combs from Frisia, wine amphorae from Crimea, pottery from Bulgaria, glass from Constantinople and amber from the Baltic Sea.

The first important centre merchants would have reached after sailing down the Sheksna into the Volga was Timerevo, a large unfor-tified trading place about 4 miles from modern Yaroslavl, which superseded it as the main trade centre in the region in 1010. Evidence from coin hoards suggests that Timerevo was probably founded around 830. Burials indicate a considerable Scandinavian presence in the town. Grave goods included an 'Ulfbhert' sword: Viking warriors prized these exceptionally high quality Frankish swords inlaid with their maker's name. Several Frankish swords have been found in Scandinavian burials in Russia, but they were not just imported for Rus warriors, they were also greatly prized by their Arab trading partners. Not far from Timerevo was another important Rus centre, Sarskoye Gorodishche on Lake Nero, near modern Rostov. This was originally a centre of the Finnish Merya tribe, which was taken over by the Rus in the early ninth century. Sarskoye Gorodishche declined in the late tenth century after the foundation of the mainly Slav town of Rostov around 963.

Bulgaria on the Volga

A few days' journey from Timerevo the merchants would have left territory controlled by the Rus. For the next 500 miles, the merchants had to pass through sparsely populated territory until they reached Bolghar, about 20 miles downstream from the confluence of the Volga and the Kama rivers. Bolghar was the trading place of the Volga Bulgars, a Turkic nomad tribe from central Asia who had arrived in the area under their leader Kotrag around 660. At around the same time another group of Bulgars migrated to the Balkans, where they founded the precursor of the modern Bulgarian state. When the Rus first made contact with the Volga Bulgars in the ninth century, they were pagan shamanists but they converted to Islam in the tenth century. Until a fort and a mosque were built there in the early tenth century, Bolghar had few permanent buildings and was probably occupied only on a seasonal basis. Bolghar was as far as most Rus merchants ever needed to go. The town was one terminus of the trans-Asian Silk Road and the major centre for fur trading with the Samoyedic peoples of the White Sea and northern Urals regions. To the south, the Volga linked Bolghar to the Khazar Khaganate and the Caspian Sea. Arab merchants travelled either the Volga or the Silk Road to Bolghar to buy slaves, furs, beeswax and honey, Baltic amber and Frankish swords from the Rus. As well as those desirable silver dirhems, Arab merchants also traded in silk, spices and fragrances, and colourful ceramic beads, which Rus women found irresistible. Local interpreters were available to help the Rus and the Arabs communicate with one another. The Bolghar khagan taxed merchants at the rate of 10 per cent of the value of their goods. The khan in his turn paid a proportion of the tax revenues to the powerful Khazar khagan who was his overlord. The Rus had their own quarter at Bolghar, close to the river, where they built wooden huts for themselves and set up a shrine and a wooden idol. The Rus believed that success in trade was a gift of their gods. Before trading, a Rus merchant would prostrate himself before the idol and recite what goods he had brought to sell, make an offering of food, and pray that he would be sent 'a merchant who has large quantities of dinars and dirhems and who will buy everything that I want and not argue with me about my price'. If trading went well, the merchant would sacrifice a number of sheep and cattle at the shrine as a thanks offering.

One of the Arab visitors to Bolghar, Ahmad ibn Fadlan (*fl. c.* 922), wrote a detailed account of his encounters with the Rus there. A devout and cultured Muslim, Ibn Fadlan made no attempt to disguise his disgust for the pagan Rus, comparing them to wandering asses because of their failure to wash after urinating or defecating, or having sex, and for not washing their hands after eating. The Rus did wash every morning but in water that was filthy because the same bowl was shared by many people who thought nothing of spitting or blowing their noses in it before passing it on to the next person. The Rus shunned the sick and treated their slaves badly (other Arab writers disagree, however, saying that they treated slaves well so that they could get the best price for them). The sex lives of the Rus both revolted and fascinated Ibn Fadlan, particularly the perfunctory way that they had sex with their slave girls in public, even while they were doing business with customers. Ibn Fadlan could not help admiring the appearance of the Rus. 'I have never seen bodies more perfect than theirs,' he writes. 'They were like palm trees. They were fair and ruddy.' The Rus wore cloaks, other Arab writers comment on their baggy trousers, and at all times they carried with them an axe, a sword, and a knife. The Rus were heavily tattooed, a custom they had probably adopted from contacts with Turkic nomad peoples like the Bulgars and Khazars. He was no less impressed by Rus women, describing the round brooches that they wore on their breasts, as made of copper, silver or gold depending on their status. Keys, symbols of a Viking woman's control of the household, hung from rings attached to the brooches. The women also wore neck rings made of silver or gold. Ibn Fadlan said as soon as a Rus man had 10,000 dirhems, he melted them down to make a neck ring for his wife. Every time he made another 10,000 dirhems, he gave his wife another neck ring. Vikings liked to wear their wealth both to show it off and for security, and it was the fate of most of the millions of dirhems the Rus received to be melted down and recast into arm and neck rings.

Ibn Fadlan also describes the magnificent appearance of the Rus king, who at the time of his visit would have been Igor. The king sat on a huge jewel-encrusted throne, surrounded by forty slave girls who were his concubines. The king rarely left his throne. If he wanted to empty his bowels a servant brought him a bowl and he would even have sex with his slave girls while he sat on the throne. If the king wanted to ride anywhere, his horse was brought into the hall, so he could mount – or dismount – directly from the throne. The king kept 400 warriors in his hall. These were the warriors of his *druzhina*, the king's personal warrior retinue. Like the Viking warriors of a *lið*, the warriors of the *druzhina*, were supposed to be loyal to their own death or that of the king. Each warrior, Ibn Fadlan says, had a personal slave girl to wash and dress him and serve him at table, and another to have sex with. Ibn Fadlan was clearly impressed by all the sex the Rus got to have.

A Viking ship burial

The burial customs of the Rus interested Ibn Fadlan greatly and he was pleased to have the chance to witness the funeral of one of their chiefs. The chief's body was placed in a temporary grave for ten days while preparations for a ship burial were made. It was Rus practice to sacrifice a slave to accompany the chief into the afterlife. The chief's slaves were asked if one of them would volunteer and one of the slave girls agreed. Ibn Fadlan says that it was usually slave girls who volunteered to be sacrificed. Whether they did this out of affection or because life as a sex-slave of the Rus was just so awful that a trip to Paradise seemed like an attractive option, he doesn't say. For the last ten days of her life, the slave girl was well treated but was also supervised at all times to make sure she did not try to run away if she had a change of heart. Meanwhile, special funerary clothes were made for the chief, and his ship was hauled out of the river and set up level on a funeral pyre. An old woman called the 'Angel of Death' oversaw all the funeral arrangements. Ibn Fadlan described her as a witch, 'thick-bodied and sinister': she was probably a *völva* (a seeress), who Vikings believed could practice magic and foretell the future. On the day of the funeral the chief's body was dressed and removed from its temporary resting place, then placed on a made-up bed in a tent on his ship with his weapons beside him. Offerings of food and alcoholic drink were placed in the ship, together with the dismembered bodies of a sacrificed dog, two horses, two cattle, a cock and a hen.

While this was taking place, the slave girl was passed around the chief's male relatives, each of whom had sex with her, telling her to tell her master that 'I only do this for my love of him'. When evening came, the slave girl took part in a ritual in which she was lifted up three times to look over a wooden frame. The first time she was lifted she said 'there I see my father and mother'. The second time she said 'there I see all my dead relatives sitting'. The third time she said: 'there I see my master sitting in paradise and it is green and beautiful. There are men and young people with him and he is calling me. Take me to him.' At that she was taken to the ship. She took off two bracelets she was wearing and gave them to the Angel of Death, whose job it was to kill her. The girl was then lifted onto the ship and given an intoxicating drink, which she sang over before drinking. The drink probably cont-ained a narcotic because she soon began to behave in a confused manner. Once the girl was thoroughly intoxicated she was taken into the tent. Now the chief's warriors began to bang staves on their shields to drown out the girl's cries so that the other slave girls would not be frightened and deterred from volunteering to die with their masters. A ritualised gang-rape followed. Six men entered the tent and had sex with the girl after which she was laid next to the chief. Four of the men held the girl's arms and legs, the other two held the opposite ends of a rope that had been tied around her neck so they could pull on them. All was now ready and the Angel of Death stabbed the girl repeatedly between the ribs while the two men strangled her to death. The girl's body was left next to the chief's.

The funeral ceremony now reached its climax. The chief's closest male relative, stripped naked, walked backwards towards the ship holding a burning torch and set light to the pyre. Then people app-roached the ship with more wood, each of them holding a burning brand which they threw onto the pyre. The ship and the tent were soon ablaze. One of the Rus told Ibn Fadlan that the Arabs were fools to put the bodies of those they loved most into the ground to be eaten by worms and insects. 'We burn them in the fire in an instant so that they enter paradise immediately and without delay.' After the fire had burned out, an earth mound was erected over the ashes and a wooden post erected on top, inscribed with the name of the chief, presumably in runes.

To the Khazar Khaganate

Adventurous Rus merchants could choose to continue another 900 miles down the Volga to trade at Itil (or Atil), the capital of the Khazar Khaganate. The location of Itil has not been identified for certain but it is very likely to have been near the village of Samosdelka in the Volga Delta, where excavations in 2008 revealed the remains of a substantial early medieval town. Rus merchants from Kiev could reach Itil by a shorter route if they sailed down the Dnepr to the Black Sea, and then into the Sea of Azov and the River Don to reach the Khazar border fortress of Sarkel, now lost under the waters of Stalin's Tsimlyansk reservoir. Upstream from Sarkel, the course of the Don comes to within 40 miles of the Volga. Today the Volga-Don canal links the two rivers at this point, but the Rus had to carry or drag their ships overland into the Volga to complete their journey by sailing downstream to Itil.

Arab visitors to Itil described it as being divided into three parts by two channels of the Volga. The western part of the city was the administrative centre, with law courts, a fortress and a military garrison. The eastern section was the commercial centre where the Rus and Arab merchants would have done business. Tolls levied at 10 per cent of the value goods sold in the markets here were the khaganate's main source of income. Between the eastern and western parts, on an island, was the royal centre with the palaces of the khagan and the bek. The Arabs described the khagan as a spiritual leader who lived in seclusion, while the bek was a vizier or prime minister who was responsible for the actual running of the khaganate and for leading military expeditions. While the royal palace and associated buildings were built of brick and stone, most of Itil's population lived in traditional felt yurts. Many people spent only the winter in the city, returning to the steppes in the summer to follow their herds. The khaganate was a tolerant and religiously diverse state. The khagan and the ruling classes had converted to Judaism in the earlier eighth century but most of their Khazar subjects remained loyal to their traditional shamanistic beliefs. Itil had communities of Christians, Muslims and pagans, most of them foreign merchants, who all had their own places of worship. A panel of seven judges – two Christians, two Muslims, two Jews, and one judge to represent the shamanists and pagans – sat to adjudicate in disputes between believers of different religions.

Serkland

For some Rus merchants, Itil was just a staging post on the long journey to the Abbasid Caliphate or, as the Vikings called it, Serkland (probably meaning 'shirt-land' from the loose-fitting Arab clothing). By taking a ship from Itil and crossing the Caspian Sea to reach the cities of Abaskun and Ardebil in present-day Iran, Rus merchants could pick up the caravan routes across the Iranian plateau and the Zagros Mountains and descend to the hot, dry plains of Mesopotamia to reach Baghdad. For a merchant who had originally set out from Sweden, this would be the end of a two- or even three-year journey. What he would have made of his first encounter with a camel is not known. Writing in the 840s the Persian geographer Ibn Khurradadhbih says that the Rus who traded in Baghdad tried to pass themselves off as Christians for political reasons, because Christians were more acceptable to Muslims than pagans, and that they paid the *jizya* tax that was levied on non-believers. The Arabs relied on Slav eunuchs to interpret for them when they wanted to do business with the Rus. The Arabs generally thought of their Rus visitors as a kind of *Saqaliba*, which was a term they used to describe fair-skinned, light-haired peoples like the Slavs. Other Arab writers, like the well-travelled al-Mas'udi (d. 957), recognised that they were the same people as the *Majus* who sometimes raided Muslim Spain.

Although it was only founded in 763, Baghdad had grown explosively and by the early ninth century it was the world's largest city with a population of over one million. Baghdad was chosen as the capital of the Abbasid Caliphate for political, economic and agricultural reasons. Baghdad was close to the geographical centre of the caliphate and was surrounded by the fertile irrigated farmland of the Mesopotamian plain. This allowed the large urban population to be supported without relying on food imports. The city was on the Silk Road, the major caravan route to China, and was also on the navigable River Tigris, giving easy access to Basra and the Persian Gulf, and beyond that to the trade routes to India and the Spice Islands of the East Indies. Rus merchants who made it this far must have been overwhelmed by the sights, smells and tastes of the produce on sale in the city's dozens of specialist markets, selling meat, vegetables, fruit, textiles, books, slaves, metalwork, Chinese goods: there was even a flower market. However, Baghdad does not seem to have captured the Viking imagination in the way Constantinople did. Perhaps too few made the long and arduous journey there, or it may just have been that Baghdad was hot, dusty and built mainly of dull mud brick so it just failed to impress in the same way that Constantinople's mighty stone and brick walls and vast cathedrals did.

Rus raiders on the Caspian Sea

On a few occasions Rus fleets reached the Caspian Sea and raided Muslim cities along its southern and western shores. These raids were made possible by the co-operation of the Khazars, whose territory they had to pass through to reach the Caspian Sea. The earliest recorded raid took place some time between 864 and 884 and was an unsuccessful attack on Abaskun. Abaskun was raided again, with more success, by a fleet of sixteen Rus ships in 910 and a third raid in the area was recorded in 911 or 912. In 913 the Rus returned in strength, with a fleet said by al-Mas'udi to number 500 ships, each crewed by 100 men. The fleet sailed down the Dnepr from Kiev, into the Black Sea and around the Crimea into the Sea of Azov. In return for a 50 per cent share of the plunder, the Khazar khagan agree to allow the Rus to sail up the Don past Sarkel and portage their ships overland into the Volga and so sail into the Caspian Sea.

The Rus first attacked Abaskun and then began to work their way west along the coast of Tabaristan and then north to the coast of Azerbaijan, which was also known as the Naphtha Coast because of its many natural oil wells. In Azerbaijan they raided inland, three days from the coast, to sack the caravan city of Ardebil. The coast was undefended and unprepared. The Rus plundered and burned, took captives and 'spilled oceans of blood' without meeting any effective opposition. When the Rus seized some islands off the coast of Shirvan, the emir marshalled every ship he could find and attacked their fleet. Lacking any experience of fighting on board ships, the Muslims were no match for the Rus and thousands were killed or drowned in the battle. On their return to the Volga, the Rus sent messengers to the khagan to tell him that they were on their way with his share of the plunder, but he was no longer in a position to guarantee their safe passage. The khagan's Muslim subjects, outraged by reports of their atrocities, attacked the Rus as they sailed up the Volga, killing, according to al-Mas'udi, 30,000 of them. The survivors continued their flight up the Volga only to be ambushed and massacred by the Bulgars. The leader of the Rus expedition is not known but it is likely to have been Oleg: quite possibly he was killed in these battles as he is said to have died in 913.

After this disaster, the Rus did not return to the Caspian Sea until 943, when they raided Azerbaijan again. The name of the expedition's leader is not known but Igor was ruler of the Kievan Rus at this time. The Rus rowed up the Kura river over 100 miles to the city of Barda. Greatly underestimating their strength, the emir confronted the Rus with an army of 600 Iranian and Kurdish mercenaries and 5,000 of the city folk outside the city walls. Faced with a ferocious onslaught by the Rus, the untrained city folk fled, quickly followed by the rest of the soldiers. Only the Iranians stood their ground and most of them were killed. After the Rus took the city, they did their best to calm the people, telling them that they had no quarrel with Islam and that they would treat them well if they were loyal to their new rulers. The wealthier city folk, who had something to lose, made no trouble for the Rus, but when the emir's forces tried to retake Barda, the common people rose up and attacked them. After this, the Rus gave the population three days to leave. Most ignored the ultimatum – they probably had nowhere to go – and on the fourth day the Rus turned on them, massacring thousands and taking 10,000 people captive. The Rus separated the adult men from the women and children and imprisoned them in the city's main mosque, demanding that they ransom themselves. A Christian civil servant negotiated a ransom of twenty dirhems a head. Some paid up but many Muslims refused because they did not think they should have been valued the same as *jizya*-paying Christians. The Rus eventually lost patience and massacred them. Those who did ransom themselves were given a clay token, which gave them safe passage. The Rus kept the women and children who, according to the Iranian writer Ibn Miskawayh (d. 1030), were raped and enslaved. The Vikings have a popular reputation for 'rape and pillage', but this actually is one of very few instances where a contemporary explicitly accuses them of raping women. The silence of the sources suggests that Vikings were neither better nor worse than most warriors of their day in this regard, not that rape itself was uncommon. Whoever they were owned by, enslaved women had no rights and it was taken for granted that they could be used for sexual gratification: they were, after all, just property.

Barda's ordeal came to an end when dysentery broke out among the Rus, steadily depleting their numbers. This encouraged the emir to lay siege to Barda. One night the Rus sallied out against the besiegers but were heavily defeated, losing 700 men. The Rus retreated to the city's citadel but the epidemic continued to take its toll. Under cover of night, the surviving Rus slipped out of the city with as much plunder as they could carry and, dragging their slaves with them, made for the River Kura and their ships. These had been kept under guard, presumably in a *longphort* type of fortification. After the Rus had departed for home, the Muslims dug up the graves of the warriors who had died in the epidemic to recover the swords that had been buried with them.

The raid on Barda needed the co-operation of the Khazars, but it must have caused considerable tensions with their Muslim neighbours and subjects. In about 960, the khagan Joseph wrote to Abd ar-Rahman III, the caliph of Córdoba, telling him that he was now preventing Rus ships entering the Caspian Sea to raid the Muslims. He had to do this, he said, because 'if I would give them any chance at all they would lay waste the whole land of the Muslims as far as Baghdad.' The Arabs would probably have agreed. The two Rus raids on the Caspian had created a very strong impression on the Muslim world. Ibn Miskawayh thought them formidable fighters, 'they do not recognise defeats,' he said, 'no one turns back until he has killed or been killed.' Another writer, Marwazi, praised their courage, saying that one Rus 'is equal to a number of any other nation'. He was grateful that the Rus fought on foot, 'if they had horses and were riders, they would be a great scourge to mankind'.

The road to Mikligarðr

Known simply as *Mikligarðr*, the 'great city', Constantinople held the Vikings in thrall more than any other place. With half a million inhabitants, Constantinople was Europe's largest city, and by a long way its most magnificent. It is not known exactly when the first Rus reached Constantinople, but it must have been before 839 when a group of them arrived at the Frankish court with a Byzantine diplomatic mission. A Byzantine hagiography *The Life of St George of Amastris*, written before 848, describes Rus raids on Amastris (now Amasra) on Anatolia's Black Sea coast not long after the saint's death in 806, which implies that they must have found their way to Constantinople some time in the early ninth century at the latest.

The main route to Constantinople from Staraja Ladoga followed the River Volkhov upstream to the fortified settlement of Gorodische ('fortress'), close to the point where the river flows out of Lake Ilmen. In the Viking Age the site of Gorodische was a low island, for which reason the Vikings knew it as *Holmgarð* ('island city'). Gorodische was a small Slav settlement that appears to have come under Scandinavian control around the middle of the ninth century, making this the most likely site of Rurik's capital. Many Scandinavian artefacts have been found on the site, including two amulets inscribed with runic charms. Around 930, Gorodische was abandoned in favour of a new site 2 miles downstream: this was Novgorod, the 'new city'. The Volkhov divided Novgorod in two, the Sofia bank on the west and the Merchantsi bank on the east. Late in the Viking Age, the two banks were linked by a bridge. On the Sofia bank merchants' and craftsmen's quarters huddled around the heavily fortified kremlin (citadel) where, in the eleventh century the cathedral of St Sofia was built. On the Merchantsi bank a colony of mainly foreign merchants developed around a royal palace. The whole of this area was protected by a rampart. Novgorod grew quickly to become the dominant Rus centre in north-east Russia, sending Staraja Ladoga into decline. Novgorod's connections with Scandinavia continued after the Viking Age, when its trade came to be dominated by merchants from the Hanseatic town of Visby on Gotland. Novgorod has seen extensive archaeological excavations. Waterlogged conditions have resulted in excellent preservation of clothing, furniture and other artefacts made from organic materials. The most important finds have been more than 1,000 merchants' letters and accounts, written on birch-bark in Old Russian using the Cyrillic alphabet. Few specifically Scandinavian artefacts have ever been discovered, however, suggesting that Novgorod's population was mainly Slavic, at least in material culture, from the start.

The route onwards from Novgorod crossed Lake Ilmen and followed the River Lovat to its headwaters, where there was a portage across into the Western Dvina river. A secondary route from Scandinavia to Constantinople, which avoided Novgorod, joined the Lovat about halfway between the lake and its headwaters. This route began in the Gulf of Finland and followed the River Narva (the modern border between Estonia and Russia) to Lake Peipus and the towns of Pskov and Izborsk. Izborsk, the older of the two towns, began as a small hill-top settlement with a mixed population of Finns, Slavs and Scandinavians. The settlement was protected with an earth and timber rampart in the tenth century and in the eleventh century the whole hilltop was surrounded by a stone wall. Though it remained an important border fortress, in the tenth century Izborsk was gradually supplanted as a commercial centre by nearby Pskov, on the banks of the River Velikaya. This river was followed upstream to a portage over into the valley of the Lovat to join the route south from Novgorod. Around 10 per cent of excavated graves in Viking Age cemeteries around Pskov contained Scandinavian artefacts: the rest of the population were Slavs or Finns.

The Western Dvina flows west to the Baltic Sea at Riga (as the Daugava). The river was a trade route but the Letts controlled its outlet to the sea and it was not a major Rus route. On reaching the Western Dvina, Rus merchants sailed downstream as far as Vitebsk, where they began another portage, which took them to the River Dnepr near Gnezdovo, the forerunner of modern Smolensk. Halfway between Novgorod and Kiev, Gnezdovo was an important staging post for Rus merchants. Outside the town there was a massive cremation cemetery of over 4,000 burial mounds. The cemetery has produced more Scandinavian artefacts than any other site in Russia but, despite this, about 95 per cent of the burials belonged to members of the local Slav tribe, the Krivich. The cemetery contained several Scandinavian warrior burials, with weapons, boats and sacrificed slave girls, as described by Ibn Fadlan. Seven hoards of Arabic and Byzantine coins, Frankish swords and a Crimean wine amphora are evidence of the town's long-distance trade links.

Kiev

From Gnezdovo, the Dnepr could be followed all the way to the Black Sea but the main destination for many merchants would have been Kiev, by the late ninth century, the main Rus power centre. Along the way, they would have passed close to Chernigov, on the River Desna, an eastern tributary of the Dnepr. No Rus settlement has yet been identified here but a large Viking Age cemetery has, implying that one existed close by. The cemetery contains the 'Black Mound', the largest known pagan Rus burial mound. The mound was 36 feet (11 m) high and contained the ashes of a funeral pyre on which had been cremated the bodies of a warrior and a woman. After the cremation, a mound was raised over the ashes and the chief's weapons and armour were placed on top, with a cauldron containing the bones of a goat, two drinking horns, and a figurine of the Scandinavian thunder god Thor. The mound was then built up to its full height and a pillar was erected on top. The burial is probably that of an important Rus chief in the service of the ruler of Kiev. Now the capital of Ukraine, Kiev – *Kœnugarð* to the Vikings – was built on three hills overlooking the Dnepr. Archaeological excavations have shown that Kiev was already an important Slav town, with a pagan temple, before it came under Rus control in the second half of the ninth century. The town was centred on the Starokievskaya Gora hill and its strongly fortified kremlin where the ruler and his retinue lived. In the tenth century a large settlement of merchants and craftsmen developed on the low-lying Podol on the riverbank below the kremlin. Few Viking Age burials have been discovered in Kiev, probably because later expansion of the city has destroyed the earliest cemeteries.

After Kiev, the journey down the Dnepr became increasingly dangerous because the lower reaches of the river were in territory controlled by hostile Pecheneg nomads. In the twentieth century the course of the Dnepr was transformed by vast hydro-electric reservoirs, but in the Viking Age the passage downriver was obstructed by 50 miles of rapids south of the modern city of Dnepropetrovsk. The rapids had to be bypassed by a series of portages, during which the Rus were very vulnerable to ambush by the Pechenegs. Because of the dangers, merchants gathered at the fortress of Vitichev, 25 miles south of Kiev, in the spring to sail downstream in large parties for mutual protection. It took five to six weeks to reach Constantinople so the expeditions had to leave before the end of June in order to make the return trip before the river froze again. New boats for these expeditions were built every year. No Rus boats have ever been found but Greek and Arab sources suggest they were large expanded log-boats, probably not dissimilar to the chaikas used by the Cossacks in the same region in the early modern period. The boats were built by hollowing out a tree trunk. This was done by the Rus-Slav tributaries in forested areas north of Kiev over the winter. As soon as the ice on the rivers broke up they were floated downstream to Kiev, where planks were added to the sides and to raise the freeboard and rowing benches, masts and sails were fitted.

From Vitichev, it was about ten days sailing to the first of the Dnepr rapids. The Byzantine emperor Constantine VII Porphyrogenitus (r. 913–59) recorded the Old Norse names of the rapids in a government policy manual, De Adminstrando Imperio ('On the Administration of the Empire'), that he wrote c. 948. The first rapid, called Essupi ('sleepless') was passable with care: the Rus manhandled the boats through the shallows by the riverbanks. The next two rapids, Ulvorsi ('island falls') and Gelandri ('roaring falls'), were passed in the same way. The fourth rapid, Aïfor ('impassable falls'), was the biggest and had to be avoided by a 6 mile portage. Some of the crew always needed to stand guard against Pecheneg ambushes, while the rest drew the boats on shore and unloaded them. This had to be done not only to lighten the boats for dragging or carrying but also because, without water to support it, the weight of the cargo could break a boat's back. Slaves were led around the rapids in neck chains, no doubt carrying the rest of the cargo. A rune stone at Pilgards on Gotland commemorates a Viking called Rafn who drowned trying to run these rapids. The next two rapids, Baruforos ('wave falls') and Leanti ('laughing falls'), could be passed in the same way as the first three. At the foot of the final rapids, Strukun ('the courser'), was the Kichkas ford, a major crossing place where the river ran broad but shallow. Cliffs near the ford were a favourite vantage point for Pechenegs planning to ambush the Rus in the shallows. After passing Kichkas the Rus hauled in at Khortytsya Island where they made offerings of thanks to their gods at an enormous oak tree.

Below Khortytsya, the Dnepr widened so the Rus could sail out of bow-shot from the shore, safe from the Pechenegs, who always shadowed the convoys from the riverbanks. After another four days sailing, the Rus reached the Black Sea and Berezan Island, where they stopped and rested for two or three days and made such repairs as were necessary. The Rus continued their journey towards Constantinople by sailing south along the coast. The Pechenegs continued to shadow the convoys as far as the mouth of the Danube, hoping to seize any boats that were blown onshore. Once past the mouth of the Danube the main dangers of the journey were behind them and the Rus sailed in easy stages to the Bosphorus straits and Constantinople where, as Constantine put it, 'their voyage, fraught with such travail and terror, such difficulty and danger' was finally at an end.

The city of Constantine

Constantinople (modern Istanbul) was founded in 324 by the Roman emperor Constantine the Great (r. 306–37) on the site of the ancient Greek port of Byzantium. The first Roman emperor to convert to Christianity, Constantine intended his new city, which he modestly named after himself, to be a new Christian capital for the empire, untainted by Rome's paganism. When the Roman Empire was permanently divided on the death of Theodosius I in 395, Constantinople became the capital of the Eastern Roman Empire, which, because of its predominantly Greek language and culture, historians conventionally call the Byzantine Empire. Byzantine emperors would not have recognised this name, however: they always maintained that they were Roman emperors. Constantine's choice of site was a stroke of genius. Constantinople stands on the narrow Bosphorus straits that separate Europe from Asia and link the Black Sea and the Mediterranean. Its position at this natural crossroads quickly made Constantinople into a wealthy trade centre. The city was built on a peninsula with the Bosphorus on one side and a vast sheltered natural harbour, the Golden Horn, on the other. This was not just convenient for visiting merchant ships, it also gave the city a very strong defensive position. Constantine closed off the landward side of the peninsula with a stone wall but the city soon outgrew it. Between 404 and 413, new walls were built more than a mile further out. About twenty-five years later, walls were built around Constantinople's seaward sides to protect them against naval assaults. In wartime, the Golden Horn was closed to shipping by an iron chain stretched across its mouth, giving the city even more protection from attack from the sea. When the land walls were damaged by an earthquake in 447, the emperor Theodosius II (408–50) ordered them to be rebuilt with a moat and three parallel walls, giving Constantinople the most formidable defences of any city in the world at that time. Theodosius's walls were arguably the best investment in fortifications ever made: they were breached only once, when the city fell to the Ottoman Turks in 1453.

Despite the strength of Constantinople's defences, the Rus found its enormous wealth too tempting not to try to seize it by force. The Rus first attacked Constantinople on 18 June 860, while the emperor Michael III was absent from the city on campaign in the Abbasid Caliphate. The powerful Byzantine navy was also away, fighting Arab pirates in the Mediterranean. The Greeks were taken completely by surprise – the patriarch Photius described the attack as 'a thunderbolt from heaven' – and there was little they could do to prevent the Rus plundering Constantinople's suburbs before sailing through the Bosphorus to raid around the Sea of Marmora, burning and plundering houses, churches and monasteries, and killing and captive-taking. However, the Rus did not attempt to attack Constantinople's walls, so the city itself remained safe. The Rus faced little or no resistance and the Byzantines ascribed their eventual withdrawal on 4 August to the miraculous intervention of the Mother of God. They were probably really just making sure that they had plenty of time to get home before the rivers froze and left them at the mercy of the Pechenegs.

According to the Russian *Primary Chronicle*, the second attack on Constantinople was Oleg's, in 907. Oleg sailed to Constantinople with a fleet of 2,000 ships but found the entrance to the Golden Horn blocked with an iron chain. Undaunted, the Rus hauled their ships ashore, fitted wheels to them and dragged them overland around the chain and into the Golden Horn, just as they would have dealt with impassable rapids at home. Oleg fastened his shield to the city gates but the Byzantines beat off his attacks. Impressed by the ferocity of the Rus, the Byzantines subsequently agreed the trade treaties of 907 and 911. The problem with accepting this account is that no Byzantine writer makes any mention of it, which would seem unlikely if an attack of that scale really did take place. A third attempt to take the city was made by Igor in 941. A fragmentary letter from an unnamed Khazar to an unidentified Jew, known as the Schechter Letter, suggests that the attack was incited by the Khazars who wanted revenge on the emperor Romanos Lecapenus (r. 920–44) for pursuing anti-Jewish policies. Igor (called Helgu in the letter) agreed to the attack as the price of his liberty after he had suffered a defeat by the Khazars. Igor's fleet, claimed to be 1,000-ships-strong, landed on the Anatolian coast in May and plundered widely before moving on to Constantinople. Both the Byzantine fleet and army had gone on campaign leaving Constantinople unguarded except for fifteen old dromons, which the emperor fitted out with Greek Fire projectors. The Byzantines kept the formula for Greek Fire a closely guarded secret, but it was an incendiary weapon probably based on naphtha. The Rus had never experienced this weapon before and their ships swarmed around the dromons as they sailed out to do battle. The Rus were in for a nasty surprise:

> 'As their galleys lay surrounded by the enemy, the Greeks began to fling their fire all around: and the Rus seeing the flames threw themselves in haste from the ships, preferring to be drowned in the water than burned alive in the fire. Some sank to the bottom under the weight of their armour: some caught fire as they swam among the waves; not a man escaped that day save those who managed to reach the shore. For the Rus ships by reason of their small size can move in very shallow water where the Greek galleys because of their greater draught cannot pass' (Liudprand of Cremona, *The Embassy to Constantinople*, trans. F. A. Wright, Routledge, 1930.)

The Byzantine victory was not so decisive as this account implies. Sufficient Rus survived for them to spend weeks plundering on the Asian coast of the Bosphorus, raiding inland as far as Nicomedia (now Izmit). The Rus only withdrew in September when reinforcements finally reached Constantinople. The Rus then sailed to the coast of

Thrace (modern Bulgaria) and continued their plundering. Almost at the moment when they were ready to sail for home the Byzantine fleet fell upon them by surprise and only a handful of ships escaped. Those Rus who were captured were taken to Constantinople to be publicly beheaded.

Assimilation and conversion

By the middle of the tenth century, the Rus were becoming assimilated with the native Slavs through intermarriage and were losing their Scandinavian culture and identity. Svyatoslav was himself a sign of that assimilation: all previous Rus rulers had had Scandinavian names, his name was Slavic. Slavs, or at least men with Slavic names, were also achieving high rank. The names of the Rus witnesses to the trade agreements with Byzantium made in 907 and 911 all had Scandinavian names. Half the witnesses to Igor's new trade treaty of 945 had Slavic names. Even by 907, the Rus appear to have adopted native religious beliefs, swearing to uphold the treaties by the Slavic gods Perun, a thunder god, and Veles, a chthonic deity. A steady trickle of Viking warriors still came east to serve in the *druzhina* of the Rus rulers but these native Scandinavians were now known by a new name to distinguish them from the Slavicised Rus – Varangians. The word is thought to be derived from Old Norse *vár*, meaning 'pledge', after the Viking custom of forming sworn fellowships when embarking on a common enterprise such as a Viking raid or a trading expedition.

Despite his Slavic name, Svyatoslav was very much a traditional Viking warlord. After he attained his majority c. 963, Svyatoslav spent most of his reign campaigning against the Pechenegs, Volga Bulgars and Khazars. Svyatoslav's motives were probably twofold: to secure complete control of the Volga and Don river trade routes, and to force the Slav tributaries of the Pechenegs, Khazars and Volga Bulgars to pay tribute to the Rus instead. In his greatest campaign, c. 965, Svyatoslav reduced both the Volga Bulgars and Khazars to tributary status. Bolghar, Sarkel and Itil were all sacked and plundered. An eyewitness told Ibn Hawqal soon after the attack on Itil that there was: 'not enough left of a vineyard or a garden worth giving to a beggar. If a leaf were left on a branch, the Rus would carry it off. There is not a grape or a raisin left in the country.' The attack permanently broke the power of the Khazars, Rus pirates were free to operate on the Caspian Sea again and a number of small-scale raids are recorded up to around 1030. After destroying Itil and Bolghar, Svyatoslav turned his sights on the Volga Bulgars' cousins in the Balkans. He was encouraged in this by the Byzantine emperor Nikephoros Phokas (r. 963–9) who, in 967, offered him 1,500 pounds (680 kg) of gold to assist him in a campaign against Bulgaria. This began an entanglement with Byzantium's proverbially devious politics that would ultimately cost Svyatoslav his life. Kalokyros, the Byzantine ambassador charged with negotiating with Svyatoslav, had ambitions to seize the imperial throne for himself. Kalokyros reached a secret agreement with Svyatoslav: if he helped him become emperor, he would allow Svyatoslav to keep Bulgaria if he conquered it. In August 967, Svyatoslav invaded Bulgaria and captured the important trade centre of Pereyaslavets near the mouth of the Danube. Had he held it, Svyatoslav would have gained control over the important Danube river trade route through central Europe. However, the Bulgars recaptured it when Svyatoslav was forced to withdraw in 968 after news reached him that Kiev was under siege by the Pechenegs. Svyatoslav returned to Bulgaria in 969, recaptured Pereyeslavets, and quickly went on to capture the Bulgar capital at Preslav and the fortress of Dorostolon (Silistra, Bulgaria). However, by this time there had been a change of regime at Constantinople. Kalokyros' treachery had been discovered, and Nikephoros had been deposed and murdered by his wife's lover John Tzimiskes (r. 969–76).

John offered to continue with the payments of gold offered by Nikephoros if Svyatoslav would withdraw from Bulgaria. Svyatoslav refused to negotiate and contemptuously told the emperor he would meet him at the gates of Constantinople. In 970, Svyatoslav crossed the Balkans and sacked the Byzantine city of Philippopolis (Plovdiv, Bulgaria). The Byzantine historian Leo the Deacon, who later met Svyatoslav in person, accused him of impaling 20,000 captives outside the city. Svyatoslav now advanced towards Constantinople, but he was still several days' march away when a smaller Byzantine army defeated him at Arcadiopolis (Lüleburgaz, Turkey) and forced him to retreat back over the Balkans. At Easter 971, John took the offensive and recaptured Preslav after a short siege. At the same time, 300 Byzantine warships with Greek Fire projectors took control of the Danube, capturing Pereyslavets and cutting off Svyatoslav's retreat. Svyatoslav fell back to Dorostolon, where he was blockaded by the Byzantine army on land and by the Byzantine warships on the Danube. Desperate Rus attempts to break the siege failed and, after two months, hunger forced Svyatoslav to negotiate for peace. In return for renouncing his territorial ambitions in Bulgaria, John allowed Svyatoslav to withdraw with his forces, even providing his army with rations for the journey. This was just a front, however: John was also negotiating with the Pechenegs. As Svyatoslav's fleet made its way back up the Dnepr towards Kiev, it was ambushed by the Pechenegs, probably at the Kichkas ford. Svyatoslav and most of his army were killed. In what was the ultimate accolade one barbarian leader could pay to another, the Pecheneg khagan Kurya had Svyatoslav's skull made into a prestige drinking goblet.

Svyatoslav's empire was ephemeral. Soon after his death, civil war broke out between his teenage sons, Yaropolk, Oleg and Vladimir ('the Great'). After Yaropolk killed Oleg, Vladimir fled to Sweden. In 980 Vladimir returned with an army of 6,000 Varangians and drove Yaropolk out of Kiev. Vladimir lured his brother into a peace conference, where two Varangians murdered him. Vladimir's reign (980–1015) was one of the most important in Russian history, marking the end of Kievan Rus as a Viking state. In his early years, Vladimir was a devotee of the thunder god Perun, but in 988 he made the momentous decision to convert to Orthodox Christianity.

The *Primary Chronicle* tells a rather fanciful story about Vladimir's conversion. In 987, Vladimir sent envoys around the world to learn about the monotheistic religions, Judaism, Islam, and Roman Catholic and Orthodox Christianity. Vladimir rejected Judaism on the grounds that they had lost their homeland and must, therefore, have been abandoned by God. Islam was rejected because of its ban on the consumption of pork and alcohol. Especially alcohol. The envoys Vladimir sent to Germany to learn about Roman Catholicism reported unfavourably on their drab churches but those he sent to Constantinople to learn about Orthodoxy gave glowing reports about the beauty of the service they had attended in the vast Hagia Sophia cathedral. They apparently no longer knew whether they were in heaven or on earth. Impressed, Vladimir agreed to convert in return for the hand of the emperor Basil II's sister Anna. It is not known how Anna felt about being married off to a barbarian warlord who reportedly had several wives and 800 concubines already, and leaving behind the sophisticated comforts of Constantinople for the timber halls of Kiev. Vladimir was baptised at the Byzantine city of Cherson in Crimea in 988 and on his return to Kiev he destroyed the pagan shrines, threw the idol of Perun into the Dnepr, and ordered his subjects to accept baptism, starting with his twelve sons. Significantly, Slavic was adopted as the language of the Russian church, a clear sign that by now the Rus elite were Slavic speakers.

Greek and Arabic sources paint a rather different, and altogether more credible, picture of the conversion of the Rus. In the early Middle Ages, Orthodox and Roman Catholic missionaries competed with one another for the souls of Europe's last pagans. Byzantine efforts to convert the Rus to Orthodox Christianity were actually begun by the patriarch Photius in the 860s. According to the *Primary Chronicle*, Askold and Dir became converts in 867, and there were sufficient converts by 874 for the patriarch to appoint an archbishop to the Rus. Christianity did not spread quickly among the Rus, but the Rus-Byzantine trade treaty of 945 mentions that there was a substantial Christian community and at least one church at Kiev. Probably in 957, Olga of Kiev visited Constantinople and became an Orthodox Christian. Her son Sviatoslav, however, refused to convert because he thought he would lose credibility with his *druzhina*. This suggests that the warrior aristocracy was still mostly pagan. Vladimir's decision to abandon paganism was most likely made for reasons of political advantage. In 987, Basil II was faced with a serious uprising and he appealed to Vladimir for military assistance. Vladimir's price was marriage to Anna, but this was politically impossible while Vladimir was a pagan, so he converted and forced his subjects to do so too. Baptism was a small price to pay for an alliance with Europe's most powerful state. The agreement with Basil solved an immediate problem for Vladimir. He still had with him the 6,000 Varangians he had recruited in Sweden to help him win power and they were getting restless because he could not afford to pay them. By sending them off to fight for Basil, Vladimir rid his kingdom of a possible destabilising influence.

The Varangian Guard

Basil II made good use of Vladimir's 6,000 Varangians, throwing them into battle against the rebels almost as soon as they arrived in Constantinople in the summer of 988. Their ferocity impressed Basil so much that he decided to create an elite unit of imperial lifeguards to be manned exclusively by Varangians, his own Greek lifeguards having proved disloyal. The Varangian Guard subsequently fought in every major Byzantine campaign until Constantinople was captured by crusaders in 1204. Early recruits to the guard were mostly Swedes and Rus, but by the early eleventh century Danes, Norwegians and Icelanders were making the long journey through Russia to Constantinople, attracted by the generous pay. Regarded as outstandingly loyal, Varangian Guardsmen were the highest paid mercenaries in Byzantine service, receiving the equivalent of between 1⅓ to 2½ pounds of gold a year, a one-third share of the Byzantine army's war booty, and frequent gifts of treasure and fine clothing from the emperors. They even got to wear silk clothes when off-duty: this at a time when a king back home in Scandinavia would have been satisfied with decorative silk trim on his best clothing. With incentives like these, the emperor could afford to be fussy. Applicants had to prove that they were men of substance by paying an entry fee, and they needed to prove their battle skills by serving in a regular army unit before being admitted to the guard. Appearance mattered too, as the emperor wanted to surround himself with tall, well-built men who would look both magnificent and intimidating.

The most famous member of the guard was Harald Hardrada, a future king of Norway, who served as an officer from 1034 to 1043 on campaigns in Sicily, Bulgaria, Anatolia and the Holy Land. Harald's saga probably exaggerates the favours shown to him by the emperors to flatter the Norwegian monarchy with this tenuous imperial connection, but he certainly made enough money during his service to finance his successful bid to seize the Norwegian throne. Few others did quite so well but even ordinary guardsmen like the Icelander Bolli Bollason (d. *c.* 1067) could cut quite a dash when they returned home:

> 'Bolli rode from the ship with eleven companions. His companions were all wearing scarlet and rode in gilded saddles; they were all fine looking men, but Bolli surpassed them all. He was wearing clothes of gold-embroidered silk which the Greek emperor had given him, and over them a scarlet cloak. He was girt with the sword 'Leg-Biter', its pommel now gold-embossed and the hilt bound with gold. He had a gilded helmet on his head and a red shield at his side on which a knight was traced in gold. He carried a lance in his hand, as is the custom in foreign lands. Wherever they took lodgings for the night, the womenfolk paid no heed to anything but to gaze at Bolli and his companions in all their finery.' (*Laxdaela Saga*, trans. Magnus Magnusson and Hermann Pálsson, Penguin, 1969.)

The Varangian Guard probably had a formal establishment of 6,000 men, divided into twelve divisions of 500. Strict discipline was imposed by a regimental tribunal. The guard's commander, the Akolouthos, was usually a Greek. His status reflected that of the guard itself; he held the first rank in the hierarchy of imperial offices and in processions he walked immediately behind the emperor himself. The Varangians were not encouraged to learn Greek – it probably suited the emperor to maintain a communication barrier between the guardsmen and his Greek subjects – so commands were relayed through a corps of interpreters. The guard's primary function was to protect the emperor, wherever he was. When he was based in Constantinople the guard also acted as a special police force, suppressing civil unrest and arresting suspected traitors, killing, torturing or blinding them as required by the emperor. Having no local sympathies, the Varangians could be trusted to carry out their duties without regard to the rank or family connections of their victims. If the emperor went on campaign, part of the guard was always left behind to garrison Constantinople. In camp, the Varangians' tents surrounded the emperor's tent; if the emperor was staying in a city, the keys to its gates were entrusted to the Varangians. In battle, the emperor kept the Varangians with him to the rear of the main battleline, holding them in reserve until the battle reached a critical point. The Varangians made highly effective shock troops, fighting on foot using traditional Viking weapons and tactics. The two-handed broadaxe was their favoured weapon and because of this they were often described as 'the emperor's axe-wielding barbarians' (or, on account of their heavy drinking, 'the emperor's wine-swilling barbarians'). The Varangians' reputation for ferocity and their disregard for the pain of wounds in battle suggests that many must have been practicing berserkers.

In 1071, the Byzantine army suffered a catastrophic defeat at the hands of the Seljuq Turks at the Battle of Manzikert (Malazgirt, Turkey). The emperor Romanos IV was wounded and captured and most of the Varangian Guard were killed, remaining loyal to the emperor after most of the Byzantine army had fled the battlefield. The depleted ranks of the guard were filled, in part, by English warriors who had gone into exile following the Norman conquest. The Varangian Guard still remained attractive to Scandinavians, however. When the Danish king Erik the Evergood visited Constantinople in 1103, many of his retinue stayed on and joined the guard. The same thing happened when King Sigurd of Norway stopped by in 1110 on his way home from a crusade in the Holy Land. When jarl Rognvald of Orkney set out for the Holy Land in 1153, six ships broke away from his fleet as soon as it entered the Mediterranean and went straight to Constantinople where their crews joined the guard. The guard survived until 1204, when Constantinople was captured by crusaders. The guard's final hour was not its finest: the Varangians refused to fight the crusaders until they were offered an extortionate pay rise. After 1204, English and Scandinavian mercenaries, described as Varangians, continued to serve in Byzantine armies but they were treated no differently to any other mercenaries. The ranking of the Akolouthos says it all – he had fallen in rank from first to fiftieth.

Yngvar the Widefarer

By the later tenth century, the Islamic world's silver mines were becoming exhausted and the flow of dirhems through Russia gradually declined. Fewer and fewer Scandinavian merchants came east to trade but the memory of Serkland's fabulous wealth lingered on to inspire a new generation of adventurers. Around 1041, Yngvar the Widefarer, a Swede, led an expedition east to try to re-open the trade routes, but he met with disaster somewhere in the Caspian region and he and most of his men were killed. Yngvar's expedition is known from a group of twenty-six rune-stones in central Sweden that commemorate men who 'fell in the east' with Yngvar. A highly fictionalised account of Yngvar's expedition survives in the thirteenth century *Yngvars saga víðförla* ('The Saga of Yngvar the Widefarer'), a translation into Old Icelandic of a lost twelfth-century Latin work by an Icelandic monk Odd Snorrason. The Yngvar of the saga is a warrior in the service of the Swedish king Olof Skötkonung (r. *c.* 995–1022). When the king refuses to grant Yngvar a royal title, he raises an expedition to go to the east in search of a kingdom for himself. Yngvar goes first to the court of kniaz Yaroslav the Wise (r. 1019–54) in Russia and after three years presses on with thirty ships along an unnamed river into the east. From this point onwards, Yngvar's adventures become increasingly fantastic, with encounters with giants, dragons, witches and, inevitably, a beautiful queen, Silkisif of Gardariki, who falls in love with him. Finally, Yngvar dies in an epidemic that decimates his expedition and his body is returned to Silkisif, who sends the survivors home with instructions to send missionaries to convert her country to Christianity. According to the saga, Yngvar died in 1041 aged twenty-five, in which case he would have been no more than six when he set out from Sweden.

It is almost impossible to disentangle fact from fiction in Yngvar's saga, but events during Yaroslav's reign provide it with a credible context. Jaroslav was the last ruler of Kievan Russia to maintain close links with Scandinavia. One of Vladimir's many sons, Yaroslav, was appointed governor of Novgorod by his father. After his father's death in 1015, Yaroslav's older brother Sviatopolk murdered three of their brothers and seized power in Kiev. Supported by the people of Novgorod and an army of Varangians, Yaroslav defeated and killed Sviatopolk in 1019 to establish his rule over Kiev. In the same year Yaroslav married Ingigerd, the daughter of King Olof

Skötkonung, establishing an alliance with Sweden. When his brother Mstislav challenged him for control of Kiev in 1024, Yaroslav was able to call on the support of his brother-in-law King Önund Jacob (r. 1022–50), who led an army of Varangians over from Sweden. Many other Varangians broke their journeys to Constantinople at Yaroslav's court at Novgorod, often signing on in his *druzhina* for a few years before moving on. One of these was Harald Hardrada, who spent three years (1031–4) in his *druzhina* before he left to join the Varangian Guard. When he returned to Russia in 1041, on his way to claim the Norwegian throne, Harald married Yaroslav's daughter Elisleif (Elizabeth). Yngvar is likely to have been one of these adventurers, like Harald, who served Yaroslav for a number of years before travelling on. But where did Yngvar go? Several of the Yngvar runestones state that he and his men died in Serkland. This is usually taken to mean the Abbasid Caliphate, but it may be that in this case it means the kingdom of Georgia. Georgian chronicles state that in 1042 a group of Varangians landed at the mouth of the River Rioni on Georgia's Black Sea coast and joined the army of King Bagrat IV (r. 1027–72), who was fighting a civil war against a rebel general. The rebels defeated Bagrat and his Varangian allies at the Battle of Sasireti in the Caucasus Mountains. The defeat was so severe that Bagrat lost control of half his kingdom and it is likely that his Varangians suffered heavy casualties. The date of the battle is so close to the date given for Yngvar's death in the saga that there must be a possibility that this was the disaster that cost him and so many of his men their lives. However, the saga says that Yngvar died of sickness. This was the fate of another Varangian, Önund, a son of King Emund of Sweden (r. 1050–60), who, according to Adam of Bremen (d. *c.* 1080) was sent overseas 'to extend his dominions'. Önund fell ill and died in 'the land of the Amazons', which in the Middle Ages was thought to be on the steppes north of the Black Sea and the Caspian Sea, after drinking from a well that had been poisoned by the warrior women. Are Yngvar and Önund the same person, or has the saga conflated the stories of two separate ill-fated Varangian expeditions to re-open the routes to the east?

Fading contacts

While Yaroslav's Scandinavian connection was important to him, it is also very clear that there was no longer a special relationship. The relations he cultivated with other European states, such as the Byzantine Empire, Germany, France and Hungary, were just as important to him as those with Scandinavia. After Yaroslav's reign, the links between Russia and Scandinavia faded. Aspiring Scandinavian recruits for the Varangian Guard began to travel to Constantinople by sea or through Germany and Hungary rather than by the old river route through Russia. The last time Varangian mercenaries fought in any numbers for the Rus was during an unsuccessful attack on Constantinople, commanded by Yaroslav's son Vladimir in 1043. Just as in 941, the Rus fleet was destroyed by dromons spewing Greek Fire. Changing trade patterns also weakened the links between Scandinavia and Russia. Novgorod went from strength to strength as Russia's main outlet to the west, but by the thirteenth century German merchants from Baltic cities like Lübeck had taken control of its trade, excluding Scandinavians through monopolistic practices.

Ultimately, the Viking contribution to the development of Russian civilisation was very slight. Tellingly, despite over 200 years of close interaction, less than a dozen Scandinavian loan words were adopted into the developing Russian language. Nor did the Vikings leave any clear genetic traces in the modern Russian population. Probably, the most important Viking impact was on urbanisation. Many of the eastern Slavs' fortified settlements were already beginning to develop into towns by the beginning of the Viking Age, but there can be no doubt that the arrival of Scandinavian merchants gave the process enormous impetus by greatly expanding east–west trade links, turning small towns like Kiev into prosperous cities in less than a century. Far more significant to the development of early Russia, was Vladimir's adoption of Orthodox Christianity, which opened Kievan Russia to the powerful influence of Byzantine civilisation. Byzantine culture shaped Russia for centuries to come and, just as significantly, created an ideological barrier between it and the Catholic west. Kievan Russia's alphabet, art, architecture, law, music and political ideologies were all essentially of Byzantine origin. Tsargrad ('city of the emperors'), as Constantinople came to be known to the Russians, was regarded as the cultural and religious capital of the world. When the Byzantine Empire fell to the Turks in 1453, the Russians were entirely justified in seeing themselves as its cultural and political successors.

CHAPTER 8

THINGVELLIR, BRATTAHLID AND L'ANSE AUX MEADOWS
THE NORSE IN THE NORTH ATLANTIC
835–1000

I t was in the North Atlantic that the Vikings showed the full potential of their seafaring abilities. Using islands like stepping stones, the Vikings gradually explored the North Atlantic, sailing in stages from Norway to Shetland, the Faeroe Islands, Iceland, Greenland until, finally, around 1000, they became the first Europeans to set foot on the North American continent. Unlike the Viking expansion in Britain, Ireland and Frankia, which was initially motivated by plunder, or the expansion into Russia, which was motivated by trade, the expansion into the North Atlantic was from the beginning a search for land to settle. Successful Viking colonies were founded in the Faeroe Islands and Iceland, and these became the only permanent extensions of the Scandinavian world to emerge from the Viking Age. Everywhere else that Vikings settled they were assimilated by the native populations within a few generations. In the Faeroes and Iceland, however, there were no native populations to assimilate the settlers and Scandinavian cultural traditions continued to flourish and evolve.

Although they made it their own, the Vikings were not the first explorers of the North Atlantic. For at least two centuries before the beginning of the Viking Age, Irish monks had been setting out in their curachs in search of remote islands where they could contemplate the divine in perfect solitude, disturbed only by the cries of seabirds and the crashing of the waves on the shore. The monks developed a tradition of writing *imrama*, travel tales, the most famous of which is the *Navigatio sancti Brendani abbatis* (The Voyage of St Brendan the Abbot). The *Navigatio* recounts a voyage purported to have been made by St Brendan (d. *c.* 577) in search of the mythical Isles of the Blessed, which were believed to lie somewhere in the western ocean. The *imrama* certainly show a familiarity with the North Atlantic – the *Navigatio*, for example, describes what are probably icebergs, volcanoes and whales – but they also include so many fantastical and mythological elements that it is impossible to disentangle truth from invention. There is no evidence to support claims that are often made that St Brendan discovered America before the Vikings, but Irish monks certainly did reach the Faeroe Islands and Iceland before them. Ash from peat fires containing charred barley grains found in windblown sand deposits at Á Sondum on Sandoy in the southern Faeroes has been radiocarbon-dated to between the fourth and sixth centuries AD. Although no trace of buildings has yet been found, the ash probably came from domestic hearths and had been thrown out onto the sand to help control erosion, which was a common practice at the time. As peat was not used as a fuel in Scandinavia at this time but was widely used in Britain and Ireland, this evidence suggests that seafaring Irish monks had discovered the Faeroes not long after Ireland's conversion to Christianity. No physical traces of an Irish presence in Iceland have been found in modern times, but early Viking settlers claimed that they found croziers and other ecclesiastical artefacts there. There are also two *papar* place-names (see ch. 4) associated with Irish monks, Papos and Papey, in the east of Iceland. The monks, all being celibate males, did not found any permanent self-sustaining communities in either place: they were always visitors rather than settlers.

The settlement of the Faeroe Islands

The Viking expansion into the North Atlantic was originally a by-product of the raids and settlements on the Scottish islands, which began around the end of the eighth century. There the Vikings came into contact with Irish monks and it was probably from them that the Vikings learned about the existence of other islands to the north. Just two full days' sail north-west of Shetland, Vikings reached the Faeroes early in the ninth century. Writing around 825, the Irish monk Dicuil says that the Vikings had already forced his brother monks to stop using the islands as a retreat. The Vikings found the islands well populated with sheep, which had probably been introduced by the monks as a ready source of food. These sheep gave the islands their name, the *fær-øer*, the 'sheep islands'. Though mountainous, windswept and treeless, the islands have a mild climate for their northerly latitude and have good pastures and plenty of rough grazing land. This made them attractive to settlers from western Norway and the Hebrides, where pastoralism was more important than arable farming. The islands' huge seabird colonies offered a rich seasonal source of meat and eggs (though seabirds are very much an acquired taste), and pilot whales were also hunted.

According to Icelandic and Faeroese historical traditions, the first Viking settler of the Faeroes was Grímur Kamban. Grímur was said to have settled at Funningur, by a sheltered bay on Eysturoy, the second largest of the Faeroe islands. As Grímur's second name is of Gaelic origin (from cambán, meaning 'crooked one'), he had probably spent some time living in the Hebrides. He was probably not unusual in this. Recent DNA analysis of the Y chromosomes of modern Faeroese men indicates that 87 per cent of them have Scandinavian ancestry. Analysis of modern Faeroese women's mitochondrial DNA, which is passed down only through the female line, indicates that 84 per cent of them have British or Irish origins. As it was in the Hebrides, the majority of Viking settlers in the Faeroes must have been single men who acquired wives en route. The number of settlers is not known but by the end of the Viking Age, the islands' population was probably between 2,000 and 4,000. The isolation and small size of the Faeroese population has left it unusually vulnerable to diseases caused by recessive genes. One potentially fatal genetic disorder, carnitine transporter deficiency, is 1,000 times more common in the islands than anywhere else in the world.

The Viking discovery of Iceland

The Vikings' next step out into the Atlantic – the discovery and settlement of Iceland – is one of the best documented events of the Viking Age. Medieval Icelanders were fascinated by genealogy, not only because, as emigrants, they wanted to know where their families came from, but because such knowledge was essential when it came to establishing property rights. To begin with, family traditions about the settlement period were passed down orally from one generation to the next, but in the early twelfth century they were committed to writing in the two earliest works of Icelandic history, *Landnámabók* and *Íslendingabók*, both of which were written in the Old Norse language. *Íslendingabók* ('The Book of the Icelanders'), a short chronicle of Icelandic history from the discovery of Iceland to 1118, was written between 1122 and 1132 by Ari Thorgilsson, a priest from Snæfellsness. Ari relied on oral traditions and, for more recent events, on eyewitnesses, but he took care to establish the reliability of his informants, naming many of them, and avoiding Christian prejudice and supernatural explanations of events. Though not proven, it is generally thought that Ari was also the author of *Landnámabók* ('The Book of the Settlements'), which gives details of the names, genealogies and land claims of hundreds of Iceland's original Norse settlers.

The first Viking to visit Iceland was Gardar the Swede, who in *c.* 860 set out on a voyage from Denmark, where he had made his home, to the Hebrides, to claim some land his wife had inherited. While passing through the Pentland Firth, the straits that separate the Orkney Islands from the Scottish mainland, Gardar's ship was caught in a storm and blown far out into the Atlantic. Gardar eventually sighted the mountainous coast of an unknown land. What Gardar saw was not at all inviting, it was the rugged Eastern Horn on Iceland's forbidding south-east coast, guarded by high cliffs and huge scree slopes tumbling into the sea. Undeterred, Gardar began to follow the coastline westwards, eventually circumnavigating Iceland and establishing that it was an island. Gardar spent nearly a year exploring his new-found land, wintering at Husavik on Iceland's north coast. When he set sail in the spring, Gardar was forced to abandon a man called Nattfari, together with a male slave and a bondswoman, when the small boat they were in went adrift. These three survived, inadvertently becoming Iceland's first permanent inhabitants. Naming his discovery Gardarsholm (Gardar's island) after himself, Gardar sailed east to Norway, where he began to sing its praises.

Another accidental visitor to Iceland around this time was Naddod the Viking. He was sailing from Norway to the Faeroe Islands when he was blown off course and made landfall in Iceland's Eastern Fjords. Naddod climbed a mountain to look for signs of habitation and, seeing none, left in the middle of a heavy snowstorm. Naddod too gave favourable reports of the island, which he decided to call Snæland (Snowland). Shortly after Naddod's return, the Norwegian Floki Vilgerdarson set out from Rogaland with the intention of settling in Naddod's Snæland. Floki had a reputation as a great Viking warrior but he was a hopeless settler. Floki spent his summer hunting seals at Vatnesfjörður on Breiðarfjörður in north-west Iceland but he neglected to make any hay, with the result that all the livestock he had brought with him starved to death over the winter. This doomed his attempt at settlement but pack ice in the fjord prevented him sailing for home. By the time the pack ice finally broke up it was too late in the year to risk trying to return to Norway, so Floki was forced to stay another winter, this time at Borgarfjörður further to the south. Thoroughly disillusioned by his experiences, Floki decided to re-name Snæland 'Iceland'. Floki's name was the one that stuck even though his men gave more favourable reports of the island: the most enthusiastic of them, Thorolf, swore that butter dripped from every blade of grass. For this reason he was known ever afterwards as Thorolf Butter.

Thorolf must have been a born optimist. Iceland is a large volcanic island lying exactly on the mid-Atlantic ridge, where magma welling up from the mantle is gradually pushing Europe and America apart. Despite lying only just south of the Arctic Circle, the influence of the warm Gulf Stream current keeps the climate mild for the latitude. Glaciers and ice sheets on the mountains cover about 14 per cent of Iceland but the rest of the island is free of permafrost. Iceland's combination of ice and fire must have reminded the settlers of the Viking creation myth, in which the world emerges in the void between the fire realm of Muspel and the frozen realm of Niflheim. Today, less than a quarter of Iceland is vegetated, the remainder of the unglaciated area being mainly barren lava fields and ash deserts. However, when it was discovered by the Vikings, around 40 per cent of Iceland was covered with low, scrubby, birch and willow woodland, so it would have looked considerably less bleak than it does today. Even so, Iceland turned out to be a distinctly marginal environment for European settlement and the settlers were very vulnerable to the vagaries of the weather and volcanic eruptions.

Hearing the reports circulating about Iceland, two Norwegian foster-brothers, Ingolf and Hjorleif, made a reconnaissance trip to the Eastern Fjords in the late 860s to assess the prospects for settlements. The foster-brothers had lost their estates paying compensation to jarl Atli of Gaular for killing his sons and they urgently needed a safe refuge. Liking what they saw the foster-brothers made preparations to emigrate. Ingolf had the resources to fund his expedition, but Hjorleif did not, so he set out on a *víking* trip to Ireland. Even the Viking settlement of an uninhabited land involved violence. In Ireland, Hjorleif plundered a hoard of treasure from a souterrain and captured ten Irish slaves to take with him to Iceland. According to the *Lándnámabók*, Ingolf and Hjorleif set out for Iceland again in 874. Study of layers of volcanic ash called tephra confirm the date. One of these layers, known as the *landnám* layer, which is found over almost all of the island, has been dated to 871–2. Evidence of human impact on the environment is found above the layer but not below it. Ingolf sacrificed to the gods and gained favourable auguries. Hjorleif did not bother: he never sacrificed. The two sailed in company until they sighted land and then split up. Hjorleif settled at once on the south coast at Hjörleifshöfði ('Horleif's Head'). Ingolf, seeking the guidance of the gods, cast the carved pillars of his high-seat overboard, vowing to settle wherever they were washed ashore. Finding the pillars would take Ingolf all of three years.

After spending the first winter at Hjörleifshöfði, Hjorleif wanted to sow crops. He had only brought one ox, so he made his slaves drag the plough. It wasn't long before the slaves had had enough of this: they murdered Hjorleif and the other men in his party, and sailed off with his possessions and the women, to a group of islands off Iceland's south-west coast. These became known after them as the Vestmannaeyjar ('isles of the Irish'). Shortly after this, two of Ingolf's slaves, who were following the coast looking for his high-seat pillars, came to Hjörleifshöfði and found Hjorleif's body. Ingolf was saddened by the killing, 'but so it goes,' he said, 'with those who are not prepared to offer up sacrifice.' Ingolf guessed that the Irish had fled to the Vestmannaeyjar and went after them. Surprising the Irish while they were eating a meal, Ingolf slew some of them. The others died leaping off a cliff in their panic to escape.

After spending a third winter in Iceland, Ingolf finally found his high-seat pillars. Ingolf named the place Reykjavik, the 'bay of smoke', after the many steaming hot springs in the area. It is now Iceland's capital. Ingolf took into possession the whole of the Reykjanes peninsula west of the River Öxará as his estate and settled his followers and slaves on it as his dependents. More settlers soon followed. The *Landnámabók* gives us the names of 400 leading settlers, and over 3,000 other (mainly male) settlers, who migrated to Iceland in the settlement period. As the named settlers brought wives, children, dependents and slaves with them, it is possible that around 20,000 people had migrated to Iceland by around 900. By the eleventh century the population had probably reached about 60,000, though there was little fresh immigration after *c.* 930, by which time all the best grazing land had been claimed. Most of the named settlers came from western Norway but there were also a few Swedes and Danes, as well as a significant number who came from the Norse colonies in the Hebrides. Many of this last group were second-generation emigrants and several of them, such as the powerful matriarch Aud the Deep-Minded, were already Christian, while others, like Helgi the Lean, who worshipped both Christ and Thor, were partly so. However, the religion did not take root in Iceland and it died out with the first generation of settlers. Even Aud was given a pagan ship burial by her followers. Some of this group were the product of mixed Norse-Celtic marriages and two of the leading settlers, Dufthakr and Helgi the Lean, claimed descent from the Irish king Cerball mac Dúnlainge (r. 842–88). Many settlers, like Hjorleif, also took with them significant numbers of British and Irish slaves.

Recent analysis of the DNA of modern Icelanders has revealed just how significant the British and Irish contribution to the settlement of Iceland was. Analysis of the Y chromosomes of Icelandic men indicate that 75 per cent have Scandinavian origins, while 25 per cent have British or Irish origins. Strikingly, analysis of mitochondrial DNA of Icelandic women shows that the majority – 65 per cent – have British or Irish origins, with only 35 per cent having Scandinavian origins. The sexual imbalance suggests that, as in the Hebrides and the Faeroes, a majority of the Viking settlers were single men of relatively low social rank, who perhaps had been unable to marry at home because they had no access to land. Although only a bare majority of the settlers were Scandinavian, their social, political and cultural dominance was total. This is most clearly seen in the Icelandic language which, apart from some personal names, shows only insignificant Celtic influences. As a result of Iceland's isolation and cultural conservatism, modern Icelandic remains close to the *dönsk tunga* ('Danish Tongue'), the common Old Norse language spoken by all Scandinavians in the Viking Age.

According to the traditions recorded in *Landnámabók*, *Íslendingabók*, and the later Icelandic family sagas, the settlers of Iceland and the Faeroes were exiles fleeing the tyrannical rule that King Harald Fairhair (d *c.* 930) is supposed to have imposed on Norway after he defeated his rivals at the battle of Hafrsfjord. This is unlikely to be true. The date of Harald's victory is not known but it is unlikely to have taken place before 885 and was perhaps as late as 900. By this time the Faeroes had been long settled and the settlement of Iceland was already in full swing. Iceland was not fully settled until around 930, so Harald's rule could have played a part in sustaining emigration but certainly cannot have been the initial cause. However, the Icelandic traditions probably do contain a deeper truth. The leaders of the settlement of Iceland were all members of the *hersir* class, local chieftains who made up the lower ranks of the aristocracy: there were no jarls or kings among the settlers. The *hersir* were the main losers in the growth of centralised authority in Scandinavia during the eighth and ninth centuries, as it steadily undermined their local autonomy and began to turn them into agents of the crown. For men of this class, the opportunity to emigrate to a land that was beyond the reach of kings must have been an attractive one. Those settlers who came from the Hebrides may have found Iceland attractive also because it was unpopulated, and so would be able to hold their land in greater security than in the isles, where they were always exposed to attack by the Gaels.

The land-taking

Most of the leading settlers, or *lándnámsmenn* ('land-takers'), arrived in their own ships. These were not longships but sturdy merchant ships called *knarrs*. With shorter, broader and deeper hulls than longships, knarrs relied on sails alone, carrying only a couple of pairs of oars for manoeuvring in harbour. At the time of the settlements, knarrs probably had a cargo capacity of 25–30 tons; later in the Viking Age knarrs were being built that could carry up to 50 tons of cargo. Sea trials with modern replicas have proved that knarrs were very seaworthy ships. *Saga Siglar*, a replica of a 50-foot long knarr, known as *Skuldelev* 1, found in Roskilde Fjord in Denmark, circumnavigated the world in 1984–6 (though it later sank off the Spanish coast in 1992). The voyage to Iceland could take two to three weeks, often with stop-overs in Orkney, Shetland and the Faeroe Islands. The voyage cannot have been a comfortable experience. Knarrs were basically just large open boats without cabins to give crew and passengers shelter in bad weather. Tents were stretched over ships' decks to provide shelter in harbour but it is unlikely that this could be done at sea because the tent would catch the wind and drive the ship off course. People probably had to huddle under sealskin or greased leather cloaks in the hold, along with the livestock, to keep warm. Nor was there any possibility of enjoying any hot food on the high seas. Shipwreck was a real possibility. In one bad year, of the thirty-five ships sailing to Iceland all but eight were wrecked.

In the early years of the settlement the *lándnámsmenn* found plenty of land to go around and they needed no formal legal institutions for establishing ownership. Possession was all. The *lándnámsmenn* claimed as much land as they thought they needed to support themselves and their free and servile dependents. One of the most prominent *lándnámsmenn* was a woman, Aud the Deep-Minded, the daughter of the famous Hebridean Viking Ketil Flatnose and widow of King Olaf the White of Dublin. After her husband's death, Aud left Dublin and settled with her son Thorstein in Caithness in northern Scotland. After Thorstein was killed fighting the Scots, Aud took over leadership of his dependents and made the decision to emigrate to Iceland. While Viking Age Norse society was male dominated, it was not unusual for a woman to exercise authority, even though she had no formal role in public life. Norse society was hierarchical and, while an aristocratic woman might be inferior to an aristocratic man, she was always superior to everyone of lower social rank, whether they were men or women. Free-born Norse women of all social ranks enjoyed higher legal status than they did in Christian Europe. Women had the right to inherit property and a woman retained her property rights after marriage – her property did not become her husband's as it did in Christian countries. Women also had the right to divorce their husbands if a marriage was unsuccessful. Once Christianity had become established in Scandinavia, women's rights were gradually undermined as laws were bought into line with those prevailing in the rest of Europe.

Gender roles were clear-cut. Men ploughed, hunted, fished, traded and fought. Physically demanding crafts like blacksmithing and carpentry were also male preserves. Women's lives were mainly confined to the home or family farm: they baked, brewed, spun thread, wove cloth, made clothes, milked the cows, churned butter, nursed the sick and looked after the children and, in wealthier households, managed the servants and slaves. Women wore the keys to the house and family strongbox on their belts as a symbol of their domestic authority. When their husbands were absent on business or campaign, women held full authority over the family estate and if they were widowed they took the place of their husbands unless they remarried. As the widow of a king, Aud's authority over her followers and dependents would have been unquestioned. However, there was one male role she could not fulfil – she could not offer leadership in war, and it was undoubtedly this that lay at the root of her decision to emigrate.

Aud claimed several hundred square miles of land around Breiðarfjörður, settling where her high-seat pillars came ashore at

Hvamm. The *Laxdæla Saga* describes how Aud divided out the land between her followers:

> 'The same spring that Aud set up household at Hvamm, Koll [one of her Norwegian followers] married her grand-daughter Thorgerd. Aud gave, at her own cost, the bridal-feast, and let Thorgerd have for her dowry all Laxárdalur ('salmon-river valley'); and Koll set up a household there on the south side of the Laxá river.

> 'After that Aud gave to more men parts of her land-take. To Hord she gave all Hörðudalur as far as Skraumuhlaups River. He lived at Hörðubolstaðr, and was a man of the greatest mark, and blessed with noble offspring... Aud spoke to her men and said: "Now you shall be rewarded for all your work, for now I do not lack means with which to pay each one of you for your toil and good-will. You all know that I have given the Irishman named Erp, son of Jarl Meldun, his freedom, for far away was it from my wish that so high-born a man should bear the name of slave." Afterwards Aud gave him the lands of Sauðafell, between Tunguá River and Midá River... To Sökkolf Aud gave Sökkólfdalur, where he lived to old age. Hundi was the name of one of her freedmen. He was of Scottish kin. To him she gave Hundadalur. The fourth of Aud's slaves was called Vifil and to him she gave Vifilsdalur.' (trans. Magnus Maguusson and Herman Pálsson).

Aud was not unusual in freeing her slaves. Iceland's cool climate is unsuitable for intensive agriculture and the land was most economically used as pasture with widely dispersed farmsteads. Slaves could not be closely supervised under these circumstances so it made more sense to free them and make them rent-paying tenants instead. Slavery soon died out as a result. Except in the south-west, which became the most densely populated part of Iceland, most of the settlements were close to the sea: the interior was, as it still is, uninhabited.

The Icelandic economy depended mainly on animal husbandry, primarily cattle and sheep but with some pigs. Cattle needed to be kept indoors during the long winters and needed good fodder if they were to continue to provide milk. For this reason the hay crop was of crucial importance. Horses were bred both for transport and meat. Barley was grown on a small scale in sheltered areas near the south coast but grain and flour were mostly imported luxuries. This provided a diet rich in meat and dairy products but with little bread or fresh vegetables. Fishing, hunting of seals, seabirds and waterfowl, gathering seabirds' eggs, berries and shellfish, and scavenging beached whales provided a significant supplement to the Icelanders' diet. Despite the unbalanced diet, studies of the skeletal remains of early Icelanders show that the population was well-nourished and healthy. Timber was the main building material in Scandinavia, but it was in short supply in Iceland. The settlers adapted, building the walls of their longhouses out of blocks of turf laid on stone foundations, so that wood was only needed for the roofs (which were covered with turf). The turf gave excellent insulation against wind and cold.

Founding the Althing

As Iceland began to fill up with settlers it became increasingly lawless, as disputes easily escalated into protracted blood feuds. Local leadership was assumed by the *goðar*, a small group of wealthy chieftains who could offer advocacy and protection to smaller landowners in return for their political and military support. *Goðar* literally means 'priest', and the word is used as such in Scandinavia, but in Iceland it was a wholly secular hereditary office. However, it was not a closed class and men could rise into it or fall out of it according to their fortunes. Without the support of a *goði* it was all but impossible for an ordinary freeman to hold on to his land, but this did not mean that the *goðar* could take the loyalty of their followers for granted. As freemen they could, and did, transfer their allegiance to another *goði* if their opinions were not taken into account or their interests were neglected. A consequence of this was that Icelandic chieftaincies were political rather than territorial units, as a *goði's* followers could be scattered over a wide area.

The most important governmental institution of Viking Age Scandinavia after monarchy was the thing, an assembly of freemen at which local disputes and criminal offences were judged and at which new laws were made. Vikings took this institution with them when they emigrated and thing place-names are common in the areas of Britain where they settled, for example Tynwald (Isle of Man), Thingwall (Wirral), Dingwall (Ross and Cromarty), and Tingwall (one each in Orkney and Shetland). In Iceland the *goðar* set up district things to settle local disputes within a few years of the initial settlement. However, by the early tenth century the *goðar* recognised that there was a need for a higher authority to deal with wider disputes that the district things could not resolve. Appealing to the king of Norway was a possibility, but that would have limited Iceland's independence, so around 930 the *goðar* set up an all-Iceland assembly, the Althing (*Alþingi*). An issue that had to be addressed before the Althing could meet was that Iceland had no national law. The settlers came from many different places and had brought with them their own local laws and customs, creating endless problems when trying to resolve disputes. In preparation for the setting-up of the Althing, a man called Ulfljot was sent to Norway for three years to adapt the Gulathing laws of western Norway to Icelandic conditions.

The law codes of Viking Age Scandinavia were not based on general principles but on specified penalties for specified offences. The bulk of law concerned the payment of *mannbœtr* (compensation) for injuries and killings. Penalties were usually financial, requiring compensation to be paid, for example in the case of injuries, so much for the loss of a hand, so much for the loss of an arm, and so on. The scale of compensation depended on the severity of the injuries and on the status of the victim. This last principle was not adopted by the Icelanders, all freemen were treated as being of equal worth. In the case of slaves, it was their owners who were compensated if they were killed or injured. Theft was usually punished by hanging as it was assumed that thieves would be too poor to pay compensation for their crime. The most serious penalty, outlawry, was reserved for those who refused to accept judgment or pay compensation. Outlawry literally placed the offender outside the protection of the law and meant that he could be killed with impunity by anyone. In Iceland, an outlaw could pay ransom for his life (usually a heavy silver ring), in which case his outlawry was limited to three years exile, and the outlaw continued to enjoy legal protection in specified places for up to three years while he arranged passage out of the country. If he failed to leave after three years, he was then sentenced to full outlawry, which was for life and involved total rejection from society. It was illegal to help a full outlaw in any way, including giving him food or shelter, and he was not safe even abroad. It was hard on his family too. He lost all his property and his children were declared illegitimate and lost their inheritance rights. The Icelandic laws allowed a full outlaw to redeem himself by killing another outlaw. This was a calculated measure to sow mistrust among outlaws and discourage them from forming bands. Scandinavian laws allowed cases affecting the honour of the disputants to be settled out of court by judicial duels. In Iceland, this was known as *hólmgangr* ('island-going'), because the duels were usually held on islands in rivers. It was a right that was easily abused by good warriors.

Thingvellir

While Ulfljot was learning about Norwegian law, his half-brother Grímur Geitskör was sent to survey Iceland to find a suitable site to hold the Althing. The site he chose was Bláskógar, afterwards known as Thingvellir ('thing plain'), a dramatic place of ravines and waterfalls in the valley of the Öxará River in south-west Iceland. Thingvellir is a remarkable place in a country that is not short of remarkable places and it would be nice to think that Grímur was motivated by aesthetic considerations. However, the reasons for his choice were altogether more prosaic: the owner of the land had recently been outlawed for murder so the site could be taken over without paying anyone compensation. Being in the heart of the most densely part of Iceland also meant that most Icelanders would not have to travel too far to attend the Althing. Thingvellir is a lava plain lying almost right over the rift where the Eurasian and North American tectonic plates are being forced apart. As the lava plain was stretched by the movement of the tectonic plates, its surface cracked forming chasms and ravines and it was in the shelter of one of these, on the western edge of the plain, that the Althing was held. The Althing met annually for two weeks during June, when travelling was easiest and there was almost twenty-four hour daylight. Meetings were always held in the open air. People attending the Althing lived in temporary booths, the turf foundations of some of which can still be seen, or in tents. Until a church was built there in the eleventh century, there were no permanent structures on the site. The main business of the Althing was conducted from two different locations, the Lögberg ('Law Rock'), a natural platform for making speeches, and Neðri-Vellir, a level place on the west bank of the Öxará, where the *Lögretta* ('Law Council') met.

All freemen had the right to attend and speak, but the Althing was essentially an aristocratic and oligarchic form of government. All judicial and legislative power was in the hands of the thirty-six *goðar*, who alone had the right to vote in the *Lögretta*, the Althing's legislative council (the number of *goðar* was increased to thirty-nine in 965 and to forty-eight in 1005). The Icelandic Free State (also described as a Commonwealth) had only one public office, that of the Lawspeaker (*Lögsögumaðr*). There are no precedents for this office in Scandinavia, so it was a uniquely Icelandic institution. The *goðar* elected the Lawspeaker on the first day of the Althing for a three-year renewable term immediately after the outgoing Lawspeaker had opened proceedings. It was quite common for Lawspeakers to be re-elected: the longest serving Lawspeaker, Skapti Thórodsson, served for nine successive terms (1004–1030). The Lawspeaker's most important duty was to recite the Icelandic laws from the Law Rock. Until the Icelandic laws were written down in 1117–18, the Lawspeaker had to recite the laws from memory: one third of the laws were recited in each year of the Lawspeaker's term of office. If in doubt, the Lawspeaker could consult with five or more *lögmenn* (legal experts) before reciting the laws. The Lawspeaker was also chairman of the *Lögretta* but he had no executive authority.

Although the Althing was ultimately controlled by the *goðar*, decision-making tended to be consensual as they needed to consider the opinions of their 'thingmen' (followers). Failure to do this might lead them to transfer their allegiance to another *goði*. From around 965, legal disputes that could not be resolved at the district things were heard at the Althing's *fjórðungsdómar* ('quarter courts'), named after Iceland's four geographical quarters, the Court of the North Quarter, East Quarter, South Quarter and West Quarter. Around 1005 a fifth court was constituted to adjudicate in cases that had become deadlocked in the Quarter Courts. The *goðar* were expected to argue the cases of their followers at the Althing. The *goðar* were also expected to help enforce judgments on behalf of their followers as the Icelandic state had no law enforcement officers. In return for their advocacy and protection, the *goðar* could call upon the armed support of their followers in their feuds with other *goðar*. And those *goðar* with the largest numbers of followers to back them up, naturally enjoyed more influence at the Althing. For many of those who attended the Althing, however, legislation and litigation were side issues. The Althing brought the widely dispersed people of Iceland together like no other occasion, making it the most important social event of the year. There people could meet their friends and relatives, strike business deals and arrange marriages. Tradesmen and entertainers flocked to Thingvellir to tender to their every need.

Conversion to Christianity

The Althing was highly successful at resolving problems: not the least of its achievements was ensuring a peaceful conversion to Christianity in 999 or 1000. In 995 Olaf Tryggvason became king of Norway. Only a year before, Olaf had converted to Christianity and he now set about persuading his subjects of the virtues of the new religion by force rather than preaching. Like other Christian medieval European rulers, Olaf saw pagans as fair game, exempt from the normal rules of diplomacy. In 995 Olaf had intervened in Orkney to impose Christianity and it was clear that he would do the same in the Faeroes and Iceland as soon as the opportunity arose. By this time, many Icelanders had converted to Christianity as a result of missionary activity. The first missionary was a young Icelander called Thorvald Kodransson ('the Far-Travelled') who had converted while in Germany. He returned to Iceland around 981, but enjoyed little success and was eventually outlawed after killing two men, ending his days in a monastery in Russia. Other equally violent missionaries soon followed. Early in his reign, King Olaf sent Stefnir Thorgilsson, an Icelandic convert, to convert the Icelanders. He set about destroying pagan temples and in response the Althing called on families to prosecute any family members heard blaspheming the old gods. After Stefnir failed to make progress, Olaf sent an intemperate German priest called Thangbrand, who travelled the countryside with a small band of converts, preaching and killing anyone who

spoke against him. Thangbrand's mission also failed and, in 999, King Olaf turned to economic sanctions and hostage-taking. He closed Norwegian ports to Icelanders – a severe blow because Norway was Iceland's main trading partner – and imprisoned all the Icelanders then in Norway. Olaf threatened to maim or kill his prisoners unless Iceland accepted Christianity.

Under this intense pressure, the Icelanders divided into pro- and anti-Christian camps. The Christians threatened to set up their own parallel system of things and courts, pushing the country to the edge of civil war. Things came to a head at the Althing in 1000, but violence was averted by treating the issue like a blood feud that needed settling and submitting it to arbitration. Mediators chose the Lawspeaker, Thorgeir Thorkelsson, to settle dispute. Thorgeir was a pagan but had strong links with Christians too, making him acceptable to both sides. According to the account of the conversion in *Íslendingabók*, Thorgeir spent a day and a night huddled under a cloak while he deliberated his decision. After receiving assurances from both sides that they would abide by his ruling, Thorgeir announced 'that all people should become Christian and that those who here in the land were yet unbaptised should be baptized...' If they wished, people might sacrifice to old gods in private but it would be outlawry if this practice were verified by witnesses. Even though pagans were in the majority, Thorgeir's compromise was accepted peacefully and there was no pressure to revert to paganism, even when King Olaf was killed later that year. When he returned to his home in the north of Iceland, Thorgeir demonstrated his own commitment to the decision by demolishing his pagan shrine and throwing its idols into a waterfall, known since as Goðafoss ('falls of the gods'). A few years later, with the crisis safely passed, pagan worship was outlawed completely.

By following their traditional methods for resolving disputes the Icelanders not only avoided violence but also denied King Olaf the pretext, which a civil war might have offered, to assert any kind of sovereignty over their country. Olaf was more successful in the case of the Faeroe Islands. In 1000, Olaf commissioned Sigmundur Brestisson, a Faeroese exile in Norway, to convert the Faeroe islanders to Christianity and to bring them under Norwegian sovereignty. The leader of the pagan party was Tróndur of Gøtu, who publicly cursed Christianity by Thor's hammer. Sigmundur and his men broke into Tróndur's home one night and offered him the choice of conversion or having his head cut off. Confronted with such a persuasive theological argument, Tróndur chose Christianity and the rest of the islanders took the hint and followed suit. Sigmundur's methods of conversion made him a hated figure and he was murdered in 1005, but the islands remained under Norwegian sovereignty.

The Gunnbjorn Skerries

Once the Norse had settled Iceland, it was probably only a matter of time before some storm-driven seafarer discovered Greenland. Some time between 900 and 930, Gunnbjorn Ulf-Krakuson was blown off course on a voyage from Norway to Iceland and sighted a group of islands to the west of Iceland, known after him as the Gunnbjorn Skerries. This is generally reckoned to be the first European sighting of Greenland and, as Greenland is geologically part of North America, of the American continent. The exact location of the skerries is uncertain. Ivar Bardarson, a fourteenth-century Norwegian traveller, located them two days sail due west of Snæfellsnes on Iceland's west coast. This makes it most likely that the skerries were the Sermiligaaq archipelago, a group of ice-free islands east of Angmagsalik on Greenland's heavily glaciated east coast. Gunnbjorn did not land on the skerries and his discovery excited little interest at the time because there was still good land to be had in Iceland: Gunnbjorn himself settled there. As the Icelandic population grew, people were forced onto more marginal land. In 975–6 there was a cold summer and the grass didn't grow well enough for many farmers to harvest enough hay to keep their livestock alive through the winter. People died of starvation. Gunnbjorn's skerries began to look more attractive and in 978 Snæbjorn Galti set off to look for them with twenty-four followers. They built a house on the skerries and spent a dreadful winter completely snowed in until the beginning of March. Confinement did no one's mood any good, quarrels broke out, turned bloody and after Snæbjorn was murdered the would-be colonists left for Norway.

Brattahlid

The first successful Norse settlement in Greenland was led by the red-bearded, red-haired Erik Thorvaldson, better known as Erik the Red. Born in Norway, Erik emigrated to Iceland while still a child, after his father was exiled for a blood feud. As all the best land was claimed, his family were forced to settle on Iceland's barren and icy south-east coast. When he grew up, Erik's attempts to claim better land for himself involved him in many disputes and several killings and in the early 980s he was outlawed for three years. As he had to leave the country anyway, Erik sailed off to look for Gunnbjorn's skerries, promising to return if he found them. Erik made land on Greenland's east coast, near a prominent glacier, which became known as Blåserk ('blue shirt'), probably Rigny Bjerg, well north of the Arctic Circle. Erik followed the inhospitable coast south, eventually rounding Cape Farewell, Greenland's most southerly point. Sailing north again Erik discovered Greenland's eastern fjords, in the sheltered reaches of which he found good grazing land and birch woods. The land was completely uninhabited but Erik found the remains of boats and dwellings along the shores. These were relics of the prehistoric Dorset Inuit people who had abandoned the area a century before because of climate change. The Norse expansion into the North Atlantic coincided with the beginning of the Medieval Warm Period, a period lasting from c. 900–c. 1250 when the climate of the North Atlantic region was warmer than the long-term average. The Inuit way of life depended on seal hunting, which was best done in late winter and spring when the seals were exposed on sea ice. In the warmer climate, the eastern fjords had become largely ice-free so the Inuit retreated north to better hunting grounds.

Erik spent three summers exploring Greenland before returning to Iceland, where he hoped to persuade others to join him in colonising the eastern fjords. A born salesman, Erik decided to call his discovery Greenland 'because men would be drawn to go there if it had an attractive name'. Thanks to the recent famine, many families were interested and when Erik headed back to Greenland next summer, twenty-five ships set sail with him. *Íslendingabók* mentions that this happened fourteen or fifteen years before Iceland accepted Christianity, that is around

985–6. Of the twenty-five ships that set out with Erik, only fourteen made it safely to the eastern fjords: the rest turned back or were lost at sea. Thorbjorn, a friend of Erik's who emigrated to Greenland a few years after the initial settlement, brought thirty people with him in his ship. If this was typical, the Greenland colony would have started with little more than 400 people. However, this was still enough to found two settlements, the larger Eastern Settlement (Eystrbyggð) in the south around modern Qaqortoq, and the smaller Western Settlement (Vestribyggð) 300 miles further north around Nuuk. Later, a small Middle Settlement was founded half way between the two. The settlement was organised on Icelandic lines with an annual thing that Erik presided over in a role similar to the Lawspeaker's.

Erik's own estate was at Brattahlið ('steep slope'), about 60 miles from the open sea at the head of Tunuliarfik Fjord, which in his day was known as Eriksfjord. Erik's descendents continued to live at Brattahlið until the fifteenth century. Excavations at Brattahlið have uncovered the stone foundations of three longhouses with associated outbuildings, a probable thing place, a probable forge, and the foundations of a stone church. All of the stone structures date probably to the thirteeth or fourteenth centuries. In all likelihood, Erik's farm was built of turf, like contemporary buildings in Iceland, and its traces have been destroyed by the later buildings. The church had an associated burial ground containing around 144 burials, some of which had gravestones: one was engraved with a short runic inscription reading 'Ingibjørg's grave'. In the middle of the burial ground excavators discovered the traces of a very small turf church with an interior space of little more than 6 feet broad and 11 feet wide. The turf walls are so thick that its external dimensions are around 12 feet broad by 15 feet long. This building can be directly connected to Erik's wife, Thjodhild (another Icelander who could trace her descent back to Cerball mac Dúnlainge). While visiting King Olaf's court in Norway in c. 1000, Erik's son Leif converted to Christianity. When he was ready to return home, King Olaf asked Leif to preach Christianity in Greenland and provided him with a priest to baptise and instruct the people. Erik was not pleased by his son's conversion and refused to accept the new faith. Thjodhild, however, embraced Christianity at once and built a small church near their farm, where she and other new converts prayed. Erik became even more unhappy after Thjodhild's conversion: she refused to sleep with him any more because he was a pagan.

To begin with the Greenland colony flourished. By around 1100, the colony's population had grown to around 4,000 people. The Eastern Settlement had 190 farms, twelve parish churches, an Augustinian monastery, a Benedictine nunnery, and a rather modest cathedral at Garðar (now Igaliku). The Western Settlement had ninety farms and four churches, while the Middle Settlement had twenty farms. Sheep, goat and cattle rearing formed the basis of the economy, but in sheltered areas it was even possible to grow a little barley. The colony was not self-sufficient as it lacked timber, grain and iron. Fortunately, the colony had unique access to valuable resources that were much in demand in Europe: walrus ivory and hide (used for making ships' ropes), sealskin (for waterproof cloaks and boots), polar bear skins, and gyrfalcons. Gyrfalcons were the most expensive of all birds used for the elite medieval sport of falconry. In the Islamic world a gyrfalcon cost around 1,000 gold dinars, the equivalent of £120,000 ($186,000) today. Narwhal tusks were even more valuable: medieval Europeans believed them to be the horns of the mythical unicorn and would pay more than their weight in gold for them. The Greenlanders obtained these products on annual hunting expeditions to the Norðsetr, the area around Disko Island, about 250 miles north of the Arctic Circle. Recently, a probable Norse camp has been found at Tanfield Valley on Baffin Island's south coast, suggesting that hunting expeditions may have been made to this area too.

Viking navigation

The Norse Greenland colony was medieval Europe's most remote outpost. To reach it from the European continent seafarers needed to cross almost 2,000 miles of open ocean. At the time, only the Malays in the Indian Ocean and the Polynesians in the Pacific undertook longer oceanic voyages, but they did so in warmer and more predictable seas. In the Icelandic sagas, Viking seafarers seem to show an almost casual confidence in their ability to make long open sea voyages but in reality

Viking navigation was not an exact art. Viking skippers recognised this and whenever they could they hugged the coast, keeping a safe distance offshore to avoid shoals and reefs, and navigating using landmarks on shore. At night, or if bad weather was setting in, they would seek a safe anchorage, rather than risk getting lost or running aground in darkness or poor visibility. Danes and Swedes, who sailed mostly in the North Sea and the Baltic, very rarely had to sail out of sight of land: Norwegians, setting out for Shetland, the Faeroes, Iceland or Greenland had no choice. When they had to make an open sea crossing, Viking navigators used a technique known as latitude sailing. Leaving his home port, the navigator would sail north or south along the coast to reach a point he knew to be on the same latitude as his intended destination. He would then wait until there was a favourable wind blowing in the right direction and head out onto the open sea and try to follow a heading due east or west to his destination.

In European waters, at least, Viking navigators were heirs to a vast body of seafaring lore and sailing directions that had been passed down orally from generation to generation for centuries. Navigation was a specialised occupation and the *leiðsagnarmaðr* (pilot) might be the only professional seaman on a ship. This did not mean he was the captain: the ship's owner was always the captain irrespective of how competent a sailor he was. Successful navigators were experts at reading sea and weather conditions, interpreting the movements of wildlife, which could reveal the direction of land, and observing the positions and altitudes of the sun and stars to determine latitude accurately. However, in common with all navigators before the eighteenth century, Vikings had no means of determining their longitude. The best they could do was to estimate their position based on their speed and direction of travel. It is not known how Viking navigators estimated speed, as there is no evidence for use of the ship log before the fifteenth century, but the evidence of the sagas shows that they could do this with tolerable accuracy. In conditions of poor visibility even the most experienced navigators could suffer from *hafvilla* ('confusion'), that is completely losing their bearings. This was most likely to happen when a ship was becalmed for a long period in fog, when it could drift imperceptibly far off its course on the ocean currents.

A navigator's most reliable guide was the Pole Star, which, north
of the Tropics, is always above the horizon and always points due
north. The Pole Star is also a reliable indicator of latitude. As the still
point around which the other stars rotate, the altitude of the Pole Star
remains constant all night and, when viewed from any fixed location,
remains the same all year round. From night to night a navigator could
estimate the height of the Pole Star above the horizon: if it was higher
than the previous night, the ship had sailed further north; if it was
lower, the ship was further south. In summer in high latitudes the Pole
Star could be invisible during the night long twilight. At such times
navigators had to rely on the sun, which is due south at noon, for
directions. The height of the sun at noon can also be used to determine
latitude, though in this case higher means further south, lower means
further north. Through observations like these, Norse navigators knew
that Cape Farewell in Greenland (59° 46′ N) was almost at the same
latitude as Bergen, the main port in western Norway (60° 4′ N). Sailing
directions in one copy of *Landnámabók* advised navigators heading to
Greenland to sail a slightly more northerly course, approximately 61°,
in order to avoid the Shetland Islands, which share the same latitude
as Bergen. A ship from Bergen should first sail north along the coast
to Hernar (60° 36′ N), then: 'sail west but keep far enough north of the
Shetlands so that these islands are barely visible in clear weather. One
should stay far enough south of the Faeroes so that their steep and
high mountains are just halfway up over the horizon. In addition, one
should stay far enough south of Iceland so that you can't see land but
just the coast-bound birds. When you reach the east coast of Greenland
you should keep a lookout for landmarks and follow the current
west around Cape Farewell to the villages on the south-west point.'

The sailing directions do not rely on latitude sailing alone: the
navigator is expected to know important landmarks and understand
the movements of seabirds. These could provide important clues about
the direction of land. During the breeding season (April-August),
which was much the same as the Vikings' sailing season, seabirds feed
at sea but return regularly to land to feed their young and to roost at
night. Different birds range further to feed than others. Kittiwakes may
travel over 100 miles from land to feed, while smaller seabirds such as

puffins and guillemots rarely travel more than 6 miles. Observing the flight of seabirds in the morning and evening gives reliable indications of the direction of land. In poor visibility, the presence of puffins and guillemots would also give early warning that land was very close. Some navigators took caged birds with them. When Floki Vilgerdarson set out for Iceland he took three ravens with him. When he released the first, it flew away in the direction of the Faeroe Islands, their last port of call. When he released the second, it circled round for a while before returning to the ship. When he released the third, it flew away straight ahead and by following in that direction Floki found land.

There were many other environmental clues for the navigator who knew how to read them. Whales have regular migration routes and feeding grounds. For instance, there is one south of Iceland, roughly halfway between the Faeroe Islands and Greenland. A build-up of cloud on the horizon may indicate the presence of land. If the sea suddenly slackens in a storm it may be a sign that the ship has sailed into the lee of an island hidden by rain, fog or darkness. The colour and clarity of the sea can provide further clues about a ship's position. Rivers wash silt into the sea, sometimes clouding it for miles offshore. A seafarer sailing to Greenland would expect to see ice floes when he approached its coast.

Navigation aids

Viking navigators were under no illusions about the dangers of seafaring and it is likely that for many the most important navigation aid was a Thor's hammer amulet, the thunder god Thor being a protector of travellers and seafarers. Compasses or lodestones were unknown to the Vikings but they may have used other simple navigation aids. One of these was the sounding line, which the Vikings are thought to have adopted from the English late in the Viking Age. This was simply a rope with a weight tied on to one end that was lowered from the ship into the sea to measure its depth. It was especially useful in the shallow shoally waters of the Baltic or southern North Sea. English navigators liked to keep about 10 fathoms (60 feet/18.3 m) of water under their keels when coasting.

Vikings may have used two other navigation aids, the so-called sun stone, and a sun compass. The sun stone is mentioned in a small number of saga sources and is supposed to have been a crystal that was used to locate the position of the sun on overcast days. *The Story of Rauð and his Sons* describes the use of the sun stone on land:

'The weather was thick and snowy as Sigurd had predicted. Then King Olaf summoned Sigurd and Dagur to him. The king made people look out and nowhere could they see a clear sky. Then he asked Sigurd to tell where the sun was at that time. He gave a clear assertion. Then the king made them bring the sun stone and held it up and saw where light radiated from the stone and thus directly verified Sigurd's prediction.' (trans J. E. Turville-Petre, Viking Society for Northern Research 1947.)

The sun stone is thought to have been the transparent crystalline form of calcium carbonate known as Iceland Spar, which is known for its polarising qualities. However, modern experiments indicate that the polarising effect is not strong enough to locate the sun's position under a heavy overcast and works only under a clear sky or light overcast when the sun's position can be seen with the naked eye anyway. No sun stone has ever been found in a Viking context but one has been recovered from an Elizabethan shipwreck off the Channel Island of Alderney, though this does not prove that it was being used for navigation.

The existence of the sun compass rests on even more slender evidence than the sun stone. In 1948, excavations of a Norse monastery at Narsarsuaq on Uunartoq Fjord in Greenland uncovered half of a small wooden disc, around 2¾ inches in diameter (7 cm) with a hole in the centre and equidistant notches cut around the edges. When complete, there were probably thirty-two notches. The surface of the disc is incised with lines, some of which are parabolic. It is these parabolic lines that have led to the disc being interpreted as part of a sun compass. *If* the disc had at its centre a gnomon, then these parabolic lines might represent the course of the sun's shadow through the day. These devices are easy to make and would have been a useful aid to latitude sailing. If the course of the sun's shadow was plotted onto the disc at the port of departure, a ship's latitude relative to the starting place could easily be determined by measuring the length of the sun's shadow daily at noon. If the shadow falls short of the line, the shorter shadow shows that the sun is higher in the sky, meaning that the ship has sailed south relative to its starting point. If the shadow crosses the line, the longer shadow shows that the sun is lower in the sky, meaning that the ship has sailed north relative to its starting point. Because the altitude of the sun varies with the time of year as well as with latitude, the device would have been absolutely accurate only on the day it was made and it would have become increasingly unreliable the longer a voyage was, limiting its usefulness. Another limitation is that the compass has to be held absolutely level while a reading is being taken – no easy thing in a small ship on a choppy sea. Floating the compass in a bucket of water might have solved this problem, but only if some way could be found to stop it spinning. The disc may simply have been part of a child's toy or was perhaps a 'confession disc', similar to those used by Icelandic priests to count the number of people taking confession. In any case, the monastery at Narsarsuaq was built after the end of the Viking Age, so even if the disc was part of a sun compass, it is not evidence that they were used by Vikings.

It is possible that by the end of the Viking Age, navigators had access to written tables of astronomical observations. An Icelander called Oddi Helgasson (*c.* 1070/80–*c.* 1140/50), whose knowledge of astronomy earned him the nickname Star Oddi, compiled a chart showing the direction of sunrise and sunset through the year from different harbours in Iceland, which enabled navigators to take directions. It is very likely that such knowledge was also transmitted orally, from one generation of navigators to the next.

The Vinland voyages

The final step on the Vikings 'stepping stone' route across the Atlantic was from Greenland to the North American continent. The story of the Norse discovery of America is told in the two 'Vinland sagas', *Grænlendinga saga* ('The Saga of the Greenlanders'), written *c.* 1200, and *Eiríks saga rauða* ('Erik the Red's Saga'), written *c.* 1265. The Greenlanders' saga is generally thought to be the more reliable and is the one generally followed here. Erik's saga, which actually does not have much to say about Erik the Red, includes several fantastical elements, such as an encounter with a uniped (a mythical one-legged creature), which undermine its credibility. Once again, this step was made by accident. Bjarni Herjolfsson, an Icelandic merchant, returned home from a trip to Norway in 986 and found that his father had emigrated to Greenland with Erik the Red. Knowing nothing about Greenland other than that is was a mountainous land with glaciers, no trees and good pastures, Bjarni immediately set off after his father. It was a reckless thing to do. Three days into his voyage the weather turned, fog and a north wind set in and for many days he was unable to get his bearings. When at last the weather cleared, he found himself off the coast of a densely forested, hilly land. This was obviously not Greenland, so Bjarni turned his ship north and after two days made another landfall, this time off a flat, forested land. Bjarni's crew wanted to land but he refused and continued to the north-east, and after three days encountered a rocky, mountainous and heavily glaciated land. This land seemed to Bjarni to be too barren to be Greenland. Putting it astern, Bjarni sailed west for four days and finally reached the Eastern Settlement and his father's farm at Herjolfsnes.

Bjarni came in for a lot of criticism for his lack of curiosity about the lands he had discovered, but he was a merchant not an explorer. When Bjarni gave up trading, Leif Eriksson bought his ship and began to prepare an expedition to follow-up on his discoveries. This took place shortly after Greenland became Christian. Leif set off with thirty-five men, including Tyrkir the Southerner, who was probably a German. Leif asked his father to be joint leader of the expedition with him but he refused, citing that he was too old. Leif began by reversing Bjarni's voyage. Sailing north-west, Leif first came to a land of bare rock and glaciers. Leif was determined to go one better than Bjarni; he went ashore and gave the land a name, Helluland ('Slab Land'). Sailing south, they came to a low wooded land with white sand beaches. After going ashore to explore, Leif called this Markland ('Forest Land'). Leif pressed on still further south and discovered a land where grapes grew wild and the rivers teemed with salmon. Leif decided to call this land Vinland ('Wine Land'). The party built houses at a place afterwards called Leifsbuðir ('Leif's booths'), where they spent a comfortable winter. There was no frost and the days were much longer than they were in Greenland. In the spring Leif and his crew loaded a full cargo of timber and set off back to Greenland. On the way, Leif rescued fifteen shipwrecked Norwegian sailors from a reef near the Greenland coast. This earned him his nickname Leif the Lucky, though it was the shipwrecked sailors who were really the lucky ones. Or perhaps not; most of them died of an epidemic in the winter, along with Erik the Red.

The locations of Leif's discoveries will probably never be known for certain. Leif's description of Helluland is a good fit for Baffin Island in the Canadian Arctic, and Markland is almost certainly Labrador. Vinland is much harder to identify. The Hudson River is the southern limit of Atlantic salmon, while the St Lawrence is the northern limit of wild grapes, which would place Vinland in New England or the Canadian Maritimes. However, winters in these areas are certainly not frost free. According to *Grænlendinga saga*, Leif observed that on the shortest day the sun rose before 9 a.m. and did not set until after 3 p.m. but these are not clock times, as the Vikings did not have clocks, so they cannot help us determine Vinland's latitude. What is certain, however, is that Leif and his crew were the first Europeans to set foot on the North American continent.

Leif's voyage was followed-up by his brother Thorvald. Thorvald spent a winter at Leifsbuðir. The next summer Thorvald explored the coast to the north-east. The ship broke its keel when it was driven ashore in a storm. The party had to spend some time repairing the ship: they left the old keel on a headland that Thorvald decided to call Kjalarnes ('Keel headland'). Sailing further east, the party landed to explore at the mouth of a fjord. Returning to the ship, they saw three humps on the beach. These turned out to be canoes, each with three men hiding underneath. So began the first encounter between Europeans and Native Americans. It did not go well. The Native Americans tried to run away from the strangers but Thorvald's men captured eight of them and killed them, apparently without any provocation. Unfortunately for Thorvald, the ninth escaped in one of the boats and raised the alarm. Further up the fjord, the Norse could see low humps which they surmised to be houses. Soon a swarm of canoes was heading down the fjord towards them. The heavily outnumbered Norse defended themselves with their shields and the natives soon withdrew but not before Thorvald had received a fatal arrow wound. He died soon after and became the first European to be buried in North America. The rest of the party returned safely to Greenland.

The identity of the unfortunate native Americans is unknown: if Vinland really was as far south as Leif's account implies, they would have belonged to one of the many Algonquian-speaking peoples who inhabited the east coast between Chesapeake Bay and the St Lawrence before European settlement. In the Icelandic sources, all native peoples encountered in North America and Greenland are described simply as Skrælings. The origins of the name are uncertain. One is that it means 'screamers', perhaps because the Norse found their language completely incomprehensible. Perhaps more likely, it may be derived from the Old Norse word *skrá*, meaning skin. This would probably be a reference to their animal skin clothing, which would have contrasted with the woven woollen clothing worn by the Norse.

A few years later Thorfinn Karlsefni set out from Greenland to found a permanent colony at Leifsbuðir. He took with him his wife Gudrid, sixty men and five women, and a variety of livestock. The party spent an uneventful winter during which Gudrid gave birth to a son, Snorri, the first European to be born in America. The following spring saw their first encounter with Skrælings, who came to Leifsbuðir to trade furs. The Greenlanders' iron tools and weapons must have fascinated the Skrælings, who still had a Stone Age culture (small artefacts of native copper and meteoritic iron were used), but Karlsefni forbade his men to trade any of them. During a second encounter later in the year, one of Karlsefni's men killed a Skræling for trying to steal some weapons. The rest fled but soon returned to get their revenge. Expecting this, Karlsefni had prepared an ambush and the Skrælings were easily driven off. Nevertheless, the next spring Karlsefni abandoned the settlement and returned to Greenland. He eventually bought lands in Iceland.

Erik's saga adds that on the return voyage a ship owned by Bjarni Grimolfsson was blown far off course into Irish waters. The ship's hull became infested with driftwood-eating worms and began to leak. The ship's boat was only large enough to take half the crew. Bjarni decreed that lots would be drawn to decide who would go in the boat, and who would remain behind. Bjarni was one of those who drew a place in the boat. As Bjarni prepared to depart with the boat, a young Icelander asked:

> 'Are you going to leave me here Bjarni?'
> 'That is how it has to be,' replied Bjarni.
> The Icelander said, 'But that is not what you promised when I left my father's farm in Iceland to go with you.'
> 'I see no other way,' said Bjarni, 'what do you suggest?"'
> 'I suggest we change places, you come up here and I shall go down there.'
> 'So be it,' said Bjarni, 'I can see that you would spare no effort to live and are afraid to die.' (trans. Magnus Magnusson & Hermann Pálsson.)

With that, Bjarni climbed back into the sinking ship and the Icelander took his place in the boat. Those in the ship's boat reached safety in Ireland; Bjarni and everyone left with him in the ship were never seen again and presumably drowned. Bjarni was within his rights to refuse to change places with the Icelander, but could not have done so without also appearing to be afraid of death. The Icelander, perhaps intentionally, had put him in a difficult situation. Bjarni could save his life or save his honour, but not both. For a proud man like Bjarni, it was not a difficult dilemma to resolve. By giving up his place in the boat Bjarmi saved his honour, secured his posthumous reputation, and was remembered by future generations. No one knows the name of the cowardly Icelander, he was *niðing* and would have lived the rest of his life as a social outcast.

A second attempt at settlement was led by Leif's half-sister Freydis, who, according to Erik's saga, had already been to Vinland as part of Karlsefni's expedition. She invited two brothers called Helgi and Finnbogi to join her, but she was a difficult, uncompromising woman who seemed set on causing conflict with them from the very start. Ill feeling grew during the winter and in the spring Freydis sent her men to kill the brothers and their followers after an argument over a ship. None of the men were willing to kill the five women so Freydis took an axe and did the job herself. Despite threatening to kill anyone who told of her evil deeds when they got home, people inevitably talked. Leif, who was now leader of the Greenland community, was horrified when he heard the rumours, but had not the heart to punish his sister, only predicting that her sins would blight her descendents' fortunes.

The failure of Freydis' expedition ended Norse attempts at settlement in America. The distances involved were too great and the small Greenland colony simply did not have the resources or the surplus population to support a colonisation effort so far away. Though iron weapons gave the Norse a military advantage over the natives, it was not marked enough to prevail against their superior numbers. The immediate consequences of the Norse discovery of North America were slight. The existence of Vinland soon became known in Europe but it was thought merely to be another island in the Atlantic Ocean, like Iceland or Greenland, so its significance was not understood. Erik Gnupsson, the bishop of Garðar, set off on a new expedition to Vinland in 1112 but its fate is not recorded. As a new bishop was sent to Greenland in 1115, Erik may not have returned and been given up for dead. After this interest in Vinland faded and by the time the Vinland sagas were written, it had largely been forgotten outside Iceland and Greenland. There is no evidence, for example, that Columbus knew of Vinland's existence when he set off on his voyage across the Atlantic in 1492 in search of a route to China, only to find America in the way.

Voyages from Greenland to Markland and Helluland continued at least until the fourteenth century. The last recorded expedition was in 1347, when a small ship with seventeen Greenlanders was blown off course to Iceland while returning from cutting timber in Markland. As far as Native Americans were concerned, the Vinland voyages might as well have never happened: they had no impact whatsoever on North America's cultural development. Despite this, the Norse discovery of North America does mark a significant moment in world history: it was the end of humanity's 70,000 year journey out of Africa. The descendents of peoples who had left Africa and migrated east through Asia to the Americas had finally met the descendents of people who had left Africa and migrated west. The circle of the world was closed.

L'Anse aux Meadows

The first archaeological evidence for the Norse presence in North America was a runestone found at Kensington, Minnesota, in 1898, or so it briefly seemed. The text purported to describe the journey of eight Goths (i.e. Swedes) and twenty-two Norwegians from Vinland to Minnesota via the Great Lakes in 1362. Closer examination revealed that the runes were a mixture of types used from the ninth to the eleventh century and homemade symbols. The language used was the distinctive Swedish-Norwegian dialect spoken by Scandinavian settlers in Minnesota in the 1890s, while the date was based on the Arabic system of numeration that was not used in fourteenth-century Scandinavia. Although it still has its advocates, academics quickly recognised that the Kensington runestone was a forgery, presumably made by local Scandinavian settlers either as a joke or for reasons of ethnic prestige. The stone was the beginning of a minor tradition of providing the missing evidence that would prove beyond doubt that the Vinland sagas were not just romantic travellers' tales about imaginary lands. Runic inscriptions have even been found in Oklahoma.

Real archaeological evidence of a Norse presence in North America finally came to light in 1961 with the discovery of a Norse settlement at L'Anse aux Meadows in Newfoundland. L'Anse aux Meadows is a shallow, sheltered cove at Newfoundland's northern tip. The cove faces west, with a clear view of the hills of Labrador 30 miles away across the Strait of Belle Isle. Although the landscape is open grassland, the name actually has nothing to do with meadows, it is an English corruption of the name given by early French settlers, L'Anse-aux-Méduses, meaning 'Jellyfish Bay'. L'Anse aux Meadows was uninhabited when the Norse arrived but they were not the first to spot its attractions; there had been several phases of occupation by early Inuit seal hunters spread over thousands of years.

The Norse settlement consisted of eight buildings, all of them built of turf and lined with timber. Three of the buildings were long-houses, the others were probably workshops. The settlement could have accommodated up to about ninety people. Longhouses may have been the typical Viking dwelling but they are not unique to them.

Longhouses were built by several Native American peoples including the Inuit; indeed, the foundations of long-abandoned Inuit longhouses in the Canadian Arctic have sometimes been mistaken for Viking longhouses. However, the large numbers of metal artefacts excavated from the settlement prove beyond any doubt that L'Anse aux Meadows was a Norse settlement. The majority of these objects were wrought iron ship rivets, suggesting that ship repair was a major activity on site. The rivets may have been manufactured at a small forge that was built a small distance from the settlement, probably as a precaution against fire. Native Americans made small tools from meteoritic iron and by cold-hammering native copper, but they lacked the technology to smelt iron. A typically Scandinavian bronze ring pin was also found on the site. The discovery of a soapstone spindle whorl confirmed the saga accounts that women went on the Vinland voyages as spinning was a female activity. Stone weights found in one building may have been part of a loom. A glass bead, a broken bone needle and a whetstone for sharpening needles and knives are also all typical of the sort of artefacts that are found in Norse settlements of the Viking Age. Radiocarbon-dating of organic materials indicates that the site was occupied *c.* 980-1020, which accords well with the saga traditions.

Even though the sagas say that the Norse took livestock with them, the excavations at L'Anse aux Meadows provided no evidence of farming or the presence of European domesticated animals. The settlers were, however, active hunters. The bones of caribou, wolf, fox, bear, lynx, marten, seal, whale and walrus and of many species of fish and wildfowl have been found on the site. The environment around L'Anse aux Meadows bears little resemblance to that of Vinland. Winters are severe and there are no wild grapes so, unless Leif greatly exaggerated the delights of Vinland, which is not impossible – his father had taught him the importance of good marketing – L'Anse aux Meadows is unlikely to be Leifsbuðir. It seems more likely that L'Anse aux Meadows was a base for expeditions further south. That such expeditions took place is proven by the presence of butternuts among food remains on the site. An American species of walnut, butternuts grow no further north than southern New Brunswick and the lower St Lawrence, more than 500 miles south of L'Anse aux Meadows.

So far, only one Norse artefact that is generally accepted as genuine has been found in the United States. This is a worn silver penny minted during the reign of the Norwegian king Olaf Kyrre (r. 1067–93) that was found during excavations of a large Native American village at Goddard Point on the coast of Maine. The exact circumstances in which the coin was found are undocumented and the possibility that it was introduced to the site to manipulate the evidence cannot be ruled out. Even if this was not the case, it is not evidence that Norse seafarers visited Maine. The Goddard site provided abundant evidence that it was at the centre of an extensive trade network that extended as far as Arctic Canada. As the Greenland Norse continued to visit Labrador until the fourteenth century, the coin could originally have been acquired as an exotic curio by an Inuit and found its way to Maine along the native trade routes, probably changing hands many times.

Vikings and Skrælings in the Arctic

The Norse Greenlander's hunting expeditions to the Norðsetr continued long after the end of the Viking Age proper (c. 1100). The farthest north that the Norse can be proven beyond doubt to have got is Kingigtorssuaq, a small, rocky island about 72° north. Some time in the mid- to late thirteenth century, three Norsemen made a runic inscription on a small flat stone and placed it in a cairn on top of the island, where it was found in 1824: 'Erlingur the son of Sigvaths and Baarne Thordars son and Enriði son, Washingday [Saturday] before Rogation Day [25 April], raised this mound and rode...' The inscription ends with six unique runes presumed to be a secret code. For the inscription to have been made so early in the year, before the sea ice began to break up, the Norse must have spent the winter in the area. It is likely, however, that the Norse did sail much further north than this. In 1876, a British oceanographic expedition discovered two ancient cairns on Washington Irving Island, off northern Greenland, around 79° north and over 1,000 miles north of the Western Settlement. The British dismantled the cairns to see if earlier explorers had left a message hidden in them. Finding none, and not knowing of any other Europeans who had ventured so far north, the British concluded that the cairns must have been built by the Norse. If so, this may be where the Viking expansion finally fizzled out, less than 800 miles from the North Pole. Modern researchers who have examined the cairns agree that they are unlikely to be of Inuit construction.

At first the Norse had the Norðsetr to themselves but around 1170 they made contact with the Thule Inuit, who had recently migrated into the high Arctic from Alaska, displacing the earlier Dorset Inuit. The ancestors of the modern Inuit peoples, the Thule were superbly adapted to life in the high Arctic. The secret of their success was their mastery of whale hunting – earlier Inuit cultures could only exploit beached whales. The Thule pursued whales at sea in umiaks, open hide-covered boats, about 30 feet long, driven by paddles. Whales were killed using a toggling harpoon. These have detachable points that lodge inside the whale's body and cannot fall out. The points are attached by ropes to inflated sealskin floats, which prevent the whale from diving and from sinking when it has been killed. This technology gave the Thule access to far more abundant resources than were available to earlier Inuit peoples, who had depended on seals. The Thule also used the bow and arrow, which earlier Inuit had not.

The initial encounters between the Norse and the Skrælings, as the Norse called the Inuit, are not recorded. Hunter-gatherer peoples vigorously defend their hunting grounds against interlopers and, as Thorvald had shown in Vinland, the Norse also had an instinct to fight first and ask questions later. Norse artefacts have been found on many Inuit archaeological sites in the Canadian Arctic and northern Greenland so there may also have been trade: there are however other explanations for their presence. The Inuit site that has so far produced the greatest number of Norse artefacts is Skraeling Island, a small island off Ellesmere Island nearly 78° north, which was occupied repeatedly by early Inuit peoples over a period of over 5,000 years. The Inuit were drawn to the island because of its proximity to the North Water Polynya, a large permanently ice free area in northern Baffin Bay (between Ellesmere Island and Greenland), which attracts large numbers of seals and whales. The Thule arrived on Skraeling Island in the thirteenth century and built a cluster of winter houses from stones, turf and whalebones.

The Norse artefacts from Skraeling Island include pieces of woven woollen cloth, iron ship rivets, knife and spear blades, a carpenter's plane (with its blade missing), an awl, iron wedges (for splitting wood), pieces of mail armour, and fragments of boxes and barrels. Inuit artefacts included harpoon heads, pieces of meteoritic iron blades, and a small wood carving of a face with non-Inuit features. Similar carvings, known as *kavdlunaits* from the Inuit word for 'foreigner', have been found at other Inuit sites. Some are depicted wearing European-style hoods and cloaks and are thought to be Inuit portrayals of the Norse. Radiocarbon-dates for some of the Norse artefacts cluster around the middle of the thirteenth century. A similar range of Norse artefacts found at an Inuit site on Ruin Island, about 60 miles away on the Greenland side of the Nares Strait, has been dated to the same period.

Trade or shipwreck?

The presence of Norse artefacts on these Inuit sites is usually interpreted as evidence of trade between them and the Norse. This may not be the case, however. The Inuit did have the furs, hides and ivory that the Norse needed to maintain their trade links with Europe but what could the Norse offer in return? Wood was a precious commodity this far north but the Greenland Norse were always short of timber too. Iron tools might have been traded but this was also always in short supply in the Norse colonies. The Inuit had access to meteoritic iron from northern Greenland, which they worked into blades by cold hammering. Norse wrought iron was better quality but might have been harder to work with without the technology of forges. Rather than indicating a regular trade, an alternative explanation for the presence of these artefacts is that they all come from a single Norse expedition to the far north, perhaps the same one that built the cairns on Washington Irvine Island. The ship rivets were not new when they came into Inuit hands, they look as if they have been salvaged from ship's planks. The Norse would hardly trade the planks of their own ship so they were probably salvaged from a shipwreck along with the other artefacts. Or perhaps the Inuit fought the trespassing Norse and captured and looted the ship. Back in the settlements, this was just another expedition that set out on the dangerous Arctic seas bound for the Norðsetr and was never heard of again.

CHAPTER 9

MALDON, LONDON AND STAMFORD BRIDGE

ENGLAND'S SECOND VIKING AGE
978–1085

or England's King Edgar 'the Peaceful' (r. 957–975) the year 973 was one of stage-managed triumphalism. Edgar was the first English king for over 150 years who did not have to face a Viking invasion: not a single Viking raid was recorded during his reign. Free from external threats, Edgar could concentrate on building the authority of his government and with restoring the damage done by the Vikings to the English church. Edgar also had wider ambitions. England was the largest, richest and most powerful kingdom in Britain and Edgar fancied himself not just as king of the English but as an emperor of the whole island. His first triumphal act of 973 was to hold a coronation ceremony, though Edgar had already been king for fifteen years and his coronation was a celebration rather than the prelude to his reign. By choosing the old Roman city of Bath for his coronation, Edgar was quite deliberately trading on its imperial associations to add lustre to his own kingship. These imperial pretensions were displayed even more clearly later in the year when he held court at Chester, a former Roman legionary fortress. There, in a magnificent piece of theatre, Edgar was rowed on the River Dee by six or eight British kings (the chronicles differ on just how many) including Kenneth II of Scotland, a Viking king called Maccus from the Isle of Man or the Hebrides, Malcolm of Strathclyde, and three or five Welsh kings, while Edgar held the tiller. The symbolism was obvious: Edgar's was the hand that guided all of Britain.

Edgar's triumphalism proved premature. After his death in 975, aged only thirty-two, there was not a single uncontested succession to the English throne until after the Norman Conquest. Edgar was survived by two sons, the eldest Edward by a concubine, the younger Æthelred by his wife Ælfthryth. Edward was about thirteen years old, Æthelred about seven. Edward would normally have inherited the throne unopposed but because he was illegitimate, an influential faction favoured Æthelred. Edward's supporters were stronger, but he reigned for only three years before he was murdered while he was visiting Æthelred at Corfe in Dorset. Æthelred (r. 978–1016) now became king, but the suspicion that he had instigated his brother's murder hung over him for the remainder of his life, undermining his subjects' trust in him and making it difficult for him ever to assert his authority effectively. Edward, in life a violent and intemperate young man, came to be regarded as a martyr by his supporters. This was a lot to live down, but Æthelred did not help himself either by his unwillingness to listen to his advisors, for which he posthumously earned the nickname 'the Unready', from Old English *unræd*, meaning 'ill-advised' rather than unprepared. It was also a disadvantage that in an age when kings were expected to lead armies in battle, Æthelred lacked any military abilities whatsoever. Æthelred was, however, an able administrator and it is possible that, given peace, he might have become a successful ruler.

The Battle of Maldon

Unfortunately for Æthelred, and England, the Vikings were adept at detecting political weakness and a new wave of attacks was not long in coming. Less than two years into his reign, in 980, Vikings sacked the port of Southampton, killing many of the townsfolk and taking most of the survivors captive. In the same year, the always-vulnerable Isle of Thanet in Kent was raided and a fleet from the Hebrides or Orkney raided Cheshire. England's quarter-century of peace was over.

The raids seem to have begun on a relatively small scale – seven ships raided Southampton and three are recorded attacking Dorset in 982 – but they soon escalated. In 991, Olaf Tryggvason, an ambitious sea-king with a claim to the Norwegian throne, landed at Folkestone with a fleet of ninety-three ships. After ravaging the town and its hinterland, Olaf moved on to Sandwich and crossed the Thames estuary to Ipswich before advancing to Maldon in Essex. Here Olaf made camp on Northey Island in the estuary of the River Blackwater. Byrhtnoth, the ealdorman of Essex, took up position on the mainland opposite the island with his household warriors and the local levies. Olaf offered to withdraw and sail home if he was paid tribute. Byrhtnoth refused, saying that he would pay the Vikings only with spear points and sword blades.

The battle that followed is the subject of one of the finest Old English poems, known as 'The Battle of Maldon', a moving expression of the heroic values shared by both English and Viking warriors. A causeway joined Northey Island to the mainland, but it could only be crossed at low tide. As the tide ebbed, the Vikings tried to cross the causeway to attack the English, but they were easily held off by just three English warriors. The Vikings taunted the English that they lacked the courage to fight them on equal terms on level ground. At this point, Byrhtnoth made the fateful decision to pull his forces back and allow the Vikings to cross the causeway and form a shield wall on the mainland. The size of the two armies is unknown but, given the size of Olaf's fleet, it is not unrealistic to assume that he commanded 3,000 to 4,000 men. There is no evidence at all for the size of Byrhtnoth's army, but one late source, the twelfth century *Book of Ely*, says that he was outnumbered by the Vikings. The battle soon began to go against the English. Many (probably all) of the levies were untried in battle and did not even know how to hold their shields and spears properly in the shield wall. When Byrhtnoth, fighting in the front rank, was fatally wounded, some of the English warriors began to lose their nerve. According to the poem the first to flee was Godric, who stole Byrhtnoth's horse – though he had ridden to battle, the ealdorman was fighting on foot as was usual for English warriors – and galloped off the battlefield, followed by his brothers. Others, recognising Byrhtnoth's horse, thought he was abandoning them and fled too. Only Byrhtnoth's household warriors stood their ground, fighting on around his fallen body. In the poem, the warriors encouraged one another in the hopeless fight. 'Let us call to mind,' one says, 'those declarations we often uttered over mead, when from our seat we heroes would put up pledges about tough fighting: now it can be proved who is brave.' They died to a man.

The poet who composed 'The Battle of Maldon' criticised Byrhtnoth for allowing the Vikings to cross the causeway, ascribing it to his *ofermode*, the kind of pride that got Satan expelled from Heaven. This almost certainly does not do justice to Byrhtnoth. Byrhtnoth must have recognised that, although his presence with an army certainly prevented the Vikings ravaging the countryside around Maldon, their ships gave them the tactical initiative: they could simply sail off and plunder an undefended settlement. By deliberately bringing on a battle, Byrhtnoth gambled on being able to destroy the Viking army and so save the whole country from a ravaging. In accepting Byrhtnoth's challenge, Olaf made similar calculations. If he succeeded in destroying the English army, he would be free to plunder wherever he liked.

Æthelred buys off the Vikings

The consequences for England of Byrhtnoth's defeat were very serious. Olaf demanded that Æthelred pay 10,000 pounds (4536 kg) of silver as tribute in return for peace. Archbishop Sigeric advised Æthelred to pay up and on this occasion, at least, he listened to a counsellor. The tribute, called *gafol* but more commonly known as Danegeld, was raised by introducing a general tax and by sales of land and privileges. This payment did get rid of Olaf but only served to advertise England's weakness and attract other raiders. Vikings returned to the Thames estuary the next year. Æthelred ordered the fleet to gather at London to cut off the Viking fleet from the sea. Æthelred put Ælfric, the ealdorman of Hampshire, in command but instead Ælfric warned the Vikings of the impending attack and then joined forces with them. This set the pattern for the remainder of Æthelred's reign: English efforts to fight the Vikings would be continuously undermined by disloyalty.

In 994, Viking raids on England became more intense. Olaf Tryggvason returned in alliance with Svein Forkbeard, the king of Denmark. The two were unlikely allies as Olaf's ambitions posed a direct threat to the Danish domination of Norway established by Svein's father Harald Bluetooth in 970. On 20 September, Olaf and Svein sailed up the Thames with ninety-four ships and attacked London, apparently thinking that they would capture the prosperous town easily. However, the townsfolk fought back ferociously and drove the Vikings off with heavy losses. Svein and Olaf moved on and ravaged Essex, Kent, Sussex and Hampshire before Æthelred resorted to the familiar expedient of buying them off, this time for 16,000 pounds (7,257 kg) of silver. Olaf spent the winter in England and was feted by King Æthelred, who stood as his godfather when he was baptised by the bishop of Winchester at Andover. Olaf swore, too, that he would never return to England again in hostility, a promise he kept. In 995 he returned to Norway and was accepted as king. Svein, who was already a Christian, also returned home and was too busy for the next five years trying to dislodge Olaf from Norway to raid England. The absence of these two dominant figures left the field open for lesser chiefs to lead raids on their own account and to form the kind of coalitions that had proved so successful for the Vikings in the ninth century. The English suffered defeat after defeat, but they did keep fighting. On 23 May 1001, the Vikings defeated the levies of Hampshire at *Æthelingadene*. For once, the *Anglo-Saxon Chronicle* gives casualty figures that have the ring of precision about them. English casualties were eighty-one killed, including five members of the nobility. The chronicle says that the Danes had many more killed, but it was still the English who gave up the battle first. The English were failing not for lack of courage but for lack of co-ordination. Æthelred provided little overall direction for the war effort and seems to have left every shire to fend for itself. In an age when warriors expected their leaders to fight in the front ranks, the king's reluctance to take the field in person was utterly demoralising. For Æthelred's opponents, England's defeats had nothing to do with a failure of leadership, however, they were manifestations of God's anger over Edward's murder.

Some of the raids against England were launched from bases in

Normandy. It is not certain that this was with the agreement of Duke Richard the Good, but he did have a Danish mother and had other ties with the Vikings (see ch. 4). Æthelred sent a fleet on an abortive mission to attack these bases in *c*. 1001–2. Æthelred then tried instead to use diplomacy to deny the Vikings bases in Normandy. In 1002 this resulted in a diplomatic marriage between Æthelred and Duke Richard's sister Emma. Emma had two sons by Æthelred, Edward (later to become known as 'the Confessor') and Alfred. It does not appear that Æthelred received any immediate benefits from this relationship and it further destabilised his government by threatening the position of his sons by his first marriage. In the long term, however, the creation of a dynastic link between England and Normandy had far-reaching consequences for both.

In 1000, Svein Forkbeard triumphed over Olaf Tryggvason and re-established Danish domination over Norway. Victory had come at a price and Svein needed to refill his coffers so, in 1003, he returned to England. Svein's government was rudimentary and he did not have either the right or the administrative expertise to levy general taxation on his subjects. Instead, Svein became a parasite on Æthelred's own efficient administration by launching systematic plundering and tribute-gathering raids against England. Once terms had been agreed, Æthelred's tax collectors gathered the tribute and delivered it to Svein. Svein's armies differed from the Viking armies that had plundered in England previously. Viking hosts of the ninth century were loose coalitions of warbands, often with joint leadership, whose warriors fought for an agreed share of the plunder: they were partners in the enterprise, albeit junior ones. Svein was the sole commander of his army and his warriors fought for pay: they were employees. The number of ships in Svein's fleets seems small in comparison to the big raiding fleets of the ninth century, putting a mere ninety-four ships to sea in 994, but they would have included several *drakkars*, a new type of very large longship with crews of sixty to eighty oarsmen and the capacity to carry up to 500 warriors on a short voyage. Drakkars were so expensive to build that they were the preserve of kings and jarls, and they were often fitted out with lavish decorations to further enhance their owners' status. Another difference from the ninth century was

that the Danes, most of them at least, were now Christian, their conversion having begun in earnest some thirty years earlier.

The St Brice's Day massacre

Svein's appetite for tribute may have been sharpened by one of the most
curious episodes of Æthelred's reign. England was severely raided in
1002, and the Vikings were paid off with 24,000 pounds (10,866 kg) of
silver. Then, as the *Anglo-Saxon Chronicle* puts it, 'the king ordered to
be slain all the Danish men who were in England – this was done on St
Brice's Day [13 November] – because the king had been informed that
they would treacherously deprive him, and then all his councillors, of
life, and possess his kingdom afterwards.' The order cannot have been
directed against the people of the Danelaw, if only because it would
have been completely impractical to carry out a genocide on that
scale in a single day. The probable target was the Danish mercenaries
in royal service whose loyalty was suspect. One such was Pallig, who
had collaborated with Viking raiders in Devon the previous year.
Pallig was a man of high rank, married to King Svein's sister Gunhilde,
who was also killed in the massacre. The twelfth-century chronicler
Henry of Huntingdon wrote that as a child he had talked to old men
who remembered the massacre. They told him that Æthelred had sent
letters to every town with orders that the Danes were to be attacked
on the same day and at the same hour to achieve complete surprise.
How promptly the king's orders were carried out is unknown. One
town where they were acted on was Oxford. Æthelred referred to the
massacre in a charter of 1004 in which he explained that the church of
St Frideswide needed to be rebuilt because the local Danes:

> 'striving to escape death, entered this sanctuary of Christ, having
> broken down the doors and bolts, and resolved to make a refuge
> and defence for themselves therein against the people of the town
> and the suburbs; but when all the people in pursuit strove, forced by
> necessity, to drive them out, and could not, they set fire to the planks
> and burned, as it seems, this church with its ornaments and books.'

Æthelred described the massacre as 'a most just extermination'.

Excavations at St John's College in Oxford in 2008 uncovered a mass grave containing the skeletons of between thirty-four and thirty-eight well-built young men, all bearing the marks of violent death. Many of the wounds were to their backs, showing that they had been killed while fleeing. Several of the bodies were charred, indicating that they had been burned before burial. The bones have been radiocarbon-dated to between 960 and 1020, and chemical analysis of collagen in the bones and tooth enamel shows that these men grew up in countries colder than Britain. Though certainty is not possible, this is compelling evidence that these men were Danish victims of the St Brice's Day massacre.

In 2009, evidence of another massacre from this period was discovered during road building on Ridgeway Hill, overlooking the port of Weymouth in Dorset. This mass burial, in an abandoned Roman quarry, contained the skeletons of fifty-four young men, all of whom had been decapitated in an unusual way, using a sword blow to the front of the neck, rather than the more usual strike from the back. The skulls were piled separately from the skeletons and only fifty-one were found: it is likely that the missing skulls were displayed on stakes. Execution with a sword was usually a privilege reserved for people of high status, so the victims were not likely to have been ordinary criminals, who would have been hanged. Chemical analysis of the bones and teeth shows that these men, like those in the Oxford mass burial, grew up in cold climates and are likely to have been Vikings: one of them came from north of the Arctic Circle. Another of the victims had incisions filed into his front teeth, a painful procedure, and it is thought that these incisions would have been filled with pigment to give their owner a fierce appearance. Svein Forkbeard's father Harald Bluetooth may have acquired his nickname after enduring a similar procedure. The method used to kill these men was described in the thirteenth-century *Saga of the Jomsvikings*, about a semi-legendary band of elite Vikings said to have been founded by Harald. A Jomsviking who was about to be executed was asked what he thought about dying. 'He said:

> "I think well of death, as do all of us. But I am not minded to be slaughtered like a sheep, and would rather face the blow. You hew into my face and watch closely if I flinch." ... They did what he asked for and let him face the blow. [The executioner] stepped in front of

him and hewed into his face; and he did not flinch a whit except that
his eyes closed when death came upon him.' (trans Lee M. Hollander,
University of Texas Press, 1955.)

The bones have been radiocarbon-dated to 980–1030 but, as is the
case with the Oxford burial, it is impossible to say with any degree
of certainty that the Ridgeway Hill grave contains victims of the St
Brice's Day Massacre. It is perhaps more likely that they were Vikings
captured during an unsuccessful raid. The English may, therefore,
have enjoyed more successes against the Vikings than the relentlessly
negative narrator of the *Anglo-Saxon Chronicle* was willing to admit.

Svein apparently faced little resistance to his campaign in 1003. An
army gathered to confront him in Wiltshire but at the last moment its
commander, the unreliable ealdorman Ælfric, feigned illness and no
battle took place. Svein returned in 1004 and raided in East Anglia,
sacking the important town of Norwich. The ealdorman Ulfcytel, who
was probably of Danish ancestry, tried to buy Svein off, but he soon
broke the truce. Ulfcytel raised what forces he could and fought back:
both sides suffered heavy casualties but once again the Danes prevailed.
The *Anglo-Saxon Chronicle* blames the defeat on the failure of the East
Angles to give Ulfcytel the support he needed. Famine forced Svein to
withdraw from England in 1005, but he was back the next summer,
overrunning the south of England before withdrawing to the Isle of
Wight for the winter. Æthelred asked for a truce, negotiations followed and in 1007 Svein received an enormous *gafol* of 36,000 pounds
(16,329 kg) of silver. This was enough to satisfy Svein and he returned
home to Denmark. Æthelred used the respite to build more ships and
manufacture more armour. There is also archaeological evidence that
town defences were strengthened around this time, often with new
stone walls replacing earth and timber ramparts.

Thorkell the Tall

In 1009 the new fleet, the largest ever raised in England, was mustered
at Sandwich in Kent in readiness for further Danish attacks. Æthelred
himself took command. Danish fleets did not usually attempt to sail
to England directly across the North Sea, preferring to hug the coasts

of Denmark, Germany and Frisia until they reached the mouth of the Rhine and made the short crossing to Kent. Sandwich was, therefore, the ideal place to station the fleet if it was to have any chance of intercepting a Danish fleet before it even landed. However, at the muster a dispute broke out between two leading nobles, Brihtric and Wulfnoth Cild. Accused by Brihtric of unspecified offences, Wulfnoth seized twenty ships and set off on a plundering expedition along the south coast. Brihtric set off in pursuit with another eighty ships, but these were caught in a storm and wrecked. When news of the disaster reached Sandwich, the king fled and the remainder of the fleet broke up in confusion. 'And the toil of all the nation thus lightly came to naught,' lamented the chronicler. Then, at the beginning of August, a large Danish fleet landed at Sandwich completely unopposed: it was soon reinforced by a second Danish force. The leader of this new Danish army was Thorkell the Tall. The son of a Danish jarl, Thorkell had been a commander in Svein's army but was now acting on his own behalf. Thorkell may simply have been out to enrich himself, but it is equally possible that he intended to use success as a Viking leader as a springboard to seize power at home, as Olaf Tryggvason had done.

The arrival of Thorkell's army marked the beginning of the end for Æthelred's regime. As the *Anglo-Saxon Chronicle* tells it, the story has a clear villain: Eadric Streona, the ealdorman of Mercia. Eadric found royal favour by acting as Æthelred's hit-man, murdering Ælfhelm, the ealdorman of Northumbria, who had backed the wrong side in a power struggle at court. Eadric's reward was to be appointed to govern Mercia, one of the most senior offices in the land. Eadric went on to earn an unenviable reputation for base treachery. Eadric was first singled out for criticism in the *Chronicle's* entry for 1011. The English army, led by Æthelred in person, had succeeded in cutting the Danes off from their ships and the men were eager to attack, but Eadric somehow persuaded Æthelred against it and the Danes escaped. Thorkell spent the next two years criss-crossing Wessex and East Anglia, plundering and burning. English resistance became increasingly disorganised. The *Anglo-Saxon Chronicle* paints a picture of complete chaos:

> 'When [the Danes] were in the east, the English army was kept in the west, and when they were in the south, our army was in the north.

Then all the councillors were summoned to the king, and it was then to be decided how this country was to be defended. But even if anything was then decided, it did not last even a month. Finally there was no leader who would collect an army, but each fled as best he could, and in the end no shire would even help the next'.

Archbishop Ælfheah's murder

In September 1011, Thorkell laid siege to Canterbury. The city fell three weeks later: a traitor opened the gates. Thorkell took a good haul of valuable captives, including Ælfheah, the archbishop of Canterbury. Æthelred finally called for a truce over the winter and at Easter Thorkell was paid *gafol* of 48,000 pounds (21,772 kg). England's defences might have been collapsing but its bureaucracy was still functioning efficiently and Æthelred's tax collectors had no difficulty raising even this enormous amount of money from his long-suffering subjects. The payment did not save Ælfheah. The Danes wanted another 3,000 pounds (1,361 kg) ransom for his release, but the archbishop refused to allow anyone to pay it, apparently so as to spare the peasantry further burdens. On the Saturday after Easter (19 April 1012), Ælfheah's captors got good and drunk and gave vent to their frustration with their unco-operative prisoner. They battered the archbishop with bones and ox heads and then one of the Danes killed him with an axe blow to the head. Thorkell seems to have tried to save the hostage, promising his men silver and gold if they would spare him, but to no avail. Even in such violent times, the murder of an archbishop was a shocking event. The next day, Ælfheah's body was taken to London for burial in St Paul's cathedral: he was immediately recognised as a martyr. Once the *gafol* was paid and shared out, the Danish army split up. Most headed home with their loot, but Thorkell entered Æthelred's service with forty-five ships, promising to defend his kingdom in return for which he and his men would be fed and clothed. To cover the costs Æthelred introduced an annual land tax called the *heregeld* ('army-tax'). Like many taxes introduced as a temporary expedient, the *heregeld* became permanent and was not officially abolished until 1052. Thorkell's decision is sometimes presented as being motivated by remorse for Ælfheah's murder, but putting his army up for hire was probably a commercial decision: in 1014 Æthelred paid him 12,000 pounds (5,443 kg) of silver raised by the *heregeld*.

Back in Denmark, King Svein must have watched Thorkell's growing wealth and influence with suspicion. What might he do if he returned to Denmark with a ship full of treasure and a loyal army at his back? It was scarcely credible that he would just retire quietly to his family estates. Svein must also have been well-acquainted with the chaotic condition of England's defences and, as there was no shortage of experienced warriors now that most of Thorkell's army had come home, he decided that the time was right for him to launch a new invasion on his own account. This time, however, he was planning to conquer England.

In the high summer of 1013, Svein's fleet landed at Sandwich and then followed the coast north, round East Anglia and into the Humber estuary, then up the River Trent to Gainsborough, where he made his headquarters. There the Northumbrians and the Danish settlers of the Danelaw submitted to him and gave hostages. Svein left the hostages and the fleet in the care of his son Cnut at Gainsborough, took horses and set off south plundering and burning as he went. Town after town submitted. Only at London did Svein meet resistance.

London resists the Danes

The Londoners had already seen off Olaf Tryggvason and several attacks by Thorkell's army. Now with Æthelred and Thorkell inside the city walls, Svein's army also failed to break through. London was not yet England's capital – Winchester in Hampshire was the Wessex dynasty's main political centre – but it was by now its largest and most prosperous city. Though the Vikings sacked London a number of times in the ninth century, they indirectly helped set the city on the road to national pre-eminence. After he seized control of London in 886, Alfred the Great rebuilt the old Roman walls and installed a garrison. New streets and wharves were built and the trading community at Lundenwic (at Aldwych) was relocated within the protection of the walls. Around 915 another fortified settlement was founded on the south bank of the Thames at Southwark. It was probably around this time that London Bridge was built, not just to link both sides of the river but also to control shipping and prevent hostile fleets sailing up the river. In this way London became critical to the defence of the kingdom against the Vikings.

Repulsed from London, Svein headed west to Bath, where the nobles of Wessex submitted to him. London, now the only place that still had not recognised Svein as king, bowed to the inevitable, submitted and gave hostages. Svein returned to Gainsborough and demanded that the English pay and feed his army. Æthelred took refuge with Thorkell and his army at Greenwich on the Thames. He then went to the Isle of Wight, where he spent Christmas before going into exile with his brother-in-law Duke Richard in Normandy. Svein did not enjoy his victory for long. He fell ill and died at Gainsborough at Candlemas, 3 February 1014. The Danish army elected Cnut as king, but the English recalled Æthelred from exile with a message saying 'that no lord was dearer to them than their natural lord, if he would govern them more justly than before'.

Come Easter, Cnut was still at Gainsborough. The people of Lindsey, a Danish-settled district of Lincolnshire, agreed to supply Cnut with horses and join him on campaign. However, Æthelred behaved with uncharacteristic decisiveness and marched north before Cnut was ready. Cnut took to his ships and abandoned the people of Lindsey to savage retaliation. Cnut sailed south to Sandwich, where the hostages who had been given to his father were put ashore, but only after their hands, ears and noses were cut off. Returning to Denmark, Cnut found that his brother Harald had been made king. Harald refused Cnut's request to divide Denmark with him but did agree to help him conquer England.

Æthelred soon showed that he would not govern his people any more justly than before. At the assembly at Oxford in 1015, ealdorman Eadric murdered two thegns from the Five Boroughs, Sigeferth and Morcar, so that the king could seize their property. Before that happened, Æthelred's eldest son, the atheling (crown prince) Edmund Ironside, rebelled, married Sigeferth's widow and seized the properties for himself. Edmund's motive was probably to forestall a claim on the throne by his younger half-brother Edward. While this dispute was going on, Cnut arrived back at Sandwich with a very large fleet. Writing very shortly after Cnut's invasion, the German chronicler Thietmar of Merseburg (d. 1018) gives the strength of the fleet as 340 ships, each with eighty men, which adds up to a force of 27,200 men. Viking armies of this size are not credibly attested elsewhere but, while Thietmar's numbers are almost certainly exaggerated, it is likely that Cnut's army was impressively large by the standards of the day. This time Cnut had some heavyweight allies, jarl Erik of Lade (Hlaðir) (d. c. 1023), the most powerful magnate in Norway, and Thorkell the Tall, both of whom could raise large armies in their own right. Thorkell had decided that it was time to patch things up with Cnut and had travelled to Denmark during the winter to offer to serve him with his army. With the fate of a kingdom at stake, Cnut's army attracted warriors from all over Scandinavia, not just Denmark.

Æthelred chose this moment of crisis to fall sick and utterly failed to offer his divided kingdom any inspiring leadership. Edmund raised forces in the north and Eadric raised an army in the south. The two agreed to collaborate, but they did not trust each other and separated without engaging the Danes. Eadric then changed sides, going over to Cnut and taking a unit of Danish mercenaries with him. Edmund's efforts to organise an effective defence against Cnut came to naught because no one was willing to take the field unless the king himself would lead them. Æthelred, now becoming increasingly frail, refused to leave the safety of London.

Edmund Ironside

Æthelred finally died on 23 April 1016 and was buried in St Paul's. Such magnates as were present in London, together with the people of the city, chose Edmund as their new king. Edmund had the appetite for war that his father had so conspicuously lacked and he inspired the English to renew their resistance to the Danes. Two weeks after Æthelred died, Cnut's fleet sailed up the Thames to Greenwich. Edmund hurriedly left to raise forces in Wessex while the Londoners prepared to resist the Danes once again. The widowed queen Emma remained in London with her sons throughout the siege, encouraging the defenders. The

Danes could not get past London Bridge so they dug a canal around Southwark and dragged their ships to the west side of the bridge, then surrounded the city with a ditch to prevent anyone getting in and out, but the townsfolk continued to resist fiercely. Edmund's presence in Wessex forced Cnut to go after him, leaving only a small force to maintain the siege of London. Edmund and Cnut pursued each other across the breadth of southern England, fighting two bloody battles, at Penselwood and Sherston before midsummer. Though inconclusive, they allowed Edmund to relieve the siege of London, but the Danes escaped in their ships. Edmund won a battle at Brentford but not decisively enough to prevent the Danes making another assault on London from both the river and from land. Once again, London put up a stout defence and the Danes withdrew, setting off on a march that took them in a great loop through southern Mercia, south into Wessex and east to Kent. Edmund caught up with them again at Otford, where he inflicted another reverse on the invaders. Edmund was beginning to look as if he might succeed in defeating Cnut. Ealdorman Eadric predictably offered to change sides again and Edmund took him back into favour. 'No greater folly was ever agreed to than that was,' said the Anglo-Saxon chronicler, plainly believing that it was safer to have Eadric as an enemy than a friend. Later chroniclers, such as Henry of Huntingdon and William of Malmesbury, claim that Eadric changed sides with Cnut's agreement so that he would have the opportunity to betray Edmund.

In the autumn, Cnut's army went into Essex. Edmund gathered his forces and clashed with Cnut at Ashingdon on the morning of 18 October. As soon as the battle started Eadric began to spread alarm and defeatism and took flight with the Mercian levies. With Edmund in command, Eadric's betrayal was not enough to precipitate a general rout. The rest of the English stood their ground and fought until long after dark, suffering very heavy casualties, including the stalwart ealdorman Ulfcytel of East Anglia. Under cover of darkness, Edmund was able to disengage in reasonably good order and he retreated to Alney in Gloucestershire. Here Eadric presented himself again, urging Edmund to reach a negotiated settlement with Cnut. After such a punishing campaign, Edmund probably had little choice but to agree.

By the Treaty of Alney, Cnut and Edmund divided England between them. Edmund kept Wessex, Cnut was granted everything north of the Thames. Only now did the Londoners finally submit to Cnut and paid him unspecified tribute for peace. Cnut moved his fleet to London and took up winter quarters there with his army.

Cnut becomes King of England

On 30 November 1016, a matter of weeks after agreeing to the division of the kingdom, Edmund Ironside died. No contemporary source says what caused Edmund's death but later chroniclers, all too plausibly, blamed Eadric. Eadric is alleged to have concealed an assassin – in one version, his own son – in the pit of the king's privy. When Edmund went to empty his bowels, the assassin struck, stabbing him from below. After Edmund's death Cnut, by agreement, became king of all of England. There was no opposition; English resistance was broken and leaderless. Significantly, Cnut chose London for his coronation, rather than Winchester or any other place associated with the Wessex dynasty. The surviving English claimants to the throne, King Edmund's brother Eadwig and Emma's two young sons by Æthelred, Edward the Confessor and Alfred, went into exile in Normandy. Emma probably went with them. Eadric advised Cnut to kill Edmund's infant sons, Edward the Exile and Edmund, but he sent them into exile in Sweden and from there they went to Kiev and, eventually to Hungary. Several high ranking English nobles were executed as were some of Cnut's own commanders. Cnut divided England into four. Keeping Wessex for himself, he left Eadric with Mercia, and rewarded Thorkell the Tall with East Anglia and jarl Erik with Northumbria.

By the end of 1017, Cnut felt secure on his throne and he decided that he no longer needed the dubious benefit of Eadric's support. At Christmas that year Cnut summoned Eadric to London. Eadric expected to be further rewarded for helping Cnut win the throne but the king upbraided him for his treachery and ordered jarl Erik to cut his head off, 'so that soldiers may learn from this example to be faithful, not faithless, to their kings'. Cnut could now pay off his army. To do this he levied an exceptionally heavy tribute on the English of

82,500 pounds (37,421 kg), to be paid at Easter 1018. London's share of the tribute was 10,500 pounds (4,763 kg), a sign of just how important and wealthy the city was becoming. Many of Cnut's commanders were rewarded with lands and titles, establishing a new Anglo-Danish aristocracy, but there was no large scale Danish settlement as there had been in the ninth century. Cnut's warriors were mercenaries serving for pay and now that the campaign was over most went home. Cnut retained forty ships' crews as his housecarls (*huskarlar*), his household warriors. They were paid by continuing to levy Æthelred's heregeld. Despite a heavy burden of taxation, Cnut's rule was not unpopular in England. He made few changes to the traditional institutions of the country and the English welcomed the peace and security he brought after so many years of violence and instability.

After his coronation, Cnut began to negotiate an alliance with Richard of Normandy, which resulted in his marriage to Queen Emma in 1018. Cnut's main motive for the marriage was to prevent Æthelred's sons seeking Norman support against him, but he may also have seen her experience as queen of England as an advantage. During his campaigns in England, Cnut had already acquired an English consort in the shape of Ælfgifu of Northampton, with whom he already had two sons, Svein Alfivason and Harold Harefoot. Although he put Ælfgifu aside so that he could marry Emma, Cnut continued to show her favour and she continued to be influential throughout his reign. Later in 1018, Cnut's brother Harald died and the following year he sailed to Denmark to claim the throne. Cnut always recognised that England was the most valuable of his kingdoms and he soon returned, leaving Denmark to be ruled by a regent.

Cnut's foreign policy

Cnut pursued a far more active foreign policy than any ruler of England had done previously. In 1026 and 1028, Cnut returned to Scandinavia to restore Danish control of Norway, which had been lost to Olaf Haraldsson (St Olaf) after Svein Forkbeard's death. By 1030, the Swedish king and the earls of Orkney recognised Cnut as overlord making him, at least nominally, the ruler of almost the whole Scandinavian world.

Little is known about Cnut's relations with Wales and Ireland: it is possible that he allied with the Dublin Vikings to pillage Wales in 1030. Lothian was lost to the Scots following the Northumbrian defeat at the Battle of Carham in 1016. A peace of sorts was patched up through the diplomacy of Queen Emma and Duke Richard, but it did not last. Cnut invaded Scotland in 1031, and though he did not recover Lothian he accepted the submission of three Scottish rulers named in the *Anglo-Saxon Chronicle* as King Malcolm II, Maelbeth (probably Macbeth, then the *mormaer* of Moray), and the unidentified Iehmarc, who was probably a Gaelic-Norse ruler from the Hebrides.

Cnut was arguably the greatest of all the Viking kings but, though he won power as a Viking, he ruled as a Christian European king. In England he assiduously performed those duties most expected of a Christian king, making laws and supporting the church through donations and privileges. In 1027, Cnut made a pilgrimage to Rome to attend the coronation of the Holy Roman Emperor Conrad II. As well as demonstrating his piety, this helped establish Cnut as a figure of European stature. Cnut cultivated friendly relations with Conrad, whose empire bordered Denmark in the south. The two rulers eventually arranged a diplomatic marriage: Cnut's daughter Gunnhild married Conrad's son, the future Emperor Henry III. As part of the agreement, Conrad recognised the River Eider as Denmark's southern border.

Impressive though it was, Cnut's empire lacked any institutional unity and it did not survive his death in 1035. Cnut's intention was that Svein Alfivason, his elder son by Ælfigifu, would rule Norway. Around 1030, Cnut made Svein king of Norway with his mother as regent, but Ælfgifu quickly made herself unpopular by her efforts to centralise power. Around the time of Cnut's death, the Norwegians rebelled and invited Magnus the Good (r. 1035–47), Olaf Haraldsson's son, to become king. Svein fled with his mother to Denmark, where he died early in 1036. Cnut intended that Harthacnut, his son by Emma, would inherit both England and Denmark, but his accession was opposed in England and instead Harold Harefoot, Cnut's second son by Ælfgifu, became king. Queen Emma was forced into exile in Flanders. Only after Harold died, at Oxford, in March 1040, was Harthacnut able to succeed to the English throne. Harthacnut was unmarried, childless and in poor health. While drinking heavily at a wedding feast in London, Harthacnut suffered a stroke and died on 8 June 1042. With him, Cnut's dynasty came to an end. By an agreement reached in 1036, the Norwegian king Magnus the Good was accepted as king in Denmark, but the English chose the exiled Edward the Confessor (r. 1042–66), so restoring the Wessex dynasty.

Edward's reign was peaceful but his marriage was childless and, as he grew older and his health began to fail, the problem of the succession became acute. This set the stage for the final acts of England's Viking Age. By the time Edward died on 4 or 5 January 1066 at his new palace at Westminster – London had now become England's most important political centre as well as its main commercial centre – three leading claimants to the throne had emerged: Harold Godwinson, the powerful Anglo-Danish earl of Wessex; William duke of Normandy; and Harald Hardrada (r. 1046–66), the king of Norway. There was also Edgar the Atheling, Edward the Exile's son: as a member of the Wessex dynasty he had the strongest hereditary claim but he was only fourteen and lacked any influential supporters at court. Harold had no royal blood but he had for many years dominated the English court and he had a proven record as a soldier, having led several successful campaigns against the Welsh.

William's candidature was based on his claim that King Edward had promised him the throne after his death. This is not impossible. Edward had formed a friendship with William when he was in exile in Normandy and he was known for his pro-Norman sympathies. However, the English did not share their king's tastes. Edward had invited a number of Norman nobles to settle in England, but their high-handed arrogance had soon made them unpopular. Harald Hardrada had inherited his claim from his predecessor Magnus the Good (who had inherited his claim through his agreement with Harthacnut). In a career that had taken him across most of the Viking world, Harald had more than earned his reputation for being the greatest warrior of his day, but, like William, he had no supporters in England.

Harold Godwinson had the advantage over his rivals of being present while Edward lay on his deathbed. With no factions at court pushing for William, Edgar or Harald, Edward had little choice when he nominated Harold as his successor a few hours before he died. Harold may have been the king the English wanted but they were under no illusions that this settled the matter. A comet that appeared on 24 April was not seen as a good omen. Both Harald and William began to gather forces to invade England and make good their claims on the throne. Both men had earned formidable military reputations: Harald was described as 'the thunderbolt of the north' by Adam of Bremen, because of his prowess in war, while William was already being called 'the Conqueror' for his many victories. Harold mobilised his forces in late spring and waited, not knowing who would strike first. Unexpectedly, the first invasion came from Harold's younger brother Tostig, who had been exiled to Flanders in 1065 for misgoverning his earldom of Northumbria. With an army and sixty ships provided by Count Baldwin of Flanders, Tostig raided along the south coast from the Isle of Wight to Kent before sailing north to Northumbria, where he was defeated by local forces. Fleeing to Scotland, Tostig transferred his allegiance to Harald Hardrada.

The Battle of Stamford Bridge

The winds through the summer of 1066 blew persistently from the north. These held William's fleet in port but carried Harald's fleet of 300 ships south from Nidaros (now Trondheim) to Shetland and Orkney and along the British coast to Tynemouth, where it was joined by Tostig's Flemish fleet. Tostig's presence added some much-needed credibility to Harald's claim to the throne. From Tynemouth, Harald continued south into the Humber, finally landing on 16 September at Ricall on the River Ouse, 9 miles south of York. Leaving his teenage son Olaf and jarl Paul of Orkney to guard the ships, Harald set off for York on 20 September but was confronted at the village of Fulford Gate by an English army under earls Edwin and Morcar. Harald defeated them, inflicting heavy casualties on the English. Why the earls chose to fight when they could have awaited reinforcements behind the walls of York remains a mystery. York surrendered immediately and agreed to give hostages, and provide supplies and men to support Harald's bid for the throne. While he awaited the promised support, Harald withdrew to Stamford Bridge, on the River Derwent about 7 miles east of York.

Harold, who had been warned of Harald's approach as soon as his fleet had appeared off the English coast, was already marching north with his army. On 24 September Harold reached Tadcaster just 10 miles south-west of York. The next day, he marched his army straight through York and on to Stamford Bridge where he caught Harald's army completely by surprise. The weather was warm for the time of year and the Norwegians, including King Harald, had left their armour with the ships at Riccall, 13 miles away. The English slaughtered the Norwegians on the west side of the river but a single brave Norwegian axeman made a stand on the bridge, killing everyone who approached and buying time for the rest of the army on the east bank to form a shield wall. The English crossed only after a warrior climbed under the bridge and speared the axeman from below. The battle raged for hours but their lack of armour put the Norwegians at a fatal disadvantage and their shield wall gradually began to give way. King Harald was killed by an arrow in the throat and Tostig also became a casualty. Late in the day reinforcements arrived from the Norwegian ships and briefly halted the English advance. They had run all the way to Stamford Bridge in full armour and were so exhausted that their stand was short-lived. The Norwegians fled back towards Ricall with the English in hot pursuit: many of the Norwegians drowned trying to cross the river. The English paid a high price for their victory but Harald's army was all but annihilated. When, after the battle, King Harold allowed Olaf and jarl Paul to leave with the survivors, they needed only twenty of the 300 ships that had transported their late comrades. The scale of Harald's defeat was such that it took Norway a generation to recover.

A few days later the winds finally changed to the south and on 28 September, William the Conqueror landed at Pevensey. Harold hurried south to defeat and death at the Battle of Hastings on 14 October. With Harold dead English resistance quickly crumbled and on Christmas Day 1066, William was crowned king of England in Westminster Abbey. The Norman conquest had much more far-reaching consequences than the Danish conquest fifty years earlier. William and many of his followers may have been of Viking descent, but by 1066, Normandy was linguistically and culturally a French principality. The conquest decisively drew England out of its north European orbit and turned it into a political and cultural satellite of France. It would be the end of the fourteenth century before England again had a king whose first language was English. The native English aristocracy who survived the battles of 1066 were within a few years either executed or exiled, and almost every English landowner was dispossessed. The English peasantry were forced into serfdom. The conquerors expropriated the wealth of the English on such a vast scale that even today, 950 years later, people in England with surnames of Norman-French origin are, on average, 20 per cent richer than the national average.

The end of England's Viking Age

The Battle of Stamford Bridge is widely seen as marking the end of England's Viking Age, but the Vikings were not quite finished with England. William was quite the most brutal man ever to rule England and the atrocities he meted out to the defeated English were such that, even in an age inured to violence, they shocked Europe. Two years after William's accession fierce but unco-ordinated English rebellions erupted across the country and these brought the Danes back to England. After his death at Stamford Bridge, Harald Hardrada's claim to the English throne had passed to the Danish king Svein Estrithsson (r. 1046–74/6), and it was to him that the English rebels turned for support, offering to accept him as king. In 1069, Svein sent his son Cnut to England with a fleet of 240 ships. Cnut landed at Dover in September and then sailed north, meeting with little success until he reached the Humber in October where he joined up with a large English rebel force. The Danes and the English marched on York and wiped out the Norman garrison there. William acted quickly and recaptured York in December. A campaign of savage retaliation, known as the 'Harrying of North', followed. William's forces spread out across the countryside, burning and killing people and livestock, reducing the survivors to beggary. The *Domesday Book*, compiled in 1086, lists hundreds of villages across the north as still being waste and uninhabited, and worth only a fraction of their value twenty years earlier. William's brutality served the double purpose of punishing the rebels and depriving the Danes of supplies. William literally made a desert of the north and called it peace.

In the spring of 1070, King Svein joined his son on the Humber and in June sailed to the Wash to join the English rebels under Hereward the Wake in sacking Peterborough. However, Svein was reluctant to face the Normans in open battle. When a force of just 160 Normans arrived at Ely, the Danes took to their ships. With English resistance collapsing, Svein reached an agreement with William and went home with his plunder. Five years later, Cnut returned to England with 200 ships at the invitation of two rebellious Norman earls. By the time he arrived, the rebellion was over and, apart from sacking York, he achieved nothing. In 1080, Cnut became king of Denmark (r. 1080–86) and revived his claim to the English throne. In 1085 he allied with Count Baldwin of Flanders, one of William's French rivals, and raised a large invasion fleet. William prepared for the invasion by bringing over troops from Normandy, taxing the English, and by laying waste England's coastal districts so that the Danes would find nothing with which to supply their army. 'And people had much oppression that year,' lamented the *Anglo-Saxon Chronicle*: being protected by William was probably considerably worse than being raided by Vikings. The English suffered for nothing: the threat of a German invasion of Denmark prevented Cnut's fleet from sailing and at the end of the summer it dispersed. Cnut planned to try again but he was murdered in Odense in July 1086 and his successor Olaf had other priorities. With Cnut's death, England's Viking Age truly came to an end. True, England continued to suffer Viking raids from Orkney and Norway until the middle of the twelfth century and as late as the 1150s the Norwegian king Eystein II took advantage of a civil war to plunder England's east coast. However, these were mere pinpricks and the country never again faced the threat of a serious Viking invasion.

CHAPTER 10

HEDEBY, JELLING AND STIKLESTAD
THE SCANDINAVIAN KINGDOMS TO 1100

istories of the Vikings tend to concentrate on their impact on
Europe and the wider world. The untold story of the Vikings
is the impact that Europe had on them. At the beginning of
the Viking Age, Scandinavians were still prehistoric, pagan
barbarians: by its end, they were fully integrated into the cultural
mainstream of Roman Catholic Christian Europe. For all their energy
and aggression, the Vikings did not Scandinavianise Europe; Europe
Europeanised the Vikings. This process of assimilating Scandinavia into
Christian Europe, which mirrors on a much larger scale the assimilation
of Scandinavian settlers into their European host communities, was
inextricably linked to the culmination of the state formation process,
which saw the emergence of stable kingdoms in Denmark, Norway
and Sweden. Just as it was the emergence of states in these countries
that triggered Viking exploration and raiding, it was the end of the
state-building process, not more effective defences by the Vikings'
victims, that led to the decline of their freebooting ways. Once kings
had built effective governments, they could prevent their subjects from
causing diplomatic problems with neighbouring states, and they could
also offer them alternative routes to social advancement through royal
service, so reducing the incentive to go on Viking raids. And because

they now had other forms of income from taxation and trade, kings did not have the same pressures to lead plundering raids themselves. As was the case in the Viking colonies, conversion to Christianity was the main vehicle of cultural assimilation.

The Danes and Charlemagne

Because it was blessed with the greatest area of good arable land, Denmark was the wealthiest and most populated country of Viking Age Scandinavia. It was also the smallest and most compact, with good internal communications. The two largest regions of Viking Age Denmark were the Jutland peninsula in the west and the two provinces of Skåne and Blekinge in the east (both of which came under Swedish rule in the seventeenth century). In between them lay a scatter of dozens of low-lying islands, linked rather than separated by shallow, sheltered channels of the sea. Because there were no large forests or high mountains as there were in Norway and Sweden, there were few obstacles to travel on land. Because of its land border with Germany in the south, Denmark was also the Scandinavian country in closest contact with Christian Europe. These geographical circumstances alone made it likely that Denmark would be the first of the Scandinavian countries to be welded into a unified kingdom, but there was also an important external factor driving the Danes towards unity: their powerful Christian neighbour, the Frankish empire.

According to the *Frankish Royal Annals*, the king of the Danes at the time of the earliest Viking raids was Sigfred, who probably ruled from around 770 to 800. The first recorded Danish king since the time of Angantyr, little more is known about Sigfred than his name. Nothing is known about his ancestry – was he a descendent of Angantyr or did he belong to another dynasty? – nor is it known if he ruled all of the Danes or just those who lived in Jutland. Despite that, it is not unreasonable to imagine that the steady expansion of the Frankish Empire towards the Danes' southern borders caused Sigfred great unease. In 734, the Franks had begun to spread east along the North Sea coast and had conquered Frisia. Then, in 773, the Frankish king Charlemagne began the conquest and conversion to Christianity of the pagan Saxons, whose territory bordered directly on Denmark in the south. The Danevirke, which guarded the Danes' border with the Saxons, would not have been built if relations between the two peoples had always been friendly. It must have been clear to Sigfred, however, that the mighty Franks would make altogether more dangerous enemies, so he supported the Saxons in their struggle to preserve their independence and provided a refuge for their leader Widukind.

Sigfred's support was not enough to stop the Frankish steamroller and by the time he was last heard of, in 798, Charlemagne had subjugated all the Saxons who lived west of the Elbe river. Saxon resistance continued north of the Elbe until 804, when Charlemagne finally secured their submission, bringing the Frankish empire to the Danish border. That Charlemagne gave the newly conquered lands to the Abodrites, a Wendish tribe allied to the Franks, rather than incorporate them into his empire (the Wends were a group of Slav tribes whose lands extended along the Baltic coast from the neck of the Jutland peninsula east to the river Vistula), suggests that he had no immediate plans to conquer the Danes but their new king, Godfred, could hardly be sure about that. Charlemagne invited Godfred to a meeting, perhaps to reassure him about his intentions, perhaps not. Godfred brought his fleet and army to the border as a show of strength but came no further. Charlemagne was a militant Christian and he had justified his conquest of the Saxons on the grounds of their paganism as well as their raids on Frankish territory. The Danes were pagans too: would Charlemagne demand Godfred's baptism and co-operation in evangelising his subjects? If Godfred refused, would Charlemagne see this as a sufficient *casus belli*, especially as his subjects were now launching pirate raids on the Frankish empire? Godfred had good cause to be suspicious of Charlemagne.

In 808, Godfred led a fleet to attack the Abodrites in alliance with one of their Wendish rivals, the Wiltzians. Godfred captured and sacked many of the Abodrites' fortified towns, levied tribute, and captured and hanged one of their chiefs. It's very likely that Godfred sacrificed this chief to Odin as hanging was the usual way that the god's sacrificial victims were killed. Before sailing for home, Godfred destroyed the town of *Reric*, which was one end of an overland trade route between the Baltic and the North Sea. Reric's location is not known for certain, but it was most likely at Groß Strömkendorf on Wismar Bucht, where the remains of a substantial planned Slavic settlement of the eighth century have been discovered. Reric was under Godfred's control, and it provided him with substantial income from tolls and taxes, but it was now no longer secure. Godfred ensured that Reric would be of no benefit to the Abodrites by rounding up its merchants and craftsmen and taking them back to Denmark with him: he had plans for them.

Hedeby: the town on the heath

Anticipating Frankish reprisals for his attack on their ally, Godfred set about refurbishing the Danevirke rampart when he returned home. At the same time, Godfred resettled Reric's merchants and craftsmen at Hedeby ('heath-town'), at the eastern end of the Danevirke, by the head of the Schlei Fjord, a narrow, reed-fringed, 15-mile long inlet of the Baltic. The feared reprisals fell upon the Wiltzians rather than the Danes and Hedeby quickly began to flourish, becoming the most important town in Viking Age Scandinavia. Hedeby's location, right at the neck of the Jutland peninsula, made it the natural focus for trade between the southern North Sea and Baltic Sea regions. Merchants could avoid the long and dangerous voyage around Jutland by offloading their cargoes at Hedeby and carting them 9 miles overland to Hollingstedt on the River Treene. Here, cargoes could be transferred to another ship and sailed down the Treene, into the River Eider and so into the North Sea. Some historians have suggested that the ships themselves might have been portaged from one sea to the other, much as the Rus carried their boats from one river system to another in Russia, but there is no hard evidence for this. Hedeby also lay on the *Hærvej* (the 'Army Road'), an ancient north-south route running from Viborg in north Jutland to Hamburg on the River Elbe. Despite its name, the road was mainly a trade and cattle droving route.

At its peak in the tenth century, Hedeby covered an area of about 15 acres (6 hectares) and had a population of around 1,000 to 1,500 people. The town was protected from attack by land by a semi-circular earth and timber rampart, which was 1,400 yards (1,280 m) long and is still over 10 feet (3 m) high. Today, this rampart is the only visible evidence of Hedeby's existence. The waterfront was open but the entrance into the harbour was protected by a barrier of wooden stakes that had been driven into the bed of the shallow fjord. A channel through the barrier could be closed off in wartime with chains or floating logs. Such barriers were a common precaution against pirate raids in Viking Age Denmark and Sweden. The Schlei Fjord also gave the town a measure of protection – no pirate fleet would be able sail down its 15-mile length unseen and launch a surprise attack.

On its low-lying site by the fjord, Hedeby was probably a damp and muddy place to live. The small town was laid out in an orderly way on either side of a small stream using a grid of narrow fenced rectangular building plots along two main streets running roughly parallel to the waterfront. Like many other Viking Age towns, the streets were paved with split logs to stop them becoming completely impassable in wet weather. The town's single-storey houses were built with timber posts, walls of lattices of branches made windproof with a coating of clay, and thatched roofs. A typical house had a single room, which functioned as both family dwelling and workshop. Inside, the houses were dark, with the doorway being the only source of daylight, and smoky. Families lived and worked around a hearth in the centre of the floor and, as there were no chimneys, smoke had to find its way out under the eaves or through the thatched roof. The houses had small enclosed yards containing wells and latrines in close proximity to one another. Many of the buildings were German or Slavonic in style, suggesting that the town had an international population. Hedeby's houses were not built to last – most would have needed to be completely rebuilt every ten to thirty years. The town's waterfront was lined with timber quays, some of which extended almost 200 feet (60 m) out into the fjord. The quays were strongly built and many had warehouses and other structures built on top of them. There is archaeological evidence of craft activities, including metal-, bone- and amber-working, glass-making, pottery, weaving and ship repair. By around 825, Hedeby also had a mint, which produced imitations of Frankish silver *deniers* bearing representations of Viking longships and trading *knarrs*.

Apart from a possible toll house near the harbour and a meeting hall, no administrative buildings have been identified in Hedeby. The town was probably governed from the high-status settlement at Flüsing, about 2½ miles away on the north shore of Schlei Fjord, not far from Schleswig. This settlement, which was only about one-fifth the size of Hedeby, focused on a great feasting hall and had a mainly military character. It was probably here that Godfred gathered his forces in 804. The site continued to be occupied until the middle of the tenth century, when the hall burned down. Iron arrowheads embedded in burned timbers show that this was no accident but the result of a violent attack.

Hedeby's main trade links were with the eastern Baltic and Norway, and with England and the Rhineland. Two merchants who are known to have visited Hedeby were Ottar and Wulfstan. Both men visited King Alfred's court in England, where scribes wrote down their accounts of the trade routes they followed. Wulfstan, who was probably English, used Hedeby as his base for trading voyages to the Wendish ports along the Baltic's southern coast. Ottar was from Hålogaland in Arctic Norway and he spent his summers hunting walrus in the White Sea, heading south to Hedeby to sell their ivory teeth. It was a lucrative trade because disruption to Mediterranean trade routes meant that the better quality elephant ivory was almost unobtainable in early Medieval Europe. Some merchants came from much further afield, however. A Jewish merchant from Córdoba, al-Tartushi, who visited around the middle of the tenth century, thought Hedeby a poor and squalid place and he hated the singing of the townsfolk, which he thought was 'worse than the barking of dogs'. Around this time, his home town of Córdoba was one of the world's largest cities, with great mosques, palaces, libraries and universities so Hedeby was little more than a farming village in comparison.

A fragile kingdom

Godfred did not live long enough to see his new town flourish. Charlemagne's response to Godfred's attack on the Abodrites was to build a fort at Itzehoe, north of the Elbe and less than 40 miles from the Danish border. In 810, Godfred retaliated by raiding Frisia with a fleet of 200 ships. The raid was successful: Godfred extracted 100 pounds (45 kg) of silver in tribute and long before Charlemagne's forces arrived on the scene he was back home. And then, apparently at the peak of his power, Godfred was murdered by one of his retainers. Events of the next few years fully demonstrated the fragility of the early Danish kingdom. Godfred's successor, a nephew called Hemming, survived two years and was succeeded by two brothers Harald Klak and Reginfred after a brief civil war that left two other claimants dead. Such arrangements were not uncommon in Viking Age Scandinavia: joint kingship was a practical way of resolving competing claims where two or more claimants had equal support. In 813, a third brother, another Hemming, turned up to share the throne. Hemming had been in the service of Charlemagne and this seems to have made him suspect in the eyes of the Danes, who transferred their allegiance to four of Godfred's sons, who had been in exile in Sweden. Hemming fled back to the Frankish court, where he was promised help to regain the Danish throne. A long struggle between the two fraternal factions followed until by around 834 all the rivals were dead or permanently exiled bar one, Horik, the last of Godfred's sons.

At first Horik maintained friendly relations with Charlemagne's successor Louis the Pious and on occasion even captured and executed pirate leaders who had raided Frankia. Horik's main concern was to consolidate his own authority and he did not want his subjects provoking Frankish interventions. The civil war that broke out in the Frankish empire after Louis' death in 840 emboldened Horik. In 845, he sent a large fleet to sack Hamburg and two years later Horik refused demands by the emperor Lothar that he prevent his subjects raiding the Frankish lands. Horik was in any case far too insecure to enforce any such prohibition. In 850, Horik was forced to share his kingdom with two nephews. Then, in 854, a third nephew, Gudurm, turned up to claim a share of the kingdom too. Gudurm was every Viking Age Scandinavian king's worst nightmare – a successful pirate leader with royal blood, a hoard of plunder and a large and loyal warrior band to back him up. Gudurm's arrival threw the kingdom into a vicious civil war in which Horik and most of the rest of the extended royal family, including his three nephews, all perished. Stability did not return to Denmark for nearly a century.

Virtually nothing is known about events in Denmark in the second half of the ninth century. Writing in his *Deeds of the Bishops of the Church of Hamburg*, our best informed source for the early Danish kingdom, the German ecclesiastical historian Adam of Bremen summed up the confusion: 'How many Danish kings, or rather tyrants, there were indeed, and whether some of them ruled at the same time or lived for a short time one after the other, is uncertain.' Adam was commissioned to write his history by archbishop Adalbert of Hamburg (d. 1072) and had access to a wide range of sources, including the archives of the archbishopric of Hamburg-Bremen, which had led efforts to evangelise Scandinavia. Adam even visited Denmark himself in 1068–9 and met King Svein Estrithson (r. 1047–74), whom he cites as a major informant for his work. If Adam had no idea what was going on, probably no one else did either.

By around 890, part of Denmark, at least, had come under the control of a Swedish king called Olof. Two runestones commemorating Olof's grandson Sigtrygg have been found at Hedeby, suggesting that the town was the dynasty's main powerbase. Hedeby returned to Danish control in the mid-930s when Sigtrygg was overthrown by another obscure ruler called Harthacnut Sveinsson. In saga traditions, Harthacnut was said to be a grandson of the legendary Viking Ragnar Lodbrok, but Adam of Bremen says he came from *Nortmannia*, by which he probably meant Normandy or maybe northern Jutland. Harthacnut's main claim to fame is that he was the father of the man Danes regard as the as the real founder of their kingdom, Gorm the Old (d. *c.* 958). Gorm most likely earned his nickname not because he was particularly long-lived – it is not known when he was born – but because he was the ancestor of the medieval Danish kings. The actual extent of Gorm's kingdom is not known but he certainly did not rule all the Danes; the first king to do that would be his son Harald Bluetooth (r. *c.* 958–87), who succeeded him after his death in 958.

Consolidating royal authority

Outside their own private lands, the early Danish kings exercised authority indirectly through subordinate chieftains. This meant that royal authority was inherently weak and in many parts of Denmark completely non-existent. Whatever the claims of rulers to be kings of the Danes, chiefs in areas remote from the royal power centres ruled in effective independence. Harald's achievement was to make royal authority real throughout the whole of Denmark. It is unlikely that this was a peaceful process because the most obvious physical evidence of Harald's authority is a chain of six or seven forts that he built right across the country, at Fyrkat and Aggersborg in north Jutland, at Nonnebakken on Fyn, Trelleborg and Borrering (also known as Vallø Borgring) on Sjælland, and at Trelleborg and (probably) at Borgeby in Skåne. There was no fort in southern Jutland, where Harald's authority was strongest.

Harald's forts show clear evidence of central planning in their near identical design. All the forts are precisely circular with four equally spaced covered gateways placed on the four points of the compass. Axial streets divide the interiors into four equally sized quadrants. At Fyrkat and Trelleborg (Sjælland) each quadrant contained four three-roomed bow-sided wooden buildings arranged in a square, at Aggersborg, which at over 260 yards (240 m) was twice the diameter of the other forts, there were twelve buildings arranged in three squares. At the centre of each square was a smaller wooden building. A ring road ran around the inside of the earth ramparts, which were faced with timber to make them more difficult to climb. All the forts were encircled by a ditch. There are no exact parallels to Harald's forts anywhere in Europe but it is possible that they were modelled on circular forts built by the Franks to protect the Low Countries from Viking raids in the ninth century. Investigation of the buildings at Fyrkat has shown that while some were used as dwellings, most were workshops, stables and stores. Women and children, as well as adult males, were found buried in a cemetery outside the ramparts, which suggests that the forts were centres for royal administration, where taxes were collected, as well as strongpoints for controlling the local population. Dendrochronology shows that the timbers used for the buildings at Fyrkat and Trelleborg were felled in c. 980, that is, quite late in Harald's reign. The forts were occupied for no more than twenty or thirty years: once the Danes had accepted centralised royal government, they were no longer needed.

Denmark becomes Christian

Harald also began the cultural transformation of Denmark by converting to Christianity in 965. According to later stories, Poppo, a German missionary, probably from Würzburg, persuaded Harald to convert after he demonstrated the superior power of the Christian god by carrying red hot irons in his bare hands without suffering any injury. This missionary success had been a long time coming. Willibrord's fruitless mission to King Angantyr in the 720s was not followed-up until 822, when Louis the Pious sent Ebo, the archbishop of Reims, on the first of three missions to Denmark. Ebo was as conspicuously unsuccessful as Willibrord had been. In 826, the Danish king Harald Klak converted to Christianity while visiting the Frankish court in order to curry favour with Louis, whose support he was seeking against Godfred's sons. When Harald returned to Denmark, Louis sent the monk Ansgar to accompany him. When Godfred's pagan sons forced Harald into exile a year later, Ansgar went to Sweden where King Björn allowed him to found a church at the trade centre of Birka on Lake Mälaren. Ansgar entrusted the mission in Sweden to his kinsman Gautbert, so that he could concentrate on Denmark. In 831, he became the first bishop of Hamburg and, the following year, he was appointed papal legate for the Scandinavian and Slavonic missions. Ansgar's mission suffered severe setbacks. Gautbert was expelled from Birka a few years after his arrival and the Danish attack on Hamburg in 845 severely disrupted missionary activity. In 851–2, Ansgar led a second mission to Scandinavia, founding churches at Hedeby and Ribe in Denmark and re-establishing the church at Birka. Ansgar became known as 'the Apostle of the North' for his efforts but for all that he failed to establish any enduring Christian communities in either Denmark or Sweden. Missionary activity languished again until the German king Henry the Fowler invaded Denmark and defeated King Gorm soon after he won power. Henry's victory created the opportunity for Unni, the archbishop of Hamburg-Bremen, to launch a new mission to Denmark. Gorm gave Unni a hostile reception but, according to Adam of Bremen, young Harald was more sympathetic: 'Unni made him so faithful to Christ that, although he himself had not received the sacrament of baptism, he permitted the public profession of Christianity, which his father had always hated.' By 948 there were enough Christians in Jutland to justify its division into three bishoprics, at Hedeby, Ribe and Århus, under the control of the archbishopric of Hamburg-Bremen. When Harald finally took the plunge and was baptised in 965, along with his wife and son, Svein Forkbeard, he showed that his conversion was sincere by actively encouraging his people to adopt the new faith.

Whatever the spiritual attractions of the new faith – and it certainly offered greater doctrinal clarity than Norse paganism – an astute ruler like Harald must have been aware of the many political advantages that would come from conversion. The immediate pay-off for Harald was the prospect of better relations with his powerful southern neighbour, the German Holy Roman Emperor Otto I. Harald would have known from the experience of previous generations of Viking leaders overseas in Frankia, England and Ireland, that there could be no normal diplomatic relations with Christian rulers unless he too became a Christian. There must also have been many aspects of Christian teaching that were attractive to a state-building monarch. The many Old Testament stories of righteous kings who defeated their enemies thanks to the support of God must have given Christianity considerable appeal to a warrior king. The potential of the Christian doctrine of divinely ordained kingship for raising the status of the monarchy must have been quite obvious too. The church also brought with it literate personnel with administrative expertise, who could help a king build a government for his kingdom. While jealous of its spiritual authority, the church recognised that strong government made its own task of conversion easier and could help protect its personnel and property, so kings could usually count on ecclesiastical support. The international culture of Catholic Europe, including Romanesque art and architecture, the Latin language and alphabet and the classical literature of ancient Rome came as part of the Christian package. As the new religion spread and put down deeper roots, this gradually became the elite culture, displacing indigenous cultural traditions tainted with paganism.

Royal Jelling

Gorm and Harald ruled Denmark from their manor at Jelling, now a large village, in the gently rolling countryside of mid Jutland about 80 miles north of Hedeby on the old *Hærvej*. Jelling may have been chosen as a royal residence because it was already marked as a place of ancient power by a Bronze Age burial mound. By the second half of the tenth century, Gorm and Harald between them had provided Jelling with a remarkable collection of monuments: a massive 1,100 foot (335 m) long ship-setting, by far the largest known, two large mounds, two runestones, a wooden church and several large halls, all of which stood within a palisaded enclosure covering nearly 30 acres (12 hectares). Between them, these monuments tell the story of Denmark's transition from paganism to Christianity and its emergence as a stable territorial kingdom.

Standing nearly 30 feet (9 m) tall, the two mounds dominate Jelling even today. Traditionally they were believed to be the burial mounds of King Gorm (the south mound) and his wife Thyre (the north mound), but archaeological investigations have revealed a more complicated history. The north mound was built exactly in the middle of the huge ship-setting, so it is likely that they were built at the same time. The mound was built over the earlier Bronze Age tumulus: a large timber-lined burial chamber at its centre was partly dug into the older mound. Dendrochronological analysis shows that the timbers were felled in the autumn of 958. However, the burial chamber itself was empty. Excavations showed that the mound had been dug into around the time of Harald's conversion to Christianity and the bodies in the chamber had been removed along with any grave goods. One of the few artefacts left behind was part of a wooden wagon. These were commonly used as coffins for high status women. This supports the traditional association of the mound with Queen Thyre, who died some time before Gorm. The southern mound associated with Gorm, however, turned out never to have contained any bodies at all. If Gorm was buried at Jelling, he must have been buried in the north mound. The southern mound was built over a pile of rocks that may have been a *hørg*, where sacrificial offerings were made. Despite its pagan nature, the mound was probably not built until after Harald's baptism and its purpose remains unclear: perhaps the mound was a respectful burial for the old pagan ways that the new religion was consigning to oblivion.

A twelfth-century stone church now stands between the two mounds but excavations in the 1970s showed that it was built on the site of a substantial tenth-century timber church. A burial found within the church contained the partially preserved skeleton of a well-built man. In life, he was a little over five feet six inches (1.67 m) tall and was suffering from osteoarthritis of the lower back when he died, probably still in his forties. Only a very important man would have been buried inside a royal church but his identity is unknown. It has generally been assumed that the skeleton is that of Gorm, the theory being that after his conversion Harald had his parents exhumed from the north mound and reburied in consecrated ground, though if that was the case there is no sign of Thyre's skeleton. However, burying pagans in a church would have been against Christian doctrine, which did not allow posthumous conversions. If Gorm and Thyre really were buried in the northern mound, Harald may have exhumed them simply because he did not want pagans buried so close to his new Christian centre.

South of the church stand Jelling's two runestones. The smaller and older of the stones was erected by King Gorm as a memorial to Queen Thyre. Gorm was evidently fond of Thyre as he described her as 'Denmark's adornment'. The inscription has more than sentimental value because this is the earliest recorded use of the word Denmark ('tannmarkaR') to describe the country of the Danes. Old engravings of the monuments at Jelling suggest that this runestone may originally have stood on top of the northern mound, only being moved to its present location in relatively modern times. The second and larger of the runestones is an assertively Christian monument erected by King Harald to commemorate both his parents and his own achievements in uniting and Christianising the Danes. One face of the stone carries the runic inscription: 'King Harald ordered this monument made in memory of Gorm, his father, and in memory of Thyre, his mother; that Harald who won for himself all of Denmark and Norway and made the Danes Christian.' A second face shows a vigorously carved lion fighting a serpent and the third, a figure of the crucified Christ on a cross entwined with branches and leaves. By depicting the crucifixion this way, the stone carver may have intended to draw a deliberate parallel between Christ and Odin, who hanged himself from the world-tree Yggdrasil to learn the secret of runes. Small traces of paint show that the runestone was originally brightly coloured. Jelling's time as a pre-eminent centre of power was brief. Now in the far west of his unified kingdom, Jelling was no longer a convenient base for Harald's rule, so in the 980s he moved to Roskilde, only a few miles from the ancient power centre at Lejre, on the more centrally situated island of Sjælland.

Exile and death

Harald's authority was not confined to Denmark. Through an alliance with Håkon Sigurdsson, jarl of Lade (now a suburb of Trondheim), Harald overthrew Norway's King Harald Greycloak c. 970, taking the south of the country for himself and giving the north to Håkon. Harald also won control of a Wendish port called Jumne or Jomsborg, which is probably the modern Polish port of Wolin near the mouth of the Oder River. In the tenth century, Wolin was a strongly fortified trading and manufacturing centre with a large and well-constructed harbour. The well-travelled Córdoban merchant, al-Tartushi, thought it a more impressive place than Hedeby. Significant numbers of typically Scandinavian artefacts, such as Thor's hammer amulets, Norwegian soapstone bowls and runic inscriptions, point to the presence of a permanent Scandinavian community in the Slavic town. This may have given rise to the legend of the Jomsvikings, an elite band of Viking mercenaries who, according to romantic Icelandic saga traditions, used Jomsborg as their base.

Despite his achievements Harald's reign ended badly. Harald suffered his first setback in 975 when he lost control of Hedeby to the Germans. The previous year, Danish Vikings had raided northern Germany and, rightly or wrongly, the new emperor, Otto II, held Harald responsible and invaded Denmark in response. Harald, aided by jarl Håkon, tried to hold the Germans at the Danevirke, but was eventually forced back. Harald surrendered Hedeby, and its revenues, to Otto, who built and garrisoned a fort at nearby Schleswig to guard it. Under pressure from Otto, Harald tried to introduce Christianity to Norway. Unfortunately for Harald, this alienated jarl Håkon, a devout pagan, who rebelled and seized control of the whole of Norway.

In 982, Otto II suffered a severe defeat while campaigning in Italy. This was too good an opportunity to let pass and a Danish army under Svein Forkbeard recaptured Hedeby from the Germans, while Harald's father-in-law Mistivoj burned Hamburg. By now, however, Harald had made himself many enemies at home. Local chieftains had seen their traditional autonomy curtailed as Harald tightened royal authority and devout pagans resented the imposition of Christianity. In 987, Svein overthrew his father, who fled across the Baltic to Jomsborg, where he died soon after from wounds inflicted during the fighting. According to Adam of Bremen, Svein had never taken his baptism seriously and he was able to win power with the support of disgruntled pagans. While Svein may well have benefited from such disaffection, it is unlikely that he ever renounced Christianity. There is strong evidence that he continued his father's Christianisation policy, founding many churches during his reign, and had he really been hostile to Christianity he would hardly have allowed his father's retainers to bring his body back from Jomsborg and bury it in the church he had founded at Roskilde.

The real reason for Adam's hostility was probably that Svein rejected the authority of the archbishopric of Hamburg-Bremen. In medieval Europe, the modern distinction between church and state did not exist. Kings relied heavily on bishops to help them govern their kingdoms and always sought to influence appointments to bishoprics. The Danish church and its bishops in Harald's time were ultimately responsible to the archbishops of Hamburg-Bremen, who were appointed by the German emperors. No medieval king would have liked this situation as it represented a limitation on his sovereignty. And it was often the case that where the church led, secular authority followed. Harald was probably willing to put up with this situation because it kept the emperors off his back while he consolidated royal authority in Denmark. Svein may have overthrown his father because he saw all too clearly that a German claim to rule the Danish church might ultimately be used to support a German claim to sovereignty over the state. Throughout his reign, Svein avoided contacts with

Hamburg-Bremen and when he needed priests he brought them over from England.

Svein seized power at a time of resurgent Viking raiding, mainly against England, now seen as a soft target thanks to the weak rule of Æthelred the Unready. Svein knew that returning Viking leaders, with their newly won wealth and status, could challenge royal authority so he kept them in the shade by leading his own tribute-gathering raids (see ch. 9). Two Viking leaders who must have caused Svein much anxiety were the exiled Norwegian sea-king Olaf Tryggvason and the Danish nobleman Thorkell the Tall. According to saga traditions, Thorkell was the son of Strút Harald, jarl of Sjælland, and the brother of Sigvaldi, the supposed leader of the Jomsvikings. In other words, he was a member of the class that had lost most from Harald's centralisation of royal authority. In 1011, Thorkell received the enormous payment of 48,000 pounds (21,772 kg) of silver from Æthelred, whose service he later entered, fighting for him against Svein. Thanks to his lack of royal blood, Thorkell's threat to Svein was limited. Thorkell might be an overmighty subject but it would have been hard for him to replace Svein on the throne, and he was eventually found a role in the new order (by Svein's son Cnut). The same was not true of Olaf Tryggvason. Olaf used the proceeds of his raids on England in 991–4 to fund a successful attempt to win control of Norway in 995. However, Svein claimed to be Norway's true ruler by right of inheritance from his father Harald. This made conflict inevitable.

Harald Fairhair unites Norway

Danish ambitions to rule Norway were nothing new. Back in 813 the Frankish annals recorded that kings Harald Klak and Reginfred were fighting in Vestfold, west of Oslo Fjord, trying to impose their rule on an unwilling population. The outcome of the struggle is not recorded but they probably failed to subjugate the area for long. Two decades later two high-status women, one elderly, the other middle aged, were buried with lavish grave goods in a richly decorated longship under a barrow at Oseberg, in the heart of Vestfold. As such a burial would only have been afforded to a powerful queen, it is clear that Vestfold was at the heart of an independent kingdom. It is not known which of the two women buried in the barrow was the queen and which the sacrificial companion to join her in the afterlife – both were well-dressed – but local traditions had a name for her: Åsa, known from saga traditions as the grandmother of Harald Fairhair, the first king to rule all of Norway.

Despite Harald's importance in Norwegian history, it is not known for certain when he actually lived. The fullest account of Harald's life is his saga in *Heimskringla* ('The Circle of the World'), an epic saga history of the kings of Norway by the thirteenth-century Icelander Snorri Sturluson, but this certainly contains much legendary material. According to Snorri, Harald was a descendent of the proto-historical Swedish Yngling dynasty and through them of the fertility god Freyr. Harald's father, Halfdan the Black, was the son of Åsa and her husband King Gudrød of Vestfold. Harald inherited the kingship of Vestfold at the age of ten after his father drowned accidentally by falling through a hole in a frozen lake. It is unlikely that this could have happened much before *c.* 870. Harald's ambition was to rule all of Norway and he vowed not to cut or comb his hair until he had achieved his goal, hence his nickname 'fairhair' (*hárfagri*).

Unity was never going to come easily to Norway. The country's rugged topography and long coastline made internal communications difficult, promoting localism: at the beginning of the Viking Age almost every valley had its chief or petty king. Two areas, however, were particularly favourable for the development of regional power centres. One of these was Viken, the sheltered Oslo Fjord region in the south-east of the country, which included Harald's kingdom of Vestfold. Lying in the rain shadow of Norway's central spine of mountains, Viken has a relatively dry and sunny climate favourable to arable farming. The other was the Trøndelag, the fertile region around Trondheim Fjord, over 300 miles away across the mountains to the north. This region was dominated by Håkon Grjotgardsson, the jarl of Lade, whose pedigree was no less illustrious than Harald's. After some indecisive host-ilities, Harald and Håkon became allies, the king recognising the jarl's autonomy in the north in return for his support fighting the dozens of other local kings. Harald's campaign ended with his victory around 885 (it is hard to be precise) over a coalition of seven local kings and jarls at the sea battle of Hafrsfjord, near modern Stavanger, after which opposition to his rule collapsed. Icelandic traditions claim that some of the survivors from Hafrsfjord fled to the Scottish isles from where they raided Norway. Harald led an expedition west to bring the area under Norwegian control, establishing the Earldom of Orkney under his ally Rognvald of Møre.

Harald's tyranny

Icelandic historical traditions, epitomised by Snorri, present Harald Fairhair as a tyrannical ruler. After his victory at Hafrsfjord, Harald is said to have confiscated all the *óðal* land from the bonders (free peasant farmers), forcing them to become royal tenants, and to have imposed heavy taxation. It was to escape this oppression that medieval Icelanders like Snorri believed that their ancestors had emigrated to Iceland. However, there is no evidence that Harald attempted any such expropriation of *óðal* land: the reduction of most free peasants to tenant status seems actually to have been a phenomenon of Snorri's own age. It is also certain that the settlement of Iceland began before the Battle of Hafrsfjord is likely to have taken place. Some historians also doubt that Harald ever made an expedition to the isles because the Earldom of Orkney was established before Harald became king (see ch. 4). It is, therefore, likely that the Icelanders invented the story in order to explain why so many of the first settlers came not from Norway but from the Scottish isles. In reality, Harald's rule was much less than absolute. The jarls of Lade ruled in Trøndelag and Hålogaland in virtual independence and it is only in their title that they were anything less than kings. Harald certainly did reduce many local kingdoms to jarldoms but there were still dozens of 'valley kings' in Norway even a century later. Nor did such unity as Harald imposed survive his death some time between 930 and 940.

During his long life, he is supposed to have been eighty when he died, Harald fathered over twenty sons by at least eight different women. According to Snorri, Harald divided the kingdom between his sons three years before his death, appointing his favourite son Erik Bloodaxe as high king over them all. This did not go down well with

Erik's brothers, who all believed, as possessors of royal blood, that they were entitled to the dignity of full kingship. No sooner was Harald dead than his sons, predictably enough, sought power for themselves in the many local kingdoms their father had controlled. Thanks to his lurid nickname – earned because of his brutal rulership rather than his prowess in battle – Erik Bloodaxe is probably the most famous of all Viking leaders. Scarcely less notorious, in saga traditions at least, was Erik's wife Gunnhild, who was reputed to be a *völva* or seeress. Even before Harald died, she had been accused of encompassing the death of Erik's half-brother Halfdan by magic. No statesman, Erik tried to maintain the unity of the kingdom by violence. Egged on by Gunnhild, Erik seriously depleted the numbers of his brothers before the Norwegians tired of him and invited his younger half-brother Håkon the Good (d. 960) to come home from England, where he had been fostered by king Æthelstan, and take the throne. With the support of Sigurd Håkonarson, the jarl of Lade, Håkon was proclaimed king in the Trøndelag. When Håkon began to advance on Viken, Erik's support evaporated and he fled to Orkney. From there Erik embarked on a career as a Viking raider, which won him the kingship of York in 948 and a violent death on Stainmore six years later (see ch. 2).

Paganism prevails

Håkon could have known little about his kingdom when he arrived home. He was still an infant when his father had sent him to England, and he had never been back to Norway. Håkon's position in Norway was never strong because he lacked the local connections, friendships and prestige that would have accrued to him naturally if he had been brought up there. In most respects he was a weak ruler who exercised direct authority only in the west of the country. His nephews Gudrød Bjørnsson and Tryggvi Olafsson ruled as kings in Vestfold and Østfold, while jarl Sigurd ruled in complete autonomy in Trøndelag and Halogaland. Æthelstan had brought Håkon up as a Christian and he began his reign hoping to spread the faith in Norway. Although there had been no recorded missionary activity, many Norwegians must have been familiar with Christianity by this time thanks to their long-standing contacts with Britain and Ireland. There are likely to have been considerable numbers of Christian slaves living in Norway and many Norwegians will have had Christian relations living in the Viking colonies in Britain and Ireland. Many a homecoming warrior may have been a nominal Christian after accepting baptism for pragmatic reasons while serving Christian rulers as a mercenary or to smooth negotiations of tribute payments. However, apart from a few inscribed crosses, there is no archaeological evidence of any Christian communities in Norway before Håkon's reign.

To help him spread the faith, Håkon invited missionaries to come over from England. While a few of Håkon's personal retinue did accept baptism, they did so more out of loyalty than conviction, and most Norwegians were willing to tolerate their king's Christianity only as long as he kept his worship private. The issue came to a head when Håkon announced at the Frostathing assembly in the Trøndelag that he wished the people to be baptised and to end pagan sacrifices. This provoked an immediate rebellion by the bonders, who sincerely feared for the prosperity of the land if they were not able to perform the traditional sacrifices. Most chieftains also opposed Christianity, partly, at least, because they feared a loss of status and authority: the Norse pagan religion had no priesthood and it was the chieftains who conducted the sacrificial rituals. Supported, it seems, by jarl Sigurd, the bonders threatened that if the king did not perform the sacrifices as his father had done they would choose another king. At the harvest festival at Lade later that year, Håkon attempted a compromise by placing a linen cloth between his mouth and the sacrificial horse flesh he had been offered, but this satisfied no one. Four local chiefs in the district of Møre began killing priests and burning the churches Håkon had founded, while another group of chiefs resolved to force him to take part in the midwinter Yule sacrifice, threatening violence if he refused. Under this intense pressure Håkon finally gave in and ate some small pieces of horse liver. This token sacrifice seems to have satisfied the pagans and, after this humiliation, Håkon gave up his attempt to make the Norwegians Christian.

Håkon soon faced a greater challenge to his throne. After their father's death in 954, Erik Bloodaxe's sons had gone to Denmark and won Harald Bluetooth's support for a campaign to try to drive Håkon from the Norwegian throne. Håkon proved to be a capable warrior, inflicting a succession of defeats on Erik's sons. In 960, three of Erik's sons, Harald Greycloak, Gamle and Sigurd, landed secretly in Hordaland and surprised Håkon in his hall at Fitjar. Håkon fought off the brothers, who fled back to their ships, but it was his last victory: during the battle he received an arrow wound to his arm and he died of blood loss soon afterwards. Although Snorri says that he was still a Christian at the end of his life, Håkon may, at least publicly, have converted to paganism, if only to keep the peace. Certainly Håkon's followers gave him a traditional pagan burial in a barrow and in his funeral lay *Hákonamál*, Håkon's skald Eyvind Skaldaspillir described his welcome in Valhalla as befitting a pagan warrior who fell in battle. Despite all the opposition to his religious policies, Håkon was remembered in saga traditions as a just ruler who brought peace and good harvests and whose legal reforms made the district things more representative and easier to consult.

As Håkon had no male heirs, Harald Greycloak, the eldest of Erik's sons, succeeded to the throne with the support of Harald Bluetooth. Harald and his brothers had been baptised while they were in England and, unlike their uncle, they were prepared to use violence against those who opposed Christianity. They destroyed many pagan temples and overthrew the idols to demonstrate their powerlessness, but few Norwegians converted despite the intimidation. Harald aspired to exercise direct authority throughout Norway and dealt ruthlessly with opposition. It was clear to Harald that the most serious obstacle to achieving this was jarl Sigurd. Harald courted Sigurd's malcontent brother Grjotgard and came to a secret agreement: in return for helping to overthrow Sigurd, Harald would make Grjotgard jarl in his place. After the harvest in 962, Grjotgard sent word to Harald that Sigurd was gathered with very few followers in a hall at Aglo in north Trøndelag. Guided by Grjotgard, Harald sailed up Trondheim Fjord by starlight arriving at Aglo undetected late at night. Harald's men set fire to the hall while Sigurd was feasting with his followers. Trapped inside, the jarl and his men were all burned to death. Harald also engineered the murders of Gudrød Bjørnsson and Tryggvi Olafsson soon afterwards, but the violent elimination of his main rivals did not make Harald's position secure.

Norway comes under Danish control

Rising popular discontent with Harald's activities created an opportunity for Harald Bluetooth to intervene in Norway. Jarl Sigurd had been a popular ruler and after his killing the folk of Trøndelag rallied to his son Håkon Sigurdsson. After three years of desultory warfare, Harald was forced to accept Håkon as jarl of Lade, with the same autonomy his father had enjoyed. The peace did not last and in 968 Håkon went into exile in Denmark, where he hatched a conspiracy with Harald Bluetooth to overthrow Harald Greycloak and share Norway between them. Danish Harald lured Norwegian Harald to Denmark with offers of land, only to ambush and kill him when he landed at Hals on Limfjord in north Jutland. After the killing Håkon and Harald Bluetooth took a large fleet to Viken and divided the country between them. Håkon received back his ancestral jarldom in the north, which he ruled in complete autonomy, and the west coast districts of Rogaland, Hordaland, Sogn, Møre and Romsdal, which he ruled as Harald's vassal. Harald took control of the rest of the country except for Vestfold and Agder, which he gave to Harald Grenske, the son of the murdered king Gudrød Bjørnsson.

At first Håkon was true to his arrangement with Harald and loyally brought ships and men to defend Denmark against the emperor Otto II's attack in 975. While Håkon was in Denmark, Harald forced him to accept baptism and agree to take a party of priests with him to Norway to begin missionary work. A devout pagan, Håkon's conversion was insincere and he had no intention of helping Harald Christianise Norway. Håkon took the priests onboard his ship as Harald demanded but, as soon as he got a favourable wind for home, he disembarked the priests and made good his escape, plundering Danish territory on the way. Preoccupied with the threat from Germany, Harald was unable to prevent Håkon seizing control of all of Norway on his return and for the next ten years or so he enjoyed undisturbed possession of the country. Late in Harald's reign or early in Svein Forkbeard's – the sources are contradictory and none can be considered to be really reliable – the Danes attempted to win back control of Norway by sending a fleet of sixty ships to attack Lade. According to saga traditions the fleet was led by the elite Jomsvikings, but it never reached its destination. Deliberately misled by a captured herdsman, the Danes blundered unwittingly into a much larger Norwegian fleet under jarl Håkon and his son Erik at Hjørungavåg in Sunnmøre and was crushingly defeated in a battle fought in a heavy hailstorm. Only about half the Danish fleet escaped.

According to the saga traditions, Håkon became increasingly over-bearing after his victory at Hjørungavåg and began to tax the bonders so heavily that his support ebbed away. So unpopular had Håkon become that when Olaf Tryggvason unexpectedly arrived in Norway in 995, fresh from his triumphs in England, he was immediately accepted as king. Håkon fled but was murdered soon after by one of his retainers while he was hiding in a pigsty: when Olaf later displayed his severed head, it was pelted with stones by a mob of angry bonders. Håkon's son Erik Håkonarson escaped however, and, like many an exile before him, became a Viking leader.

Olaf's rapturous welcome soon began to turn sour. Olaf's upbringing had made him ruthless even by the standards of a ruthless age. Olaf was still a young child when his father, King Tryggve Olafsson, was murdered, forcing him into exile with his mother. Crossing the Baltic Sea on their way to Russia, their ship was captured by Estonian Vikings and Olaf fell into the hands of a slave dealer called Klerkon. Luckily for Olaf, he was sold to kind-hearted owners who looked after him well as he grew up (Klerkon exchanged him for a good cloak). When Olaf was eight, he was found by his cousin Sigurd who bought his freedom and took him to Novgorod. It was there that the then nine-year-old Olaf ran into Klerkon again and promptly split his head in two with a small axe. As a teenager Olaf became a warrior in Vladimir the Great's *druzhina,* but left when he was eighteen to begin a career of Viking raiding. As a man of royal blood, Olaf easily raised a warrior band despite his youth and, as was still the custom, this entitled him to call himself a king. All he needed to do now was to win a kingdom. Eight years of ceaseless raiding in the Baltic and England provided him with the wealth, the reputation and the loyal warrior band to do just that: he was still only about twenty-seven years old.

Convert or die

While Olaf had been in England in 994, he had been baptised by Ælfheah, the archbishop of Canterbury, who was later martyred by the Danes in 1012, and he was determined to break pagan resistance to Christianity once and for all. Olaf was not a patient man and he seems to have concluded from the start that force would bring quicker results than argument. Olaf began his campaign of Christianisation in Viken, where he could count on the support of his father's family. Olaf treated those who opposed him harshly, killing some, mutilating others, and driving some into exile. Olaf tied practitioners of traditional pagan *seiðr* magic to rocks by the sea at low tide and left them to drown. The folk of Viken found Olaf's approach persuasive and by early 997 most had been baptised. That summer Olaf moved to the west of the country, taking a large army with him to quell any opposition. There was none, in part thanks to Olaf's maternal family, which used its influence in the area to soften up the opposition to Christianity. In the autumn, Olaf moved to the still staunchly pagan Trøndelag and burned the temple at Lade. This was a step too far for the locals and they rose in arms forcing Olaf to withdraw to Viken for the winter. This was only a temporary setback. The following year Olaf returned to the Trøndelag. At first Olaf adopted a conciliatory approach, offering to learn about pagan customs, but this was only to lull his opponents into a false sense of security. At the district thing, Olaf and his men killed the leader of the pagan faction, Járn-Skeggi, in the temple of Thor. Though the pagans had come well-armed, the loss of their leader broke their resistance and they tamely agreed to baptism.

To better consolidate his authority in the all-too independent Trøndelag, Olaf built a palace and a missionary church on a peninsula by the mouth of the Nidelva river, with the river on one side and Trondheim Fjord on the other. As it was almost completely surrounded by water, the site was easy to defend and had good access to sea. It was also only 2 miles from Lade: so closely associated with local independence but now very obviously under royal control. Olaf called the place Kaupangen ('trading place'), perhaps to attract merchants and the taxes and tolls they could be made to pay, but it soon became known as Nidaros ('mouth of the Nidelva'). Since the nineteenth century, however, it has been known as Trondheim, now Norway's third largest city. Olaf also tried to strengthen his authority in the region by marrying Járn-Skeggi's daughter Gudrun. This turned out to be an almost fatal error of judgment on Olaf's part: Gudrun did not have a forgiving nature and she tried to stab him to death on their wedding night. After that the saga notes laconically: 'Gudrun never came into the king's bed again.' In spring 999, Olaf completed the conversion of Norway's coastal districts when he sailed to Halogaland, north of the Arctic Circle, but only after he had defeated the Halogalanders in a sea battle. Around the same time, the Icelandic Althing bowed to Olaf's pressure and adopted Christianity as the island's official religion.

Christianisation was only one means by which Olaf hoped to strengthen royal authority. Coinage was an important way that medieval monarchs promoted their image and authority: Olaf opened a mint at Trondheim and issued Norway's first coinage. He also introduced the office of district governor. However, Olaf's reign was destined to be a short one. After several years of successful raiding in the Baltic, Erik Håkonarson went to Denmark, where he was welcomed by Svein Forkbeard. In alliance with the Swedish king Olof Skötkonung (r. c. 995–1022), who had his own designs on Norwegian territory, the pair began to plot Olaf's downfall. Their opportunity came in 1000, when Olaf sailed south, through Danish waters, to raid the Wendish lands on the south coast of the Baltic.

According to saga traditions Olaf was goaded into the raid by his new wife Thyre, Svein Forkbeard's sister. This was no diplomatic marriage: against her brother's wishes, Thyre had abandoned her pagan husband, a Wendish king, and married Olaf instead. Thyre demanded that Olaf go to Wendland to recover property she had been forced to abandon when she fled from her husband. Against his counsellors' advice, Olaf is alleged to have agreed. A more plausible scenario is that Olaf believed that a profitable raiding expedition would help heal the wounds of his forced Christianisation and bind the warrior aristocracy in loyalty to him. And as pagans, the Wends were fair game.

Battle at sea

Olaf's expedition went well enough but King Svein's spies observed his movements closely. As Olaf sailed home that September, Svein and his allies ambushed him at Svöld with a superior force. Svöld has never been identified: some historians favour the German Baltic island of Rügen, others the Øresund, the narrow channel that separates Denmark and Sweden. With sixty-four oars Olaf's gilded flagship, the drakkar *Long Serpent*, was one of the largest longships ever built but Olaf had eleven ships, his opponents over seventy and the result was never in doubt.

The exact course of the battle is not known for certain but it probably did not involve individual ship-to-ship actions. Viking Age sea battles were usually fought in much the same way as land battles, but with the ships themselves forming the battlefield. The opposing fleets formed up in line, bows-on to the other. The largest ships were always stationed in the centre. Masts and sails were taken down before battle to clear the decks for action and all manoeuvring was done under oars alone. The defending fleet, as Olaf's fleet did at Svöld, often used the masts and spars to lash its ships together so that they formed a solid fighting platform on which warriors could move quickly from ship to ship to where they were most needed. The attacking fleet could also do this but only after it had made contact with the enemy. Tactics were simple. The first step was to fasten onto the enemy ships with grappling hooks and anchors, and then board them. Once the deck had been cleared in hand-to-hand fighting, the ship would be cut loose and rowed away. Size was always more important in sea battles than speed and manoeuvrability. The larger a ship was, the more men it carried and the taller it was. A high-sided ship offered better protection from missiles for its crew and it was harder for attackers to board. Its crew could in turn rain missiles down onto the crew of a smaller ship and they were also more easily able to board it.

At Svöld Erik Håkonarson took the lead in the fighting on his own flagship, the *Iron Beard*, which rivalled Olaf's *Long Serpent* in size and splendour. According to Snorri's account of the battle in his saga of the king's life in *Heimskringla*, Erik laid his ship:

> 'alongside the outermost of King Olaf's ships, thinned it of men, cut the cables, and let it drift free. Then he laid alongside the next, and fought until he had cleared it of men too. Now all the people who were in the smaller ships began to run into the larger and the jarl cut them loose as soon as he cleared them of men... At last it came to this, that all King Olaf's ships were cleared of men except the *Long Serpent*, on board of which gathered all who could still use their weapons. Then *Iron Beard* lay side to side with the Serpent and the fight went on with battle axe and sword.'

Numbers told and eventually Olaf made a last stand at the stern of *Long Serpent*. Seeing that death or capture were inevitable Olaf, in full armour, jumped over the side of his ship and sank without trace. Norwegians proved reluctant to accept their king's death and Olaf became a 'king in the mountain' like Arthur, Frederick Barbarossa and many others who are still awaiting the right moment to reclaim their kingdoms. Soon after his death stories began to circulate that Olaf had swum underwater to another ship and sailed to Wendland, and from there travelled on to the Holy Land. But, as Snorri put it, whatever the truth of the stories 'King Olaf Tryggvason never came back again to his kingdom of Norway'.

Danish interlude

With Olaf dead, Norway was divided between Svein Forkbeard, Erik and King Olof. Svein took Viken as his share, while Erik, now jarl of Lade, ruled most of the north and west as his vassal. King Olof received inland districts in central Norway but gave these to his son-in-law, Erik's brother Svein Håkonarson, to rule as his vassal. Erik and his brother may have converted to Christianity during their exile but if they did they did not try to impose it on their subjects and many Norwegians relapsed to paganism. Danish domination of Norway restored, Svein spent the remainder of his reign plundering England to finance his state-building, ultimately conquering the country in 1014. In Denmark Svein was succeed by his elder son Harald II (r. 1014–18) and his younger son Cnut inherited his claim to England. Cnut had to fight for his inheritance but England was such a prize that he attracted the backing of both his father's old enemy Thorkell the Tall, and jarl Erik of Lade, who made his lands over to his son Håkon. Erik's absence provided the opportunity for another exiled Norwegian royal, Olaf Haraldsson (r. 1016–28), to return home, restore his country's independence, and complete Olaf Tryggvason's Christianisation of his people.

Olaf Haraldsson's ultimate fate was to become a martyr and a saint and, thanks to this, he is without doubt the best documented of all Viking Age Scandinavian kings, a popular subject for hagiographers and royal biographers alike. Dozens of skaldic poems, composed during his lifetime, and within a few years of death, have been preserved in later sagas of his life. However, Olaf's perceived sanctity also means that objectivity is in short supply: who could criticise a saint in the Middle Ages? When he came to write the *Saga of St Olaf*, the longest of the kings' sagas in *Heimskringla*, Snorri Sturluson drew on a wide range of earlier sources and deliberately omitted sources he considered too fanciful, but he was a product of his age and even this relatively sober saga comes close to hagiography at times.

Born around 995, Olaf was the posthumous son of Harald Grenske, the king of Vestfold and Agder and a direct descendant of Harald Fairhair. Olaf was probably baptised, with his mother Åsta and step-father Sigurd Syr, the king of Ringerike, as a child during Olaf Tryggvason's Christianisation campaign, but the Norman writer William of Jumièges (died *c.* 1070) states that he was baptised in 1013 by the bishop of Rouen during a visit to Normandy. Olaf was as precocious as Olaf Tryggvason had been and at the age of twelve his step-father gave him a ship and warrior band so that he could embark on a career as a Viking raider. This made Olaf a king even though he as yet had no kingdom. It is hard today to imagine that grown men would follow a twelve-year-old boy into battle, but that was how strong the charisma of royal blood was. In a Viking career that took him from the Baltic to Spain, Olaf more than justified his men's faith in him. Olaf spent much of his time in England, fighting in alliance with Thorkell the Tall some of the time, at others serving King Æthelred, earning a fortune in the process from tribute and payment for mercenary service.

Soon after jarl Erik left to join Cnut in England, Olaf returned to southern Norway and was proclaimed king with the support of his step-father and a coalition of petty kings. On learning of Olaf's arrival in Norway, Svein Håkonarson raised a fleet in the Trøndelag and set off south to confront him. Olaf and Svein met in a sea battle at Nesjar in Oslo Fjord on Palm Sunday 25 March 1016. Svein was defeated and fled to take refuge with his father-in-law in Sweden, where he died soon afterwards. When he learned about his uncle's defeat, Håkon too took flight, going to England where Cnut, now king, welcomed him and made him Earl of Worcester. His power now unchallenged in Norway, Olaf resumed Olaf Tryggvason's Christianisation and state-building policies and, like him, he based himself at Nidaros, so that he could keep a close eye on this, the most independent-minded part of his kingdom. Despite some reversion to paganism under the rule of the jarls of Lade, Christianity remained firmly established in coastal areas, so Olaf focused his efforts on the uplands, where there were as yet few Christians. Olaf's approach to evangelisation was, if anything, even more brutal than his predecessor's. Those who converted enjoyed royal favour, those who resisted suffered death, torture, mutilation or blinding. Many of the petty valley kings lost their little kingdoms and were exiled from Norway, not always retaining all their body parts.

Advised by an English bishop called Grimketel or Grimkell, Olaf made the first steps towards giving Norway an established ecclesiastical structure and in Christianising Norway's pagan laws. At the Moster thing in western Norway in 1024, he proclaimed new laws on religious observance. Observance of Christian fast and feast days was made compulsory as was baptism of all healthy infants. Christian laws of marriage were imposed. The whole community was made responsible for paying for the upkeep of churches and the clergy. The introduction of the Christian calendar ensured that the practices of the church began to dictate the rhythms of daily life. Copies of the Moster Law, as it became known, were read out at all the local things, which were ordered to approve them.

Olaf inevitably made enemies, especially among the chieftain class, who probably objected to the centralisation of royal authority as much as his religious revolution. Many of them yearned for a return to the days of weak, indirect rule when their king lived far away. After some early conflicts, Olaf made an ally of the Swedish king Olof Sköttkonung by marrying his daughter Astrid, but Cnut, who had added Denmark to his domains when his brother died in 1018, was not so easily out-maneouvred. Cnut believed that Norway was his by right and he sent letters to Olaf telling him that, if he wanted to avoid conflict, he should travel to England and submit to him as his overlord. Olaf refused and, to pre-empt any attempt by Cnut to invade Norway, he allied with his brother-in-law, the new Swedish king Önund Jacob (r. 1022–c. 1050) in an attack on Denmark. The allies awaited Cnut's inevitable retaliation on the Helgeå ('Holy River') in Skåne. When Cnut sailed into the river, his large Anglo-Danish fleet was thrown into disarray when Olaf and Önund broke down an earth and timber dam they had constructed upstream, releasing a violent torrent of water that overturned ships and drowned hundreds of his men. Somehow, Cnut managed to regain control of his forces and prevent the battle turning into a rout, but at the end of the day he had to abandon the battlefield to the Swedes and Danes. As it turned out, Helgeå proved to be a hollow victory for Olaf and Önund: they had suffered such severe casualties that they could not continue their campaign and their alliance broke up as each hurried home, fearful that Cnut might get there before them.

Their fears were justified. Within four years Önund was Cnut's vassal and Olaf was dead. When Olaf returned to Norway after his Danish campaign, he found that his support was evaporating and he felt that of the leading chieftains there were only four he could be sure of. That proved to be over optimistic. When Cnut arrived off the coast of Viken with an Anglo-Danish fleet of fifty ships in 1028, the whole country rose against Olaf, who fled with a few loyal retainers first to Sweden and from there to the court of King Yaroslav in Russia. In Olaf's place, Cnut restored Håkon Eriksson to his family's jarldom of Lade and appointed him regent of Norway. The arrangement was not destined to last. In 1029, Håkon was lost at sea returning to Norway from a trip to England to visit Cnut. News of jarl Håkon's disappearance quickly reached Olaf and in spring 1030 he set out to reclaim his throne, leaving his five-year-old illegitimate son Magnus the Good in Yaroslav's care.

The Battle of Stiklestad

Olaf returned to Norway through Sweden, where he gathered an army of, according to Snorri, around 3,600 men, crossing the Kjølen Mountains into the Trøndelag. With the benefit of hindsight, Olaf's court skald, Sigvat Tordsson, thought that if the king had been freer with his wealth he could have raised a larger army. However, it might have proved difficult to feed a larger force on its long march through the sparsely populated mountains on the way to Norway. News travelled fast along the Viking trade routes, giving Olaf's enemies in Norway ample time to prepare for his arrival. As he descended the valley of the Verdalselva river towards Trondheim Fjord he met a much larger army of bonders near the farm of Stiklestad. While Olaf's army probably included a high proportion of professional warriors, including the housecarls of his personal retinue, the peasant farmers he faced were not fighting with scythes and pitchforks. All freemen in Viking Age Scandinavia had to be equipped for military service so all would have had at least a shield and spear, and known how to use them, while the wealthier bonders would have been a great deal better equipped than that. The battle probably took place on 29 July 1030, and did not start until the day was well advanced. Olaf attempted to seize the initiative with a headlong downhill charge against the bonders' army, hoping that if he broke their shield wall the bonders would lose confidence and run. The bonders gave ground but they did not break and run – too many of them remembered Olaf's brutal rule to want to give in easily – and their superior numbers quickly began to tell. In desperate hand-to-hand fighting, Olaf was, we are told by Snorri, disabled by a wound to the leg, then speared in the guts by Thore Hund, the leader of the bonder army, and finally finished off by a blow to the neck. Now that Olaf was dead his army began to break up and flee: the battle had lasted about an hour and a half. Among the fugitives was Olaf's fifteen-year-old half-brother Harald Hardrada. Though wounded, the young man was given refuge and treated by a sympathetic peasant, who helped him escape to Sweden once he recovered. Harald travelled on to Russia and then Constantinople, where he joined the Varangian Guard.

After the battle, some loyal peasants hid Olaf's body from his enemies and secretly buried it on the banks of the Verdalselva. But though Olaf had lost his life and kingdom, he did in a real sense win the peace. Olaf had broken the back of pagan resistance to Christianity. When Olaf fled into exile in 1028, there was no return to paganism under Cnut's equally militant Christian regime. The bonder army at Stiklestad was given spiritual encouragement by a Danish bishop: if anyone prayed to Odin for victory they did so privately. Olaf's achievements were irreversible and Norway was now set in its course to become an integral part of Roman Catholic Christendom.

Norway's royal saint

Miracles were soon reported at Olaf's burial place and increasing numbers of people claimed that prayers addressed to him had been answered. A year after Olaf's death, bishop Grimkell exhumed his body and reburied it in or near St Clement's church in Nidaros. Olaf's body was found to be uncorrupted, an incontrovertible sign of sanctity to the medieval Christian mind, and Grimkell declared him to be a saint on the spot. Even though the papacy never officially recognised Olaf as a saint, his cult spread rapidly, aided by the unpopularity of Danish rule and a series of bad harvests, which were widely interpreted as a sign of divine anger over Olaf's killing. This does not mean that Norway was now deeply Christian. Pagan beliefs and sentiments persisted for generations. The church expected this – it was the case with all newly converted populations – and, where it could, it adopted or adapted earlier beliefs to Christian practices to make it easier for converts to engage with the new religion. As a saint, Olaf acquired many of the characteristics of the fertility god Freyr and the popular giant-slaying thunder god Thor. Farmers prayed to St Olaf for a good harvest as they would once have prayed to Freyr, while folk tales proliferated about his battles with malevolent trolls and giants.

The bonders had expected Cnut to rule them with a lighter hand but they were soon disillusioned. There was no magnate of comparable status to replace the drowned jarl Håkon, so Cnut had little choice but to try to rule Norway more directly, rather than relying on informal power-sharing as his father and grandfather had done. To this end, Cnut sent his teenage son Svein to rule Norway under the regency of his English mother Ælfgifu of Northampton. Ælfgifu proved such a harsh ruler that 'Alfiva's time', as her regency was remembered in Norway, became a byword for oppressive government. Olaf's own brutality was soon forgotten and he became instead a symbol of national unity. In 1034, two Norwegian chiefs who had taken Cnut's side against Olaf, Kalv Arneson and Einar Tambarskjelve, became so disenchanted with Danish rule that they travelled to Russia to bring back Olaf's son Magnus. When he arrived in Norway, a popular uprising broke out, forcing Ælfgifu and Svein to flee to Denmark. Svein died there soon afterwards.

Cnut passed away in 1035 and his Anglo-Scandinavian empire fell apart. Harold Harefoot, Cnut's second son by Ælfgifu, became king of England, while Harthacnut, his son by Emma of Normandy, became king of Denmark. Harthacnut immediately recognised Magnus as king of Norway and the two kings agreed that whoever outlived the other would rule both Denmark and Norway. Accordingly, when Harthacnut died in 1042, Magnus became king of Denmark, appointing Cnut's nephew Svein Estrithson to rule as his regent. Unusually, Svein took his surname from his mother, Cnut's sister Estrith, to emphasise his connection to the royal house and to disassociate himself from his father jarl Ulf, who Cnut had executed for treason. Svein had a credible claim on the Danish throne through his mother and rebelled against Magnus and at the Viborg thing in northern Jutland the Danes paid him the homage due to a king. Magnus reacted swiftly and when he arrived in Denmark with a large fleet Svein fled into exile with King Önund in Sweden.

The Danes stayed loyal to Magnus because he proved himself to be a good defender of Denmark. For two centuries and more, Scandinavians had sailed out to plunder the Wendish tribes of the southern Baltic with complete impunity. By the early eleventh century, however, the Wends had learned Viking shipbuilding methods and were launching pirate raids of their own on Scandinavia, and the Danish islands proved particularly vulnerable. In summer 1043, Magnus led a fleet across the Baltic and sacked the Wendish stronghold of Jumne – Viking Jomsborg

– in retaliation. Later in the year, he crushed a Wendish invasion of Jutland at the battle of Lyrskov Heath, to the north of Hedeby. An anonymous history of Norway known as *Ágrip*, written around 1190, tells the story that the night before the battle Magnus's father appeared to him in a vision, reassured him of victory over the pagan Wends, and instructed how to deploy his army for battle. Being the son of a saint only added to Magnus's lustre.

While Svein Estrithson was in Sweden, contemplating his next move, Harald Hardrada turned up, fresh from his service with the Varangians, with a claim to the Norwegian throne, a chest full of money, and a fearsome reputation as a war leader. Svein and Harald immediately formed an alliance but Magnus just as quickly broke it up by offering Harald a share of Norway. Magnus fell ill and died in Sjælland in 1047 aged only twenty-four: he had no male heirs. On his deathbed he expressed the wish that Harald should inherit Norway but that Svein should have Denmark. Svein was delighted but Harald's ambition was not satisfied with Norway alone. For the next four years Harald fought to dislodge Svein from Denmark, launching great Viking raids every summer, culminating with the sacking of Hedeby in 1050. This was intended to strike a blow to Svein's revenues, but Hedeby was not as important as it had been. The larger ships that were coming into use in the eleventh century found it increasingly difficult to reach Hedeby and after it was sacked again in 1066, this time by the Wends, it was abandoned in favour of Schleswig, which was built near deeper water across the Schlei Fjord.

Harald won every battle he fought against Svein but a decisive victory eluded him. Defeat never discouraged Svein, whose humane spirit endeared him to his subjects. In 1050, Svein went so far as to throw away a military advantage during a sea chase when he stopped to rescue drowning captives who Harald had thrown into the sea even though he knew this would allow his mortal enemy to escape. To fund his wars, Harald imposed a heavy burden of tax on the Norwegians and it was the ruthless way he dealt with opposition that earned him his nickname Hardrada, meaning 'hard-ruler'. Harald gave Denmark ten years of peace while he fought over Norway's border with Sweden, but he returned to the attack again in 1060. At the River Niså (now the River Nissan), near Halmstadt in Halland, Harald destroyed the Danish fleet in a night-long sea battle. Svein was lucky to escape with his life but even this disaster did not break Danish resistance. By now Harald's subjects were getting restive and in 1064 he finally made peace and recognised Svein as king of Denmark. This was a decisive moment for both kingdoms, a parting of the ways. By the time dynastic marriages reunited the two kingdoms under a common ruler in 1380, each had acquired its own indelible national consciousness.

After his setback in Denmark, Harald Hardrada did not opt for the quieter life his subjects so obviously wished for. When King Edward the Confessor died in 1066, Harald gathered an army and sailed to England to pursue the tenuous claim to the English throne he had inherited from Magnus the Good only to meet with defeat and death at Stamford Bridge. Harald was succeeded jointly by his two sons Magnus II and Olaf III (r. 1067–93). Magnus died young in 1069 leaving as sole king Olaf, who gave up his father's aggressive foreign policy, made peace with England and Denmark, and spent the remainder of his long reign in Norway improving the administration of his kingdom. His grateful people remembered him as Olaf Kyrre, Olaf the Peaceful. It was in Olaf's time that Norwegian laws were first committed to writing and it was he who introduced the system of trade guilds to Norway, which formed such an important feature of urban life in medieval Western Europe. Since St Olaf's time, bishops had been part of the royal household: Olaf gave Norway a regular diocesan structure, with bishoprics at Nidaros, Oslo and the newly founded town of Bergen. By the time Olaf fell ill and died in 1093, Norway was, to all intents and purposes, a regular medieval European kingdom.

The same could also be said of Denmark by the time Svein Estrithson died around 1074. Not the least sign of Svein's own personal assimilation to Christian European culture was that he was the first Scandinavian king who could read and write. Although Svein pursued, in a halfhearted way, his claim to the English throne, supporting the English rebellion against the Normans in 1069–70, his reign after the end of the conflict with Harald Hardrada was mostly peaceful and dominated by efforts to build friendly relations with the Holy Roman Emperor Henry III and with the papacy. In his dealings with the popes, Svein, a prolific church-builder, had two main objectives, both of which would ultimately be achieved by his sons. Firstly, he pressed for the Danish church to have its own archbishop so that it would be independent of the German archbishopric of Hamburg-Bremen. This ambition was finally fulfilled under his son Erik the Evergood (r. 1095–1103) in 1103, with the elevation of the bishopric of Lund to an archbishopric with responsibility for all of Scandinavia (Norway and Sweden got their own archbishoprics in 1152 and 1164). A second ambition was to have his great-grandfather Harald Bluetooth canonised for his role in converting the Danes, so that the Danish monarchy would have its own royal saint to bolster its authority. This would be fulfilled rather too literally by Svein's son Cnut the Holy (r. 1080–86).

Denmark's last Viking king

Cnut succeeded after the brief reign of his brother Harald III (1074/6–1080). A popular ruler who was remembered as a legal reformer, Harald brought the end of the Viking Age a step closer by making piracy effectively a licensed activity, permissible only if the crown was given a share of the plunder. As a youth, Cnut had led Viking raids against the Wends, and led two invasions of England in 1069 and 1074 in support of his father's claim to the English throne. Cnut ended the crown's dependency on war booty by increasing the royal revenues from taxes and tolls, and enforced the payment of tithes (one tenth of income) to support the church. Cnut also cracked down on freelance Viking raiding, hanging Egil Ragnarsen, the jarl of Bornholm, for piracy. Not surprisingly, Cnut's reforms made him unpopular with his subjects. Their discontent was magnified in 1085, when Cnut introduced a poll tax to pay for a planned invasion of England to pursue his claim to the throne. The fleet gathered in Limfjord but the threat of a German invasion kept Cnut in Schleswig, and in late summer his army broke up as his discontented warriors went home to see to the harvest. When Cnut ordered the fleet to gather again in 1086, a rebellion broke out in Jutland. Cnut fled to Odense where, on 10 July, the rebels killed him, together with his brother Benedict and seventeen of his followers, in front of the altar of St Alban's priory. No Danish king would ever again raise a fleet to invade England.

Denmark had been officially Christian for 120 years when Cnut was killed, yet the aftermath of his death hints that pagan sentiments were not entirely extinguished. Cnut was succeeded by his brother Olaf Hunger (r. 1086–1095). Under Olaf, Denmark suffered several consecutive years of crop failures, widespread famine and starvation, earning him his unenviable nickname. To the Danes, it was all too obvious that the disaster was an expression of God's anger over the sacrilegious killing of Cnut on consecrated ground. When Olaf died in August 1095, it was in very strange circumstances. According to the chronicler Saxo Grammaticus, Olaf 'willingly gave himself to rid the land of its bad luck and begged that all of the guilt [of Olaf's killing] would fall upon his head alone. So he offered his life for his country-men.' This mysterious explanation of Olaf's death has clear echoes of the fate of the semi-legendary Swedish king Domalde, who was sacrificed to appease the gods after two years of failed harvests (see ch. 1). Could it be that Olaf was sacrificed as a scapegoat for the guilt of the Danes? Or might Olaf have tried to atone for their sins by committing suicide (a very un-Christian act in itself)? Saxo's statement certainly implies that Olaf met his death voluntarily and that he was neither murdered nor died of natural causes. It only adds to the mystery that Olaf's burial place is unknown. It has been suggested that his body was cut up and distributed throughout Denmark in the belief that in some way this would help restore the fertility of the land. The sequel to Olaf's death was, however, unambiguously Christian. His successor Erik the Evergood lobbied the papacy to have their brother Cnut recognised as a martyr and he was canonised in 1102. Erik had already begun to build a cathedral, in the pan-European Romanesque style, to house Cnut's remains, close to the site of his martyrdom. Cnut's skeleton, and that of his brother Benedict, can still be seen in the cathedral's crypt: the bones show only too clearly evidence of the violent death of Denmark's last Viking king.

The kingdom of the Swedes

Sweden was the last of the Scandinavian kingdoms to emerge as a unified state and, compared to Norway and Denmark, relatively little is known about its early development. Swedes did not participate in any great numbers in the settlement of Iceland, so their history was of peripheral interest to medieval Icelandic historians and saga writers who had so much to say about the kings of Norway. Nor do the Swedes feature much in contemporary annals from Western Europe because their main field of activity was in the east.

The earliest Swedish king we know much about was Erik the Victorious (r. *c.* 970–95). Erik's own ancestry is difficult to trace because the sources are confused and contradictory. There is no evidence that either he or his immediate successors claimed to be members of the Yngling dynasty and the semi-legendary saga traditions hold him to be a descendent of Sigurd Ring, the victor of Brávalla, who founded a new dynasty at Uppsala around the middle of the eighth century. Erik earned fame for his victory over his nephew Styrbjorn Starki and his Danish allies at the Battle of Fyrisvellir, a marshy plain near Uppsala, some time in the 980s. No truly reliable account of the battle exists but it is described in several Icelandic sagas and in the Danish history of Saxo Grammaticus. In addition, two late tenth-century runestones in Skåne (now in Sweden but then in Denmark) commemorating men 'who did not flee at Uppsala' probably refer to this battle, as may a contemporary runestone on the island of Öland, commemorating a Danish chief who was buried there, perhaps after dying on his way home from wounds suffered in the battle. Even more convincing is a runestone at Högby in Östergötland that commemorates Asmund, 'who fell at Fœri' (i.e. Fyris), perhaps on Erik's side.

The exact boundaries of Erik's kingdom are still hazy. In the Viking Age, Sweden 'proper' consisted roughly of the modern Swedish province of Svealand, with its heartland around Uppsala and Lake Mälaren, and the far southern part of Norrland (roughly the modern provinces of Gästrikland and Hälsingland). The area to the north, extending up beyond the Arctic Circle was populated mainly by Sami reindeer hunters and only became incorporated into Sweden later in the Middle Ages. The Swedes traded with the Sami and also raided them to collect tribute in furs. Between Sweden and the Danish provinces of Skåne and Blekinge was Götaland, the homeland of the Götar (the Geats of 'Beowulf'). Despite inhabiting a large area and being an apparently numerous people, virtually nothing is known about the Götar in the Viking Age. There is no archaeological evidence of political centralisation to compare with the royal centres at Jelling or Uppsala, so they were probably divided into many local chiefdoms or petty kingdoms. The Götar do not feature prominently in saga traditions, are not mentioned in contemporary literary sources as taking part in any Viking raids, and even those who actually visited the Baltic, such as Rimbert (the biographer of St Ansgar) and the merchant Wulfstan, had almost nothing to say about them. This may simply be a result of confusion over identities – the Götar were not culturally or linguistically distinct from the Swedes – or, more likely, that they were under the political domination of the Swedes. Legendary traditions, like those preserved in 'Beowulf', certainly refer to wars between the Swedes and the Götar; and some kings of the Götar, such as Alrik, who, according to the Sparlösa runestone, ruled in Västergötland *c*. 800, were members of Swedish royal dynasties. Also in a loose association with Sweden was the large Baltic island of Gotland, whose inhabitants were independent but paid tribute to the Swedish kings in return for rights of free travel and free trade. Gotland would not be fully incorporated into Sweden until the thirteenth century, by which time the Viking Age was over.

Birka

Viking Age Sweden benefited from its proximity to the important trade routes across the Baltic to Russia and beyond to the Islamic world and the Byzantine Empire. While Uppsala was the kingdom's main political and religious centre, its main trading centre was Birka on the island of Björkö near the mouth of Lake Mälaren about 20 miles west of Stockholm. Birka developed around 800, replacing the earlier Vendel period trading place at Helgö, about 5 miles to the south-east. Birka covered around 17 acres (7 hectares) and probably had a permanent population of between 700 and 1,000 people. In the tenth century,

Birka was protected by a rampart and a small hillfort, and a row of wooden stakes restricted access to the main harbour. Further barriers of wooden stakes and rocks were used to obstruct access channels to prevent pirate fleets making quick attacks on the town. Such defences were necessary as the many islands and inlets along the approaches to Birka were notorious hiding places for pirates. Among their victims was the missionary St Ansgar, who was robbed of all his belongings while sailing to Birka in 829.

The organically-rich occupation deposits at Birka, known as *Svarta Jorden* ('Black Earth'), are up to 6 feet thick and have produced abundant information about the buildings and daily life of the town. It was divided into plots of land, delineated by passageways flanked by ditches. Each plot contained one or two houses and several outbuildings used as workshops and stores. The buildings were timber-framed with walls of wattle-and-daub and roofs of thatch, wood and, occasionally, turf. Many of the inhabitants were merchants but there were also craftsmen in metals, jewellery, bone and antler, and furs, and even some warriors, perhaps a small permanent garrison to protect the town and keep order. Considerable quantities of Arab coins confirm that Birka's most important trade links were with the east, especially after *c.* 900, but there was also Rhineland pottery and glass and scraps of Frisian woollen cloth. Birka is surrounded by cemeteries containing over 3,000 graves, of which about 1,100 have been excavated. The graves indicate that Birka had a mixed population of Scandinavians and foreigners. Native graves, the majority, were cremations under small mounds or in stone settings shaped like ships or triangles. The rich grave goods found in these burials are unparalleled for quality and include large quantities of imported glass, weapons, jewellery and pottery. The foreign graves were inhumations in coffins or stone chambers without grave goods. These were on the outer edges of the cemeteries and are thought to have belonged to Christian and Muslim merchants and craftsmen and their families. Adam of Bremen said that Danish, Norwegian, Wendish and 'Scythian' (probably Rus) ships sailed to Birka annually for commerce. Some of the inhumations might also belong to native converts to Christianity, of whom there were a few at Birka.

The missionary St Ansgar met Swedish kings at Birka when he visited in 829–30 and 851–2, but there is no evidence of a royal residence on the island. Birka was probably administered from a royal estate at Hovgården on the neighbouring island of Adelsö, a couple of miles away, rather as Hedeby was administered from the royal estate at Flüsing. One of the five large burial mounds at Hovgården, known collectively as the Kungshögar ('the kings' barrows'), was excavated a century ago and was found to contain the remains of a high status male who had been cremated in a boat along with horses, cattle and dogs some time around 900. Birka seems to have been abandoned quite abruptly during the reign of Erik the Victorious. A complete absence of Anglo-Saxon coins suggests that this must have happened before Æthelred II began paying enormous sums in Danegeld to the Vikings in the 990s: thousands of his coins have been found in Scandinavia and some of them, at least, would have found their way to Birka had it still been occupied. There is no evidence that Birka met a violent end so it is likely that trade simply shifted to the new town, founded by Erik c. 980, of Sigtuna on the northern shore of Lake Mälaren about 15 miles south of Uppsala.

Union of the Swedes and Götar

Sweden comes more fully into the light of recorded history during the reign of Erik's son Olof Skötkonung ('treasure king') (r. 995–1022). Olof's reign is enormously significant both because he was Sweden's first Christian king and because he was the first king who is known to have ruled both the Swedes and the Götar, so laying the foundations of the medieval Swedish kingdom. However, those foundations were very shaky and it was well into the twelfth century before Sweden was a fully Christianised, unified kingdom. The paucity of sources for Viking Age Sweden makes it impossible to know how Olof actually came to rule over both the Swedes and the Götar. Presumably dynastic connections between the two peoples already existed and there may have been earlier kings who ruled over both areas: there is certainly no reason to assume that Olof's achievement was unprecedented or that he came to rule the Götar by conquest rather than by election at the regional things held annually in Västergötland and Östergötland. However, Olof's union of the two people was also not final because many of his successors did not exercise authority over the Götar. Sometimes, the Götar elected different kings to the Swedes, on other occasions they did without a king altogether and were ruled by their own chiefs and lawspeakers. The achievement of stable dynastic rule was made more difficult in Sweden because, unlike in Denmark and Norway, it was not necessary to have royal blood to be chosen as a king. The Viking Age was a distant memory when the Swedes and Götar were at last permanently united in 1173 by Knut Eriksson (r. 1167–96).

The fragility of the Swedish kingdom contributed to the slow acceptance of Christianity. In Denmark and Norway forceful action by kings overcame pagan opposition to Christianity, but Swedish kings had to act with greater circumspection. Pagan Swedish kings did not actively oppose missionary activity. The kings who Ansgar met at Birka gave him permission to preach after consulting the local thing, but they showed no interest in converting themselves and, without royal backing, he failed to found lasting Christian communities. The missionary effort was renewed by Unni, like Ansgar an archbishop of Hamburg-Bremen, but he died at Birka in 936 with little to show for his efforts. The conversion of the Danes under Harald Bluetooth gave missionary efforts in Sweden a new impetus. During Erik's reign a Danish missionary, Bishop Odinkar Hvite the Elder, began the conversion of the Götar from his base at Skara in Västergötland. Adam of Bremen believed that Odinkar enjoyed so much success because, as a Dane, 'he could easily convince the barbarians of everything about our religion'. Erik was himself baptised when he was in Denmark in the 980s or early 990s, but Adam says that he renounced Christianity as soon as he returned to Sweden. The traditional story of Olof Skötkonung's conversion is that he was baptised by St Sigfrid, an English missionary from Glastonbury, in 1008 at Husaby, not far from Skara. This date is probably too late: Olof used Christian imagery on the coins issued at the new town of Sigtuna right from the beginning of his reign, so he may really have been baptised before he became king. It is possible that the young Olof was baptised at the same time as his father, but was

more receptive to the new religion. 'God's Sigtuna', as Olof called the
town on his coins, seems to have had a largely Christian population
right from its foundation, because few pagan burials have been discovered in its extensive cemeteries. It was probably Olof's intention
that Sigtuna would be a Christian counter-balance to the nearby pagan
cult centre at Uppsala and he founded several churches there. Olof
began to give Sweden a formal ecclesiastical organisation, founding
a bishopric at Skara in 1014, but the strength of pagan sentiment was
such that he never risked trying to convert the Swedes by force. Olof's
softly-softly approach to promoting Christianity was still too much for
devout pagans and towards the end of his reign he was forced to share
power with his son Jacob, who succeeded him after his death in 1022.
The pagans detested Jacob's biblical name and they forced him to adopt
the proper Swedish name Önund when he became king.

Changing his name was about the limit of Önund's compromise
with the pagans. He and his immediate successors continued to
co-operate with the church, encourage missionary activity, and
extend the country's diocesan structure. By around 1080, paganism
was dying out among the Götar, and missionaries were travelling
the countryside destroying the last temples and pagan idols. The
Swedes, however, stubbornly resisted conversion. Missionary bishops
believed that paganism would never collapse unless the temple at
Uppsala was destroyed, but Swedish kings refused to sanction the use
of force. Önund did not retaliate when an over-enthusiastic English
missionary called Wilfrid was hacked to pieces by a pagan mob after he
provocatively destroyed an idol of Thor at Uppsala in the 1030s. Thirty
years later, king Stenkil (r. 1060–66) refused to allow Adalvard, the
newly appointed bishop of Sigtuna, to destroy the temple at Uppsala,
fearing that this would provoke a pagan uprising. He was right to be
wary. Stenkil's son Inge the Elder, who became king around 1080, was
a more militant Christian, but when he tried to outlaw paganism at the
thing at Uppsala, he was pelted with stones and had to flee into exile
in Västergötland. In Inge's place, the Swedes chose his brother-in-law
Blót-Sven ('sacrifice-Sven'), who agreed to reinstate paganism and
perform the traditional sacrifices. Immediately, a horse was brought
and cut into pieces for eating and a sacred tree was smeared with its

blood. Sven reigned only for about three years. In exile, Inge raised a small mounted force and invaded Svealand, taking Sven by surprise in the early hours of the morning in his hall. After surrounding the place, Inge's men set the hall on fire. The few who managed to get out of the burning building were butchered by Inge's men. Sven's death broke pagan resistance to Christianity. Restored to the throne, Inge resumed his anti-pagan crusade and soon afterwards the cult centre at Uppsala was destroyed and replaced with a church. By the time Inge died in 1105, Sweden was mainly Christian. The death of the old gods, so long prophesied, had finally come to pass.

CHAPTER 11

PALERMO, JERUSALEM AND TALLINN

FROM VIKING TO CRUSADER

By the twelfth century, the Scandinavian kingdoms were beginning to look much like the rest of the Catholic west. Castles and Romanesque churches and cathedrals impacted on the landscape like no Viking Age building had ever done. European fashions in the decorative arts and clothing predominated, and Latin became the language of high culture. The military aristocracy trained as knights and began to fight on horseback. Most of the population was now Christian by conviction rather than compulsion and it shared in the excitement and religious fervour of the crusading movement. As relatively new recruits to western Christendom, who had leaned heavily on Christian concepts of kingship to build their authority, Scandinavian kings were among the first to see that crusading was good politics as well as good religion. Yet, although the cause was new, it would often have been hard to tell the difference between a Scandinavian crusade and an old fashioned Viking raid.

Crusading was one of the most important expressions of the Catholic west's growing self-confidence. After centuries on the defensive, the Catholic west was expanding. Scandinavia, Poland and Hungary had been brought into the Catholic fold and in Spain the Reconquista was in full swing, pushing the Muslim Moors back.

Internally, the growth of government was bringing greater political stability, population and trade was growing, and a cultural revival was underway. For the first time in centuries, western Europeans were not preoccupied with mere survival. While the west was on the rise, the Byzantine Empire, for centuries the greatest Christian power, was in steep decline after suffering catastrophic defeats at the hands of the Seljuq Turks. In 1095, the Byzantine emperor Alexius I made a plea to Pope Urban II for military support against the Seljuqs. What Alexius had in mind was that the pope would send him some mercenary knights who would sign up and fight as part of the Byzantine army. What Urban actually called for was a holy war to free Jerusalem from the infidel Muslims who had occupied it for over 450 years and restore it to Christian rule. As an inducement, Urban declared that anyone who went on the expedition would enjoy the remission of all penances due for their sins, which was popularly, if incorrectly, understood to mean a guarantee of immediate entry to Heaven if they died. The crusade was, in effect, to be a great pilgrimage in arms.

Tens of thousands responded to Urban's call, from great nobles like Duke Robert of Normandy down to humble peasants with no military experience at all. The appeal for the military aristocracy was particularly strong. For years the church had railed at them for their violent way of life and now there was a way for them to follow their profession and do God's work at the same time. Most participants in the First Crusade came from France and the Holy Roman Empire, but there were certainly some Scandinavians – a Danish noble called Svein came with his French wife Florina and a large retinue of warriors. Though countless thousands of crusaders died of hunger, thirst, disease, exhaustion and battle along the way – Svein and his wife among them – the expedition was an astonishing success and in 1099 Jerusalem was taken after a short siege. However, the crusader Kingdom of Jerusalem that was founded in the aftermath of victory needed constant support if it was to survive. Over the next 200 years, eight major crusades and dozens of minor ones were launched, though, ultimately, they failed to prevent the Muslims reoccupying the Holy Land. The First Crusade was so successful that the concept of crusading was soon extended to expeditions against those perceived to be God's enemies, whoever they were and wherever they were found. Crusading vows could be fulfilled by fighting Moors in Spain, pagan Slavs and Balts in the Baltic, schismatic Orthodox Christians in Russia and Byzantium, and Cathar heretics in the south of France. Although there had been no kings on the First Crusade, they soon realised that crusading was a potent way to enhance their prestige as defenders of the Christian people.

Only three years after the fall of Jerusalem, Denmark's king Erik Ejegod (Erik the Evergood) became the first king of any Catholic country to set out for the Holy Land. Leaving Denmark with his queen Boedil and a large retinue, Erik travelled the old Varangian route to Constantinople through Russia. This was not a crusade but a pilgrimage, performed by Erik as penance for killing four of his retainers in a drunken rage. From Constantinople, Erik sailed on ships provided by the Emperor Alexius to Paphos in Cyprus, where he and Boedil fell ill. Erik died there in July 1103: Boedil carried on to Jerusalem, where she also died later in the same year.

Four years after Erik's death, the seventeen-year-old Norwegian king Sigurd I (r. 1103–30) became the first king to lead a crusade. He was probably inspired to do this by the expedition of Skofte Ögmundsson, a Norwegian aristocrat who set out for the Holy Land with a fleet of five longships in 1102, the same year that King Erik set out on his ill-fated journey. Skofte got only as far as Rome, where he died, but his men carried on to Jerusalem and Constantinople and by 1104 they were back at home, telling exciting stories about their travels. Sigurd was the second son of Magnus Barefoot and since his father's death in 1103, he had ruled Norway jointly with his elder brother Eystein, so the decision to go on crusade was not one for him alone. Eystein agreed that Sigurd should go and he quite clearly regarded the crusade as a worthy enterprise that would benefit the kingdom as a whole because he shared the costs. As part of the preparations for the crusade the brothers agreed to a general reform of government, abolishing unjust laws and oppressive taxes so that they would secure divine favour for the expedition. There was plenty of popular enthusiasm for the crusade and no one had to be coerced into joining.

Sigurd decided to make the entire journey to the Holy Land by sea, finally setting sail in autumn 1107 with a fleet of sixty longships. Depending on the size of the ships, Sigurd's army may have been anything between 3,000- and 5,000-strong. Given the likely problems of supplying any army on a long expedition, the lower limit seems more credible than the higher. Because of the lateness of the season, Sigurd sailed only as far as England, where he spent the winter with King Henry I. The fleet set out again in the spring but by autumn it had got no further than the pilgrimage centre of Santiago de Compostela in the Spanish Christian kingdom of Galicia, where the Norwegians planned to spend the winter. The local lord had promised to provide markets where the Norwegians could buy provisions but, because of local food shortages, he held none after Christmas. Feeling that they had outstayed their welcome, the Norwegians stormed a local castle, looted its food stores and, despite the season, set sail and headed south along the coasts of Muslim Spain. From here on the crusade turned into a Christianised Viking expedition, no doubt made all the more enjoyable by the conviction that God surely approved of every injury they inflicted on the infidel. Sigurd first encountered a Moorish pirate fleet cruising off the coast of Portugal and captured eight of its galleys. Next Sigurd captured the Moorish castle at Colares, massacring its garrison after they refused to convert to Christianity, and then joined Count Henry of Portugal in an attack on nearby Lisbon. The allies took the city, and a great amount of plunder, but not the citadel, so Lisbon was soon back in Moorish hands: the Moors were finally driven out by English, Frisian and Flemish crusaders in 1147. Crossing the Tagus river estuary, the Norwegians sacked another Moorish town, Alcácer do Sol, and massacred so much of its population that it was abandoned for years. Sigurd continued plundering his way along the Spanish coast and, after another battle with a Moorish fleet, sailed through the Straits of Gibraltar and into the Mediterranean. Formentera, Ibiza and Minorca, all at this time occupied by the Moors, were then each plundered in turn. In late spring 1109, Sigurd arrived at Palermo in Sicily, where he was welcomed by the twelve-year-old Norman count Roger II (r. 1105–54).

Norman Italy

Count Roger was the grandson of a minor Norman baron called Tancred de Hauteville (d. 1041). Nothing certain is known of Tancred's ancestry but, according to the chronicler Geoffrey of Malaterra (d. 1099), he was descended from one of Rollo's Viking warriors called Hiallt, who gave his name to the village of Hauteville. Geoffrey had access to the Norman court in Sicily so he was probably recording Hauteville family traditions, but Hiallt is most likely an invention: Hauteville almost certainly means simply 'high village'. However, as members of the Norman military aristocracy, it would be surprising if the Hautevilles did not have Viking ancestors. Tancred married twice and fathered at least twelve sons, eight of whom, including Roger's father Roger I, left Normandy and emigrated to southern Italy to seek their fortunes. The situation in Normandy in the early eleventh century was not dissimilar to that in early Viking Age Scandinavia. The Norman dukes were consolidating their authority and competition for land and power within the Norman aristocracy was intense and often violent. Members of the lesser nobility, like the Hautevilles, feared for their future status. They also found their resources becoming too slender to provide an adequate inheritance for all their sons. Normandy, therefore, had relatively large numbers of young men with little or no land and poor prospects of ever getting any. As part of their noble upbringing they had all been trained as knights, so many left to serve as mercenaries for foreign rulers.

The most popular destination for Norman emigrants was southern Italy, which in the early eleventh century was being fought over by the Lombards, the Byzantine Empire and the Arabs. The first Normans to serve here was a band of forty who fought for the Lombard Duchy of Benevento against the Byzantines in 1017. At first, the Normans fought simply for pay, but in 1030 Sergius, the duke of Naples, made the Norman leader Rannulf count of Aversa. Now that they were established as a permanent presence in Italy, more and more Normans came out to join family members who were already living there, a phenomenon known as chain migration. In 1047, Robert Guiscard (d. 1085), one of the Hauteville brothers, arrived in Italy. After he established himself in Calabria, he was joined by his younger brothers Roger (d. 1101) and Richard (d. 1078). Together they had conquered the Lombard duchies by 1072, driven the Byzantines out of Italy altogether, and captured Messina and Palermo from the Arabs in Sicily. After the fall of Palermo, Robert invested Roger as count of Sicily and left him to complete the conquest of the island by himself, which he did by 1091, while he returned to Italy. Roger was succeed by his eight-year-old son Simon and, after his early death in 1105, by his youngest son Roger, then aged about ten. Because of Roger's age, the government was run by a regency under his mother, so he would have had plenty of time to keep Sigurd entertained. In his saga account of Sigurd's crusade, Snorri Sturluson says that the king bestowed on Roger the title of king. This may be a fiction but it was Roger's destiny as an adult to unite all the Norman principalities in Italy under his rule and in 1130 to be crowned king of Sicily with papal blessing. The culture of Roger's court at Palermo, an eclectic mix of Latin-Italian, Norman, Arab and Byzantine elements, blended to perfection in the dazzling palace chapel, was a far cry from the rough ship camps of Rollo's Vikings. This cultural eclecticism is evidence of one characteristic the Normans did share with the Vikings: they were good mixers. In the longer term, the Normans had little influence on the native Italian population. Both were Catholic Christians so there were no barriers to intermarriage and the Normans were gradually assimilated by the Italian majority. Norman rule continued in Italy until 1190–4, when the Kingdom of Sicily was conquered by the German emperor Henry VI.

To Jerusalem

Sigurd greatly enjoyed his time at Roger's court and it was not until summer 1110 that he left to complete his journey. Sailing from Sicily through the Greek archipelago, Sigurd finally landed in the Holy Land at Acre in late summer or early autumn. He had lost only one ship, wrecked on the coast of Brittany, during the whole voyage from Norway. From Acre he and his retainers rode in procession to Jerusalem, where they were greeted warmly by King Baldwin. Sigurd visited the usual pilgrimage sites and rode with King Baldwin to the River Jordan. Back at Jerusalem, Baldwin gave Sigurd many holy relics, including a precious splinter of the True Cross. Baldwin was very reluctant for the Norwegians to leave. At the end of the First Crusade, most of the surviving crusaders, having fulfilled their vows, went home, leaving all too few behind to defend what they had conquered. As a result the crusader kingdom was always chronically short of manpower. Baldwin begged Sigurd to remain: 'for a very little time to aid in extending and glorifying the Christian name. Then, having accomplished something for Christ, they could return to their own country giving generous thanks to God.' (Fulcher of Chartres). Muslim fleets were harassing Christian shipping and Baldwin wanted to eliminate the Muslim-held port of Sidon (now in Lebanon) which they used as a base. In return for supplies, Sigurd agreed to use his fleet to blockade Sidon from the sea, while Baldwin's forces besieged it from the land. The siege lasted only seven weeks. Seeing that there was no hope of relief, the garrison negotiated the surrender of the town to Baldwin on 5 December 1110 in return for safe conduct. Having now 'accomplished something for Christ', Sigurd sailed off to Constantinople via Cyprus and Greece.

At Constantinople, Sigurd and his men were lavishly entertained by the Emperor Alexius, but he does not seem to have stayed long before setting out on the journey home overland through Bulgaria, Hungary, the Holy Roman Empire and Denmark, where King Niels gave him a ship to sail to Norway: he had been away more than three years. Before leaving Constantinople, Sigurd made a gift of his ships to the emperor and gave his men leave to sign on with the Varangian Guard if they wished. The Norwegians had had ample opportunities to talk to serving Varangians and learn about their privileged lives and it seems that most of them stayed behind in Constantinople, leaving their king to travel on with only a small retinue. Sigurd's crusade made a modest but worthwhile contribution to securing the Christian position in the east and, just as important from his point of view, it considerably enhanced the status of the Norwegian crown, both at home and abroad. On his return to Norway, Sigurd was greeted rapturously as a national hero and he became known to posterity as 'Jorsalfar', the Jerusalem-farer. Such was the glamour of his expedition that his reign was looked back on as a golden age when God smiled on Norway. 'Sigurd's time was a good one,' wrote one Norwegian chronicler:

> 'both in terms of harvests and many other beneficial things, with the one exception that he could hardly control his temper when he suffered attacks as he grew older. But he was nevertheless regarded as the most splendid and remarkable of all kings, and in particular because of his journey. He was also a very fine-looking man and very tall, as his father and forefathers had been. He loved his people, and they him.' *(Agrip.)*

The Wendish Crusade

In 1144, the crusaders lost the key city of Edessa in Syria to the Turks. Pope Eugenius III's response to this setback was to call the Second Crusade, the first major crusading expedition to the Holy Land since Jerusalem was captured in 1099. The main expedition, led by kings Louis VII of France and Conrad III of Germany, was directed at the Turks (and was a disastrous failure), but Eugenius widened the concept of the crusade by offering the same spiritual incentives to knights from northern Germany who wanted to launch a campaign against the pagan Wends of the southern Baltic region. In this way the crusading movement was co-opted to support German territorial expansion in Eastern Europe. The calling of a crusade against the Wends found an immediate response from the Danes, who for well over a century had suffered from devastating Viking-style raids by Wendish pirates. Coastal areas had been depopulated, churches built to double as refuges for the local population, and fjords blocked with stake barriers to keep pirate ships out: Wendish slave markets were said to be full of Danish captives for sale. Occasional Danish retaliatory attacks had made little impact and many Danish islands now paid tribute to the Wends in return for peace.

From the start the Wendish Crusade suffered from divided leadership and while the German contingent enjoyed modest success, the Danes were defeated. It was not until 1159 that the Danes finally enjoyed a major victory, when the young Valdemar the Great (r. 1157–82) flexed his military muscles and led a successful Viking-style raid on the Wendish island of Rügen. Valdemar's success convinced the powerful Saxon duke Henry the Lion that he would make a useful ally in combined operations against the Wends, with the Saxons attacking them by land and the Danes attacking from the sea. After joint victories in 1160 and 1164, the alliance fell apart as the two rulers quarrelled over the spoils and thereafter regarded each other as rivals. But by this time Valdemar no longer needed Henry's support. Valdemar's tactics against the Wends were an almost seamless continuation of those used by the Vikings. Raiding parties made surprise landings from fleets of longships, sweeping quickly inland to plunder and return to their ships before the Wends could organise resistance. One departure from Viking traditions was that each longship carried four horses so that armoured knights could join the raids. Although they could not take the strongly fortified Wendish towns, the Danes brought them to their knees through economic warfare, burning crops and villages, taking livestock and captives, and by preying on Wendish merchant shipping. These tactics had the great advantage of being very profitable. Wendish retaliation was blunted by constructing castles at strategic locations on the Danish coast and by mounting naval patrols to look out for approaching pirate fleets. In most of his campaigns, Valdemar was accompanied by Absalon, the warlike bishop of Roskilde, who is best known today as the founder of Copenhagen. Absalon took great pleasure in destroying the idols of the Wendish gods to demonstrate their powerlessness, but religion was a secondary concern for Valdemar: his main aims were to seize plunder and territory, and end Wendish pirate raids on Denmark.

Decisive success came in 1168, when Valdemar plundered and burned the cliff-top sanctuary of the Wendish high-god Svantovit at Arkona on Rügen. The shocked Rugians surrendered, accepted Danish rule and submitted to baptism. Now joined by the Rugian fleet, the Danes destroyed the Liutizian pirate stronghold of Dziwnów on the island of Wolin near the mouth of the Oder in 1170, so removing another threat to their security. After the Danes defeated a Wendish pirate fleet in a sea battle off the island of Falster two years later, Wendish pirates never ventured into Danish waters again. By 1185 the Danish tactic of devastating Viking-style raids had forced the submission of the Liutizians and the Pomeranians to give them control of the entire Baltic Sea coast from Rügen east to the mouth of the River Vistula. Conquest was not followed by military occupation or settlement, however. The Wends simply became tributaries of the Danes, who counted on the threat of punitive raids to keep their vassals loyal.

The Livonian Crusades

Crusading in the Baltic region received a new impetus in 1193, when pope Celestine III called for a crusade against the Livonians, a group of tribes who lived in what is now Latvia and Estonia. The papacy's motive in this crusade was not simply the conversion of pagans, it was also to prevent the area coming under the influence of what it saw as the heretical Orthodox church. The Livonian Crusade was dominated from the outset by German crusading orders such as the Livonian Knights, the Sword Brothers and the Teutonic Knights, but the Danish king Valdemar II (r. 1202–41) saw an opportunity for territorial expansion and in 1218 he won full papal blessing for an invasion of Estonia. Valdemar landed at the Estonian trading place of Lyndanisse (modern Tallinn) in June the next year with a fleet of 500 longships. Longships were becoming decidedly old-fashioned by this time and this was probably the last occasion that they were used on such a large scale in the Baltic. Apart from the adoption of the stern-post rudder in place of the less-effective side rudder, longships had changed little since the Viking Age and they had long exhausted their development potential. German crusaders were now sailing the Baltic in cogs, a type of ship that probably originated in Frisia in the Viking Age. Unlike longships, cogs had no oars and relied entirely on a single square sail. Though they could not compete with longships for speed and manoeuvrability, cogs were sturdy and seaworthy, with broad, deep hulls and high sides, and were cheaper and easier to build. Cogs were first built to carry bulky cargoes – even the smallest cogs could carry twice the 20-ton cargo of a Viking *knarr* – but they proved surprisingly well-suited to war. Especially when fitted with wooden fighting platforms at the bows and stern, cogs towered over longships, giving their crews a clear advantage in a sea battle. Scandinavian technological conservatism helped the German-dominated Hanseatic League of mercantile cities – early adopters of the cog – to supplant the Scandinavians as the main trading and naval power in the Baltic in the course of the thirteenth and fourteenth centuries. Scandinavians continued to build longships for the coastal defence levy fleets until the early fifteenth century, but their ineffectiveness in battle against cogs had been demonstrated many times by then.

It is thought that Valdemar set up camp on the Toompea, a steep-sided flat-topped hill rising around 100 feet (30.5 m) above the harbour at Tallinn, giving excellent views over the sea and low lying coast-lands. As well as being a good defensive position, the hill had religious significance to the Estonians, who believed that it was the burial mound of their mythological hero Kalev. Apparently overawed by the strength of Valdemar's fleet, the Estonian chiefs agreed to submit and a few even allowed themselves to be baptised. However, this was all a ruse to lull the Danes into a false sense of security and the Estonians achieved complete surprise when they attacked the Danish camp a few days later. The battle of Lyndanisse achieved legendary stature in Danish historical traditions as the place where the country's national flag, the Dannebrog, fell from Heaven as a sign to encourage the embattled Danes to fight on and overcome the pagans. Some historians have tried to rationalise this story, explaining it away as the sighting of an unusual weather phenomenon, but it is more likely to be pure fiction. The legend cannot be traced back any earlier than the sixteenth century, and the earliest known the use of the Dannebrog dates only to 1397, nearly 200 years after the battle. After his victory, Valdemar built a castle on the Toompea which, despite being incomplete, held out against an Estonian siege in 1223. It is from Valdemar's castle that Tallinn's name is derived, from Taani-linn, meaning the 'Danes' castle': rebuilt many times, it now houses the Estonian parliament. After Valdemar's final victory over the Estonians in 1224, a stone cathedral was built near the castle and the Toompea became the main centre of Danish secular and ecclesiastical government in Estonia. Tallinn has the best harbour on the Estonian coast and it soon attracted German merchants, who settled on the lower ground between the Toompea and the harbour, creating a commercial Lower Town. In 1285 the city, known to the Germans as Reval, joined the Hanseatic League and Germans continued to dominate the city's economy until the twentieth century. Outside Tallinn, most of the land was parcelled out not to Danes but to Saxon lords, who paid a land tax to the Danish crown.

The failure to follow up conquest with occupation and settlement quickly doomed Denmark's Baltic empire. Denmark's increasingly obsolescent fleet could not dominate the Baltic sea lanes, and neither could it challenge the power of the Germans on land. The lands won during the Wendish crusades were conquered by German princes even before Valdemar's death and in 1346 Denmark sold Estonia to the Teutonic Knights after a native uprising.

The Swedish Crusades

Swedish involvement with the crusades was, if anything, an even more naked land-grab than was Denmark's. Like the Danes, the Swedes had a pirate problem: in their case the pirates were Estonians from the island of Saaremaa (Ösel in Swedish), Finns from Karelia (eastern Finland), and Curonians from modern Latvia, all of them pagan peoples. The Swedes, in turn, raided their persecutors, plundering and gathering tribute Viking-style, much as they had been doing for centuries. The Swedes were also competing for influence in the region with Novgorod, which was the most important centre for the lucrative fur trade. Swedes were as welcome as any other merchants to visit Novgorod to trade, but the city was powerful enough to prevent them raiding in Russia and gathering furs as tribute as they had done in the Viking Age. The Swedes now sought to profit from Novgorod's fur trade by controlling the Gulf of Finland, which gave the city its 'window on the west', and by plundering Novgorodian ships, as happened in 1142 when a Swedish fleet captured three ships from Novgorod and killed 150 merchants. To secure its access to the Gulf, Novgorod began the conquest and conversion to Orthodox Christianity of the Karelian Finns, and retaliated against Swedish raids on its territory by raiding the shores of Lake Mälaren. After one raid they carried the church doors of the royal town of Sigtuna back to Novgorod. The Swedes countered Novgorod's influence in Karelia with their own wars of conquest and conversion in Finland, which they justified by using the terminology of crusading. Because of its desire to limit the influence of the Orthodox church, the Catholic church supported the Swedish expeditions, but they were never given papal sanction like the crusades to the Holy Land or the Wendish and Livonian Crusades, and the Swedish crusaders were never offered the same spiritual rewards.

Later tradition has it that the first Swedish crusade in Finland was led by King Erik IX (r. 1155–60), some time around 1157. Erik is said to have brought the whole of the south-west of Finland under Swedish rule and to have converted the conquered Finns to Christianity. When Erik returned home he left behind a missionary bishop Henry of Uppsala who was later martyred by the Finns. Erik may well have campaigned in Finland, but the story of the crusade was probably invented as part of the cult that developed around his memory after he was murdered by rebel nobles as he left church after attending Mass on Ascension Day (18 May) 1160. Sweden was by that time the only Scandinavian kingdom without a royal saint, so it suited his successors to encourage his veneration as a martyr. The Swedish conquest of Finland was probably begun a long time before Erik's reign, as place-name evidence suggests that Swedes had colonised the south-west coast around Turku (Swedish Åbo) as early as the mid-eleventh century, and was a slow process marked by frequent campaigns and many reverses. Even in the late twelfth century Sweden's hold on south-west Finland was not secure. In a letter to a Swedish archbishop, Pope Alexander III (r. 1159–81) complained that: 'the Finns always promise to obey the Christian faith whenever they are threatened by a hostile army... but when the army retires they deny the faith, despise the preachers and grievously persecute them.'

Because of their frequent backsliding, Pope Gregory IX called for a formal crusade against the Finns, but the Swedes ignored it and instead attacked Novgorod in 1240 only to be defeated by Alexander Nevsky at the Battle of the Neva. The Swedish conquest of Finland was finally secured by the so-called Second and Third Swedish Crusades. The Second Swedish Crusade (c. 1248–50), led by the mighty aristocrat Birger Jarl, brought the Tavastia region of central Finland under firm Swedish control, while the Third Swedish Crusade (1292–3), aimed unashamedly at Christian Novgorod, conquered Karelia, ended the activities of Orthodox missionaries there, and established a castle at Vyborg (now in Russia). The Swedes hoped this would be a base from which to extend their conquests to the mouth of the Neva and cut Novgorod off from the Gulf of Finland. Years of raid and counter-raid followed until the Treaty of Noteborg in 1323 established a frontier between Swedish Finland and Novgorod, which left Novgorod in control of the Neva. The Swedes did eventually achieve their ambition of winning control of the Neva and cutting Russia off from the Gulf of Finland in 1595, only to lose it in 1702 to Peter the Great, the founder of St Petersburg. Unlike the ephemeral Danish conquests in the Baltic, the Swedish conquest of Finland had long-lasting consequences. This was in large part because here conquest was followed by settlement. In the wake of the crusaders, large numbers of Swedish peasant farmers, fleeing the imposition of serfdom at home, settled in southern Finland. Even though Russia ended Swedish rule in 1809, Finland still has a Swedish-speaking minority and recognises Swedish as one of its official languages.

CHAPTER 12

LARGS, REYKHOLT AND HVALSEY

THE VIKING TWILIGHT

If the growth of state power had brought the Viking Age to a close in Scandinavia by 1100, it enjoyed a lingering twilight in areas where royal authority was weak or non-existent. In Orkney and the Hebrides, Norse and Norse-Gaelic chieftains still supplemented the income from their estates by leading Viking raids, while in Iceland and Greenland an essentially Viking Age society of local chieftains and free tenant farmers continued to make their own laws and settle disputes at the representative things. However, by 1200 these societies were an anomaly in a Europe of increasingly centralised kingdoms and were living on borrowed time.

Magnus Barefoot's legacy

Magnus Barefoot's reign marked the peak of Norwegian power in the Northern Isles and the Hebrides. Magnus's campaigns more than paid for themselves with a great hoard of plunder and his conquests provided a potential source of revenue and manpower for the Norwegian crown but, and this was a big 'but', only if they could be controlled in the long term and at acceptable cost. Magnus was only able to assert royal authority in the isles because he was there in person with an army and a fleet at his back. This was not a situation that could be maintained indefinitely. Garrisoning the isles would have been prohibitively expensive and there still remained much to be done to establish royal authority firmly in Norway itself, never mind the remote islands around Scotland. Magnus's achievement, therefore, proved ephemeral and did not long survive his death in battle in Ireland in 1103.

The only measures that Magnus had taken during his short life to consolidate royal authority in the Northern Isles was to depose the joint earls of Orkney, Paul and Erlend, in 1098, and appoint his eight-year-old son Sigurd in their place. In 1102 Magnus added the Kingdom of Man and the Isles to Sigurd's nominal domains. If this arrangement had endured it might have helped create a tradition of loyalty to the Norwegian royal house, but Sigurd would have none of it. Once his father was dead, Sigurd sailed home to Norway to claim his share of the kingdom alongside his brother Eystein and he never returned. While Sigurd crusaded, his brother Eystein was focused entirely on building stable government and prosperity in Norway, so the islanders were left to fend for themselves. When Sigurd died in 1130 (he had ruled alone since Eystein's death in 1123), a civil war broke out – a consequence of the Viking Age laws of succession that so often left kings with too many heirs – and only twice in the next 150 years did Norwegian kings visit their western dependencies. In the absence of the kings, royal authority predictably withered, creating a power vacuum that no one else was in a position to fill. The kings of the Scots certainly aspired to rule all the islands around Scotland's coast, but there were still many areas of the mainland, such as Argyll, Caithness and Galloway, which they considered part of their kingdom but did not actually control. England was too distant and the Irish kings were too preoccupied with their struggles over the high kingship to try to impose any authority in the region. Within a few years of Magnus's death, the Earldom of Orkney and the Kingdom of Man and the Isles reasserted their traditional autonomy, but neither of these polities was strong enough to prevent Norse and Gaelic Norse chieftains continuing to lead Viking raids for decades to come. Despite the establishment of Christianity, even monks could not feel secure: Iona was sacked by Norse pirates as late as 1240.

Holy earls

Before setting out on his crusade, King Sigurd gave up the Earldom of Orkney to Håkon Paulsson (r. 1105–26), son of the deposed Earl Paul. Håkon was soon joined by his cousin Magnus Erlendsson (r. 1105–16), the son of Earl Erlend. The earldom was back in the hands of its original ruling family. Earls Håkon and Magnus at first ruled Orkney and Shetland amicably enough, dispensing justice and rounding up and executing many Viking pirates who were disturbing the peace. However, in 1114 the pair fell out. Though it is not clear what the cause was, there was certainly a faction among the Orcadian chiefs that was not happy with joint rulership, and they had the ear of Earl Håkon. A meeting was arranged in April 1116 on the Orkney island of Egilsay, ostensibly to patch up a peace between the two. Each earl was to be allowed to attend with two ships full of retainers, but when Magnus saw that Håkon had turned up with eight ships he knew that he meant to kill him. Magnus first tried hiding but then gave himself up to Håkon and tried to save his life by offering to go into exile or even be imprisoned. The chiefs, however, wanted a decisive outcome and demanded that one of the earls be killed. 'Better kill him then,' said Håkon. 'I don't want an early death: I much prefer ruling over people and places.' Magnus had a reputation for piety – he had been present with Magnus Barefoot at the Battle of the Menai Straits in 1098 but had refused to fight because he had no quarrel with anyone there, and had read psalms instead – and he prepared for his execution with all the humility and composure of someone who knew he was destined to become a saint. Magnus asked his executioner to strike him on the head because it was not appropriate that someone of his birth be beheaded like a common criminal. A cult soon developed around Magnus's memory but, even though he was recognised as a saint in 1135, Håkon's reputation was not tarnished at all by the killing. *Orkneyinga Saga* describes him as a popular ruler, an able administrator who brought firm peace and made good laws. For the Orcadians it probably seemed like an ideal arrangement, one earl in Heaven to care for their souls, and another on Earth to provide them with security and good government. Håkon, however, lived with a burden of guilt for the killing and later in his reign made the long pilgrimage to Jerusalem as penance.

In 1137, Magnus's nephew Rognvald Kali Kolsson (r. 1137–58), who had been born and brought up in Norway, overthrew Earl Håkon's son and successor Paul the Silent. Rognvald would have made a good PR man in the modern world: his given name was Kali and he adopted 'Rognvald' to associate himself more closely with earlier earls of Orkney, two of whom shared the same name. Among the promises that Rognvald made to the islanders to win popular support was that he would build a stone church more magnificent than any in Orkney to house Magnus's relics. Rognvald immediately ordered work to begin at Kirkwall under the direction of his father Kol. The church was built in the weighty Norman Romanesque style, using red and yellow Orkney sandstone, by masons who had learned their skills on Durham Cathedral in northern England. The stylistic similarities between the two buildings are very obvious. Though it was still far from complete, St Magnus's remains were enshrined in the cathedral when it was consecrated about fifteen years later. A skull with a prominent head wound that was found in a casket in a cavity in the cathedral's walls in 1917 is generally accepted as Magnus's. There was politics as well as piety in Rognvald's actions. The recognition of Earl Magnus as a saint put the Earldom of Orkney on a par with the kingdoms of Norway and Denmark: by giving the earldom a church to rival anything in the Scandinavian kingdoms, Rognvald was making a powerful statement about his own status.

Rognvald further emulated the Scandinavian kings by leading his own crusade to the Holy Land with a fleet of fifteen ships in 1151, in the process establishing himself as a figure of Europe-wide stature. Rognvald returned to Orkney in time for Christmas in 1153, but the situation he found was probably an unwelcome reminder that he was not, after all, a king. Rognvald had left the earldom in the care of his junior co-earl Harald Maddadsson, the grandson of Earl Håkon Paulsson (r. 1139–1206), with whom he had ruled amicably since 1139. While Rognvald was away, King Eystein II became the first Norwegian king to visit Orkney since Magnus Barefoot's death while he was on his way to plunder the east coasts of Scotland and England. In Orkney

Eystein learned that Harald was at Thurso in Caithness with only a
single ship. Eystein sent three ships to capture him: suspecting nothing
Harald was taken without a fight. The price of Harald's freedom was
a ransom in gold and an oath of allegiance to the Norwegian crown.
Worse followed when Harald's cousin Erlend Haraldsson turned up to
claim a share of the earldom, sparking a complex dynastic struggle that
was only resolved with Erlend's killing in 1161. Rognvald did not live
to see the end of the dispute: he was killed in a skirmish with outlaws
in Caithness in 1158 and was buried in the cathedral he had founded
in Kirkwall. Miracles were soon being reported and in 1192, Rognvald
was recognised as Orkney's second saint.

The last Viking

The insecurity caused by the dispute between the earls was a heaven-
sent opportunity for one of the last of the old-fashioned Viking
freebooters, Svein Asleifarson, a chieftain from the small island of
Gairsay in Orkney. In a career of piracy that lasted over thirty years,
Svein raided the coasts of Scotland, Wales and Ireland, taking ships
on the high seas, and plundering villages and (despite him being a
Christian) monasteries too. Just as it had been for the earliest Vikings,
piracy for him was a seasonal activity to be fitted into the cycles of the
agricultural year:

> This was how Svein used to live. Winter he would spend at home on
> Gairsay, where he entertained some eighty men at his own expense.
> His drinking hall was so big, there was nothing in Orkney to compare
> with it. In the spring he had more than enough to occupy him, with
> a great deal of seed to sow, which he saw to carefully himself. Then,
> when the job was done, he would go off plundering in the Hebrides
> and Ireland on what he called his 'spring-trip', then back home just
> after midsummer, where he stayed until the cornfields had been
> reaped and the grain was safely in. After that he would go off raiding
> again, and never came back until the first month of winter was ended.
> This he called his 'autumn-trip'. *Orkneyinga Saga* (trans. Hermann
> Pálsson and Paul Edwards, Hogarth Press, London, 1978).

Svein's band of eighty warriors was large enough to make him a major power in Orkney, but he seems to have had no political ambitions beyond maintaining his autonomy. When the dispute between the earls broke out, Svein sided with Erlend so that he could legitimately plunder Orkney and Shetland, capturing ships belonging to Harald and Rognvald and stealing their rents and taxes. Once Erlend was dead, he and his victims were quite easily reconciled. Svein, after all, had his uses and, as there was little they could do about him anyway, it was best to be pragmatic. Sometimes the earls loaned him ships for his raids for a cut of the plunder and, if there was someone they wanted killing, Svein was usually happy to oblige, being well-aware that such favours could always be called in. Around 1170, Earl Harald urged Svein to give up raiding, telling him that 'most troublemakers are fated to end up dead unless they stop of their own free will'. All too aware that his high status could only be maintained by a continuous stream of plunder, Svein continued, meeting a predictably violent end in 1171 when he joined Asculf Ragnaldsson, the exiled Ostman king of Dublin, in his doomed attempt to recapture the city from the Anglo-Normans.

Earl Harald's sole rule saw the gradual decline of the Earldom of Orkney. In 1194, Harald supported an unsuccessful rebellion against King Sverre of Norway and was once again forced to recognise the overlordship of the Norwegian crown. As punishment for the rebellion, Sverre took Shetland under direct royal authority. The earldom's poss-essions on the Scottish mainland, Caithness and Sutherland, also came under growing pressure from the kings of Scotland. Scottish influence in Orkney had grown almost imperceptibly as a result of intermarriage between the Norse and Scottish aristocracies. Harald himself was the product of one such marriage: his mother was the daughter of Earl Håkon Paulsson and his father was Matad the mormaer of Atholl, through whom he had inherited Scottish royal blood. Because of his family connections, Harald's claim to a share of the earldom had been supported by King David I. David's successors, likewise, used family disputes in the earldom to increase their infl-uence there. In 1201, King William the Lion of Scotland used a dispute over the rights of the bishopric of Caithness as a pretext to invade the province in overwhelming force. Harald kept the provinces but was forced to surrender a quarter of their revenues to King William. This prepared the ground for the definitive Scottish takeover of Caithness and Sutherland after Harald's son and successor Jon Haraldsson was murdered in Thurso in 1231. Jon's death brought the direct line of Norse earls to an end (his family was lost at sea on their way to Norway after his murder). In 1236, Håkon IV (r. 1217–63) appointed Magnus mac Gille Brigte, the mormaer of Caithness, as earl. Magnus was descended from the Norse earls through his mother but was culturally a Scottish Gael. For the remainder of its history the earldom would be ruled by Scottish families, although it remained Norse in culture, language and sovereignty.

Norse and Gaels

The situation further south in Man and the Hebrides in the years immediately following Magnus Barefoot's death is far from clear because the main source, the *Cronica Regum Mannie et Insularum* ('Chronicles of the Kings of Man and the Isles') is chronologically unreliable. It is likely, however, that the island was under Irish control until 1114 when Olaf Godredsson (r. *c.* 1114–53) returned from his exile in England and, with Henry I's support, restored Norse rule in Man and the Isles. Olaf strengthened his position with marriage alliances with neighbouring rulers, all of whom had an interest in containing the power of the Scots kings. Olaf's first wife was Ingibjorg, a daughter of Earl Håkon Paulsson of Orkney, and he married one of his daughters by this marriage, Ragnhild, to Somerled, the Norse-Gaelic king of Argyll. Olaf's second marriage was to Affraic, daughter of Fergus, the king of Galloway, and his wife, an unnamed illegitimate daughter of Henry I of England. Olaf's wide-ranging alliances gave his kingdom security. The Manx chronicle describes him as 'a man of peace... in such close alliance with the kings of Ireland and Scotland that no one dared disturb the Kingdom of the Isles in his lifetime.'

In 1152, Olaf sent his son Godred to pay homage to King Inge in Norway. In Godred's absence the three sons of Olaf's brother Harald, who had been exiled in Dublin, gathered a fleet and invaded the Isle of Man to demand that their uncle give them half of the kingdom. Olaf agreed to meet the brothers at Ramsey to discuss their demands.

However, the meeting was a trap and Olaf was taken by surprise and beheaded. The Haraldssons had little popular support and they did not rule the island for long. Godred returned the next year, raised a large army in the Hebrides, and captured the brothers, blinding two of them and killing the third. According to the Manx chronicle, once he had crushed all opposition, Godred began to rule like a tyrant. His popularity may also have suffered as a result of a failed attempt to seize Dublin and other unsuccessful interventions in Irish politics. In 1155, a powerful Norse-Gaelic chieftain from the Hebrides, Thorfinn macOttar, went to Somerled and asked him to make his young son Dugald king over the Isles in place of Godred. Somerled obligingly handed his son over to Thorfinn, who duly paraded the boy through the isles, subjecting them to his rule and taking hostages. Godred acted quickly when the news of Thorfinn's coup reached him, raising a fleet and sailing to the Hebrides to regain control, even though it was mid-winter. Somerled raised a fleet of eighty ships and fell upon Godred's fleet on the night of Epiphany (5–6 January) 1156. The location of the battle is not known but it has been plausibly identified as being off the west coast of Islay. The fighting was hard but the outcome was indecisive. When day dawned the two leaders negotiated an agreement by which Godred ceded all of the Hebrides to Somerled, except for Skye, Harris and Lewis. This was not enough for Somerled. Two years later he landed at Ramsey in the Isle of Man with a fleet of fifty-three ships and forced Godred to flee into exile to Norway. Although he had ostensibly gone to war against Godred on behalf of his son, it seems that Somerled took the whole of the Kingdom of Man and the Isles under his personal rule and began to style himself *Rex Insularum* – 'King of the Isles'. Somerled's victory began the final stage of the assimilation of the Norse of the Hebrides into the indigenous Gaelic population.

Several major Highland clans, including Clan MacDougall, Clan Donald, Clan MacRory and Clan MacAlister, consider Somerled to be their direct patrilinear ancestor and later clan histories have cast him in the role of champion of the Gaels against both the Norse and the feudalising Scottish monarchy. In reality Somerled was a typical chieftain of his time and place, defending his own lands and opportunistically raiding the lands of his neighbours irrespective of whether they were Gaels or Norse: his name is derived from Old Norse *Sumarliði*, meaning 'summer warrior', a common alternative name for 'Viking'. Irish annals and later clan histories preserve several, mutually contradictory, traditions about Somerled's ancestry but modern genetic studies have shown fairly conclusively that his patrilinear ancestors were ultimately Norse. Five chiefs of different branches of Clan Donald, who can all trace their descent back to Somerled, shared a distinctive genetic marker, identified as a sub-group of haplogroup (i.e. a distinctive sequence of genes) M-17, on the Y chromosome, which is inherited only through the male line. This marker is common in Norway but rare in indigenous British and Irish populations. The same marker was found to be shared by 40 per cent of men with the surname MacAlister, 30 per cent of MacDougalls, and 18 per cent of MacRorys: Somerled may have a lot of descendents. Although Somerled had Norse ancestry, his family had travelled the road to full integration with the local Gaels some generations before he was born as his father and grandfather had Gaelic names. Somerled was much more a Gael than a Norseman in language, culture and identity.

It is not known how Somerled came to be the ruler of Argyll, but he must already have been a considerable figure when he married Olaf Godredsson's daughter around 1140. The kings of Scots regarded Argyll, the heartland of the original Scots kingdom of Dál Riata, as part of their kingdom, but it is clear that from his first appearance in the historical record that he considered himself to be an independent ruler, a king in his own right. After his conquest of Man, nothing is known of Somerled's activities until 1164, when he invaded Scotland, sailing down the Clyde with a Norse-Gaelic fleet of 160 ships from Argyll, the Hebrides, Man and Dublin. Somerled's motive was probably defensive: King Malcolm IV had recently deposed Fergus of Galloway so Somerled was probably trying to pre-empt a similar move against him. At Renfrew, Somerled was engaged by a hastily gathered Scottish army and was killed in fierce fighting. As Somerled's Gaelic and Norse warriors fled back to their ships, a priest cut off his head and gave it to the bishop of Glasgow. His body was later released to his kin and taken for burial on Iona. Somerled's sea kingdom broke up after his death. In accordance with the Gaelic custom of partible inheritance, his lands were divided between his many sons, while Godred came back from exile and, with Norwegian support, recovered Man, Lewis and Harris. However, the rest of the Hebrides remained permanently under the rule of Somerled's descendents, who, though they styled themselves kings, continued to acknowledge the kings of Norway as their ultimate overlords.

It was the growing power of the kings of Scotland that finally brought Norse influence in Man and the Hebrides to an end. Around 1200, the Scots seized the island of Bute and signaled their intention to become a power in the Isles by building a state-of-the-art castle at Rothesay. The Scots king Alexander II (r. 1214–49) entered into negotiations with Håkon IV (r. 1217–63) to buy the Hebrides from Norway. The negotiations came to nothing. Håkon had restored political stability to Norway after years of civil wars and had adopted his own expansionist policy, which aimed at uniting all the Norse Atlantic colonies under his rule: giving up part of his kingdom was not part of his plan. Frustrated, in 1249 Alexander decided to seize the Hebrides by force, but his campaign was abandoned after he fell ill and died on the island of Kerrara, off Oban. Alexander's son Alexander III (r. 1249–86) made a second offer to purchase the islands in 1260 but when this was rebuffed he sent the earl of Ross to invade Skye. Another Scottish force seized the island of Arran. Lurid accounts of Scots atrocities and the political chaos in the isles convinced Håkon that he needed to intervene personally to restore royal authority in the area. Apparently, at the height of his power – Greenland and Iceland had just submitted to Norwegian rule – Håkon set sail for the Hebrides in July 1263 with what was claimed to be the most powerful fleet ever gathered in Norway. King Magnus Olafsson of Man and Dugald MacRory, whose lands had been ravaged by the Scots, both greeted Håkon warmly when he landed on the Isle of Skye. Other chiefs and petty kings, opposed equally to both Norwegian and Scottish domination, were less enthusiastic and only submitted after Håkon's forces wasted their lands. By late summer Håkon had thoroughly cowed the Hebrides and he moved his fleet to Lamlash Bay on Arran in the Clyde estuary, where it was well-placed to strike into the heartland of the Scottish kingdom. Alexander III sent a party of Dominican friars to negotiate with Håkon, but this was just a delaying tactic. The Scots deliberately drew out the negotiations, making offers that they knew would be unacceptable, waiting for the onset of autumn to force Håkon's withdrawal. Some bored members of the Norwegian army carved their names in runes on the wall of a local cave to entertain themselves while they waited. When Håkon became impatient of making any progress he sent sixty ships to sail up Loch Long to Arrochar. From there, their crews dragged the ships across a narrow isthmus into Loch Lomond, whose shores they plundered for weeks. The rest of Håkon's fleet anchored off the Cumbrae Islands, close to the Ayrshire coast.

The Battle of Largs

At the end of September the weather turned bad. Ten ships returning from the raid on Loch Lomond were wrecked in a storm and on the night of 30 September/1 October a supply ship and a longship were driven ashore on the Scottish mainland at Largs, now a small seaside resort town. When day broke, the Scots tried to seize the beached ships but their crews fought them off until the main Norwegian fleet arrived and chased them away. The next morning King Håkon came on shore to supervise the recovery of the ships. While this was proceeding a large Scots force arrived and fierce fighting broke out as it tried to surround an isolated Norwegian scouting party on a hill overlooking the shore. The outnumbered Norwegians began to run back towards the ships in disarray, suffering many casualties, but they somehow managed to regroup and counter-attack. The Scots fell back under the unexpected assault, gifting the Norwegians enough time to reach their ships and escape. The Norwegians waited at anchor overnight and in the morning recovered their dead and sailed for home. The Battle of Largs had been in reality little more than a skirmish but, with the benefit of hindsight, it came to be seen as a decisive Norwegian defeat.

As he sailed north back through the Hebrides Håkon must have felt that his great expedition had been in vain. King Alexander's delaying tactics had worked perfectly, he had reached no diplomatic agreement that would prevent the Scots interfering in the Isles and he had been forced to withdraw without even fighting a proper battle.

He must have been painfully aware, too, that his authority over the chiefs and petty kings of the Isles would last no longer than it took him to sail home to Norway. Shortly after he arrived in Orkney in early November, Håkon was taken ill and, sending most of his fleet home, he took up residence for the winter in the bishop's palace at Kirkwall. Håkon's condition steadily deteriorated and he was soon bed-ridden. As the king lay dying, he gathered the shades of his Viking ancestors around him. He could not sleep, so to help the long winter nights pass more easily, Håkon asked his attendants to read him all the sagas of the kings of Norway beginning with the legendary Halfdan the Black, the father of Harald Fairhair. Shortly after he had finished listening to the saga of his grandfather King Sverre, Håkon lost the power of speech and three days later, in the early hours of the morning on 16 December, he died aged fifty-nine: he was the last Norwegian king to lead a hostile fleet into British waters.

Within a few months of Håkon's death, Alexander led a fleet to the Isle of Man and forced King Magnus Olafsson to become his feudal vassal. When Magnus died in November 1265, leaving only an illegitimate son called Godred, the rule of Norse kings over Man came to an end. Alexander also sent fleets to plunder and burn their way through the Hebrides. Håkon's successor, his son Magnus VI (r. 1263–80), concluded, rightly, that trying to maintain sovereignty over Man and the Isles would cost far more than they were worth. By the Treaty of Perth in 1266 Magnus gave up all claims to the Kingdom of Man and the Isles in return for a payment of 4,000 marks (approximately 20,000 pounds of silver), an annuity of 100 marks, and a Scottish recognition of Norwegian sovereignty over Orkney and Shetland. It is thought that Norse language in the kingdom died out soon after the Scottish takeover.

It proved to be just as hard for the kings of Scotland to control the Isles as it had been for the kings of Norway. The Scots easily crushed a Manx rebellion under Godred Magnusson in 1275, but in 1290 the Isle of Man was occupied by the English. Thereafter the island changed hands several times before passing permanently to the English crown in 1399. The Gaelic chieftains of the Hebrides defied pacification and in the fourteenth and fifteenth centuries the area was effectively autonomous under the MacDonald Lords of the Isles, who ruled from Finlaggan Castle on Islay. The lords maintained their authority with fleets of galleys called *birlinns*, direct descendants of the Vikings' long-ships from which they differed only in having a stern-post rudder in place of a side rudder. Even after the lordship collapsed in 1493, the Hebrides remained turbulent and they did not finally come under firm government control until after the crushing of the 1745 Jacobite rebellion. The Scots king James VI (r. 1567–1625) even considered genocide as a way to bring the islands under effective royal control.

The cession of the Kingdom of Man and the Isles to Scotland left Orkney and Shetland as the last Norse possessions in the British Isles. Although the islands were ruled by Scottish earls after 1236, their Norse character remained unaltered. In 1380 Norway and its Atlantic possessions came under the Danish crown through a dynastic union. The Danes took little interest in the islands until 1468 when King Christian I arranged the marriage of his daughter Margaret to the Scottish king James III. The cash-strapped Danish king could not afford to pay his daughter's dowry and so offered the Orkney Islands to King James as surety for a loan of 50,000 Rhenish guilders. The following year Christian added Shetland to the bargain for an additional 8,000 guilders. It was Christian's firm intention to redeem the islands as his agreement with King James included guarantees to preserve Norwegian law and customs, but the money was never paid so the arrangement became permanent. In 1471 King James abolished the earldom and annexed the islands as crown lands. The following year the bishopric of Orkney passed from the control of Nidaros to St Andrews. Gradually the islands became more Scottish in character. In 1611, Norwegian law was abolished and Norn, the local Norse dialect, finally died out in the eighteenth century, supplanted by English.

Hard times in Iceland

Though they did not lose their Norse culture and identity, the Norse colonies in Iceland and Greenland also lost their independence to the growing power of kings. Both also suffered severe population declines, which in Greenland's case proved fatal, as a result of plague, economic isolation and climate change. Around 1250, the climate in the North Atlantic began to deteriorate as the Medieval Warm Period came to an end. By 1350, average temperatures had fallen substantially below those of the present day, beginning a period of intensely cold winters and cool summers to North America and Europe, which has become known as the Little Ice Age. During this period, which lasted until around 1850, the River Thames froze so hard in winter that Londoners held fairs, and even lit bonfires, on it; Venetians skated on the Lagoon; and once the Bosphorus froze at Istanbul so that it was possible to walk across it from Europe to Asia. Harvests often failed in the cool summers, bringing hunger to millions. One of the reasons why the Black Death which ravaged Europe in 1347–51 caused such massive mortality (up to 50 per cent of the population died) was that it fell on a weakened population.

The Little Ice Age hit Iceland hard, but this was only part of its problems. As well as climatic deterioration, medieval Icelanders also had to cope with the consequences of major volcanic eruptions and serious environmental problems of their own making. The human impact on Iceland was massive and rapid. Most of Iceland's woodlands had been felled for fuel and building materials by the end of the Landnám period (c. 930) and over-grazing by sheep and cattle prevented any regeneration. Continued over-grazing began to expose the thin Icelandic soils to erosion by wind and rain. The impact was worst in the highlands, where large areas became cold deserts, but by 1300 soil erosion was also affecting the lowlands and it continued into modern times, causing a serious decline in the farming economy due to the poorer quality grazing. Only in the last few decades has this process been reversed with an ambitious woodland restoration programme. Volcanic eruptions also damaged agricultural productivity both by smothering grazing land with ash and by causing destructive flooding by melting the glaciers, which capped so many volcanoes. One of the worst incidents came in 1362 when an eruption burst through the vast Vatnajokul ice cap triggering massive floods that swept away two entire parishes and buried hundreds of square miles under knee-deep ash. The combined impact of these environmental disasters caused frequent famines that halved Iceland's population by the fifteenth century.

By this time Iceland had lost its independence. The Althing provided Iceland with stable government while all the *goðar* were of roughly equal status, but it proved unable to cope with the emergence in the early thirteenth century of six pre-eminent chieftains, the *stórgoðar* ('great chieftains'). These families competed for power, taking over the chieftaincies of lesser *goðar* in their attempts to create regional lordships, and imposing heavy burdens of taxation and military service on their followers. The country was riven by blood feuds and civil wars that eventually destroyed the Free State. To strengthen their positions many of the *stórgoðar* sought the support of Norway's expansionist King Håkon IV and became royal vassals in return for promoting his ambitions to rule Iceland. Håkon steadily extended his influence over Iceland and in 1263 the Althing voted to accept Norwegian sovereignty. The rule of the *goðar* was abolished and, though the Althing continued to meet annually at Thingvellir until 1798, the members of the *Lögretta* were now royal appointees, whose decisions were subject to royal approval. Along with the loss of political independence, Iceland lost its economic autonomy. After the end of the Landnám period, Icelanders became increasingly dependent on foreigners to maintain their trade links. The lack of timber suitable for shipbuilding meant that once the original settlers' ships had rotted they could not be replaced allowing Norwegian and, later German and English, merchants to take over Iceland's trade and impose their own terms. Until it regained its independence in 1944, Iceland would remain one of Europe's poorest countries.

In stark contrast to the political decay, the thirteenth century was also the age of Iceland's greatest cultural achievement, its saga literature. Perhaps more than anything else, the sagas have helped give the Vikings, despite their many unsavoury habits, an undeniable aura of romance. Without the sagas, the Vikings would probably be just one more half-remembered bunch of barbarians like the Vandals and the Goths. In Icelandic, *saga* means 'what is said', so the tradition probably grew out of the oral storytelling that must have been a major source of entertainment on the long winter nights. Sagas cover many different subjects, including myths and legends, romances and saints' lives. However, the two most important genres are the Íslendingasögur ('sagas of Icelanders') and royal biographies or *konungasögur* ('kings' sagas'). The anonymous Íslendingasögur are historical novels, in the form of family histories, based on the real people and events of Viking Age Iceland. The Íslendingasögur were a powerful response to Iceland's troubled times, and they catered for an escapist desire to recreate a 'golden age' of a more heroic past while, at the same time, addressing present-day anxieties. It is no surprise that in such a strife-torn society, a common theme of these sagas is the working out of a blood feud and its tragic consequences across the generations. In *Njáls saga*, which many critics regard as the finest of all the Íslendingasögur, ties of kinship, personal loyalty and friendship inexorably draw Njal, a good and peaceable man, into other people's disputes, leading him ultimately to his own violent death when his enemies trap and burn him in his hall. Though the authors of the sagas are much concerned with the workings of fate, their characters are rarely helpless victims, they are in control of their own destinies, they have choices, and they usually meet their ends as a result of their own flawed characters and misjudgements. This gripping psychological realism gives the Íslendingasögur a strikingly modern feel, especially when compared with the chivalric romances then fashionable in Europe, with their stereotyped characters and frequent supernatural and fantastical elements.

The most consistently entertaining of the Íslendingasögur must be *Egils saga,* which is based on the life of the tenth-century skald Egil Skalla-Grímsson. How closely the Egil of the saga resembles the real-life Egil is unknowable, but he is a larger than life character who embodies in a single person all of the contradictory faces of the Viking Age, appearing in turn as a warrior, merchant, farmer and skald, a man of remorseless violence who was nevertheless capable of composing verse of great sensitivity about the loss of his children. Like all the Íslendingasögur, *Egils saga* is anonymous, but it is generally thought on stylistic grounds that it was written by Snorri Sturluson (*c.* 1179–1241), medieval Iceland's leading literary figure. Like Egil, Snorri was a man of many parts, a poet, historian, lawyer and politically ambitious chieftain of the powerful Sturlung family who dominated western Iceland. From the age of three, Snorri was fostered by Jón Loftsson of

Oddi, the most influential chieftain of southern Iceland. This fostering was the most decisive event in Snorri's life. Oddi was Iceland's main cultural centre and Jón, a learned man in his own right, saw to it that Snorri received a good education in theology, law and Latin literature. When Snorri was nineteen, his foster-brother Sæmundr arranged for him an advantageous marriage to Herdís, the only child of Bersi the Wealthy, through whom he inherited his first chieftaincy in 1202. Over the following years Snorri acquired many more chieftaincies, making him one of Iceland's most influential *stórgoðar*. Elected three times as Lawspeaker, Snorri's legal skills helped him advance his interests and those of his friends, but his ambitions inevitably made him enemies. Snorri was not a violent man and many of his contemporaries thought him to be a coward at heart. Unfortunately for Snorri, in thirteenth-century Iceland, the politically ambitious could not afford to be squeamish about violence.

Reykholt

In 1206, Snorri settled at the bleak manor at Reykholt, in Reykholtsdalur in western Iceland, and set about improving his new home. Snorri built a channel from a nearby hot spring to feed an outdoor hot tub and, a sign of the times, he also built substantial fortifications of turf and timber to protect his home. The timbers of Snorri's home have long rotted and the turf walls have slumped into low banks that today give no impression of what archaeological investigations have revealed to have been an impressive castle-like home. The stone-lined hot tub alone remains. It was at Reykholt that Snorri wrote his major works, *Heimskringla* and the *Edda*, each of which has, in very different ways, contributed mightily to our knowledge of the Viking Age.

Snorri's *Heimskringla* ('The Circle of the World') is a monumental history of the kings of Norway from legendary times down to the death of Magnus IV in 1177, written as a sequence of sixteen *konungasögur*. Drawing on a multitude of histories, genealogies and skaldic poems (he quotes from the works of more than seventy skalds), Snorri created for Norway a thrilling national epic that sustained Norwegian national identity through centuries of foreign rule but questions remain about its reliability. His vivid battle scenes and convincing dialogue are mostly invented. Like the Classical historians he read in his youth, Snorri used dialogue as a dramatic rhetorical device for analysing the motives and characters of his subjects, so it cannot be taken literally. Few modern historians would put as much faith in the veracity of skaldic poems as Snorri did – they were propaganda rather than history – but he brought a keen understanding of human psychology to his work and his marked reluctance to invoke supernatural causes makes *Heimskringla* one of the most impressive, coherent and readable works of medieval historiography: despite its shortcomings all historians of the Viking Age rely on it heavily.

Snorri was also the author of a unique handbook to the Viking art of composing skaldic verse. This was a genre of alliterative verse that was composed and publicly recited by skalds to praise the deeds of their royal patrons. Good skaldic verse was committed to memory and passed down through the generations, helping to secure their subjects' posthumous reputation – something that was always close to a Viking ruler's heart. Skalds were usually also warriors. They accompanied Viking armies into battle and composed verses on the spot to encourage their fellow warriors to greater feats of heroism: skaldic poems are, therefore, often the nearest thing we have to eyewitness accounts of the Vikings in battle. By Snorri's time, skaldic verse was a dying art. Young poets no longer understood the allusions to pagan mythology that provided the genre with much of its colour and vitality. It was with the intent of reviving the art of the skalds that Snorri wrote the *Edda* (the meaning of the title is uncertain), providing his readers with a full account of Scandinavian mythology from the creation of the world to Ragnarok, the doom of the gods, as well as a discussion of poetical devices, such as metre, alliteration and kennings (poetic similes). Snorri prefaced his work with a Christian rationalisation of the pagan religion, presenting the old gods merely as deified ancient heroes, so protecting himself from any accusation of apostasy. As with his historical writing, Snorri drew on a variety of oral and written sources, some of which are preserved in an anonymous collection of mythological and heroic verse known as the *Poetic* or *Elder Edda*. The most important of these poems are 'Voluspá' ('The Prophecy of the

Seeress'), which Snorri quotes in his *Edda*, describing the creation of the world and Ragnarok, and *Hávamál*, a collection of short verses offering common-sense wisdom about everyday social conduct in Viking society, along with spells and verses about the high god Odin. Snorri's *Edda* failed to revive skaldic verse – soon after his death, the Icelanders were writing and reading the chivalric romances that Snorri so obviously disapproved of – but without it our knowledge of Scandinavian paganism would be much poorer.

It is perhaps ironic that Snorri played a significant role in the downfall of the Icelandic Free State: he was the first of the *stórgoðar* to become a vassal of the king of Norway, accepting a knighthood from Håkon IV while visiting Norway in 1220. Snorri shamelessly flattered the young king and the powerful jarl Skuli Bardarson by writing skaldic praise poems for them. Jarl Skuli was so pleased he gave Snorri a ship and other fine gifts. Before he returned home, Håkon commissioned Snorri to use his influence in the Althing to bring Iceland under Norwegian rule. This had predictably destabilising consequences. Snorri's attempts to consolidate his power caused a civil war and in 1237 he was forced to flee to Norway. Håkon was less than pleased to see him; Snorri had opened the door to royal influence but now he had outlived his usefulness. Håkon switched his support to Gissur Thorvaldsson, chieftain of the rival Haukadalur family. Håkon ordered Snorri not to return to Iceland, which, as Snorri's feudal lord, he had every right to do. However, Snorri felt compelled to return home to protect his own interests there and in 1239 he fled Norway with the help of his friend jarl Skuli. Snorri's association with Skuli proved fatal. After Skuli attempted to seize the throne later that year, Håkon ordered Gissur to kill Snorri. A sympathiser sent Snorri a coded warning of the intended attack, but he was unable to decipher it and took no special precautions to protect himself. Backed by sixty men, Gissur broke into Reykholt on the night of 23 September 1241. Taken completely by surprise, Snorri was chased into a cellar and killed. True to his nature, he offered no resistance. Snorri's killing caused outrage in both Iceland and Norway, but it showed how great Håkon's influence in Iceland now was. Conflict continued for another twenty years, but the struggle now was not for Iceland's independence, only for which family should exercise the greatest influence when it finally was annexed by Norway. The Icelanders' Viking ancestors had emigrated to escape the rule of kings but they had, in the end, fallen victim to the same centralising forces. Competition for power had torn their society apart, the rule of kings was the only way to restore peace and in 1263, the Althing voted to accept direct Norwegian rule.

Darkness falls on the Norse Greenland colony

Even during the Medieval Warm Period Greenland had been a very marginal environment for European colonisation: the onset of the Little Ice Age pushed the Norse colony over the edge into extinction. The climatic deterioration undermined the Greenland colony at several different levels. The Thule Inuit began to migrate south and took over the vital Norðsetr hunting grounds by around 1300. Without the Norðsetr's valuable commodities to attract European merchants the colony's trade links to Europe began to fade. These were already in decline in the thirteenth century, because increased trans-Saharan trade gave European craftsmen access to plentiful supplies of elephant ivory, which was much superior to Greenland's walrus ivory. Grain, iron and salt were everyday essentials in medieval Europe, but they must have become increasingly scarce luxuries in Greenland. In 1261, the Greenlanders acknowledged Norwegian sovereignty in return for a guarantee of one trade ship a year from Bergen. Increasing sea ice made it harder for the few ships that still set out for Greenland to get there. Ivar Bardarson, a priest who was sent to Greenland in 1341, wrote that the old route to the Greenland settlements, via the Gunnbjorn Skerries, had been given up because of pack ice. Ships now had to sail much further south to get around Cape Farewell. The increasing pack ice also reduced the Greenlanders' already limited wood supply by preventing driftwood reaching the shore. The voyage to Markland in 1347 (see ch. 8) was probably an attempt to improve the situation. Without the ability to build ships, the Greenlanders' dependence on the annual ship from Norway was absolute.

The colder conditions adversely affected the Greenlanders' farm-ing economy and animal bones from middens show an increasing dependence on wild caribou and seals. Skeletal remains from cemeteries show that the Greenlanders became prey to diseases associated with poor nutrition, such as chronic inner-ear infections, and had a reduced life expectancy. Everything depended on the hay harvest. The longer winters meant that livestock had to be kept in the byres for longer so the Greenlanders' dependence on hay was increasing even as their ability to provide it was declining. If the summer was too cool for the grass to grow well, there would not be enough hay to feed the livestock through the winter, and if the livestock starved so too, soon after, would the people. At Sandnes in the Western Settlement, archaeological evidence suggests that the entire parish starved to death in a hard winter in the mid-fourteenth century. At the chieftain's farm, the skeletons of nine hunting dogs were found on a stable floor: they had been butchered. This was an act of desperation indeed. When the houses of the parish were abandoned, even the valuable timbers were left. With wood in such short supply in Greenland, this would not have happened if there had been survivors. When Ivar Bardarson visited the Western Settlement in the 1340s, he found it completely uninhabited. By around 1380, the Middle Settlement had been abandoned too.

Although the archaeological evidence says otherwise, Ivar Bardarson believed that the Western settlement had been destroyed by the Inuit. The potential for conflict was clearly there, over hunting grounds, for example, and, as they did not own domestic animals themselves, the Inuit may have seen the Norse Greenlanders' livestock as just another kind of game to be hunted. There certainly was some violence between the Norse and the Inuit, though how serious a factor it was in the decline of the colony is impossible to judge. The Icelandic annals record that in 1379 Skraelings killed eighteen Greenlanders and took two boys into slavery. Inuit folk tales collected by Danish missionaries in the nineteenth century tell of conflicts with the Norse, but also of friendships. One tale tells how the Inuit avenged a Norse attack on one of their villages. Using white skins to make their kayaks look like icebergs, the Inuit approached a Norse farm undetected. When everyone had retired inside the house for the night, the Inuit packed bundles of juniper branches around it and set them on fire. Those Norse who tried to escape were shot down with arrows as they emerged from the house, the rest perished in the flames. In contrast, another tale tells how the Inuit agreed to help the Norse against pirates who had raided the settlements. When the pirates returned the Inuit rescued five women and two children. When the Inuit discovered that the pirates had carried off the rest of the Norse as captives, the survivors were adopted into their community. English, German and Moorish pirates raided Iceland in the fifteenth century, seizing people to sell as slaves on the Barbary Coast, and there is one record in a papal letter of a pirate raid on the Eastern Settlement in 1418, so the tale has the ring of truth about it. The impact of a slave raid on the small Norse community could have been much more devastating than any skirmishes with the Inuit.

A wedding at Hvalsey

In the later fourteenth century, contacts between Greenland and Norway became increasingly sporadic. In 1367, the official trade ship was lost at sea and there is no evidence that the Norwegian crown replaced it. Álfur, the bishop of Garðar, died in 1378, but it was not until 1385 that the news reached Norway. A new bishop was duly appointed, but he never sailed to take up his seat. One of the last recorded ships to visit the Greenland settlement arrived in 1406, after it was blown off course on a voyage from Norway to Iceland. Pack ice in the fjords prevented it from setting sail again for four years. While there, the ship's captain Thorstein Olafsson married Sigrid Bjornsdottir in the small stone church at Hvalsey, in the Eastern Settlement. Many guests attended the ceremony, which was held on 16 September 1408. The banns had been read publicly on three Sundays before the wedding and afterwards the priest Paul Hallvardsson gave the happy couple a marriage certificate: it is the only document written in the Norse Greenland colony that has survived. At this time, it would seem that all was well with the Eastern Settlement. It was a fully functioning medieval European community in which the church enforced conformity to Christian values. Only a year before the wedding a man called Kolgrim had been burned alive after being found guilty of using black arts to seduce a widow. This may be behind the Norse Greenlanders' striking failure to learn anything from the Inuit. Inuit hunting technology was far superior to that used by the Norse but even as their dependence on seal meat increased – isotope analysis of skeletal remains indicates that by this time Greenlanders relied on seal meat for 80 per cent of their nutrition – they adopted none of it. Inuit clothing was wonderfully adapted to survival in Arctic conditions but items of clothing recovered from a cemetery at Herjolfsnes in the Eastern Settlement show that the Norse continued to wear European-style woollens. Perhaps their Christian way of life was so central to the Norse that adopting Inuit ways would have challenged their sense of identity.

There are few recorded contacts with Greenland after Thorstein and his wife left for Norway in 1410. The Danish cartographer Claudius Clavus visited Greenland around 1420, travelling as far north as the Nordsetr and encountering Inuit, and it was probably he who took news of the pirate raid in 1418 to the outside world. In 1426, a Greenlander called Peder visited Norway, but it is not known if he ever went home. Clothing preserved in graves from the cemetery at Herjolfsnes shows that the Greenlanders were still managing to keep up to date with European fashions until around 1450, but there is no evidence for contacts after that time. By the late fifteenth century, the Norse Greenland colony had become a distant memory. No sea captains who knew the way to Greenland could be found at Bergen in 1484. In 1492 Pope Alexander VI wrote about Greenland as a lost land:

> 'The people there have no bread, wine or oil but live on dried fish and milk. Very few sailings because of the ice on the sea and these only in the month of August, when the ice has melted. It is thought that no ship has sailed there for eighty years and that no bishop or priest has lived there during this period. Because there are no priests, many of the people there who were formerly Catholics, have renounced the sacrament of baptism and have nothing else to remind of the Christian faith than a sacred altar cloth which is exhibited once a year, which was used by the last priest to say mass a hundred years ago.'

Ironically, Alexander was writing in the same year that Christopher Columbus made his first trans-Atlantic voyage. Europeans now possessed the technology to achieve what had been beyond the resources of the Greenlanders' Viking ancestors, the colonisation of the Americas.

The fate of the last Norse Greenlanders may never be known for certain, but it is likely that, by the time Pope Alexander was writing, their settlements were already deserted and abandoned. Certainly, seafarers who visited Greenland in the sixteenth century met only Inuit. It is romantic to imagine the last Norse Greenlanders, doomed by their cultural conservatism, struggling stubbornly to maintain their European ways as every winter the glaciers advanced a little further down the valleys. Forgotten and abandoned by the outside world, they died one by one of malnutrition and cold until none were left or until a few desperate survivors begged the Inuit to take them in. The fate of the settlement might have been altogether less desperate, however. Among fifteenth-century burials in the settlements there is a marked lack of women of child-bearing age. Death of complications associated with childbirth was sadly very common in Medieval Europe, so this absence must be significant. Sigrid Bjornsdottir had relations in Iceland and that was where she eventually settled after she left Greenland with her husband. Faced with increasing social and economic isolation and a choice between living on seal meat or starving, was Sigrid the only young woman who, seeing a way out, took it? The evidence of the cemeteries suggests not. This is part of a pattern of rural depopulation the world over. The young men, who stood to inherit farms, would have stayed longer, but as it became impossible for them to find wives, they would have begun to drift away too, perhaps signing on as crew on the few ships that still came to Greenland. Only those who felt too old to start a new life would have remained and, with the young people gone, the extinction of the colony was just a matter of time. The last outpost of the Viking world may simply have died of old age.

CHRONOLOGY

c. 1800 BC	Beginning of the Scandinavian Bronze Age.
c. 500 BC	Beginning of the Scandinavian Iron Age (to *c.* AD 800).
c. 320 BC	Pytheas of Massalia visits Thule.
c. AD 1–400	Emergence of a warrior aristocracy in southern Scandinavia.
c. 400–800	The first kingdoms develop in Denmark, Norway and Sweden.
425–500	Anglo-Saxon migrations from Denmark and Germany to Britain.
c. 528	Hygelac, king of the Geats, leads a Scandinavian pirate raid on the lower Rhine.
c. 725	St Willibrord leads the first Christian mission to Scandinavia.
737	The first phase of the Danevirke rampart is completed.
c. 750	Swedes established at Staraja Ladoga in Russia.
c. 789	Norwegian Vikings sack Portland in Dorsetshire.
793	Vikings plunder the Northumbrian monastery of Lindisfarne.
795	First recorded Viking raids on Scotland and Ireland.
799	Vikings raid Aquitaine.
800	Charlemagne organises coastal defences against the Vikings.
810	Danish king Godfred ravages Frisia.
822–3	Archbishop Ebo of Reims undertakes a mission to Denmark.
c. 825	First Danish coins are minted at Hedeby.
c. 825	Irish monks driven out of the Faeroe Islands by Vikings.
826	Danish king Harald Klak is baptised at Mainz. St Ansgar's first mission to Denmark.
829–30	St Ansgar's first mission to the Svear at Birka.
832	Armagh in Ireland is raided by Vikings three times in one month.
834–7	The port of Dorestad on the Rhine is raided annually.
c. 835	The Oseberg ship burial in Norway.
c. 839	The Rus reach Constantinople.
841	Viking *longphort* is established at Dublin.
843	Treaty of Verdun partitions the Carolingian empire.
844	Viking army in Spain is defeated at Seville.
845	The Danes sack Hamburg and Paris.
851–2	St Ansgar's second mission to Denmark and Sweden.
859–62	Hastein and Björn Ironside raid in the Mediterranean.
c. 860	Gardar the Swede explores the coast of Iceland.
860	The first Rus attack on Constantinople is driven off.
862	Charles the Bald, king of the West Franks orders the construction of fortified bridges against the Vikings.
c. 862	Rurik becomes ruler of Novgorod; Askold and Dyr seize Kiev.
865	Danish 'Great Army' invades England.

867	The Danes capture York.
870	The Danes conquer East Anglia.
c. 870–930	The Vikings settle Iceland.
c. 870	The Earldom of Orkney is established by Rognvald of Møre.
874–914	The 'Forty Years Rest': a lull in Viking raids against Ireland.
876-9	The beginning of Danish settlement in eastern England.
878	Alfred the Great of Wessex defeats the Danes at Edington.
c. 882	Oleg unites Novgorod and Kiev.
c. 885–90	Harald Fairhair wins the battle of Hafrsfjord, uniting most of Norway.
885-6	Unsuccessful Viking siege of Paris.
891	Arnulf king of the East Franks defeats the Vikings at the Dyle.
c. 900	Norwegian settlement begins in north-west England.
902	The Irish expel the Vikings from Dublin.
c. 900–905	The Gokstad ship burial in Norway.
907	After their attack on Constantinople is defeated the Rus agree a trade treaty with the Byzantine empire.
911	Rollo is made count of Rouen, founding Normandy.
912–54	Wessex conquers the Danelaw.
914–36	Vikings occupy Brittany.
917	Vikings under Sihtric Cáech recapture Dublin.
930	Foundation of the Icelandic Althing.
934	Henry the Fowler leads a German invasion of Denmark.
937	English defeat a Scottish-Norse alliance at Brunanburh.
948	First Scandinavian bishoprics founded at Ribe, Århus and Schleswig.
954	Erik Bloodaxe, last Viking king of York, is killed at Stainmore.
964–71	Svyatoslav of Kiev campaigns against the Bulgars, Khazars and Byzantines.
965	Harald Bluetooth of Denmark is converted to Christianity.
c. 965	Exhaustion of Muslim silver mines leads to the decline of Viking trade routes to the east.
974–81	Germans occupy Hedeby.
c. 980	Harald Bluetooth constructs the Trelleborg forts in Denmark.
c. 986	Erik the Red leads the Norse settlement of Greenland.
988	Byzantine emperor Basil II founds the Varangian Guard.
988	Vladimir the Great of Kiev converts to Orthodox Christianity.
991	Olaf Tryggvason defeats the English at Maldon.
995	Olaf Tryggvason wins control of Norway. Adopts a policy of forcible Christianisation.
995	Olof Skötkonung becomes the first king to rule both the Svear and Götar.

1000	Olaf Tryggvason is killed at the Battle of Svöld.
1000	The Icelanders accept Christianity.
c. 1000	Voyages to Vinland begin.
1002	St Brice's Day massacre of Danes living in England.
1014	Svein Forkbeard of Denmark conquers England.
1014	Brian Boru, High King of Ireland, defeats Norse-Leinster alliance at Clontarf.
1015	Olaf Haraldsson (St Olaf) becomes king of Norway.
1016	Cnut becomes king of England.
c. 1027	First stone church built in Denmark at Roskilde.
1030	Olaf Haraldsson killed at the battle of Stiklestad.
1030–5	Battle of Tarbat Ness: Thorfinn the Mighty, earl of Orkney wins control of northern Scotland.
1042	End of Danish rule in England.
1043	Magnus the Good defeats the Wends at the battle of Lyrskov Heath.
1066	Harald Hardrada killed at the battle of Stamford Bridge. Battle of Hastings begins the Norman conquest of Britain.
1075	Last Danish invasion of England.
1079	Battle of Skyhill. Godred Crovan unites the Isle of Man and the Hebrides.
1086	Cnut the Holy of Denmark is murdered after abandoning a planned invasion of England.
1098	Magnus Barefoot establishes Norwegian authority in the Scottish isles.
1103–4	Lund becomes the first Scandinavian archbishopric.
1107–11	Norwegian king Sigurd Jorsalfar leads a crusade to the Holy Land.
1122–32	Ari Thorgilsson writes *Íslendingabók* (The Book of the Icelanders).
1147	The Danes join a crusade against the pagan Wends.
1156	Somerled wins the southern Hebrides from Godred II of Man.
1171	Asculf, last Norse king of Dublin, captured and executed by the Anglo-Normans.
1241	The Icelandic poet and historian Snorri Sturluson is murdered.
1261	Norse Greenland colony comes under direct rule from Norway.
1263	Iceland comes under Norwegian rule.
1263	Scots defeat Håkon IV of Norway at Largs.
1266	Norway cedes Man and the Hebrides to Scotland.
c. 1340	Inuit occupy the Western Settlement in Greenland.
1397	Union of Kalmar unites Denmark, Norway and Sweden.
c. 1450–1500	Extinction of the Norse Greenland colony.
1469	Denmark cedes Orkney and Shetland to Scotland.

VIKING KINGS AND RULERS
c. 800–1100

KINGS OF DENMARK
Early kings
c. 720	Angantyr
c. 777	Sigfred
d. 810	Godfred
810–12	Hemming
812–13	Harald Klak
812–13	Reginfred
813–54	Horik
819–27	Harald Klak (restored)
854–7	Horik II
c. 873	Sigfred
c. 873	Halfdan
d. *c.* 900	Helgi (possibly legendary)
c. 900–36	Swedish Olaf Dynasty (Olaf, Gnupa, Gerd, Sigtryg)
c. 936	Hardegon

The Jelling Dynasty
c. 936-58	Gorm the Old
958–87	Harald Bluetooth
987–1014	Svein Forkbeard
1014–18	Harald II
1019–35	Cnut the Great (king of England 1016-35)
1035–42	Harthacnut
1042–6	Magnus the Good (king of Norway 1035-46)

Dynasty of Svein Estrithson
1046–74	Svein Estrithson
1074–80	Harald III
1080–6	Cnut the Holy
1086–95	Olaf Hunger
1095–1103	Erik the Evergood

KINGS OF NORWAY
d. *c.* 880	Halfdan the Black
c. 880–930	Harald Finehair

c. 930–6	Erik Bloodaxe (deposed, king of York 948, 952–4)
c. 936–60	Håkon the Good
c. 960–70	Harald Greycloak
995–1000	Olaf Tryggvason
1015–28	Olaf Haraldsson
1030–5	Svein Alfivason
1035–46	Magnus the Good
1045–66	Harald Hardrada
1066–9	Magnus II
1067–93	Olaf the Peaceful
1093–5	Håkon Magnusson
1093–1103	Magnus III Barefoot

KINGS OF THE SVEAR

c. 829	Björn and Önund
c. 850	Olaf
c. 935	Ring
	Erik Ringsson
	Emund Eriksson
c. 980–95	Erik the Victorious
995–1022	Olof Skötkonung
1022–50	Önund Jacob
1050–60	Emund the Old
1060–6	Stenkil Ragnvaldsson
1066–7	Erik and Erik
1066–70	Halsten
c. 1070	Önund Gårdske
1070–?	Håkon the Red
?–1080	Inge I (deposed)
1080–83	Blot-Sven
1083–1110	Inge I (restored)

KINGS OF DUBLIN

853–*c.* 871	Olaf
863–7	Auisle
c. 871–3	Ivar I
873–5	Eystein Olafsson
877–81	Bardr
883–8	Sigfred
888–93	Sihtric I (deposed)
893–4	Sigfred jarl

894–6	Sihtric I (restored)
896–902	Ivar II
917–21	Sihtric Cáech (king of York 921–7)
921–34	Guthfrith (king of York 927)
934–41	Olaf Guthfrithsson (king of York 939–41)
941–45	Blacaire
945–80	Olaf Sihtricsson
980–9	Járnkné Olafsson
989–1036	Sihtric Silkbeard
1036–8	Echmarcach mac Ragnaill (deposed)
1038–46	Ivar Haraldsson
1046–52	Echmarcach mac Ragnaill (restored) (king of Man 1052–4)
1052–70	*Murchad mac Diarmata*
1070–2	*Domnall mac Murchada* or *Diarmit mac Máel*
1072–4	Gofraid
1074–86	*Muirchertach ua Briain*
1086–9	*Enna* or *Donnchad*
1091–4	Godred Crovan (king of Man 1079–95)
1094–1118	*Domnall mac Muirchertaig ua Briain*

KINGS OF YORK

876–7	Halfdan
c. 883–95	Guthfrith
c. 895	Harthacnut
c. 895–901	Sigfrid
c. 900–02	Cnut
d. 903	Æthelwold
902–10	Halfdan II
902–10	Eowils
902–10	Ivar
c. 911, 919–21	Ragnald
921–27	Sihtric Cáech (king of Dublin 917)
927	Guthfrith (king of Dublin 921)
927–39	*Athelstan* (king of Wessex 924–39)
939–41	Olaf Guthfrithsson (king of Dublin 934)
941–4	Olaf Sihtricsson (king of Dublin 945–80)
943–4	Ragnald Guthfrithsson
944–6	*Edmund* (king of England 939)
946–8	*Eadred* (king of England 946–56)
948	Erik Bloodaxe (deposed, king of Norway *c.* 930–6)
949–52	Olaf Sihtricsson (restored)
952–4	Erik Bloodaxe (restored)

KINGS OF MAN

c. 971	Maccus mac Arailt (Magnus Haraldsson)
d. 989	Gofraid mac Arailt (Godfred Haraldsson)
d. 1004-5	Ragnall
d. 1014	Brodir?
1052-64	Echmarcach mac Ragnaill (king of Dublin 1036–8, 1046–52)
c. 1066–75	Godred Sihtricsson
c. 1075–9	Fingal Godredsson
1079–95	Godred Crovan (king of Dublin 1091–4)
1095–6	Lagmann Godredsson
1096–8	*Domnall mac Muirchertaig ua Briain* (king of Dublin 1094–1118)
1098–1103	Magnus Barefoot (king of Norway 1093–1103)

JARLS OF LADE

d. *c.* 885–90?	Håkon Grotgarðson
d. *c.* 963	Sigurd Håkonsson
c. 963-995	Håkon Sigurdsson
1000–1015	Erik Håkonsson
1015	Svein Håkonsson
1028–9	Håkon Sveinsson

EARLS OF ORKNEY

c. 870	Rognvald of Møre
d. *c.* 892	Sigurd the Mighty
c. 893	Guttorm
c. 894	Hallad
c. 895–910	Torf-Einar
d. 954	Arnkell
d. 954	Erlend
d. 963	Thorfinn Skullsplitter
	Arnfinn Thorfinnsson
	Havard Thorfinnsson
	Ljot Thorfinnsson
	Hlodver Thorfinnsson
c. 985–1014	Sigurd the Stout
1014–18	Sumarlidi
1014–20	Einar Falsemouth
1014–*c.* 1030	Brusi
c. 1020–65	Thorfinn the Mighty
1037–46	Rognvald

1065–98	Paul
1065–98	Erlend
1098–1103	Sigurd (king of Norway 1103–30)

DUKES OF NORMANDY

911–c. 928	Rollo
c. 928–42	William Longsword
942–96	Richard I
996–1026	Richard II
1026–27	Richard III
1027–35	Robert the Magnificent
1035–87	William the Conqueror (king of England 1066–87)
1087–1106	Robert Curthose

PRINCES OF KIEVAN RUS

c. 860–79	Rurik (semi-legendary ruler of Novgorod)
c. 879–913	Oleg
913–45	Igor
945–72	Svyatoslav I
972–80	Yaropolk I
980–1015	Vladimir I
1015–19	Svyatopolk I
1019–54	Yaroslav the Wise
	Muscovite branch of the dynasty survives until 1598

FURTHER READING

PRIMARY SOURCES IN TRANSLATION

ANNALS, CHRONICLES, LIVES AND LETTERS

Adam of Bremen, *History of the Archbishops of Hamburg-Bremen*,
    trans. F. J. Tschan (New York, 1959)

Allott, S. (trans.), *Alcuin of York: His Life and Letters* (York, 1974).

Anglo-Saxon Chronicle, trans. M. Swanton (London, 1996).

Annals of Fulda, trans. T. Reuter (Manchester, 1992).

Annals of St Bertin, trans. J. L. Nelson (Manchester, 1991).

Annals of Ulster, trans. S. Mac Airt and G. Mac Niocaill (Dublin, 1983).

Book of the Icelanders (Íslendingabók) by Ari Thorgilsson, ed. and trans. H.
    Hermannsson (Islandica 20, Cornell University Library, New York, 1930).

Book of Settlements: Landnámabók, trans. H. Pálsson and P. Edwards
    (Winnipeg, 1972).

Chronicles of the Kings of Man and the Isles, ed. and trans. G. Broderick
    (Douglas, Isle of Man, 1995).

Dudo of St Quentin: History of the Normans, trans. H. Christiansen
    (Woodbridge, Suffolk, 1998).

Encomium Emmae Regina, ed. and trans. A. Campbell, Camden Society 3rd
    Series 72 (London, 1947, reprint 1998).

Heimskringla: History of the Kings of Norway, trans. L. M. Hollander (Austin,
    Texas 1964).

Ibn Fadlan and the Land of Darkness: Arab Travellers in the Far North,
    trans. P. Lund and Stone (Penguin, 2012)

Keynes, S. and Lapidge, M. (trans), *Alfred the Great: Asser's Life of King Alfred
    and Other Contemporary Sources* (Harmondsworth, 1983).

King, P. D. (trans.), *Charlemagne: Translated Sources* (Lambrigg, Cumbria, 1987).

Orkneyinga Saga, trans. M. Magnusson and H. Pálsson (London, 1978).

Rimbert, *Life of St Ansgar*: translated in C. H. Robinson, *Anskar, Apostle of the
    North, 801-65: Translated from the Vita Anskarii by Bishop Rimbert, his
    fellow Missionary and Successor* (London, 1921).

Russian Primary Chronicle: Laurentian Text, ed. and trans. S. H. Cross and
    O. P. Sherbowitz-Wetzor, Medieval Academy of America Publications 60
    (Cambridge, Mass., 1953).

Scholz, B. W. and Rogers, B. (trans), *Carolingian Chronicles* (Ann Arbor, 1972).

Somerville, A. A. and McDonald, R. A., *The Viking Age: a reader* (Toronto, 2010)

The War of the Gaedhil with the Gaill, ed. and trans. J. H. Todd (London, 1867,
    Cambridge University Press reprint 2012).
Whitelock, D. (ed. and trans.), *English Historical Documents, Vol. 1 c. 500–1042*
    (2nd edn, London, 1979).
Vikings in Russia: Yngvar's Saga and Eymund's Saga, trans. H. Pálsson and P.
    Edwards (Edinburgh, 1989).
Vinland Sagas, trans. M. Magnusson and H. Pálsson (Harmondsworth, 1965).

SAGAS OF ICELANDERS

Egil's Saga, trans. H. Pálsson and P. Edwards (Harmondsworth, 1977).
Eyrbyggja Saga, trans. H. Pálsson and P. Edwards (Edinburgh, 1973).
Göngu-Hrolf's Saga, trans. H. Pálsson & P. Edwards (Edinburgh, 1980).
Laxdæla Saga, trans. by M. Magnusson & H. Pálsson (Harmondsworth, 1969).
Njal's Saga, trans. M. Magnusson and H. Pálsson (Harmondsworth, 1960).
Saga of Grettir the Strong, trans. G. A. Hight, edited and introduced by Peter
    Foote (London, 1965).

POETRY, LEGEND AND MYTHOLOGY

Beowulf: a new translation, Seamus Heaney (Faber and Faber, London, 2000).
Battle of Maldon, ed. and trans. B. Griffiths (Hockwold-cum-Wilton, Norfolk,
    1995).
Hollander, L. M. (trans.), *The Skalds, a Selection of Their Poems, with Introduction
    and Notes* (2nd edn, Ithaca N.Y., 1968);
Poetic Edda, translated by C. Larrington (Oxford, 1996).
Saga of the Volsungs: the Norse Epic of Sigurd the Dragon Slayer, trans. J. L. Byock
    (Berkeley, Los Angeles and London, 1990).
Saxo Grammaticus: The History of the Danes, Books I-IX, ed. H. Ellis Davidson,
    trans. P. Fisher (Woodbridge, Suffolk, 1996).
Snorri Sturluson, *Edda,* trans. A. Faulkes (London, 1987).

Secondary sources

The following is a selective list for the general reader, concentrating on recent works in English only. Readers of the Scandinavian (and other) languages are referred to the extensive bibliographies in Roesdahl and Wilson (1992).

GENERAL SURVEYS

Ferguson, R., *The Vikings* (London-New York, 2009).

Foote, P. G. and Wilson, D. M., *The Viking Achievement* (2nd revised edn, London, 1980).

Forte, A., Oram, R., and Pedersen, F., *Viking Empires* (Cambridge, 2005).

Graham-Campbell, J., *The Viking World* (2nd, rev. edn., London, 1989).

Haywood, J., *The Vikings* (Stroud, Gloucestershire, 1999).

Hall, R., *Exploring the World of the Vikings* (London, 2007).

Jones, G., *A History of the Vikings* (Oxford, 1968).

Roesdahl, E. and Wilson, D. M. (eds), *From Viking to Crusader: Scandinavia and Europe 800-1200* (Copenhagen, 1992).

Sawyer, P. H., (ed.), *The Oxford Illustrated History of the Vikings* (Oxford, 1997).

Wilson, D. M., *The Vikings and their Origins* (3rd rev. edn, London, 1989).

HISTORICAL ATLASES

Graham-Campbell, J. (ed.), *Cultural Atlas of the Viking World* (London and New York, 1994).

Haywood, J., *The Penguin Historical Atlas of the Vikings* (London, 1995).

Hill, D., *An Atlas of Anglo-Saxon England* (Oxford, 1981).

Hooper, N. and Bennett, M., *Cambridge Illustrated Atlas: Warfare: The Middle Ages 768-1487* (Cambridge, 1996).

PREHISTORIC SCANDINAVIA

Cunliffe, B., *The Extraordinary Voyage of Pytheas the Greek* (London, 2001).

Hedeager, L., *Iron Age Myth and Materiality: an Archaeology of Scandinavia AD 400–1000* (Abingdon, 2011).

Jensen, J., *The Prehistory of Denmark: from the Stone Age to the Vikings* (Copenhagen, 2013).

VIKING AGE SCANDINAVIA

Christiansen, E., *The Norsemen in the Viking Age* (Oxford, 2002).
Lund, N., 'Scandinavia, *c. 700–1066*' in *The New Cambridge Medieval History Vol. 2*, ed. R. McKitterick (Cambridge, 1995), pp. 202–27.
Pulsiano, P (ed.), *Medieval Scandinavia: An Encyclopedia* (New York and London, 1993).
Randsborg, K., *The Viking Age in Denmark* (London, 1980).
Roesdahl, E., *Viking Age Denmark* (London, 1982).
Sawyer B. and Sawyer, P. H., *Medieval Scandinavia* (Minneapolis, 1993).
Sawyer, P. H., *Kings and Vikings* (London, 1982).

THE NORTH ATLANTIC

Batey, C. E., Jesch, J. and Morris, C. D., *The Viking Age in Caithness, Orkney and the North Atlantic* (Edinburgh 1993).
Byock, J. L., *Viking Age Iceland* (London, 2001).
Dahl, S., 'The Norse Settlement of the Faroe Islands' in *Medieval Archaeology 14* (1970), pp. 60–73.
Enterline, J. R., *Erikson, Eskimos and Columbus: Medieval European Knowledge of America* (Baltimore, 2002).
Ingstad, A. S., *The Discovery of a Norse Settlement in America: Excavations at L'Anse aux Meadows, Newfoundland 1961–68* (Oslo, 1977).
Jóhannesson, J., *A History of the Old Icelandic Commonwealth: Íslendinga Saga* (Winnipeg, 1974).
Jones, G., *The Norse Atlantic Saga* (2nd edn, Oxford, 1986).
Krogh, K. J., *Viking Greenland* (Copenhagen, 1967).

THE CELTIC WORLD

Batey, C. E., Jesch, J. and Morris, C. D., *The Viking Age in Caithness, Orkney and the North Atlantic* (Edinburgh 1993).
Crawford, B. E., *Scandinavian Scotland* (Leicester, 1987).
Davies, W., *Wales in the Early Middle Ages* (Leicester, 1982).
Fell, C. E. (ed.), *The Viking Age in the Isle of Man* (London, 1983).
Fenton, A. and Pálsson, H. (eds), *The Northern and Western Isles in the Viking World* (Edinburgh, 1984).
Graham-Campbell, J. and Batey, C. E., *Vikings in Scotland: an Archaeological Survey* (Edinburgh, 1998).
Larsen, A., *The Vikings in Ireland* (Roskilde, 2001).
Ó Cróinin, D., *Early Medieval Ireland 400–1200* (London, 1995).
Price, N., *The Vikings in Brittany*, Viking Society for Northern Research Saga Book 22 (1986–9), pp. 319–440.
Redknap, M., *Vikings in Wales* (Cardiff, 2000)

Ritchie, A., *Viking Scotland* (London, 1993).

Smyth, A. P., *Scandinavian York and Dublin* (2 vols, Dublin, 1975–9).

Smyth, A. P., *Warlords and Holy Men: Scotland AD 400–1000* (London, 1984).

Wilson, D. M., *The Vikings in the Isle of Man* (Aarhus, 2008.)

ENGLAND

Abels, R., *Alfred the Great* (London and New York, 1998).

Brooks, N. P., 'England in the Ninth Century: the Crucible of Defeat' in
    Transactions of the Royal Historical Society, 5th Series, 29, pp. 1–20.

Edwards, B. J. N., *Vikings in North West England* (Lancaster, 1998)

Hall, R. A., *Viking Age York* (London, 1994).

Hart, C., *The Danelaw* (London, 1992).

Lawson, M. K., *Cnut: England's Viking King* (Stroud, 2004).

Richards, J. D., *Viking Age England* (Stroud, 2004).

Scragg, D. G.(ed.), *The Battle of Maldon AD 991* (Oxford, 1991).

Smyth, A. P., *Scandinavian York and Dublin* (2 vols, Dublin, 1975–9).

Stenton, F. M., *Anglo-Saxon England* (3rd edn, Oxford, 1971).

FRANCIA

Bates, D., *Normandy before 1066* (London, 1982).

Logan, F. D., *The Vikings in History* (London, 1983).

McKitterick, R., *The Frankish Kingdoms under the Carolingians 751–987*
    (London, 1983).

Nelson, J. L., *Charles the Bald* (London, 1992).

Wallace-Hadrill, J. M., 'The Vikings in Francia' in *ibid.*, *Early Medieval History*
    (Oxford, 1975).

RUSSIA AND THE EAST

Blöndal, S. and Benedikz, B. S., *The Varangians of Byzantium* (Cambridge, 2007).

Dolukhanov, P. M., , *The Early Slavs: Eastern Europe from the Initial Settlement to
    the Kievan Rus* (London, 1996).

Ellis Davidson, H. R., *The Viking Road to Byzantium* (London, 1976).

Franklin, S. and Shepard J., *The Emergence of Rus 750–1200* (Abingdon and
    New York, 2013).

Martin, J., *Medieval Russia 980–1584* (Cambridge, 2007).

SHIPS AND SEAFARING

Bately, J. and Englert, A., *Ohthere's Voyages* (Roskilde, 2007).

Christensen, A. E. (ed.), *The Earliest Ships: the Evolution of Boats into Ships*
    (London, 1996).

Crumlin-Pedersen, O., *Aspects of Maritime Scandinavia AD 200–1200* (Roskilde, 1990).

Crumlin-Pedersen, O., *Archaeology and the Sea in Scandinavia and Britain* (Roskilde, 2010).

Haywood, J., *Dark Age Naval Power* (2nd revised edn, Hockwold-cum-Wilton, Norfolk, 1999).

Short, W. R., *Viking Weapons and Combat Techniques* (Yardley, 2009).

Unger, R. W. (ed.), *Cogs, Caravels and Galleons: the Sailing Ship 1000–1650* (London, 1994).

Williams, G., *The Viking Ship* (London, 2014).

MILITARY

Griffith, P., *The Viking Art of War* (London, 1995).

Harrison, M., *Viking Hersir* (London, 1993).

Lund, N., 'Danish Military organisation' in J. Cooper (ed.), *The Battle of Maldon, Fiction and Fact* (London, 1993).

Nørgård Jørgensen, A. and Clausen, B. L. (eds), *Military Aspects of Scandinavian Society in a European Perspective, AD 1-1300* (Publications from the National Museum, Studies in Archaeology and History Vol 2, Copenhagen, 1997).

Short, William R., *Viking Weapons and Combat Techniques* (Yardley, Pennsylvania, 2009).

Siddorn, J. K., *Viking Weapons and Warfare* (Stroud, 2000).

MYTH AND RELIGION

Crossley-Holland, K., *The Penguin Book of Norse Myths* (London, 2011).

DuBois, T. A., *Nordic Religions in the Viking Age* (Philadelphia, 1999).

Ellis Davidson, H. R., *Gods and Myths of Northern Europe* (Harmondsworth, 1964).

Page, R. I., *Norse Myths* (London, 1990).

Turville-Petre, E. O. G., *Myth and Religion of the North: the Religion of Ancient Scandinavia* (2nd edn, Greenwich, Conn., 1977).

VIKING LIFE AND CULTURE

Bailey, R. N., *Viking Age Sculpture in Northern England* (London, 1980)

Clarke, H. and Ambrosiani, B., *Towns in the Viking Age* (2nd rev. edn, Leicester, 1995).

Graham-Campbell, J., *Viking Art* (London, 2013).

Hadley, D. M. and Harkel, L., *Everyday Life in Viking Towns* (Oxford, 2013).

Jesch, J., *Women in the Viking Age* (Woodbridge, Suffolk, 1991).

Jochens, J., *Women in Old Norse Society* (Ithaca and London, 1995).

Karras, R., *Slavery and Society in Medieval Scandinavia* (New Haven, Connecticut, 1988).
Page, R. I., *Runes* (London, 1987).

GENETIC STUDIES

Sykes, B., *Saxons, Vikings and Celts: the Genetic Roots of Britain and Ireland* (Norton, 2008).
Wood, M., and Harding S., *Viking DNA: the Wirral and West Lancashire Project* (Nottingham, 2010).

AFTER THE VIKINGS

Christiansen, E., *The Northern Crusades* (London, 1997).
McDonald, R. A., *The Kingdom of the Isles* (East Linton, 1997).
Sawyer, B. and Sawyer, P., *Medieval Scandinavia* (Minneapolis-London, 1993).

LIST OF ILLUSTRATIONS

1. Viking gods (Werner Forman / Getty Images).
2. Viking longhouse at Borg, Lofoten Islands (John Haywood).
3. Bronze Age ships on petroglyphs (John Haywood).
4. Royal burial mounds, Gamla Uppsala (Jose Hernandez / Flickr).
5. Gokstad ship (Museum of Cultural History, University of Oslo, Norway).
6. Viking helmet from Gjermundbu, Norway (Museum of Cultural History, University of Oslo, Norway).
7. King Edmund martyred by the Danes, Pickering Church, North Yorkshire (John Haywood).
8. Irish monastic tower, Glendalough (Shutterstock).
9. Ruins of Luni, Italy (John Haywood).
10. Great Gate of Kiev (John Swift).
11. Walls of Constantinople (John Haywood).
12. Knarr ship (Viking Ship Museum, Roskilde, Denmark).
13. Haymaking on the Faroe Islands (John Haywood).
14. Thingvellir, Iceland (Ullstein Bild / Getty Images).
15. L'Anse-aux-Meadows settlement (Wolfgang Kaehler / Getty Images).
16. Aerial view of Hedeby, Denmark (Archäologisches Landesamt Schleswig-Holstein).
17. Aerial view of Trelleborg, Sjælland, Denmark (Thue C. Leibrandt / Wikimedia Commons).
18. Cnut and Aelfgifu (The British Library Board, Stowe 944, f.6).
19. Fenrir the Wolf and Yggdrasil in the *Edda* manuscript (Árni Magnússon Institute for Icelandic Studies).
20. Ruins of Hvalsey church, Greenland (Wolfgang Kaehler / Getty Images).

INDEX

Aachen 44, 69, 78, 93
Abalus 12
Abbo the Twisted 95, 97
Absalon, bishop of Roskilde 322
Adam of Bremen 37, 277, 284, 311
Aed mac Boanta 120–21
Ælfheah, archbishop of Canterbury 257, 293
Ælle 51, 69
Æthelred 52-3
Æthelred the Unready 106, 248, 250–53, 255–60, 285
Æthelstan 47, 73, 74, 123–4, 151, 288
Æthelwulf 47
afterlife 6–8, 15
Ahmed ibn Fadlan 183–6, 193
Aidan, monk 43, 112
Alcuin, scholar 42, 44, 69
Alexander III 337, 339
Alexander Nevsky 326
Alfred the Great 53, 55–60, 62–6, 123, 258
    Life of King Alfred 59
    reforms 62–3
Al-Ghazal 172–3
Alogi 27
amber 12, 13, 14, 32, 80
Angantyr 33, 35, 279
Angles 17, 20, 28, 43, 69, 132
    East Angles 51, 52, 255
Anglo-Saxons 46, 48, 58, 63, 66
    Anglo-Saxon Chronicle 62–3, 73, 251, 255, 256–7, 269
Anund 53, 55, 56
Arabs 164, 166, 175, 176, 186, 187, 188, 318–19
Armagh 139
army structure 61–2
    women 96
Arnulf of Carinthia 99, 105
Artgal 122–3
Athelney 58–9, 60
Attila the Hun 31
Aud the Deep-Minded 117, 216, 219–20

Baghdad 188
Barda 190–91
Basil II 202–3
battles 49
    Ashingdon 261
    Bråvalla 35
    Brentford 261
    Brissarthe 104
    Brunanburh 73–4, 124, 151
    Carham 264
    Clontarf 158
    Edington 59
    Ellandun 46
    Fyrisvellir 307
    Hastings 267
    Hingston Down 47
    Killineer 142
    Linn Duchaill 150
    Maldon 249
    Manzikert 205
    Menai Straits 330
    the Neva 326
    Penselwood 261
    Ragnarök 4, 73
    Santwat 133–4
    Sherston 261
    Skitten Mire 128
    Stamford Bridge 267, 268
    Stiklestad 300
    York 51–2

Benfleet 64–5
Beowulf 28–9, 33, 308
Bergen 232, 347, 350
Bernicia 55, 69, 123–5
beserkers 6, 205
Birka 308–10, 311
Björn Ironsides 169–71
Blathmac 112–13
boat-building 18
bog bodies
  Grauballe Man 19
  Tollund Man 19
Book of Kells 112
Borre
  cemetery 39
Brian Boru 155–9
Britain
  Roman and Saxon 27–8
  tin trade 10
Brittany
  raids 87
  Veneti tribe 10
  Viking colony 102–3
bronze 13–14
Bronze Age 14–15
Brynhild 31, 51
Bulgars 182–3, 184
Burgred 52, 54
Burgundians 17, 31
burial mounds
  Birka 309
  Chernigov 194
  Gamla Uppsala 36–7
  Gnezdovo 193
  Hovgården 310
  Jelling 281–2
  Vendel 36
Byrhtnoth 249–50
Byzantine Empire
  Byzantine culture 208–9
  decline of 315

Canterbury 47
Carolingian Renaissance 77
Cashel 155–6, 159
cemeteries
  Birka 309
  Borre 39
  Elblag 38
  Grobina 38
  Isle of Man 118
  Pskov 193
  Sigtuna 312
  Staraja Ladoga 180
Ceolwulf 54, 56, 63
Charlemagne 69, 77–9, 81, 85, 271–2, 275–6
Charles the Bald 82, 84–93
Charles the Fat 93, 95, 98–9
Charles the Simple 100
Chippenham 56, 59
Christianity
  conversion to 9, 25, 33, 43, 67, 103–4, 271–2, 279–80
    Angles 69
    Denmark 279–80
    Greenland 229–30
    Guthrum 59–60
    Harald 279–80
    Hastein 64
    Hebrides 117
    Iceland 225–6
    Northumbria 112
    Norway 72, 301
    Norwegian resistance 288–90, 293
    Óengus 156
    Olaf Tryggvason 251
    Olga 202
    Rollo 100
    Roric 84
    Rus 201–2
    Sweden 311
    Vladimir 201–2

Orthodox Christianity 201–2, 208, 325, 326
churches
  Constantinople 202
  Dorestad 80
  Dublin 159, 161
  Gamla Uppsala 37
  Germany 201
  Greenland 229, 230, 349
  Iceland 223
  Jelling 281, 282
  Orkney 131, 331
  Paris 89
  Roskilde 284
  Trondheim 293–4
  York 69
Cimbri 17
Cirencester 180
Cnut 72, 106, 159, 258, 259–65, 297–9, 301–2
Cnut the Holy 305–6
Coenwulf 46
coins 72
  Cuerdale 72
  dirhems 53, 174, 181, 183, 184
  Gudme 20
  Helgö 38
  Normandy 106–7
  Repton 54
  Silverdale 55
  York 70
Constantine I 122–3, 142
Constantine II 123–4
Constantine the Great 69, 197
Constantinople 177, 178, 179, 191, 196–205, 209, 320
Corded Ware Culture 12-13
Córdoba, Emirate of 164–8, 172
Cornwall 46
crafts 70, 80, 112, 118, 160, 274
creation myth 2–3, 215

crusades 314–27
  Holy Land 331
  Jerusalem 316–21
  Livonian 323–5
  Swedish 325–7
  Wendish 321–3
Cuerdale hoard 72

Dál Cais 155–7, 159
Dál Riata 110–11, 119–21
Danegeld 50, 250, 310
Danelaw 66–8, 101
Danes 26–7, 31, 47, 49–50
  Gesta Danorum 33
  invasions
    Flanders 93
    Frisia 79
    Iona 118
    Mercia 52, 54, 68, 73
    Paris 94–7
    Seine 90-92
    Wessex 53, 55, 57
    York 51–3
  raids with horses 51
  settling in Normandy 101
Danevirke 31–2, 272, 273
Denmark 31–3, 271–82, 304–6
Deira 55, 69
Diarmait MacMurchada 161–2
dísir 6, 37
Disting 37
Donald II 121
Dorestad 79–81, 82, 83, 84
Drevljane 179–80
drinking horns 30
Dublin 71, 122, 132, 140, 142–5, 150
  Viking Dublin 160–63
  and York 151, 152–3
Dudo of St Quentin 63, 98, 101, 170
Dunkeld 120, 122

Eadred 74–5
Eadric Streona 256, 259–62
Ealdwulf 46
Eamont Bridge 123–4
Ebo, archbishop of Reims 279
Ecgberht 52, 53
Edgar the Peaceful 247–8
Edmund 52
Edmund Ironside 259–62
Edward the Confessor 252, 262, 265
Edward the Elder 67–8
Einar 127–8
Emma of Normandy 106, 252, 261,
    263, 264, 302
Engelhardt, Conrad 20
England 49, 62, 89, 93, 99–100, 109,
    115
  unification of 73–6
Erik Bloodaxe 74–5, 128, 152, 287–8
Erik the Evergood 205, 305, 306, 316
Erik Håkonarson 292, 294, 295–7
Erik the Red 228–30, 237
  Eiríks saga rauða 235–6, 237, 238
Ermanaric 31
Estonians 324, 325
Exeter 56
Eystein II 331–2

Faeroe Islands 210–12
feasting halls 31, 32, 33–5, 37, 275
Fingal 132–3
Finland 325, 326–7
Finns 38, 174, 180, 193, 325, 326
Flanders 93, 99, 101, 105
Flüsig, excavations at 32
forts 278
Francia 62, 63, 83, 87, 99, 107
Franks 26, 78, 176, 272
Freyr 6, 36–7, 286, 301
Frisia 28, 79, 83, 275
Fyn 20, 24

Gaels 117, 127, 335, 336
Gainsborough 258, 259
Gallehus 30
Galloway 117, 125
Gamla Uppsala 36–7
Gammel Lejre 33–5
Gauzelin, bishop of Paris 95, 96, 97,
    98
Germanic society 25–8
  Germanic Iron Age 26, 31, 35
    Migration Period 27, 29
    Vendel Period 35
  Roman influence 25–6
  runes and writing 23, 25
Godfred 79, 272–3, 275–6
Godfred Haraldsson 132
Godred 334–5
Godred Crovan 132–3
Godred Sihtricsson 132
Gorm 279, 281–2
Gosforth cross 72
Götar 27, 29, 308, 310, 311
Goths 17, 26
Gregory of Tours 28
Greenland 227–35, 243, 244, 347–51
  Grœnlendinga saga 235, 237
Grobina 38, 174
    Scandinavian cemeteries 38
Gudme 20
Gundahar 31
Guthfrith 123–4, 150–51
Guthred 70
Guthrum 53, 55, 56–7, 59, 63, 180

Håkon IV 337–9, 342, 346
Håkon the Good 288–90
Håkon Grjotgardsson 286
Håkon Paulsson 330
Håkon Sigurdsson 283–4, 291–2
Halfdan 50, 55, 73
Halfdan the Black 286, 339

Halfdan Highleg 127–8
Harald Bluetooth 251, 254, 277–82,
    290, 291, 311
Harald Fairhair 126, 217, 286–8
Harald Greycloak 290–91
Harald Hardrada 131, 203, 207,
    265–7, 300, 303–4
Harald Hildetand 35
Harald Klak 279, 285
Harald Maddadsson 331–4
Harold Godwinson 265–7
Hastein 63–5, 169–71
Hávamál 1, 4–5, 346
Hebrides 114, 116, 118–19, 125,
    132–5, 212, 218, 328, 335, 337
Hedeby 273–5, 283
Helgö 37–8, 308
Henry of Lund 131
Heruls 27, 28, 175
Hiberno-Saxon style 30
Higbald 45–6
Hjortspring find 17–18
hørgs 34, 281
houses 274, 309
    longhouses 13, 221, 229, 241–2
Hrothgar 33, 34
Hugh Capet 105, 107
Huns 27, 31
Huseby 39
Hvalsey 349
Hygelac 28

Iceland 117, 213–27, 340–47
    Althing 223-5, 294, 342, 346, 347
    diet 220–21
    famines 341
    Íslendingabók 213, 217, 226, 228
    Landnámabók 213, 215–16, 217,
    232
    politics and justice 221–5
    saga traditions 117

Viking settlement 210, 213–21
Igor 178–9, 184, 190, 198
Ingamund 71
Inuit 11, 242, 348–9, 350, 351
    Dorset Inuit 228, 244
    Thule Inuit 244, 347
Iona 110–12, 118
Ireland 109, 111–12, 118, 136
    Irish Vikings 160
    Irish monks 210–12
    kingdoms within Ireland 136–7
Iron Age 16, 18
    Germanic Iron Age 26, 31
Islam 164
    conversion to 172, 183
Isle of Man 118, 132–4, 334
    *Cronica Regum Mannie et
    Insularum* 334
Italy 170–71, 318–19
Ivar 50, 52, 140–41

Jelling 281–3
Jerusalem 315, 319, 331
jewellery 30, 38, 117
Jordanes 17, 26
Judaism
    conversion to 187
Jutes 17, 28
Jutland 17, 273

Karelia 325
Karl Hundason 129–30
Kells 112–13
Kenneth II 125
Kenneth mac Alpin 120–21, 122
Khazar Khaganate 186–7
Khazars 189, 191, 198, 199
Kiev 177–8, 194, 200, 202, 208
kingship 40

language (see also place-names) 67, 115
  Celtic 217
  French 106
  Gaelic 117, 118, 121
  Icelandic 217
  Latin 280
  Old English 75
  Old Norse 106–7, 117, 118, 213, 238, 336
  Pictish 121
  Russian 208
  Slavic 202
L'Anse aux Meadows 241–2
Latvia 38, 323, 325
Laxdœla Saga 204, 220
Leif Eriksson 236–7, 240, 242
Life of St Neot 57
Lindisfarne 42–3, 44, 78, 114
  Lindisfarne Gospels 30, 45
Lisbon 166–7, 168, 317
Livonians 323
Loire 86-7, 89, 92, 171
London 63, 251, 258–9, 265
longhouses 13, 221, 229, 241–2
longphuirt (longphort) 138, 139, 142, 143, 144
  Linn Duchaill 144, 150–51
longships 17–18, 48, 169, 274, 295–6, 323–4, 340
  Hjortspring 17–18
  Ladby 61
  Oseberg 60
Lothar 82, 83
Louis IV 105
Louis the Pious 81–2, 104, 176, 276
Luni 170

Maccus Haraldsson 132
Máel Brigte 126–7
Máel Sechnaill 139–40, 141, 153, 157, 159
Magnus Barefoot 133–4, 316, 328–30
Magnus Erlendsson (St Magnus) 330, 331
Magnus the Good 130–31, 264–5, 299, 302
Malcolm I 124
Malcolm II 128–9, 264
Malcolm IV 336
Mathgamain 155–6
Mercia 63, 64–5, 68
missionary activity 279, 288–9, 298, 312, 327
monasteries 43, 93, 145
  Áth Cliath 138
  Auldhame 151, 152
  Clonfert 138
  Clonmacnoise 138, 139
  Fontanelle 86
  Greenland 230, 234–5
  Jarrow 45–6
  Jumièges 86
  Kells 112, 152
  Lindisfarne 43
  Lyminge 46
  Portmahomack 113
  St Columba's 43, 110–13
  St David's 154
  St Germain-des-Prés 97
  St Ninian's 115
  St Patrick's 139, 150
Moors 164, 168, 171–3, 314, 316–17

Nantes 86–7, 102
Native Americans 237–8, 240, 242, 243
navigation 230–35
Newfoundland 241
Normandy 105-7, 115, 268, 318
Norse 115–19, 125, 127, 134, 145, 151, 163, 237, 241

artefacts 245
  Orkney and Shetland 340
North America 235–46
Northern Isles 113–15, 116, 118,
  125–8
Northumbria 42, 69, 109, 112, 119,
  124
Norway 11, 27, 39, 114–16, 118, 131,
  203, 285–7
Norwegians 104, 109, 114, 137, 267
Novgorod 177, 192–3, 325, 327
Nydam Moss 20–23
  ships 20–22

oaths 55, 61
Odin 2–6, 24, 30, 35, 36–7, 51, 87,
  128, 283, 301
Odo 95, 96, 98–100
Offa 44
Oissel 89–90
Olaf 122, 140–41
Olaf Cuarán 152–3
Olaf Godredsson 334–5
Olaf Guthfrithsson 151
Olaf Haraldsson (St Olaf) 129, 263,
  297–301
  Saga of St Olaf 297
Olaf Hunger 306
Olaf the Peaceful 304
Olaf Tryggvason 249, 251, 252, 285,
  292–6
  Heimskringla saga 286, 296
Oleg 177–8, 179, 190, 197–8
Olga 179–80, 202
Olof Skötkonung 206, 294, 310–12
Orkney 130, 131, 147, 161, 329,
  331–4
  Orkneyinga Saga 330, 332
Orkney Islands 115, 126, 127
Orthodox Christianity 201–2, 208,
  325, 326

Oscetel 53, 55, 56
Ostmen 160–63
Ottar 36
Oxford 253–4

Paris 88, 89, 94–9
Paschasius Radbertus 89
Pechenegs 179, 194, 195–6, 197,
  199–201
petroglyphs 14-16
Phoceans 10
Photius, patriarch 197, 202
Picts 109, 110–11, 115-16, 119–22,
  142
Pippin 87
place-names 66, 71, 101, 111,
  114–15, 116, 118, 221, 326
  papar 111, 118, 211
Poland
  Scandinavian colony at Elblag 38
Pont de l'Arche 91, 92, 94
Pytheas of Massalia 9–12

Ragnald 73, 123, 149–50
Ragnar 88
Ragnar Lodbrok 50, 51, 88, 141, 169
raids 40, 42, 44, 46–7, 81 85, 332
  Constantinople 197–9
  Dublin 144
  Dunkeld 122
  England 252
  Frisia 275
  Hebrides 110
  Iberian Peninsula 166–73
  Iona 112–13, 114
  Ireland 137–8, 151
  reduced incentive for 270
  Scotland 114
  strandhögg 46
  Wales 154
  Wends 302–3

Rani 26, 27
Raumarici 27
Reading 53
religion 20, 73, 187, 201–2, 289, 301, 345
  and trade 20
Repton 54
Ribe 32–3
Richard the Fearless 105–6
Richard the Good 106–7, 252, 259, 263, 264
Rodulf 26, 27
Rognvald 102-3
Rognvald Brusason 130
Rognvald Kali Kolsson 331–2
Rollo 97–8, 99–103
Roman Empire 19
  collapse 40, 77
  influence 25-6
Romerike 27, 39
Romsdal 27
Roric 83–4
Roskilde 35, 283
Rouen 86, 94, 100, 106
Rugi 27
runes 23–5, 30, 118, 243
  rune-stones 206, 241, 277, 281, 282, 307
Rurik 177, 178
Rus 175–99, 208
  assimilation with the Slavs 199
  boats 197
  burial customs 185–6
  clothes 184
  conversion to Christianity 201–2
  hygiene 183
  raid on Constantinople 198–9
  sex lives 184
  trade in Baghdad 188
  wealth 184

sacrifice 51–2, 272, 312–13
  blood eagle 51, 128
  ships 20–21
sacrificial feasts 5–6
sagas 342–5
  Edda 344
  Egils saga 343
  Eíriks saga rauða 235–6, 237, 238
  Grœnlendinga saga 235, 237
  Heimskringla 286, 296, 297, 344
  Laxdœla Saga 204, 220
  Njáls saga 343
  Orkneyinga Saga 330
  Saga of the Jomsvikings 254
  Saga of St Olaf 297
  Volsunga Saga 31
  Yngvars Saga víðförla 206
St Ansgar 308, 309, 310, 311
St Brendan 211
St Brice's day massacre 253–4
St Columba 110–13, 120
St Cuthbert 43, 44, 57
  History of St Cuthbert 71
St Magnus 330, 331
St Olaf 129, 263, 297–301
Sami 307–8
Saxo Grammaticus 33
Saxons 26, 28, 31
Scandinavia
  colonisation of 12–13
  first kingdoms 31
  and the sail 22–3
Scandinavian tribes 26–7
  ancestry 212
  assimilation into Europe 270
  burials 181
Scandza 17, 26
Scotland 109–11, 125
  Scots 109, 119–21
Seljuqs 315
Seville 167, 172

Shetland Islands 115, 126, 340
ships and boats
  birlinns 340
  cogs 323–4
  drakkars 252, 295
  dromon 168, 198
  knarrs 218, 274
  longships 17–18, 48, 169, 274,
  295–6, 323–4, 340
  sacrifices 20–21
  ship settings 14, 33, 281
  size and number 60
  umiaks 244
Sicily 319
Sigeric, Archbishop 250
  Sigfred 95, 96, 97, 99, 271–2
Sigurd 329, 330
  crusade 316–21
Sigurd the Mighty 126–7
Sigurd Ring 35
Sigvatr 106
Sihtric Silkbeard 157–9, 162
Silverdale hoard 55
Sjaelland 20, 33
skaldic verse 345–6
Skjöldungs 33, 35
slave trade 116, 144–6, 169–70, 172
  Ireland 132, 144–6, 170
slavery 220
Slavs 175, 176, 177, 179, 181, 188
Snorri Sturluson 286, 287, 290, 319,
  343–6
solar cults 15
Somerled 334–5
Sorte Muld 30
Stamford Bridge 267
Staraja Ladoga 38, 174, 180, 192
  Scandinavian burials 181
stone crosses
  Gosforth 72
  Isle of Man 118

Strabo 11–12
Strathclyde 109, 119, 122–3, 142
Svein Asleifarson 332–3
Svein Estrithson 302, 303–5
Svein Forkbeard 251–3, 258, 259,
  284–5,
Svyatoslav 179, 180, 199–201
Sweden 22, 31, 35, 307–13
Swedes 26–7, 35, 37–8, 174, 307–8
  Rus 175–99, 208
  Swedish crusades 325–7

Tacitus 19, 22, 26, 126
Tallin 324
Teutones 17
Thanet 47, 49, 248
Thietmar of Merseburg 34, 260
Thor 5, 36–7, 233
  Thor's hammer amulets 6, 13, 37,
  233, 283
Thorfinn the Mighty 129–31
Thorfinn Skullsplitter 128
Thorkell the Tall 256–8, 259, 260,
  285, 297 ·
Thorstein the Red 125, 126
Thule 11
Thule Inuit 244, 347
Tostig 266–7
trade 20, 38, 53, 70, 188, 275
  Baghdad 188
  and religion 20
  Silk Road 183, 188
  Sweden 308–9
  tin 10
  and war 53
Treaty of Verdun 82, 83
Trondheim Fjord 11, 293
Trundholm Sun Chariot 15
Turgeis 139–40, 141
Tureholm hoard 29

Ubba 50, 52, 58
Uí Néill 149, 150
Ukraine 28
Unni, archbishop of Hamburg-
  Bremen 279–80, 311
Urban II, Pope 315

Valdemar II 323–5
Valdemar the Great 321–2
Valhalla 3–4, 6, 35
valkyries 4
  Brynhild 31, 51
Vandals 17
Varangians 199, 201, 202, 203–5, 207
  Varangian Guard 203–5, 207, 320
Vendel
  art-style 36
  burials 36
Venerable Bede 45, 75
  *Ecclesiastical History of the English
  People* 75
Veneti 10
Viking
  meaning xvi
  Viking Age xvi-xvii
Vladimir 201–3
Volsunga Saga 31
  Volund 89-90

Wales 154
weapons 18, 19, 205, 240
Wends 272, 302, 305, 321, 322
  Wendish crusade 321–3
Wessex 53, 65, 66, 75
William the Lion of Scotland 333
William Longsword 104–5
William of Malmesbury 65, 261
William of Normandy, the
  Conqueror 265–9
Willibrord 33, 279
Wulfstan I 75

Yaroslav the Wise 206–8, 299
Yggdrasil 2, 24, 283
Ynglings 36, 37, 39, 286
  Domalde 37
Yngvar the Widefarer 206
  Yngvars Saga víðförla 206
York 42, 51, 68–71, 73, 74, 124, 268